WITHDRAWN

Britannica
Review
of Foreign Language
Education

Britannica Review
of Foreign Language Education

Edited by Dale L. Lange

Volume 3, 1970

Sponsored by the American Council
on the Teaching of
Foreign
Languages

 Encyclopædia Britannica, Inc. *Chicago*

American Council on the Teaching of Foreign Languages

Preface

In the two years since the *Britannica Review of Foreign Language Education* was first published, educators have given it wide and enthusiastic acceptance as an authoritative reference work. The original *Review*, proposed by Encyclopædia Britannica, Inc., in 1968, has broadened in scope and purpose with each succeeding volume.

The Advisory Committee for Volume 3 of the *Review* emphasized teachers' demands for reporting of practical classroom experience, in addition to the need for continual research projects and theory development. Authors of the *Review* chapters have been encouraged to include, wherever possible, accounts of teaching practices that have proven effective in the classroom. The authors have also attempted to evaluate these practices and to augment their reports with additional information drawn from current research and theory.

It is hoped that Volume 3 of BRFLE—a continuing ACTFL service project—will be a valuable resource for those who seek to strengthen and expand the role of foreign language education.

C. EDWARD SCEBOLD
Executive Secretary, ACTFL

American Council on the Teaching of Foreign Languages

Officers for the Year 1971

President
Lowell Dunham
University of Oklahoma

President-Elect
Gail Hutchinson
Atlanta Public Schools

Executive Secretary
C. Edward Scebold

Treasurer
Kenneth W. Mildenberger

Executive Council

Edward H. Bourque
Fairfield, Conn., Public Schools

Jean Carduner
University of Michigan

Lois T. Ellsworth
Bartlesville, Okla., Public Schools

Frank M. Grittner
Wisconsin State Department of Public Instruction

Henry Hoge
Florida State University

Mari-Luci Ulibarri
University of New Mexico

John Young
University of Hawaii

Constituents

Alabama Association of Foreign Language Teachers

Alaska Foreign Language Association

Modern and Classical Language Council, Alberta Teachers' Association

Arizona Foreign Language Association

Arkansas Foreign Language Teachers Association

California Council of Foreign Language Teachers' Associations

Colorado Congress of Foreign Language Teachers

Connecticut Council of Language Teachers

Delaware Council on the Teaching of Foreign Languages

Greater Washington Association of Teachers of Foreign Languages

Florida Foreign Language Association

Foreign Language Association of Georgia

Hawaii Association of Language Teachers

Idaho Foreign Language Teachers' Association

Illinois Foreign Language Teachers' Association

Indiana Foreign Language Teachers' Association

Iowa Foreign Language Association

Kansas Foreign Language Association

Kentucky Council of Foreign Language Teachers

Louisiana Foreign Language Teachers Association

Foreign Language Department, Maine Teachers Association

Maryland Foreign Language Association

Massachusetts Foreign Language Association

Michigan Foreign Language Association

Minnesota Council of Teachers of Foreign Languages

Mississippi Modern Language Association

Foreign Language Association of Missouri

Montana Foreign Language Teachers Association

Nebraska Foreign Language Association

Nevada Foreign Language Teachers' Association

New Hampshire Association for the Teaching of Foreign Languages

New Jersey Foreign Language Teachers Association

New Mexico Foreign Language Teachers Association

New York State Federation of Foreign Language Teachers

Foreign Language Association of North Dakota

Ohio Council on the Teaching of Foreign Languages

Oklahoma Foreign Language Teachers Association

Ontario Modern Language Teachers' Association

Oregon Association of Foreign Language Teachers

Pennsylvania State Modern Language Association

Rhode Island Foreign Language Association

Association of Foreign Language Teachers of South Carolina

South Dakota Foreign Language Association

Texas Foreign Language Association

Utah Foreign Language Association

Vermont Foreign Language Teachers' Association

Modern Foreign Language Association of Virginia

Washington Association of Foreign Language Teachers

West Virginia Modern Language Teachers Association

Wisconsin Association of Foreign Language Teachers

Wyoming Language Teachers' Association

Affiliates

American Association of Teachers of Arabic

American Association of Teachers of French

American Association of Teachers of German

American Association of Teachers of Italian

American Association of Teachers of Slavic and East European Languages

American Association of Teachers of Spanish and Portuguese

American Classical League

American Philological Association

Association des Professeurs Franco-Americains

Association of Departments of Foreign Languages

Association of Teachers of English as a Second Language

Association of Teachers of Japanese

Central States Conference on the Teaching of Foreign Languages

Chinese Language Teachers Association

Classical Association of the Atlantic States

Classical Association of the Middle West and South

Classical Association of New England

Classical Association of the Pacific Northwest

Colleges of Mid-America, Inc.

Department of Foreign Languages, National Education Association

Linguistic Society of America

Middle States Association of Modern Language Teachers

Modern Greek Studies Association

National Association of Language Laboratory Directors

National Association of Professors of Hebrew in American Institutions of Higher Learning

National Council of State Supervisors of Foreign Languages

New England Foreign Language Association

Northeast Conference on the Teaching of Foreign Languages

Pacific Northwest Conference on Foreign Languages

Rocky Mountain Modern Language Association

Société des Professeurs Français en Amérique

South Atlantic Modern Language Association

South Central Modern Language Association

Southern Conference on Language Teaching

Teachers of English to Speakers of Other Languages

Foreword

The third volume of the *Britannica Review of Foreign Language Education* (BRFLE) could not have been completed without the help of many people. The staff at Encyclopædia Britannica, Inc., is especially singled out for its guidance and help: J. Thomas Beatty, Rita Piotter, Valerie Walker, Keith Snyder, and the many others who have contributed to the completion of this volume.

To the chapter authors who have provided the content of the volume, the editor pays special tribute, because without their contribution, time, and effort, there would be no BRFLE 3. The Advisory Committee gave special help in determining the theme for the volume, in suggesting authors, and in the reading and evaluation of manuscripts. The Executive Secretary of ACTFL, C. Edward Scebold, provided encouragement to the editor and served as the necessary link between ACTFL and Encyclopædia Britannica, working out the necessary arrangements for the publication of this volume.

Thanks and appreciation are especially given by the editor to Patricia C. Maas and John A. Sánchez, his secretary and his research assistant, who spent long hours typing correspondence and retyping sections of the final manuscript in addition to critically reading the different chapters and checking references.

Most of all, the editor wishes to express his sincere thanks to his wife, Sylvia, who spent extra time with the family so that the final manuscript could be prepared on time. Her encouragement and devotion are a major factor in the completion of this editor's responsibilities.

Dale L. Lange
University of Minnesota

Contents

Introduction and overview: Pluralism in foreign language education

Purpose of the review

Dale L. Lange

University of Minnesota

As in the first two volumes of the *Britannica Review of Foreign Language Education* (BRFLE), the third volume reviews the experience, the writing, and the research in foreign language education for a particular year, 1970. Like the second volume, Volume 3 has a central theme that is exemplified broadly in each chapter. The theme, however, is not the same as in the second volume. Instead of the rather narrowly focused theme of "individualized instruction," the present "review" attempts to interpret the work of the year from an even *broader* viewpoint that includes individualized instruction. The present year's theme as indicated in the chapter heading above is "Pluralism in Foreign Language Education."

Theme for Volume 3

The theme for this year's volume was chosen by the Advisory Committee to the Editor. It developed out of the discussion of how the "profession" was no longer consciously oriented to a single approach to the learning of a foreign language and its culture. In a broad sense, recognition is given here, in choosing the theme, to the *fact* that language instruction is being adapted to serve the individual requirements of the different segments of the populations served by the nation's schools. Since there is no single curriculum or approach to foreign language instruction to fit those requirements, it must be recognized that instruction will, of necessity, be adapted to the particular school or learning situation. It is hoped that the chapters in this volume will contribute, therefore, to a broader understanding of the different needs and requirements of foreign language instruction in a society that is as pluralistic as the communities, the schools, and the learning curricula within them.

How the theme was chosen

In addition to the focus of the volume on the theme of "Pluralism in Foreign Language Education," it was felt that some effort should be spent in directing the volume more toward the practitioner, the classroom teacher. As a result, the chapter authors were instructed to bring together any and all sorts of information from as many sources as desired in order to review those

An attempt at a more practical publication

practical and useful elements of foreign language learning that might be related to their individual topics. Several authors responded with questionnaires and extensive correspondence to find such information.

The authors' task, as in the first two volumes of the *Review*, has been to analyze, synthesize, evaluate, and interpret the information they have collected on a particular topic in order to create a meaningful review.

Authors' task

The major sources of information, the *ACTFL Annual Bibliography* (Lange, 1) and the ERIC Lists 4, 5, and 6 (Mildenberger & Mazzeo, 2 and 3; Monka, 4), continue to supply basic references for chapter authors. Each author has been asked to use sources other than those indicated above and his own reading within the topic to add to the provided sources.

Information sources

Overview

The second chapter of this book, "Pluralism in Foreign Language Education: A Reason for Being" by Grittner, not only defines the theme of this volume but sets the tone for the chapters to come and thereby gives a broad unifying sense to the *Review*. Grittner suggests that "pluralism" refers essentially to the existence of subcultural groups within our society and their characteristics, such as racial inheritance, national origin, religious preference, and language dominance. But he also relates this concept to education and the role of foreign language education in a pluralistic society. He traces the role of English and other languages from the colonial days of this country to the present, showing the influences of historical events on language curricula.

Grittner's definition and background to pluralism

Grittner also displays the effect of socioeconomic forces upon the decisions that are made concerning the foreign language curriculum. He shows how compensatory education, instructional adaptation, and curriculum differentiation have been used to accommodate a multicultural student body. He notes the effect of the turning away from particular subject-matter concentration to one of process in education, of cost accountability, and of equalitarianism on foreign language programs.

Of special concern to the theme of the volume is Grittner's discussion of the contributions of psychology and psycholinguistics to the development of a pluralistic "approach" in language learning. Such an approach takes into consideration the student,

2

his environment, his aptitudes, motivations, and other characteristics and qualities in determining learning experiences.

All of this background precedes the most important part of the chapter, in which Grittner carefully examines the feasibility of using the concept of pluralism as a basic organizing factor in foreign language learning. He centers his discussion around other bases that have been used to organize curricula, such as pupil needs, societal needs, organized knowledge, interdisciplinary studies, and initiation into a given discipline. As a result of the considerations of pluralism as an organizing basis for foreign language learning, Grittner sees some major changes that must take place if such a concept is to have "a reason for being."

Similar to some of the comments in Grittner's chapter. Morain points out how the "melting pot" idea of American society no longer has validity and that the concept of pluralism in our society seems to be more relevant. She reviews the necessity of the inclusion of the cultural component in language study, including how it relates to goals and the motivation of students.

Cultural pluralism

Morain does not overlook the implications of foreign language and culture study for a better understanding of our own society, however. She shows with specific examples that the study of another language and culture is beneficial for our society as a whole. Morain also indicates that culture study is applicable across international boundaries as well as "at home." She describes how students and teachers participate in programs that relate subcultures of our society to their original sources. In that regard, she discusses the many opportunities for students to relate to African and Latin-American culture through programs such as Black studies, African literature, French and African studies, and Latin-American studies.

The most practical section for teachers, in terms of actually teaching culture, is found in the section entitled "Behind the classroom door: Strategies in action." Here Morain reviews textbooks, interdisciplinary courses, and the use of media. She also shows how grammar and literature reflect culture. This section provides a thorough review of present classroom practices in the teaching of culture.

Procedures for the assessment of cross-cultural understanding are directly related to the training of teachers. Morain shows how the profession is becoming aware of this concept and how programs of teacher education are acting to improve the situation.

Although her view is not negative, Morain believes that the

teaching of cross-cultural understanding in foreign language programs falls short of its "goals." She believes that the profession must act *soon* to correct the situation.

Bilingual education in the United States is recognized by educators and politicians as important to the welfare of a pluralistic society. As a result the federal government has supported efforts to provide bilingual education to the thousands of non-English-speaking children who enter school each year. Pacheco's chapter deals to a large extent with influences of this federal support on the development of bilingual education. He provides a rationale for bilingual programs, showing the many reasons for their existence for both non-native and native speakers of English. Such reasons include pressure from minority groups, as well as psychological, sociological, linguistic, and economic forces.

Approaches to bilingualism

This rationale allows Pacheco to proceed through an examination of current attempts to provide equal opportunity of education for the different ethnic, social, and linguistic minority groups that make up this country's pluralistic society. He reviews the many problems in materials construction and the recruitment and training of instructional personnel. He shows the necessity of community involvement for the success of such programs. The evaluation of students in bilingual programs provides another area to which some attention has been given. In terms of accountability, Pacheco discusses the relatively few attempts to evaluate bilingual curricula. In a final section of his chapter, Pacheco outlines the problems and areas of research toward which bilingual educators might direct themselves.

Interdisciplinary programs and activities are reviewed by Warriner. Her chapter is based to some degree on the results of a questionnaire that she used to get information about current programs. Warriner shows that foreign language curricula are not *uni*disciplinary but interdisciplinary in nature. She also analyzes the factors that naturally turn foreign language learning toward possessing an interdisciplinary makeup. In reviewing the literature sources, she comments on those documents that deal with advocacy of interdisciplinary programs and that describe existing programs from about 1965 to the present in the modern languages and in the classics. In addition, she also reviews interdisciplinary programs on the college level, which range from particular structures in beginning and intermediate language courses to graduate programs such as the doctor of arts degree. The results of her survey show many new and interesting pro-

Foreign language interdisciplinary programs and activities

grams that have developed in the two years since the publishing of the Ort & Smith study (5). Some planned programs are also discussed and identified. The result of the literature and program review shows that interdisciplinary curricula relate heavily to the social studies areas. This review also indicates that interdisciplinary programs play an important role in the pluralistic picture of foreign language curricula.

The chapter by Tucker and d'Anglejan specifically discusses language learning processes from a psychological viewpoint showing the interaction between the individual and his qualities with instruction and sociocultural factors. The native learning processes with language are used to examine those of second-language learning. Other factors examined in this same interaction are aptitude, intellectual potential *and* attitudes, and motivational orientation toward another culture. The chapter also points directions in which future research can proceed in the development of approaches to language learning processes. The authors especially single out immersion-type language teaching programs and the simultaneous study of linguistic and other cognitive skills as important directions in language learning research.

Language learning processes

In contrast to the study of procedures of language learning from a psycholinguistic-sociocultural viewpoint, Garfinkel presents a chapter that represents practical aspects of teaching and learning strategies in the classroom. He makes special note of the fact that the information he has reviewed concerning actual classroom behavior of teacher and student is not related to any particular theory of language learning. He reviews the literature and other sources, including a questionnaire, to relate actual teaching-learning behavior of teacher and student in the classroom environment. The author discusses the work for 1970 in terms of the development of the listening, speaking, reading, and writing skills and of general strategies in the classroom. He also presents a discussion of sources of information for the foreign language teacher.

Instructional strategies in foreign language learning and teaching

Gougher's chapter on individualized learning brings into focus the efforts of the profession to provide learning experiences that fit the individual learner. Gougher reviews the particular contribution of BRFLE 2 to the profession's understanding of individualization of learning. He shows how the contributions of different conferences and publications in foreign language education have added to the awareness of the concept and its struc-

Individualization of foreign language learning: What's being done

ture. Major sections of the chapter review attempts to define individualized learning, some theoretical bases of operation for individualization, and actual implementation of the concept in school programs. A rather large number of programs are reviewed in the latter section, giving the reader a broad cross section of practical experiences with the concept. Completing his chapter, Gougher presents a very thoughtful set of conclusions that indicate both caution and enthusiasm for the concept of individualized learning.

Cloos' chapter on in-service teacher-training programs provides another dimension to the concept of pluralism in foreign language education. His chapter deals with a wide variety of programs to fit the needs of teachers at various levels. National in-service programs, such as those under the National Defense Education Act (NDEA) and the Education Professions Development Act (EPDA) as well as those organized by professional organizations, are thoroughly discussed. Cloos also reviews the important contributions of regional in-service programs through regional conferences. State, area, and local programs of in-service training for foreign language teachers seem to have taken on the responsibilities for the continuing education of teachers, formerly the purview of national programs. Cloos also reviews a model for the individual teacher that leads to a discussion of innovations of in-service programs.

In-service programs in foreign languages at elementary and secondary levels

The chapter by Thompson, on the uncommonly taught languages, fits into the theme of pluralism in foreign language education in that it widens the perspective we may have about the languages taught in the United States. In a sense, French, German, Latin, Spanish, and perhaps Russian are recognized as *the* languages taught in schools and colleges. Thompson's chapter, however, breaks down that myth, showing that many other languages are offered in addition to the traditional ones. Like Grittner's chapter, Thompson's reviews not only the literature of 1970, but it also calls on historical events to reveal governmental, private, and professional influences on the study of uncommon languages. Thompson especially reviews the contribution of the National Defense Education Act on the teaching, learning, and preparation of materials and specialists in the non-cognate languages. He presents the "state of the uncommonly taught languages" by world area and shows how the present educational climate in the United States is particularly influencing the study of these languages.

Modern foreign language teaching in the uncommonly taught languages

The final chapter in this volume brings into focus the movement in American education for the continuing evaluation of curricular programs. Accountability is actually desired and demanded by certain segments and forces within our society. Parent and Veidt, alerted to the relative "newness" of the concept, review literature sources outside the foreign language field, as well as those within, to provide a coherent and ordered discussion of the components of accountability. They indicate how important behavioral objectives, performance criteria, and testing are to the central concept. But they also reveal that accountability raises many unanswered questions for the profession: For what and to whom should schools be accountable? How is a teacher held accountable? Who and/or what will perform the necessary evaluation?

Program evaluation: accountability

Although accountability is a rather recent development, Parent and Veidt show how it has been implemented through such structures as performance contracting, merit pay, and the voucher system. They also review recommendations for the implementation of accountability programs.

In a concluding section of the chapter, the authors particularly examine programs of accountability that have been employed. The results of this discussion show clearly the cautions with which educators must proceed with this concept.

The broad view of foreign language education suggested in this volume provides further meaning to the first two volumes of the *Britannica Review*, indicating that they must be viewed as a whole. Volume 1 sets the scene by reviewing the contributions of the individual elements of foreign language education to an understanding of foreign language teaching and learning in the late 1960s. Volume 2 provides an in-depth look at a particular movement in foreign language education, while Volume 3 shows how foreign languages fit into a multifaceted society. Thus, these three volumes together, reviewing the literature of the profession for 1968, 1969, and 1970, supply a broad base of information from which the profession might draw for its work in the 1970s.

Volumes 1, 2, and 3 considered as a whole

References, Introduction and overview

1 Lange, Dale L.,comp. "1970 ACTFL Annual Bibliography." *Foreign Language Annals* 4(1971): 427–90.
2 Mildenberger, Andrea S., and Margarita Mazzeo.

"ERIC Documents on the Teaching of Foreign Languages:List Number 4." *Foreign Language Annals* 3(1970):489–502.
3 ———— "ERIC Documents on the Teaching of

Foreign Languages:List Number 5." *Foreign Language Annals* 4(1970):95–110.
4 Monka, Carolyn. "ERIC Documents on the Teaching of Foreign Languages:List Number 6." *Foreign Language Annals* 4(1971):313–28.
5 Ort, Barbara A., and Dwight R. Smith,comps. "The Language Teacher Tours the Curriculum." *Foreign Language Annals* 3(1969):28–74.

Pluralism in foreign language education: A reason for being

Introduction

Frank M. Grittner

Wisconsin State Department of Public Instruction

Foreign language educators from Europe, after spending a considerable amount of time in the United States, are frequently struck by American preoccupation with the question, "Why study foreign languages?" To the European mind, the answer is self-evident: "One studies a foreign language in order to learn it" (Arendt, 3). In fact, it is difficult to imagine a situation in which any significant number of contemporary European educators would seriously challenge the educational value of foreign language instruction for most of their students. As the 1970 Northeast Conference Report expressed it (Sandstrom & Pimsleur, 71), ". . . It is only in the United States that a monolingual person can be considered an educated man." Fishman (24, p. 29) has noted that, while naturalization of immigrants has gone on throughout history all over the world, America represents one of the few instances in which a new nation and a new culture was created "from scratch" in the process. According to Fishman the pressures for de-ethnization and Americanization have produced an ambivalence toward foreign languages and foreign cultures in America. That is, a large percentage of Americans are in the position of wanting to identify with a non-Anglo-American heritage, while at the same time they are subjected to overt and covert kinds of pressures to conform to the Anglo-American patterns of life that supposedly represent the cultural mainstream of the nation. This phenomenon has been documented by Grittner (31, pp. 13–17) and by Wright (87), who described the virulence of the Anglicization movement in America during its westward expansion. However, despite strong negative attitudes toward immigrants, foreigners, and "hyphenated Americans" throughout much of American history, a substantial number of contemporary Americans still choose to identify themselves with a foreign heritage; in some cases, even in families with three, four, or more generations of residence in America. Fishman (24) has also documented the many persistent efforts to maintain the language as well as the cultural heritage. These

Why study foreign languages?

Pressure to conform to "mainstream culture"

9

efforts have met with varying degrees of success, but it is significant that there are such efforts and that they continue even into the present.

The term "pluralism" is commonly used in reference to subcultural groups that are defined by such characteristics as national origin, racial inheritance, religious preference, or language dominance. However, there are also those who see pluralism in its broadest possible sense; that is, they see each human being as a distinctly unique individual. Many of the advocates of individualized instruction, for example, believe that each student must be appealed to on his own terms. An illustration of this view is contained in the remarks of Tyler & Brownell (82) who state that, "Human diversity is a key to social progress and a challenge to better education. As far as the schools and instruction are concerned, we have a long way to go in making the most of the opportunities afforded in individual differences." The implications of such thinking are that, since each individual is unique to begin with, the details of his genetic heritage or socioeconomic background are merely secondary factors that, while they complicate the educational process, have no basic validity with respect to the question of pluralism in education. In this view, a good educational program will meet the student where he is and will find ways to make all desirable educational experiences available to him.

Use of the term "pluralism"

This, then, is the context in which a rationale for "pluralism in foreign language education" must be placed. There can be little doubt that America is pluralistic in many senses of the word. That is, the people who make up this nation today represent an extremely broad range of social, religious, economic, linguistic, and cultural backgrounds. In some subtle way, this mixture of circumstances has worked to the detriment of foreign language study within the American system of education. The remarks which follow will deal with the role of foreign language study in a nation that, throughout its history, has attempted to reconcile the strong pressures for pluralism inherent in its population with the powerful pressures for linguistic and cultural unification and for individual conformity to dominant group "norms."

The setting for the theme of this review

What is cultural pluralism?

As is the case with many complex social issues, a clear definition of the term "cultural pluralism" is hard to come by. Yet, since the term is being widely used by educators, it seems reasonable at the outset to attempt a definition at least in the broad functional terms that a "social model" provides. In their book, *Beyond the Melting Pot*, Glazer & Moynihan (29, pp. xxiii–xxiv) describe a model for achieving cultural pluralism among ethnic groups that, they claim, has operated successfully in large American cities in the past. This model can be summarized as having the following characteristics:

A "social model" for achieving cultural pluralism

1 There is achievement of or movement toward eventual equalization of wealth and power so that each group participates sufficiently in the goods and values and social life of a common society so as to feel that the common society is good and fair.

2 Competition between groups exists but is nonviolent; it is expressed through effectiveness of group organization and achievement.

3 Group and individual participation in the common society is by individual choice rather than being imposed by law or rigid custom.

4 Each individual in a given group is free to choose his degree of assimilation or acculturation (if any) into the dominant group.

The authors are opposed to other historical approaches to dealing with disparate cultural groups such as segregation through violent suppression or forced assimilation into the dominant culture. As the authors express it (29, p. xxiv), "We believe the ethnic pattern offers the best chance for a humane and positive adaptation to group diversity, offering the individual the choice to live as he wishes, rather than forcing him into the pattern of a single 'Americanized' society or into the compartments of a rigidly separated society. The question is, can we still convince the varied groups of the society that this is still the best solution?" Implicit in this model of cultural pluralism is the belief that subcultures can coexist peacefully with a powerful dominant culture, that members of the subculture can achieve satisfactory social and economic status, and that individuals can maintain their subculture identity while participating, if they desire, in the activities and functions of the dominant culture.

Not everyone is optimistic about this particular model. In fact, Ether (22) raises a number of questions about the feasibility of cultural pluralism. He notes that the schools have, for the past 100 years, been devoted to the task of *eliminating* differences

Questions about achieving cultural pluralism

11

"despite our politico-philosophic statements about the beauty of diversity and the contributions of all Americans. . . ." He further insists that no model for building a pluralistic society actually exists and that there is no evidence that a pluralistic society has ever existed or can exist. He concedes that such places as Hawaii, Israel, and Quebec do have functioning communities with wide cultural divergence among the inhabitants. "Yet an examination reveals that each has a dominant culture with subservient sub-cultures and that each has considerable current agitation for recognition of the subcultures" (22).

Pluralism and education

In the field of education there are many who express the conviction that the American school system can be redirected from its historical role as the "melting pot" in which nonconforming children are subjected to "acculturation" into the Anglo-American mainstream (Houts, 38). According to Ramirez (64), the change can be made only if the philosophy of public education is redirected toward "cultural democracy." As he sees it, "In the final analysis, the crucial difference between the melting pot and cultural democracy philosophies of education comes down to this: the melting pot philosophy emphasizes that the child must change to fit the educational system; the cultural democracy philosophy . . . states that the institution must change to fit the child." Bell (9) is optimistic about the role of education in creating a pluralistic society. In his opinion ". . . we *can* build a more pluralistic model of society but only through a more pluralistic education system—one that offers a great number of options to meet the needs of every individual and every individual community; one that offers greater freedom to the individual, with all the responsibilities and discipline that freedom entails."

Optimism in changing the educational system from the "melting pot" toward "cultural democracy"

From this it would appear that if education is to devote itself to achieving cultural pluralism educators must, of necessity, deal with virtually the entire school population. This means that those who control money and position in education must develop a broad tolerance for differences of all kinds, as must the teachers who are in direct daily contact with students in the classroom (Hogg & McComb, 37). In its broadest interpretation the implementation of the concept of "pluralism" would call for the toleration by the group in power of individual idiosyncrasy, of divergent subcultural behavior patterns, and of those supposedly

Implications of such a change

inherent differences that we attribute to racial inheritance. It would be superfluous to cite here the great body of facts that indicate that this kind of pluralism has not been fully achieved in America. For example, it seems quite clear that in most situations, a capable young man who has long hair and a beard, or whose first language is Spanish, or who is black is much more restricted in his opportunities than would be the case had he been a short-haired, clean-shaven, English-speaking, Anglo-American with comparable abilities. Additional problems arise if the individual is a nonconforming female. For the schools the question is, how does one educate in order to produce people who accept the divergent characteristics of others? The answer, it seems, must involve changing the attitudes and behavior patterns of a majority of people in the predominant culture as well as in each of the subcultures. Each group must learn to accept the characteristics of all other groups as being normal and perfectly valid (Frazier, 27). This kind of acceptance of other ways of life has been the stated aim of foreign language educators for many years. For example, one state's curriculum guide for all foreign languages has as the cultural goal "to evaluate the foreign culture objectively and on its own merits rather than from the standpoint of Anglo-American culture" (Grittner, 31, p. 83). The German Guide for New York City includes under cultural aims, that the student is "to develop an enlightened understanding of foreign people through a study of their contemporary life, their patterns of behavior and their national customs and observances" (59, p. 5). An examination of curriculum guides in foreign languages from the various states and municipalities across the nation will reveal a similar commitment to the development of "enlightened attitudes" toward other cultures. The possible reasons why such stated aims may not have been more widely realized will be discussed subsequently. First, however, it is important to point up another problem which relates cultural pluralism to the question of social and economic mobility.

Historically the predominant culture has often expressed its concern for subcultural groups by trying to perpetuate all of the conditions which inhere to those groups at a given point in time. To use an extreme example, one might point out that the ruling class of medieval Europe was quite intent on perpetuating the conditions of poverty, ignorance, and servitude, which were characteristics of the "subculture" of serfs. Had the ruling minority of the Middle Ages been successful in attaching perma-

Some examples of how pluralism has not been achieved

How can one educate for the acceptance of divergence?

How foreign language curricula relate to the question

Predominant culture's concern for the subcultures

nent significance to the environmentally produced characteristics of serfdom, the majority of living white Americans might today be a "subculture" of illiterate peasants to whom education would be denied as "inappropriate to their class."

In the early days of the American republic there were conservative forces who fought educational reformers on precisely such grounds. For example, on July 10, 1830, the *Philadelphia National Gazette* criticized editorially the workingman's striving for educational equality: "There will ever be distinctions of conditions of capacity, of knowledge and ignorance, in spite of all fond conceits which may be indulged, or the wild projects which may be tried, to the contrary. The 'peasant' must labor during those hours of the day, which his wealthy neighbor can give to the abstract culture of his mind" (Rippa, 66, p. 106).

Early American conservative forces against educational reform

Perhaps such examples are not so remote from present conditions as they might appear at first glance. In the late 1960s, for example, a school board member speaking for the grape growers of the San Joaquin Valley was quoted as saying, "Look, you've got to understand that we've built this Valley to what it is and we've gotten to where we are because there's always been cheap labor around. When you come in talking about raising the educational vista of the Mexican-American and helping him to aspire beyond the fields, and curing the dropout problem, you're talking about jeopardizing our economic survival" (Mangers, 52).

Present-day conservative forces of like kind

When this sort of manipulation of educational opportunity is successful, it produces cultural segregation rather than cultural pluralism. With segregation there is a minimum of social and economic mobility among the groups involved. Under these conditions mobility into the upper group can only be achieved by renouncing one's heritage, thereby earning titles such as "Uncle Tom" or "Tío Taco" for the one who capitulates. Ramirez (64) explains the high dropout rate among Chicano students as the result of emotional strains produced by conditions of cultural segregation. As he expresses it, students have "an approach-avoidance conflict with respect to education. They want to be educated; they realize its importance. But in order to achieve it they must reject themselves—an understandably painful process for any human being."

Such forces produce cultural segregation

In contrast to segregation, cultural *separatism* is the voluntary separation of a subcultural group from the predominant culture (Sizemore & Thompson, 72). Some groups (the Amish, for example) deliberately seek to locate in areas where cultural

Cultural separatism

14

separatism is possible. Groups of this type often have a strongly divergent religious orientation, with resulting behavior patterns that are incompatible with the life-style of the dominant culture. The adults in the group wish to maintain their traditions intact and to pass them on to the next generation without contamination. In this effort they frequently run into problems with certain legal requirements such as compulsory school attendance laws. Thus, at the same time that separatists are seeking to avoid public education, pluralist advocates may be seeking ways to make it more accessible. For example, Rodriguez (67), speaking for Spanish-speaking Americans, states: "We want a good education without having to surrender our culture. To refuse our Spanish-speaking children this educational opportunity is to deny them their rights as Americans."

Temporary separatism may be used for the ultimate achievement of cultural pluralism. In fact, according to Sizemore & Thompson (72), "Most previously excluded groups attempted to improve their conditions from a separated vantage point, for example, Amish, Muslims, immigrants and Catholics." Except for the Amish, for whom "improvement" was associated with continued separatism, many individuals from the previously excluded groups have learned to function successfully within the dominant culture without giving up the essentials of their heritage. Thus, separatism (even militant separatism) need not be viewed as a rejection of the goal of cultural pluralism. Quite the contrary; it can actually serve as the means to achieving mobility into the dominant culture. According to Sizemore & Thompson (72), the group cohesion that separatism produces can make mobility possible; whereas, without this group support, the individual would be unable to penetrate the walls that the "in" group has constructed. Education, of course, is a crucial factor in determining to what extent individuals within a subculture will acquire the characteristics that will enable them to function within the dominant culture. The nature, extent, and success of the individual's education will thus be of tremendous importance regardless of whether he has acquired it as a member of a separatist group, a segregated group, or the dominant group. However, in addition to its value as a vehicle for the socio-economic mobility of subculture groups, education for cultural pluralism is seen as a valuable addition to the education of students from the dominant culture. In this regard Ballesteros (6) suggests that the American myth of Anglo-cultural superiority

Temporary separatism used to achieve cultural pluralism

Education is a crucial element for cultural pluralism

15

and the monolingual orientation of the American school system "has seriously harmed this country in its dealings with other nations." According to Ballesteros, the adverse effects of American monocultural attitudes have not been limited to international relations. He suggests that, in addition, they have led to problems at home. He cites a speech by Harold Howe II, former U.S. Commissioner of Education, to make the point (6):

Effects of American monolingual attitudes

> This argument, that wider cultural exposure will help our international relations, stresses both national purposes and international amity. Perhaps the most important reason for bicultural programs, however, is not international but domestic – our relations with each other here at home. The entire history of discrimination is based on the prejudice that because someone else is different, he is somehow worse. If we could teach all our children – black, white, brown, yellow and all the American shades in between – that diversity is not to be feared or suspected, but enjoyed and valued, we would be well on the way toward achieving the equality we have always proclaimed as a national characteristic.

It is, perhaps, an exaggeration to say that "we have always proclaimed" equality "as a national characteristic." Actually, the record is somewhat clouded on that issue. As for the tradition of pluralism and tolerance, historical documents indicate that separatism and extreme intolerance of nonconformity were present through all of American history (Rippa, 66). A full exploration of these historical patterns is not within the scope of this chapter. Yet, perhaps a short survey of relevant historical developments would be useful.

The historical role of English and other languages in American education

As Ford (26) points out, the educational thrust during the Colonial Period was not motivated by a desire for pluralism. In fact, the motives were quite to the contrary. *The New England Primer*, for example, was more than a reader; it was, according to Ford, a means of indoctrinating children so that they would believe one narrow Calvinist interpretation of the Bible printed in English.

Bible versions in other languages, presumably Latin and Greek, were to be avoided according to a "Resolve of the General Court of the Massachusetts Bay" that appeared in 1647. In this

Colonial Period and the avoidance of foreign languages

Resolve other versions of the Bible were seen as products of that "ould deluder, Satan, to keepe men from the knowledge of ye Scriptures as in former times by keeping y^m in an unknown tongue, so in these latter times by pswading from ye use of tongues, that so at least ye true sence & meaning of ye originall might be clouded by false glosses of saint seeming deceivers. . . ." (Ford, 26, p. 3). The Resolve went on to order that every township with 50 households, "shall then forthwith appoint one within their towne to teach all such children as shall resort to him to write & read."

Throughout the early Colonial Period *The New England Primer* reached hundreds of thousands of New England youngsters. Following the Revolution, this and other primers began to be secularized. As early as 1790 some rather worldly middle-class motives began to appear in the primer side-by-side with the spiritual ones. For example, there was the following bit of verse (Ford, 26, p. 47):

Effects of early learning materials on the achievement of educational and cultural goals

> He who ne'er learns his A.B.C.
> Forever will a blockhead be.
> But he who learns his letters fair
> Shall have a coach to take the air.

The utilitarian rationale for education, it would appear, is deeply rooted in American culture.

At various times throughout American history powerful subcultural groups have attempted to establish primary education through languages other than English (e.g., Dutch, German, Spanish, French). Despite these efforts the pattern established by *The New England Primer* and carried on by the *McGuffey Readers* was the one that became dominant in public primary education across the United States. The educational system that emerged for grades 1–8 came to emphasize the following elements: (*1*) All instruction was to be carried on in English, and (*2*) Instruction was to include the inculcation of the Anglo-American middle-class value system and its version of the American heritage (Wright, 87). Achieving the first goal has met with serious obstacles throughout the history of the republic. An educational bulletin of the Wisconsin Department of Public Instruction (Bush, 12) that appeared during World War I (1918) is illustrative of the general problem:

The language goal was not always achieved

> The findings in our recent draft registration revealed conditions that are most startling. In one county of the state 76 men

17

presented themselves to the draft board for examination. Of these 60 spoke German only or a very few words of English. . . These men are all of voting age. What do they know of American ideals? What knowledge have they of national needs? Our state as a whole has today 32 illiterates for every group of 1,000 population.

According to the author, the solution to this was obvious: "Every teacher in Wisconsin must work untiringly to wipe out illiteracy and to encourage the use of English in every home in her community." Parents, preschool children, all must be made to work for "mastery of the new tongue (English) so that they can learn to think in the language of democracy" (Bush, 12, p. 8). Fishman (25) describes how this process of Anglicizing millions of non-English-speaking Americans took place across the country. And he notes that, "Part of the American experience with English has been to encourage, to help, to nudge, and to force millions to seemingly forget and deny parts of themselves. It is, therefore, a particularly American dilemma to have to use this same means, English, to also help these very same millions to recognize, sensitize, clarify, and intensify themselves."

Anglicizing of non-English-speaking Americans

What had happened was a gradual transformation of the early protestant concept, that each person must be literate in the vernacular in order to achieve religious salvation, into a new rationale that advocated English literacy as a vehicle for the social and economic "salvation" of the individual. It was also thought that English literacy would serve the national interest by unifying the disparate groups of immigrants and by helping to preserve "American ideals."

While English, "the language of democracy," was moving toward almost universal dominance of elementary school education, Latin, Greek, and various of the modern languages became firmly established in secondary and higher education. As was the case with vernacular literacy, foreign language learning was first offered for religious reasons. Also, in certain parts of America, a knowledge of classical languages was viewed as being part of the necessary mental equipment of the "cultured gentleman" (Grittner, 31, p. 6).

English dominates elementary education, but foreign languages firmly established at higher levels

But even though the spiritual and cultural reasons for language study tended to remain dominant in formal education through the 18th century, utilitarian reasons began to appear increasingly, notably in the writings of men such as Franklin

Utilitarian reasons for foreign language study in early America

18

and Jefferson. According to Leavitt (49) and Zeydel (88) foreign language instruction for practical purposes was first carried on by means of tutors, free-lance teachers, and study abroad. As secondary education began to expand in America, first through the Latin grammar schools and the academies and then, in the latter part of the 19th century, in the American public high school, Latin, French, and German became established as basic subjects. By the turn of the century the high school had become the predominant vehicle for the general education of those students with the ability, interest, and wherewithal to maintain themselves in school beyond the elementary level. Foreign languages, mathematics, the sciences, and the relatively new subject of English were among the subjects considered as essential preparation for life. Many foreign language educators mistakenly believe that the high school prior to World War I was largely "college preparatory." As a matter of fact, only a tiny percentage of those who attended high school actually went on into higher education. As late as 1910 enrollment figures from the federal government revealed that 80% of the students in high schools were enrolled in a foreign language (usually Latin, German, or French) (Grittner, 31, p. 8). Apparently, all but the very smallest high schools were able to obtain the services of a language teacher in one of the commonly taught languages.

However, knowledgeable educators living in the 1890s estimated the college-bound portion of the high school population to be very small (Krug, 46, p. 96). It cannot be denied that this group of secondary school students was an elite, of sorts, since it represented only about 5% of the students who had attended the elementary school (Krug, 46, p. 74). However, it is important to note that the heavy emphasis upon academic subjects was not due to the pressures for college preparation; quite the contrary, the development of trained intelligence was seen as the best possible preparation for life. As the 1894 Committee of Ten Report expressed it, "The secondary schools of the United States . . . do not exist for the purpose of preparing boys and girls for colleges. Only an insignificant percentage of the graduates of these schools go to colleges or scientific schools. Their main function is to prepare for the duties of life that small proportion of all the children in the country . . . who show themselves able to profit by an education prolonged to the eighteenth year, and whose parents are able to support them while they remain so long at school" (Krug, 46, pp. 96–97).

Reasons for heavy emphasis in 1890s on academic subjects

19

Pluralism in foreign language education/Grittner

Thus, in reality, the high school of the previous century was the common man's liberal arts college; a fulfillment of the Jeffersonian concept of democratic education which would promote a "natural aristocracy of talents and virtues" from among all classes of society (Lee, 50, p. 7). To many of the educational leaders of the 19th century it was self-evident that foreign language study should be offered as part of "preparation for life." Thus, curricular questions seldom touched upon the question of whether or not foreign languages should be offered; the discussions were more likely to be directed toward questions such as *which* languages to offer, how early to teach them, or whether to stress classical or modern languages. It was not until the second decade of the 20th century that foreign languages and certain other academic subjects were seriously threatened. The decline was attendant to the upward extension of compulsory education. As secondary education moved through the 20th century the number of students in high school grew from 250,000 in 1892 to over 21,000,000 by the end of the 1960s (Grittner, 32, p. 54).

In 19th century schools, foreign language study was part of "education for life"

Beginning with American involvement in World War I in 1917, the position of foreign language instruction in secondary and higher education began to deteriorate. The war itself resulted in the near elimination of German (then the main modern language) from the school curriculum. However, the war appears to have been only a surface reason for the rapid loss of stature of foreign language instruction. Other causes more basic to the changes in curricular rationale that led to the decline of language study include: (*1*) rapid "assembly line" industrialization with its attendant utilitarianism; (2) the push for compulsory secondary education, which brought millions of unmotivated students into the high schools; (3) the steady urbanization of the country, which created new problems for education; (4) a mechanistic version of the new behavioral psychology, which was interpreted by many educational leaders as a refutation of earlier theories of mental training in general education; (5) negative attitudes toward non-English-speaking immigrants; (6) vocationalism in secondary education; (7) isolationism in politics; and finally (8) a ten-year economic depression, which caused a shortage of funds in all areas including education. In the face of such monumental problems, American foreign language educators were apparently unable to effectively fight the charge that foreign language courses were a frill, and a highly expendable one at that (Callahan, 13).

Deterioration of foreign language study after World War I

Equalitarianism, elitism, and the academic curriculum

The preceding historical sketch outlined a few of the socio-economic factors that have helped to shape the present-day foreign language curriculum and to place foreign language instruction as an elective in the high school rather than as a required course in the elementary school. In this connection there is also the matter of changes that took place within secondary education and of the ability (or inability) of foreign language teachers to adapt to those changes. As we have seen, the high school changed from an institution whose student body was selected on the basis of ability, inclination, and parental support for academic studies to an institution charged by state legislative mandate with the responsibility of educating an increasingly large and diverse mass of boys and girls, many of whom were either indifferent to or antagonistic toward formal education. Over the past 80 years educators have tried many ways of accommodating secondary education to this multicultural student body. According to Kliebard (45), the response to this problem "may be seen as taking three forms: compensatory education, instructional adaptation, and curriculum differentiation." The first approach, compensatory education, assumes that certain curricular areas are necessary to the education of all students and that, therefore, the school has the responsibility for neutralizing deficiencies in a given student's makeup that prevent him from achieving at an acceptable level in those curricular areas. To this end, special "remedial" teachers are hired, special equipment and materials are purchased, and Head Start programs are instituted.

Changes in secondary education

Adaptation to a multicultural student body

Compensatory education

The second approach, instructional adaptation, can also be based upon a common body of curricular content. That is, all students may learn some of the same material, but they may do so at a pace or by a method that is adapted to their particular characteristics. During the 1920s and again during the 1960s and 1970s educators in several subject areas (including foreign languages) were promoting various schemes for individualizing or personalizing instruction. During the thirties and forties a number of "progressive" educators attempted to adapt the curriculum to the backgrounds of the students. In some cases, the intent was to lead the student from relevant "life-experiences"

Instructional adaptation

21

into an ever deepening understanding of intellectual subject matter. As John Dewey (19, pp. 73–74), the leading proponent of progressive education, expressed it, ". . . finding the material for learning within experience is only the first step. The next step is the progressive development of what is already experienced into a fuller and richer and also more organized form, a form that gradually approximates that in which subject-matter is presented to the skilled, mature person." For various reasons, the progressive education movement fell into disrepute as it became associated with permissiveness and chaotic, unfocused student activity. But its original intent had been to meet the student on his own terms, to begin with the interests and experiences that he had brought to school with him and to lead him from there into the organized bodies of knowledge. Where the adaptive approach was successfully implemented in the public school, foreign languages were usually omitted or were given an insignificant role. As a case in point, there was the "core curriculum" approach. In one version of the core curriculum, certain subjects would form the core around which all other subjects would revolve (e.g., there was a science core, a history-literature core, etc.). However, a perusal of the various textbooks on curriculum development reveals that foreign languages were almost never listed as either a core subject or a subordinated subject (Smith, Stanley, & Shores, 73, pp. 311–335).

The third way of coping with problems caused by diversity of student population is curriculum differentiation. With this approach, certain criteria are used to "track" or "stream" students into slots that someone deems appropriate for establishing homogeneous groups. The questions that immediately arise with this approach are, Who is to establish the criteria? and How are they to be applied? Selective criteria that have been used in the past include ability (e.g., IQ scores, grade point average, aptitude test scores) and vocational destination (e.g., commercial orientation, technical orientation, college preparatory orientation). Once the criteria have been set and the groups have been identified, then how are the results to be applied? In recent years there has been an increasing tendency to answer that question by saying that criteria shall be arbitrarily used to place students in certain courses and to exclude them from others. Thus, for example, the girl who has been identified as "secretarial material" is put into subjects such as typing, shorthand, and "business English," whereas the low-achieving, job-oriented boy is sched-

Curriculum adaptation

uled into "auto shop" or "art metal." The high ability or "college capable" students are counseled into the academic subjects including, in most cases, foreign languages; the others are counseled out. The basic problem with this approach is that, instead of promoting the neo-Jeffersonian ideal of affording social mobility for capable students through education, curriculum differentiation tends to have the opposite effect. That is, students tend to be put into tracks on the basis of socioeconomic background. And then the education that they receive makes it almost certain that they will be educationally unfit to change their subsequent socioeconomic status. In the case of the underprivileged student, this approach is often justified as being the best way to meet his individual needs. For example, according to Neff (57): "Among the so-called underprivileged youth of our country the meaning of life is usually earthy—it is defined largely in terms of job opportunities and bread-and-butter values. Life assumes meaning in so far as airy abstractions are kept to a minimum and jobs are or will be available that are commensurate with training and ability." Neff goes on to say that underprivileged students have no need for a "strictly academic brand of education"; instead what they need is "education for vocations and common life pursuits." In contrast to the ideas of progressive education, which aimed at taking the student from where he was and leading him to a higher level of intellectual and aesthetic performance, this approach looks at where the student is and provides him with the kind of training that will tend to keep him there. The implementation of this philosophy can be said to promote cultural segregation in that it contributes to the perpetuation of a lower social class whose members are largely defined by their lack of the kind of academic knowledge needed for success in middle-class occupations and cultural activities. By this process many American urban high schools may be contributing to the kind of socioeconomic stratification that, among American educators, has historically been associated with European educational systems. According to Bruner (11), one of the country's leading psychologists, this has, in fact, become a principal function of all public education in America. As he expressed it, ". . . the educational system is in effect our way of maintaining a class system—a group at the bottom. It cripples the capacity of children in the lowest socioeconomic quarter of the population to participate effectively in society, and does so early and effectively." Kliebard (45), too, is highly critical of those

This approach limits social mobility

Pluralism in foreign language education/Grittner

practices that deprive disadvantaged children of bona fide educational experiences. As he expresses it:

> . . . we lump together the disadvantaged, the unintelligent, the mechanically talented, the racial minorities, and the so-called non-college bound and *we systematically cut them off from the intellectual resources of their culture by designing a curriculum for them which minimizes intellectual content.* We rigorously exclude this group from the mainstream of intellectual life and then piously decry the lack of rationality in decision-making at the personal and national levels. We do not have the honesty to admit that we have botched the job of putting our youth in touch with the intellectual resources of our culture and instead have tried to cover this failure with a dubious doctrine which asserts that this can be accomplished with only a small proportion of the school population.

The 1970 Northeast Conference Report makes a strong case for offering foreign language to all students and for having such study available at all levels (Sandstrom & Pimsleur, 71). In addition to the promotion of pluralistic attitudes (e.g., making students more receptive "to the different cultural patterns present in our multi-ethnic society"), the report gives these reasons why all students should be included in study of foreign languages:

Foreign languages for all students

1 We do not know whom to exclude;
2 We cannot predict who will need foreign languages in later life;
3 Foreign lands are more accessible;
4 Foreign language study is educationally beneficial;
5 There are new educational and career opportunities which require foreign languages;
6 Exclusion may be damaging.

The report also contains a discussion of ways to include all students in the study of foreign languages.

There is some evidence to support the contention that languages can be taught to all students, including those who live in the less affluent sections of large urban areas. For example, Avery (5) reports that Latin has been taught successfully to thousands of elementary school children in the inner city schools in Washington, D.C., and in Philadelphia. He also reports upon a Latin Heritage Program taught at the secondary level in the inner city of Detroit.

There are, however, many within the foreign language field who are willing to exclude students from the study of foreign languages. Oliva (60, pp. 14–15), for example, lists various selective criteria for the admission of high school students to foreign language classes. These include students who are college bound, students who score high on standardized tests of verbal intelligence, and students who have high grades in English. While suggesting that standards be scaled down to accommodate students of "average intelligence," Oliva states that, "It would not be realistic to require foreign languages of all students. Most schools would not have adequate staff or facilities to provide such an expanded program even if it were educationally defensible, which it is patently not. Foreign languages constitute a part of specialized education, not general education. . . ."

Some foreign language educators hold an opposite view: an example

There appears to be a basic inconsistency between this advocacy of elitism and a statement that Oliva makes elsewhere to the effect that, "The study of the foreign language spoken by large ethnic groups within our school systems can help promote mutual understanding between peoples living side by side in our democratic society" (60, p. 17). The latter statement seems to imply that only the intelligent student (or the one who gets good grades in English) has need of those foreign language experiences which supposedly produce "mutual understanding." If so, then a very large percentage of black and Spanish-speaking children—many of whom may feel alienated from Anglo society—would be excluded, simply because they tend to do poorly in English and in IQ tests. This example is illustrative of the difficulty of reconciling the tendency toward elitism among foreign language teachers with the emerging concept of pluralism in foreign language education.

Curriculum differentiation can take place by inclusion as well as exclusion. For example, one school system reports efforts to "rewrite our 'single-track' type of 'course descriptions' which are designed basically for the high school students planning to go to college" and replace it with a three-track system (Harris, 34). This represents an attempt to broaden the acceptance of the foreign language offering by differentiating the offering according to vocational destination. The plan is to have "three learning tracks" for French, German, Latin, and Spanish, which would be defined as: (*1*) pre-college, (*2*) pre-technical (preparatory for post high school training below university level), and (*3*) pre-vocational (preparatory for immediate employment following gradu-

Curriculum differentiation by inclusion

25

ation from high school). During the 1970–71 school year, teachers were seeking to develop "terminal performance objectives," especially in areas "other than for an academic curriculum. . . ." (Harris, 34).

According to Kliebard (45), such efforts to establish elitist or differentiated groups within a school system tend to thwart the democratization function of the public school. He objects to the implication that a different kind of educational experience (practical rather than intellectual) is required for the "lower" tracks. Instead, he favors the same basic academic curriculum for all students on the grounds that, in our "much imitated" American system of education,

Elitism tends to thwart democratization of the schools

> We still offer our citizens essentially one opportunity only to become initiated into the world of ideas. In a world where ideas and intellectual competence are increasingly prized, we rarely allow a second chance. If that chance is not taken in the period of childhood through adolescence it is, for all intents and purposes, lost. Nothing could be more inimical to the American Dream than a system of schooling which acts to deny to a segment of our population that one opportunity to participate in the cultural mainstream of modern society.

The relationship of subject matter to the central purposes of education

In a similar vein, the Educational Policies Commission of the National Education Association had (in 1961) stated that the central purpose of the schools is to develop the rational and aesthetic powers of man. In the foreword to the report on *The Central Purpose of American Education* the Commission declared: "We most emphatically reject the idea that a few should be educated and that the majority should be trained. We say, on the contrary, that all have latent, unrealized powers of creativity. Our emphasis on thinking as a central outcome of education stresses the pervasiveness of rationality in all the purposes of education" (Willis, 85). The Commission's report goes on to emphasize that rationality must be a means as well as an end. Thus, while the report lists a number of subject areas that have the *potential* to develop "higher mental processes" and "creative abilities," the report also contains the statement that, "No particular body of knowledge will of itself develop the ability to

Educational Policies Commission and the purpose of schools

think clearly. The development of this ability depends instead on methods that encourage the transfer of learning from one context to another and the re-organization of things learned. The child can transfer learning when he is challenged to give thought to the solution of new problems, problems in which he becomes interested because they are within his range of comprehension. . . ." (Willis, 85). There is a point here that, although it is widely accepted in psychological and pedagogical circles, has perhaps all too often eluded the foreign language specialist. It is simply that the *process* of acquiring knowledge is held to be more important than any specific curricular *content*. Therefore, according to this interpretation, a course in industrial arts (for example) could be intellectually superior to a course in French literature. The value would lie in the degree to which each course of study involved the student in perceiving relationships, making rational decisions, developing aesthetic appreciations, and exercising his latent powers of creativity. Thus, there is implicit in the Commission report the principle that foreign languages — like other curricular areas — will tend to be accepted or rejected in accordance with the following priorities (Willis, 85):

Process versus content argument

1 Intellectual integrity: the potential of the subject matter for developing the student's rational and esthetic powers;
2 Utility: the relative importance of the knowledge in the life of the pupil and of society;
3 Methods of instruction: the ability of the teachers of the particular subject matter to teach students to use its unique curricular content in such a way that students learn to think more clearly, to demonstrate a higher degree of esthetic sensitivity, or to perform creatively within the discipline. Most important are those techniques that involve the student in transferring what he has learned to new situations.

Priorities for acceptance of any curricular area — including foreign languages

To the degree that students, parents, and educational officials perceive that a given discipline is fulfilling one or more of the above criteria, it will be considered "relevant" and will tend to flourish. As for the national emphasis upon the three criteria, this appears to be cyclical. There are periods when the intellectual side of education is emphasized. At other times, vocationalism, life adjustment, and other utilitarian curricular approaches gain ascendancy. In still another cycle the needs of the individual are emphasized and there are experiments with such innovations

Relevance and adaptability of a curricular area affects its acceptance

as "freedom schools," individualized instruction, team teaching, flexible scheduling, and other manipulations of administrative and instructional procedures. The ability of a given subject to adapt to a particular cycle will, to a large degree, determine its stability during that cycle.

Two other factors have historically assumed great importance in the rise or fall of a given curricular area. The first of these might be labeled "cost accountability." In his book, *Education and the Cult of Efficiency*, Callahan (13) shows that when the cost accountability principle is narrowly applied to education, it can override all other considerations. The second factor pertaining to the success or failure of a subject area has been discussed above at length under the term "equalitarianism." In a publicly supported educational system, it is self-evident that those subjects which benefit the largest number of taxpayers (i.e., those which reach the largest number of students) will have the best chance for survival. It is also worthy of note that the cost accountability factor and the democratization factor tend to interact with one another as follows: The larger the number of students there are enrolled in a subject area, the higher the pupil-teacher ratio will be and the lower the cost. A subject like foreign language with its elitist public image is highly vulnerable to cost accountability pressures in publicly supported educational institutions. For once it begins to decline and the per-pupil costs begin to rise, foreign language becomes an attractive item for elimination by budget analysts. Lacking broad popular support, individual languages are readily susceptible to "phase outs" based upon the kind of logic exhibited by a speaker at the National Education Association Convention in 1913 who stated: "I know nothing about the absolute value of a recitation in Greek as compared with a recitation in French or in English. I am convinced, however, by very concrete and quite local considerations, that when the obligations of the present year expire, we ought to purchase no more Greek instruction at the rate of 5.9 pupil-recitations for a dollar. The price must go down, or we shall invest in something else" (Callahan, 13, p. 73). According to Callahan (13, p. 233), even a popular language (such as German was in the early 1900s) can fall victim to the efficiency cultists "when some fortunate circumstance such as the anti-German sentiment during and after World War I occurred. . . . Significantly, when this happened the financial saving which was effected was included in the reporting of the event. Thus the *Journal of Education*

Other factors in rise or fall of curricular areas: cost accountability and equalitarianism

Foreign languages vulnerable to cost accountability pressures: examples

reported in a news item that the Cincinnati Schools had eliminated German and had saved $75,000 a year thereby."

Callahan traces the recurrent influence of the efficiency doctrine throughout the 20th century and notes that, at times, this influence has gone far beyond the mere elimination of low enrollment subject areas. In fact, it appears that an unremitting attempt has been made (and is being made) to reshape the curricula of schools and colleges to serve the purposes of business and industry and to employ the same methods and evaluative criteria (i.e., dollar criteria) to educational administration. And, when efficiency becomes the central purpose of education, then the idea that all students should be educated (rather than being trained) tends to be rejected. One cannot readily measure the things that make up the well-rounded man, and, in any case, such people are of little dollar value. "Personally," said one school administrator, "I would rather send out pupils who are lop-sided and useful, than those who are seemingly symmetrical and useless" (Callahan, 13, p. 10). And, the measure of "usefulness" for a human being is seen in terms of his utility to the world of business. As one school superintendent expressed it: "Since the school . . . really exists for the sole purpose of developing the business men and women of the future, it is evident that there should be perfect harmony between the school authorities and the business interests" (Callahan, 13). In the words of another educator, "The specifications for manufacturing come from the demands of 20th-century civilization, and it is the business of the school to build its pupils according to the specifications laid down" (Callahan, 13).

The purpose of the discussion to this point was to establish the "Reason for Being" of foreign languages in the context of the "Reason for Being" of American education. The problem is that the latter has tended to vacillate between the humanistic ideal of educating the well-rounded, autonomous, fulfilled human being and the utilitarian concept of training the socially adjusted conformist who fits neatly into one or more slots in modern industrialized society. Another problem relates to the mixing of the goals of the humanist with the techniques of the efficiency expert. For example, can one talk of "poetry input" and "learning output" in terms of "measurable overt behaviors" without in the process jeopardizing the entire humanistic "enterprise"? Or, to relate the present discussion more specifically to the topic of education for pluralism, can we really act upon President

Efficiency arguments go beyond eliminating low enrollment areas

"Usefulness" for a human being seen in his utility

Vacillation of educational system between humanistic education and utilitarian training

Pluralism in foreign language education/Grittner

Kennedy's suggestion that we "make the world safe for diversity" (Strasheim, 77, p. 18) while at the same time we adopt curriculum building techniques that call for "the precise statement of educational objectives in language which specifies expected responses, performance and outcomes which can be measured as accurately or objectively as possible" (Steiner, 75, p. 44). In short, is it possible to have "prescribed diversity" or "preplanned autonomy" all stated in terms of measurable overt behaviors that can be quantified to the satisfaction of the newest generation of efficiency experts? How does one measure a dollar's worth of diversity or two dollars' worth of autonomy? And, in any case, will this year's behavioral objectives be acceptable to next year's experts? It is precisely because such questions cannot be answered with any degree of certainty—because the goals and methods in American education are constantly shifting—that Christensen (17) sees the accountability concept as being untenable for the classroom teacher:

Prescribed diversity or preplanned autonomy; are they possible?

Accountability untenable for the classroom teacher?

> One year we are working toward "quality" education, another year toward "creative" education; and another year toward "individuating the educative process" (with 280 students?). Now we have gone gung ho on "behavioral objectives," National Assessment, and "teacher accountability through the auditing of learning output." Personally I wouldn't mind being held accountable if I knew what I was being held accountable for. But one "expert" insists that we must teach "objectively measurable skills" while another insists that students must be free to research, create, experiment, develop their own individuality. Students must be involved in planning their own curriculum, etc. So what are you supposed to "audit"? For what is the teacher to be held accountable?

Pluralism and psycholinguistic trends

Christensen (17) may, perhaps, express the type of frustration and bewilderment that many language teachers feel as they are confronted with a growing body of professional opinion that, in many cases, is a total reversal of the "basic" tenets of pedagogy that were laid down with such authority by linguists, psychologists, itinerant oracles, and methodology instructors in the NDEA summer institutes of the early 1960s. During the 1960s teachers were presented with a psychological rationale for lan-

Reversal of tenets of the 1960s foreign language pedagogy is in progress

guage acquisition in terms of the reinforcement of those "operant" responses that would lead to correct patterns of "language behavior." In foreign language instruction correct speech patterns were not to be derived from arbitrary rules, but were to come from the linguist's description of how people "really spoke." The pedagogical interpretation of all this, as far as foreign languages were concerned was that, since language is merely patterned oral behavior, the role of the foreign language teacher was basically to manipulate students so that they behaved orally, overtly, and accurately. The good teacher would set up a surrogate language environment (using himself and whatever audiovisual devices he could gather together) and he would induce students to respond. In the process he would constantly "reward" correct responses while allowing incorrect responses to "extinguish" themselves. Essentially this same process was applied to listening, speaking, reading, and writing skills. Since language was to be imposed from the outside in, the teacher was central to the learning process; *he* was in charge of controlling the "input" and monitoring the "output." This, in vastly oversimplified form, summarizes the rationale for the methodological movement of the 1960s.

Language as speech

Role of teacher to manipulate students to "behave" orally

Process applied to other skills

Midway through the 1960s a strong counter movement to the psycholinguistic foundations of audiolingualism began to gain momentum. Stephenson (76) provides a concise and detailed account of how the "post-Chomskyan revisionists" have challenged the cardinal tenets of structuralism. And Chomsky himself has made statements indicating that the behaviorist explanation for language acquisition is fundamentally wrong. One point of attack was upon the belief that language is merely a set of environmentally conditioned behaviors. For example, in 1965, Chomsky (16) stated that ". . . it may well be that the general features of language structure reflect, not so much the course of one's experience, but rather the general character of one's capacity to acquire knowledge—in the traditional sense, one's innate ideas and innate principles." Chomsky and his followers saw language as innate in the newborn child. Also, in his brilliant review of Skinner's *Verbal Behavior* (15) he gave a series of convincing arguments concerning why human language could not be explained merely in terms of a series of accidental verbal responses that had been drawn from and reinforced by the adult world. Moreover, studies of how small children learn their first language, which had been conducted in the 1960s (McNeill, 53),

Countermovement claimed language was not a set of conditioned behaviors

Chomsky

31

had tended to support Chomsky's view. These studies showed that child language contains forms and word arrangements that are found nowhere in adult speech and that, for sustained periods of time, children persist in using "nonstandard" language forms that are actually negatively reinforced by their parents. As for the view that the production of ideas is necessarily tied to language, Lado (47) has pointed out that "this view can be challenged today on the basis of the research of cognitive psychologists such as Bruner, and the works of Piaget, Furth, and others." In December of 1970, Lado (47) reported on a study that he had conducted, the results of which tended to support the belief that "thought and language are distinct and that thought is central" while language is "a symbolic system that refers to it (thought) in various ways." The pedagogical applications of the new thinking have been various. Lado (47), for example, recommends the retention of certain audiolingual techniques such as pattern practice, while suggesting the addition of "a new generation of thought exercises. . . ." Jakobovits (40), on the other hand, has concluded that language teaching as we have known it should be replaced by a radically different approach based upon the interests and learning styles of individual students. Teaching is seen more as a process of "drawing out" from the student that which he is willing and able to learn rather than as a process of "putting in" that which the teacher thinks he ought to learn. The ability of students to mimic flawlessly a corpus of genuine target-language speech patterns is considered less important than their ability to express their own ideas. This means a greater toleration of error in pronunciation and grammar so long as errors do not "seriously interfere with the goal of communication" (Jakobovits, 40). The views expressed by Jakobovits are much more adaptable to the concept of pluralism than the more rigidly structured programs of the recent past. Indeed, his approach is in essence pluralistic, since it begins with what each individual student wants to learn. (It assumes, of course, that there is something that he considers worth learning.) This meeting of individual "needs" is often assumed to be essential for present-day students. In fact there has been frequent reference in recent years to the "new student." Strasheim (77) has gone to considerable lengths to describe curricula for the "new student," as have various authors of the Northeast Conference Reports for 1970 (Tursi, 81). As one examines the meaning of "new" it becomes obvious that "new" does not signify that the present gen-

Studies of first-language acquisition

Production of ideas not necessarily tied to language

Pedagogical implications

Jakobovits: teaching is a process of "drawing out" from the student

The "new" student

eration of students has undergone en masse a biological muta-
tion. Nor does the word "new" relate to any statistical evidence
indicating that a massive proliferation of brain cells has taken
place in the collective cerebral cortexes of the younger generation. In fact, what is usually cited as "new" student behaviors
can actually be found in different forms throughout the history
of the western world. Anti-establishment attitudes, "gut-level"
reactions, and the "now" generation have "made the scene"
before. For example, the disenchantment that Socrates' students
expressed toward the Athenian establishment was apparently
intense enough to earn Socrates the death penalty for subversive un-Athenian activities. And the current youth-group rejection of mechanistic rationality in favor of spontaneous emotions
(e.g., "doing your own thing") has counterparts in history. One
could cite the *Sturm und Drang* period in 18th-century Germany
and note mottoes such as *Gefühl ist alles* (not to mention a popular novel about a mixed-up young man named Werther who could
not come to terms with the establishment). Perhaps all that is
new about the "new" students is that there are more of them,
that they are faced with a faster rate of change, and that their
lives are somewhat more complicated due to urbanization
and to the nature of modern technological society (Nelson &
Jakobovits, 58). As for the "new" education, it is possible that
educational innovations and their accompanying slogans are also
merely cyclical reactions to recurrent social, economic, and political trends (Taylor, 79). For example, when taxes are high and
money is "tight" one can predict a move toward accountability.
Similarly, when the nation is favorably competing in the international realm, foreign languages will tend to be supported.
When the international and economic picture is less favorable,
support declines and the profession seems to turn to humanistic
and personal development rationales for its self-justification. It
may also be that the theoretical underpinnings for what we do
(e.g., in the areas of epistemology, psychology, and pedagogical
theory) come as an after-the-fact explanation for that which we
are compelled to do anyhow. If such a process were operating,
intellectual figureheads would be chosen (or rejected) as needed.
And, with the American disinclination toward the study of educational history, contemporary intellectuals would be the chosen
"oracles" rather than historical ones (e.g., Chomsky rather than
Descartes; Holt rather than Dewey; and A. S. Neill rather than
Rousseau). In his history of foreign language teaching, Kelly

*Rationality exchanged for
emotion: a reoccurrence?*

*The "new" education: "old
wine in new bottles"*

33

(43, p. 363) contends that the basic corpus of ideas available to language teachers has reappeared with different labels in different contexts over the past 2,000 years. He further suggests a pattern of growth and decay:

> When an idea first appears and appeals to the most creative in the field, it is developed little by little. At all stages of the development of ideas and methods, the less original follow the successful innovators like sheep, accepting as received doctrine what is really a transitional stage. Inevitably the idea reaches the limit of its growth. At this stage, it is applied slavishly by the unoriginal, who are always in the majority, catches the attention of the interested dabbler, and repels the creative who turn elsewhere. Thus, an idea develops to sterility and dies by neglect, to be rediscovered later; and then it goes through the same cycle of tentative development, doctrinaire enforcement, and rejection.

In applying this to American education we can point to today's so-called free form schools, which have "progressive" school counterparts in the 1930s and 1940s. And the present plans for "Individually Prescribed Instruction" and the self-study guides called "unipacs" use essentially the same procedures that were followed by the Dalton Plan, the Winnetka Plan, and the student contract approach of the 1920s. The rapid emergence and disappearance of the various schemes for curriculum reform raise the suspicion that the changes actually take place in only a few pilot schools, and that they gain high visibility through speeches and publications without effecting widespread, lasting changes in education.

Emergence, disappearance, reemergence of curricular schemes

Pluralism and trends in educational psychology

As was noted earlier, foreign language education has drawn quite heavily upon behaviorist psychology for its basic learning theory. This has led to a tendency toward the belief that only those learnings which have specific applications to the real world are of value. To a considerable extent, the rationale behind training for specific behaviors can be traced to the transfer studies and subsequent writings of Thorndike and followers which were published through the early decades of the 1900s. In interpreting the ideas of Thorndike and other early behaviorists, many educators arrived at the conclusion that academic educa-

Behavioral psychology and transfer studies

tion per se had little if any transfer value into the "real world" (Joncich, 41). In part these attitudes can be attributed to an understandable reaction against the more naïve forms of 19th century faculty psychology (e.g., the mind viewed as a muscle that is developed through exposure to "hard" subject matter). However, many educators appear to have gone over to the opposite — and equally naïve — belief that there is no such thing as the development of intelligence for general purposes. In recent years there has been a return to the belief that formal education properly acquired is capable of producing people who can apply what they have learned to new and unanticipated situations.

Bruner even goes so far as to question the value of Thorndike's much quoted transfer studies and Thorndike's theory that only "identical elements" transfer. As Bruner (11) expressed it: "Look at transfer as an example of generic skill in dealing with and recognizing a broad class of problems. Learning to learn is a good case in point, and the literature on such nonspecific learning is more relevant to transfer in real life than a chapter full of quirky studies of identical elements." Bruner (11) goes on to remark that, when an educational psychologist says that transfer does not take place, "always be sure to ask him, 'And what do you transfer that statement from?' " Other well-known psychologists, such as Rogers (69), Lambert (48), and Piaget (63), have also pointed out the severe limitations of behaviorist empiricism, thereby attacking the psychological approach upon which much of the language pedagogy of recent years has been based. Like Bruner, Rogers (69) also favors nonspecific education (i.e., "learning *how* to learn") and insists that such education must be for all students. As he expresses it, "We are, in my view, faced with an entirely new situation in education. . . . The only man who is educated is the man who has learned how to learn; the man who has learned how to adapt and change; the man who has realized that no knowledge is secure, that only the process of *seeking* knowledge gives a basis for security. Changingness, a reliance on *process* rather than upon static knowledge, is the only thing that makes any sense as a goal for education in the modern world."

Contrasting with the concept of education as a process of "learning how to learn" is the concept of education as environmental enrichment. For example, laboratory experiments with a variety of animals indicate that measurable gains in the number and complexity of brain cells are registered in animals that are

Limits of behaviorism

35

raised in an educationally "rich" environment as compared with litter mates that are raised in an "impoverished" environment (Rosenzweig, 70). With regard to human beings, the weight of psychological opinion seems to favor the belief that man's abilities also are *not* permanently fixed by biological equipment (Lambert, 48, p. 235). Although certain boundaries may be fixed by biological factors there are thought to be gigantic variations that can be produced by controlling the educative process. In short, it may be that society can, if it chooses, determine patterns of ability among its members by democratized enrichment. In this regard, Gaarder (28) has stated that "current psychological theory suggests that the potential intelligence of an individual can be realized to varying degrees, depending in large part on the nature and extent of the environmental stimulation. If an individual is placed in a restricted or impoverished environment, less of his potential intelligence will develop than if he is placed in an enriching environment." If we couple these findings with those of Piaget and of certain neurologists we are led to suspect that, not only is enrichment important, but so is its *timing*. That is, learning cannot be prematurely forced; neither can it be delayed too far beyond the optimum period. Not only do *all* children appear to need "enrichment" but, also, they must have it by a certain stage in their growth or the opportunity for optimum learning is forever lost. As the Canadian neurosurgeon Wilder Penfield (61) expressed it, "What the brain is allowed to record, how and when it is conditioned – these things prepare it for the great achievement, or limit it to mediocrity. Boy and man are capable of so much more than is demanded of them! Adjust the time and the manner of learning, then you may double your demands and your expectations." Penfield concluded that foreign language study should begin prior to adolescence. This is clearly supportive of the FLES movement, and suggests that the goal of pluralism in foreign language education might best be fulfilled in early grades or at the junior high school level (Fearing, 23).

Education as process contrasts with education as environmental enrichment

Pluralism and the profession: the feasibility of establishing pluralism as a basic organizing concept for foreign language study

At various times during the past half century, educators have attempted to build curricula around various organizing principles. The curriculum can be based on: (*1*) pupil needs, (*2*) societal need, (3) organized knowledge, (4) interdisciplinary studies, or (5) initiation into a given discipline. There are, of course, other ways to organize the curriculum, but these five have been most in evidence during the half century of American education. Also, it should be noted that the various approaches can coexist. For example, in a given school, the art teacher may have a highly student-centered program based almost entirely upon the creative urges of the individual students, whereas the mathematics teacher in the same building may present his students with a highly structured curriculum based upon organized knowledge. With regard to the present discussion, it is important to consider which approach to curriculum would be most conducive to educating for pluralism and to further consider the likelihood of establishing on a widespread basis the optimum form of curricular organization. In short, what form of organization is most likely to reach all students and to promote an acceptance of, if not a sympathetic understanding for, cultures and subcultures that are different from those of the student?

The curriculum and the needs of the student

There have been many advocates of a curriculum that is built around needs that the student identifies for himself and interests that he brings with him to the classroom. For example, Jackson (39) suggests that foreign language teachers "make the study of a foreign language so pertinent to the young person's present activities and aspirations — and so rewarding in itself — that he can see its validity, even in sections of the country where English is the only language usually heard outside of the classroom." Among the ways of appealing to student interests and needs Jackson suggests contemporary studies of journalistic materials, Spanish shorthand, foreign language requests for hotel reservations, and how to say "thank you" for a gift or other kindness. In a similar vein Jakobovits recommends that teachers do everything possible to account for the different needs and backgrounds of students. In his opinion this will require the abandonment of the rigid and dogmatic instructional systems of the past regardless of how respectable the psycholinguistic or pedagogical underpinnings for such systems might be. For, while the "Old Key" was said to drive away all but a limited group of "reading oriented" students, Jakobovits (40) suggests the possibility "that the unifunctional character of the New Key

37

approach with its exclusive emphasis on audiolingualism has contributed to a significant extent to the decline of support of the curriculum on the part of students and parents." According to Jakobovits, the standard curricular approach based upon "experts'" prescriptions of skills to be acquired by students should be replaced by a multipurpose curriculum composed of specialized courses, each with a specific and limited goal. This is seen as a means of enabling the teacher to make adjustments for factors that he usually cannot control such as "perseverance, intelligence, aptitude, and opportunity to learn" (40). With this approach there would be a large number of "mini courses" that would accommodate the full range of interests and abilities of the students in the school. For example, there would be courses in learning how to read newspapers and in ordering a meal in a foreign restaurant. There would also be courses in reading literature and listening to poetry. In short, instead of first defining the curriculum and trying to make the student either fit in or drop out,

Replace prescription of skills with a multipurpose curriculum to respond to learner factors

> An effective FL curriculum is maximally responsive to the major learner factors of aptitude, intelligence, and perseverance. It will offer courses that teach specific goals in which the student is interested (so that perseverance and motivation come from within and are not externally imposed). It will use methods and techniques that take into account the individual learner's characteristics (ability to understand instructions, aptitude profile, amount of time the student is willing to spend in active study, etc.) (Jakobovits, 40).

Since the publication of Rousseau's *Emile* in 1762 there have been enthusiastic supporters of the student-centered curriculum. Nevertheless, this approach has a number of inherent problems that have never been solved. Those that are pertinent to the present discussion are: First, since the needs and interests of young people tend to be capricious, varied, and transitory, it is a difficult base upon which to build a workable curriculum. Second, because of this indefiniteness of content, students may never perceive that the goals of pluralism are among their needs or interests (or may even decide that pluralistic attitudes actually run contrary to their needs and interests). Finally, unless some structure is "imposed by experts" student learning may well involve the student in nothing more than moving from one triviality to another for a period of years without ever getting

Unsolved problems of the student-centered curriculum

deep enough into the discipline to make profitable applications of that which has been learned.

The curriculum and the needs of society

One way to put structure into the foreign language program (and thus to overcome the limitations of the student-centered curriculum) is to build the program around the needs of society. This approach begins with a value judgment to the effect that students need to behave in a certain way for the good of the social system. Implicit in this approach is the belief that it is the responsibility of teachers to instill "socially proper" behaviors into their students. With regard to the present topic, Spindler (74) is quite explicit in listing pluralism as a societal need. He has concluded that most teachers inadvertently engage in a "single-channel type of cultural transmission," which defeats the beliefs in pluralism that they often espouse. Spindler suggests that the single-channel type of cultural transmission is dysfunctional because contemporary society needs "a variety of outlooks, skills, and personality types in order to maintain its internal complexity." However, in his case studies of actual teacher classroom performance he finds that all behaviors that do not conform to the mainstream cultural pattern tend to be squelched even by teachers who had intended to accomplish the opposite purpose. To correct this he recommends a form of "cultural therapy" in all teacher-training programs "to help reduce the self-defeating effect of cultural transmission in American schools" (Spindler, 74). However, he is not at all optimistic about the possibility of implementing the needed cultural therapy in the near future, primarily for lack of trained personnel in teacher education. Spindler also points to the danger of establishing a program of cultural therapy. Paradoxically, the danger is that the therapy may simply serve to replace one set of conforming patterns of behavior with another "single-channel" set. In his words, "With the trends toward conformity that seem well established in our culture, this seems highly possible" (Spindler, 74). As Spindler views the traditional classroom in which the teacher dominates the instructional process, pluralistic attitudes are unlikely to develop.

Pluralism as a societal need . . .

. . . but it is unlikely to develop in the traditional classroom

Many people are keenly aware of the dangers of imposing educational principles upon students in the interest of society. For example, the tape-filmstrip presentation "Why Study Foreign Languages?" developed by this author (32) included societal as well as personal benefits that could derive from the study of languages. The former category included items such as translating for the military services, language uses in the Peace Corps, promotion of international understanding, and counteracting American isolationist tendencies. Among the many letters commenting on this presentation were a few that were highly critical of its propagandizing content. Significantly, one writer saw the presentation as being too supportive of the "military-industrial complex," whereas another viewed it as deliberate undermining of the American military and political systems. Most commentators recognized it as an attempt to present objectively a wide range of values—personal and societal—that may derive from foreign language study. The point is that many people see their beliefs threatened even by a statement of facts about how languages have been used, misused, or neglected in American society. One might, therefore, predict highly negative community reactions to a school program that would *deliberately* set out to inculcate pluralistic attitudes. Many people simply do not want the minds of their children to be manipulated in unfamiliar ways. A number of foreign language educators seem to be unaware of the moral question involved in shaping young minds. It is true that advocates of this approach can be found in all societies. For example, Mikhail I. Kalinin, the late president of the Soviet Union, defined education as "the definite, purposeful, and systematic influencing of the mind of the person being educated in order to imbue him with the qualities desired by the educator" (Asrael, 4).

Dangers of imposing educational principles: some examples

And, in the foreign language field there are those who advocate a similar process of imbuing students with competencies desired by the educator. In his advocacy of the systems approach, Banathy (7) ties together education for societal needs with the concept of cost accountability. He states that, in developing a curriculum "based on an analysis of the second language competencies used and needed in our society . . . first we should ask the question: What is worth learning? Second, we should investigate the least expensive way to learn whatever is worth learning. Finally, we are to find out the most productive way to pay for whatever learning is to take place." A feature worth noting in Banathy's statement is the advocacy of "activity analysis," an approach to curriculum development that was tried (and abandoned) by American curriculum specialists in the 1920s

The systems approach

Activity analysis

(Kliebard, 44). With activity analysis, the educator examines first what people do, and from the empirical data gathered by this process he builds a curriculum. To take this curricular approach seriously, one must first be willing to accept the belief that a given group of experts has the ability (and the moral right) to decide that certain behaviors in one group of people can be used as models that are then imposed upon other groups. However, many would not accept the implication that there is indeed any "we" who can answer the question: "What is worth learning?" Still others would reject the reactionary orientation of this approach, which has, in fact been its fatal flaw. Activity analysis must, by its nature, draw its models from past behaviors. And, in a rapidly changing society, by the time a cadre of teachers has been trained to implement the curricular content, that content is out of date; a new cycle of "model" behaviors will have emerged. In the final analysis, the entire approach involving prestated goals is inimical to the concept of education for pluralism. As Torrey (80) has expressed it, "It will not be possible to twist all students to any very narrow idea of what goals should be. Legitimate goals of language study are quite varied. A teacher should not make the mistake of thinking he has the right or the power to set the goals for his students."

Another way of approaching societal needs is to look to the future and to project what will be needed in the building of a better society. Kai-yu Hsu (42) expresses both the belief in the feasibility of future societal betterment and the power of foreign language education to break down "intellectual provincialism." Speaking to foreign language teachers at the third annual meeting of the American Council on the Teaching of Foreign Languages he stated that we have a responsibility "to respond to our student's desire to see relevance between his present business of learning and his future business of remaking society according to the image which we all cherish." Education for the future does eliminate the problem of obsolescence inherent in activity analysis. However, it also introduces the equally vexing problem of predicting what is needed in the future. And it fails to solve the problem of imposing values upon others that, in fact, they may not "cherish." In summary, any form of curriculum building based upon societal needs runs the risk of promoting not pluralism, but its obverse: the imposition of a set of standardized, conformist behaviors that someone deems necessary to the proper functioning of the present or future social order.

Approaching societal needs by projecting for the future

41

The curriculum as organized knowledge

It is perhaps self-evident that the predominant view of foreign language curriculum building has been the subject matter itself. As Strasheim (77) has pointed out, the most common practice of foreign language educators is to divide the foreign language content rather mechanistically into skills, or elements, or levels, and to present this material to the student on a "take it or leave it" basis. Throughout the past half century the curricular emphasis has tended to shift from reading-writing skills in one period to oral-aural skills in another. However, an elitist philosophy has remained rather constant. For example, a report published in 1929 indicated that there were many teachers "who hold that it would be better to concentrate on eliminating weaklings" in order to make faster progress with a selected group (Hagboldt, 33). And, in the 1920s, the problems of elitism and a rigid subject matter curriculum created the same kinds of drop-out problems that the profession is now experiencing. As one report from the period stated, ". . . a beginners' class in French of 100 will normally fall away to 43 at the opening of the second year, to 20 in the third year, and less than three will continue this subject into the fourth year" (Hagboldt, 33). In the 1920s, as in the present era, foreign language teachers at all levels were engaged in disputes concerning whether the emphasis should be on the language or upon the literature. It is a matter of history that during the 1930s, 1940s, and 1950s the profession decided in favor of reading skill built around literary content. During this period the students, faced with a take-it-or-leave-it choice, more often than not decided for the latter alternative.

Predominant view of curriculum building rests in the subject itself

An elitist, belletristic interpretation of the proper way to organize knowledge is still very much in evidence. For example, in an article entitled "The Treason of the Clerks: A Parable for 1970," Renoir (65) is scathingly critical of foreign language programs at all levels for their recent neglect of literary studies. He rejects out of hand any "reason for being" that is based upon utilitarian or nonliterary objectives. According to Renoir, "We must give up trying to peddle our wares on bogus grounds, and we must take our cue from Milton and Goethe to sell foreign languages for the humanistic tradition which they contain." Renoir appears to equate "humanism" with literature, which, to be appreciated fully, must be studied in the original language.

An elitist interpretation of knowledge organization

Among his suggestions for reforming the profession are burning down the language laboratory, abolishing the junior year abroad, and making classical languages prerequisite to all major programs in modern languages. The process of learning a language in itself appears to assume little importance in Renoir's value system. As he expresses it: "Literature is our subject matter, and language is merely the means whereby this subject is transmitted; when we make phonetics prerequisite to Ronsard, we fully deserve the contempt with which we are currently looked upon."

Although his rhetoric is less militant and colorful, Dow (21) also insists that the primary purpose of foreign language instruction in high school and college is to teach literature and literary appreciation. As he expresses it, "We are teaching language as a means to our actual subject: literature. For the student who is interested and has a high verbal aptitude it is a rewarding major within the humanities." In addition to the explicit elitism of the literature-based school of curriculum there is the implication that the elementary levels of instruction have little or no inherent educational value, but rather that they are merely instrumental to the higher belletristic aim. This tends to produce a "drillmaster" image for those who teach the beginning courses, which in turn implies that the high school teacher and the university teaching assistant are performing some sort of menial activity with their beginning classes whereas the "real education" takes place in the advanced levels of the university literature class. With this curricular approach there is little room for foreign languages as a vehicle for pluralism. On the contrary, the tendency is to select out those students with the background, fortitude, and unique mental equipment that suits them for the somewhat esoteric role of literary specialists.

Language as a means to an end: the study of literature

There are others who see not the literature but the language itself as the chief educative vehicle. For example, Lohnes (51) suggests that literary studies are only one aspect of the larger learning goal, which involves the gaining of insights into the culture and way of life of a foreign people through the language that they speak. As Lohnes sees it, a high level of language proficiency is neither feasible nor necessary, for "if studying a foreign language leads to a heightened awareness of the student's own language, the aim of most language teaching is fulfilled." Lohnes (51) also emphasizes the need for attitudinal changes that should result from the study of linguistic and cultural contrasts. In this regard he cites Hall's *The Silent Language* as follows:

Literature studies as one aspect of a larger goal: insight to the foreign culture

43

"The best reason for exposing oneself to foreign ways is to generate a sense of vitality and awareness—an interest in life which can come only when one lives through the shock of contrast and difference." Renoir (65) rejects this as a suitable goal for foreign language education, stating that it would be better to "take a few courses in Mathematics because mathematicians assure me that their subject provides a means of formulating concepts far more different from English than any other language and infinitely more subtle in the bargain." By his remarks Renoir reveals that he is either unaware that mathematics is a contrived and totally acultural language or else that he is indifferent to the values to be gained from cross-cultural comparisons. In either case, his approach seems antithetical to the current concept of pluralism in foreign language education.

Like Lohnes, Brooks looks to the totality of language (rather than merely to the literary segment) as a basis for the curriculum. Using the analogy of a ladder, Brooks (10) presents foreign language learning as a series of steps, all of which must be taken in their proper order. He indicates that professional agreement can and should be reached as to the nature of the various learning "rungs." Thus, Brooks holds firmly to the "organized-body-of-knowledge view" as the primary emphasis in foreign language curriculum building. With this philosophy, concessions to the student take the form of helping him cope with the subject matter that the teacher or the profession has established. It is the responsibility of the teacher at each instructional level to "know the totality of the sequence and adapt his work on the rung he is in charge of so that it may fit the ladder of his students' experience." However, Brooks does not follow the elitist view that the lower rungs are mere prerequisites for "important" rungs at the top of the ladder. On the contrary, "for the student each rung is quite as important as all others in his upward climb. . . ."

Another view of the totality of language

Van Doren also sees the language itself as the important organizing element. Speaking in favor of liberal education, Van Doren (83) views the study of language as essential to the process of learning to connect thoughts with their proper symbols. Developing the power of making language refer accurately to thought is said to come only through practice and by the study of language itself. Thus, according to Van Doren, mastery of one's own language and at least one other language is essential to a person's fulfillment as a human being, for: "The lines of any two

Language as connector of thoughts with symbols

languages converge in the structure of language itself. Without a trained sense of this structure, reason is handicapped; and to the extent that it is handicapped, the imagination is barren" (Van Doren, 83, p. 132). Van Doren goes on to express a view that was popular in the 19th century, namely that certain languages are superior to others for developing those mental processes that serve to connect thoughts and symbols. According to Van Doren (83, p. 154), ". . . Greek is still the best one for the purpose, and indeed for any purpose. . . ." Language is seen as "the mirror of the mind" and certain languages are better for keeping the mirror clean and polished. But, whichever language is chosen, its value must, according to Van Doren, be seen primarily in terms of its contribution—along with other essential disciplines—to the development of better human beings. Even the belletristic goal is secondary, for one cannot learn all languages, and, in any case, ". . . the better the book the more meaning it keeps in translation; . . . style is wonderful, but sense and wisdom are more so."

Thus Van Doren might be seen as summarizing the views of language education that were implicit in the writings of men such as Descartes, Rousseau, Goethe, and John Dewey. As Van Doren (83, p. 40) expressed it:

> The powers of the person are what education wishes to perfect. To aim at anything less is to belittle men; to fasten somewhere on their exterior a crank which accident or tyrants can twist to set machinery going. The person is not machinery which another can run. His mind has its own laws, which are the laws of thought itself.

In short, one does not teach a student to think internationally, or to think sociologically, or to think pluralistically; one merely helps the student to learn how to think. And, to do this, the student must become aware of the nature and function of language.

Language serves the function of helping the student learn how to think

The basic problem with the organized knowledge approach to curriculum in the area of foreign languages is that, whether it is built around literature or language skills or the language textbook, it tends to appear to many students as an intimidating body of content that can be learned only by the few (Baron, 8). Elitist teacher attitudes and selective guidance procedures tend to fortify this view of foreign languages, thus defeating the goals of pluralism (Mehl, 54).

Problems with the organized knowledge approach to curriculum

The interdisciplinary curriculum

Cullen (18) recommends the introduction of interdisciplinary studies in a second language at the high school and college level. This would give students the option of studying such subjects as history, biology, mathematics, and other traditional subject areas by means of a foreign language. This option would be available after two years or more of regular classroom study. According to Cullen (18): "The main objective in the class is the communication and acquiring of information; the second language is primarily a medium of communication. The famous four skills—listening comprehension, speaking, reading, and writing—are of little use unless they serve to transmit meaning accurately from one person to another." Cullen feels that by concentrating on the message rather than upon the mechanics of language learning the student is more positively motivated and, indeed, is forced to think in the foreign language. According to Cullen (18), this process produces students who are not only bilingual but who are also bicultural; that is, students who develop "a better understanding of different values, approaches, and reactions among different cultures and different ways of thinking and expressing thoughts." Although early experimentation with this approach in American schools and colleges shows promising results, the problems are formidable. The most obvious problem is the lack of teachers who are knowledgeable in a second discipline and who are, at the same time, competent in the foreign language. Then too, the implication is that foreign language is merely a "tool" with which to exchange ideas. Many foreign language teachers may tend to resent the implication that their discipline has no content worth communicating.

Studying other subjects through a foreign language

Difficulties with the interdisciplinary approach to curriculum organization

Education as initiation

There are a number of educational philosophers (e.g., John Dewey and his followers) who would reject the various approaches to curriculum described above as being simplistic and incomplete. They would, for example, consider it absurd to engage in disputes regarding whether education should be built around the needs and interests of students or around organized subject matter. Any good curricular theory would begin with that which the student wants to learn or is interested in. How-

Educational philosophers and approaches to curriculum

46

ever, any curricular theory which did not have as its aim the leading of the student away from the transitory whims of youth into a more sophisticated way of organizing his thoughts would be obviously incompetent. And a curriculum that is built mainly upon the alleged needs of society or upon the behavior patterns of some supposedly model group is beneath contempt. Peters (62) makes the point that, while educated people tend to write more books, they also tend to commit suicide more frequently. He notes that "things like increasing the suicide rate or providing employment for printers should not be built into the concept of 'education.'" According to Peters, one does not educate for extrinsic ends; in fact, it is even absurd to ask the question, "What is the purpose or goal of education?" It is as foolish as asking why one should promote good health. It is obvious that one promotes good health to be healthy; similarly, it is obvious that one engages in education to be educated. Anything that is called "education" includes as a matter of course the intent of bringing about a "desirable state of mind" in the learner. Utilitarian advantages that accrue to the learner or to others in society are merely irrelevant by-products. Peters (62) denies that it is logical to build a curriculum on these measurable by-products. As he expresses it, "In a similar way one might say that the function of the medical art is to provide employment for makers of medicine bottles or to increase the population. But this is not what the doctor conceives of himself as doing *qua* doctor, and it would be regrettable if he came to view what he should be doing *qua* doctor in terms of such remoter effects of his art." To apply Peters' line of reasoning to the present topic, one would not attempt to justify pluralism in foreign language education as a means of reducing tensions between various groups within society or of promoting international understanding, or of adding more bilingual stenographers to the job market. To the extent that a foreign language teacher views his role primarily in these terms, he is, respectively, a social worker, an instrument of the U.S. State Department, or a job-placement consultant. The criteria for determining whether a teacher is a foreign language *educator* would relate to the degree of enthusiasm that his students exhibit toward the learning of a foreign language for its own sake. In short, the main function of an educator is to get his students "hooked" on his subject matter (Strasheim, 78).

Education for education's sake

Application of the principle to pluralism in education

As for the area of "pluralism," progress in this area would be evidenced by a student's ability and willingness to make objective evaluations of a second cultural and linguistic system. Most important of all would be the student's ability to make value judgments completely on his own regardless of whether these judgments happen to conform to the beliefs of the teacher, or the community, or to any outside person or group. In summary, education as initiation refers to getting the student intellectually and emotionally involved in a discipline to the point where he has both the knowledge and the self-confidence to draw his own conclusions and to make his own decisions. This does not mean that a curriculum can be built around nothing more than autonomous growth as some "free school" advocates seem to believe. Peters (62) sees the main defects of the growth theory (and its free school manifestations) as follows: (1) its advocates have blown the concept of self-determination out of all proportion, and (2) they have evaded the fact that education involves the intentional transmission of worthwhile content. This transmission will not happen by accident according to Peters. For "the procedures of a discipline can only be mastered by an exploration of its established content under the guidance of one who has already been initiated." And although the teacher must start by appealing to the "needs and interests" of the student, ultimately "the pupil has to get the grammar of the activity into his guts so that he can eventually win through to the stage of autonomy." But he must not be deceived into viewing education as the fulfillment of discrete objectives. Education is not goal oriented simply because "education . . . can have no ends beyond itself. Its value derives from principles and standards implicit in it. To be educated is not to have arrived at a destination; it is to travel with a different view" (62).

Student progress in "pluralism"

A sketch of education as initiation

Thus, education as initiation calls for the teacher as the central figure. His role is to initiate, to inspire, to get the student interested, not in fulfilling a set of predetermined objectives, but in voluntarily taking the first firm steps into a multi-faceted and non-finite area of learning.

The teacher's role

Exploratory programs

There are some programs that are quite frankly presented as a means of promoting interest in subsequent foreign language study rather than in attempting to bring about any significant amount of learning. For example, Carney (14) reports on the use of high school students of French, German, Latin, and Spanish to teach short language units to elementary school children in the Tulsa public schools. It was claimed that this experience added excitement to the elementary school social studies program, that it convinced many children that they ought to elect foreign language study when they reached seventh grade, and that the high school language students also profited from the experience of teaching their particular language to a small group of children. A similar "exploratory" goal is expressed by Wachner (84) in the introduction to his book *General Language: English and its Foreign Relations*, which "does not presume to teach foreign language or a smattering of foreign languages. It does hope to create an attitude favorable to the study of foreign languages, to make the reader aware of the need for foreign language study, to acquaint him with the nature and development of language in general, and to give him an understanding of how it is and must be an integral part of the culture of a country."

Programs to stimulate further foreign language study

A bulletin of the Minnesota State Department of Education acknowledges the value of exploratory programs in the junior high school (or middle school) while emphasizing that such courses must offer "honest exploration." The bulletin states that, as a result of such courses, "The student should find out what language learning is really like," and "He should be able to build on this experience in a long sequence and/or learn better another foreign language" (Arendt & Fearing, 3, p. 9). The bulletin also cautions against programs that involve the sampling of a number of languages within a given school year. The exposure is seen as being too short to allow for a true exploratory experience with the foreign language. And, furthermore, such courses are "based on the false premise . . . that a few weeks contact with a number of languages will enable a student to choose the best one for him to study for a number of years." In summary, the bulletin sees the results of this *pot pourri* approach (i.e., introducing all students to a smattering of languages) as being basically negative.

Exploratory foreign language programs

Dodge (20) has drawn together a series of 11 articles that deal with the main issues presented above concerning the foreign language curriculum in secondary and in higher education. These are presented in a booklet entitled *The Case for Foreign Language Study*. The topics discussed include elitism, foreign language requirements, the dropout problem, the humanities, reorganizing the curriculum, and the need for a sound philosophical basis for justifying foreign languages in the curriculum.

Main issues in foreign language education

Pluralism, individual volition, and value systems

An essential aspect of educating for pluralism is an adherence to the principle that each student must be encouraged to generate his own value system and to use that system continuously as he is confronted with cultural patterns that differ from those that are familiar to him. According to Kai-yu Hsu (42), students should be confronted with value-laden issues without having value judgments imposed upon them. Instead the teacher has an obligation to present relevant and even controversial topics (e.g., "the French involvement in Southeast Asia" or the pros and cons of the Franco regime in Spain) and to let the discussion lead where it may. In the process it is essential to maintain the American tradition of telling students: "Each and every one of you is born of equal worth with equal dignity. You are the master of your own destiny. You must investigate and draw your own conclusions. Don't take our words, the words of another generation as unchallengeable truths." Similarly, Hechinger (35) has stated that "the desperate need today is for the intellectual leadership—in the schools, the colleges, and the communities—to teach again the importance of language—not to sell or sloganeer or deceive—but to allow us to speak to each other, to persuade, to reestablish bonds." He sees the contemporary breakdown between what is said and what is meant in the manipulative rhetoric of advertisers and political officials as being frighteningly similar to what took place in Nazi Germany and what was warned against in the "nightmare utopias" of Orwell and Huxley. The answer is to teach students to pursue relentlessly all forms of verbal deception; to test the congruency of words with meaning and of meaning with actions. Hechinger states that this would be a nonpartisan action involving "those who deal with language," who should "use as the basic materials to be tested and analyzed the words of our politicians and leaders—the political commercials and the official oratory; the executive messages and the legislative reports" (35). The use of language to scrutinize mercilessly left-wing, right-wing, and centrist propaganda (as Hechinger suggests) would doubtlessly add to the timeliness and relevance of foreign language instruction. However, how much of this sort of activity can realistically be worked into an already crowded language curriculum?

The main aspect of educating for pluralism

The importance of language and how to teach that importance

50

Perhaps all that can be done in the process of "educating for pluralism" within the foreign language class is to set the stage for making independent, individual choices based upon the examination of evidence. For example, students might learn the process of weighing evidence pro and con about the relative merits of elements of two different linguistic systems (i.e., native and target) or two divergent cultural patterns (native and target). As far as the teacher is concerned, there can be no right or wrong answers (and, hence, no "accountability" in terms of "measurable, overt responses"). For example, one student may see the paternalistic family structure of the target culture as a model of stability; another student may object that it exploits women. The important thing is that neither student should feel compelled by the instructional procedures to arrive at a particular conclusion. Neither student should be made to feel that he is more right than the other. As for whether such discussions should be carried on in English or in the target language, one can only hope that the "advanced courses" would be conducted totally in the target language. The realism that comes from visiting hundreds of foreign language classrooms leads this writer to conclude that much of the early level reading and discussing of comparative language and culture will tend to be done in English.

What can be done in educating for pluralism

The current cycle of professional opinion contains much that is supportive of an instructional approach that would involve the student in the active discussion of relevant contemporary issues. For example, there is Strasheim (78) and the various authors of the 1970 Northeast Conference Report (Tursi, 81). Moreover, the importance of language as creative self-expression has been noted by Hester (36).

Professional opinion supports active discussion of relevant issues

Summary

The problems associated with pluralism in foreign language education appear to be formidable. The educator who attempts to apply the concept to his own students may find himself under attack from many sides. For historical evidence indicates the development of a powerful force of tradition that mandates conformity to "mainstream" Anglo-American values, mannerisms, and speech patterns. Moreover this tradition is supported by claims that it serves the very practical goal of individual economic survival. In view of this, well-meaning attempts by educators to "accommodate" subcultural groups may be interpreted

Problems with pluralism in foreign language education

51

by members of the target group as a thinly disguised strategy for "keeping them in their place." Modiano (55) has noted, for example, that ghetto parents and the NAACP objected violently to textbooks prepared especially for ghetto schools. The books included illustrations depicting children in the "typical" slum environment. As it turned out, parents wanted their children to identify not with the grim realities of slum living but with an environment *outside* the ghetto, something more in line with their own aspirations. Modiano (55) also states that the gratuitous introduction into the curriculum of nonstandard language dialects, spoken by subcultural groups, might well receive the same negative response. In reference to bi-dialectal and folk dialectal programs she states that ". . . until the folk themselves, or at least their spokesmen, push for such curricula, we should be wary of instituting, even with the best of intentions, programs which are likely to go down before charges of white colonialism."

Examples of well-meaning attempts to accommodate subcultural groups

There is a middle ground that follows the approach of leaving such decisions to the subcultural group itself. In reference to non-English languages Fishman (24, pp. 373–74) suggests a program of "language maintenance" carried on voluntarily by members of "non-core cultures" who "wish to maintain institutions and organizations of their own on behalf of their languages and cultures," and who "are willing to do so within a framework of mutual interaction with American core society and its democratically maintained and developed institutions and processes." Where language is concerned, another approach is to use the nonstandard dialect, not for its own sake, but as a means of meeting a student on his own cultural, linguistic, and emotional terms with the end in mind of educating him more efficiently. The National Council of Teachers of English (NCTE) supported this second view in its adoption of Resolution 8 at the 1969 Convention in Washington, D.C. (56). The resolution calls for designing and implementing "in the pre-service education of teachers courses which reflect the cultural and ethnic plurality existing in American society today" (56). Max Rafferty, then state school superintendent of California, gave expression to a third approach to dialect differences, which is to aim at their obliteration. In an outspoken reaction to NCTE Resolution 8, Rafferty stated that the organization should be given the "Jackass of the Year" award "for conspicuous idiocy in education" (56). Rafferty went on to express the traditionalist view of language, which calls for universal conformity to the "correct" way of speaking.

A middle ground: language maintenance and use of the nonstandard dialect

A conservative educator's reaction to the use of nonstandard dialect

The toleration of nonstandard speech is unacceptable, for, as Rafferty expressed it,

> Presumably this will involve okaying all the gutter language and ghetto dialects which the kids bring with them into the schools, just as a cat brings home a very dead and somewhat over-ripe mouse. Carried to its logical conclusion, it means that linguistically anything will go if it's just multi-ethnic enough, and that anybody that objects to this debasement of the Queen's English should be "vigorously questioned" . . . I say that there is only one way to write correct English, only one way to pronounce English words properly, only one way to punctuate sentences right and only one way to conjugate verbs, compare adjectives and identify parts of speech.

Commenting upon public support for bilingualism through the provisions of the Bilingual Education Act, Roeming (68) expresses a view that lies somewhere between advocating deliberate promotion or attempted extirpation of nonstandard, non-English dialects. He sees bilingualism as a possible by-product of a more important educational goal. However, in Roeming's opinion: ". . . the primary concern of the bilingualism discussed in relation to the Bilingual Education Act is to insure a viable transition from a non-English language to English and to a well-rounded education, maintaining to whatever degree necessary the non-English language as a motivating factor in the learning process." (Questions about biculturalism and bi-dialectism are discussed pro and con in an anthology issue of the *Florida FL Reporter* under the title *Linguistic-Cultural Differences and American Education* [Aarons,1]. A comprehensive discussion of bilingualism and biculturalism is contained in the two-volume edition *Bilingual Schooling in the United States* [Andersson & Boyer, 2].

A thoughtful approach to bidialectism and bilingualism

Ultimately the concept of educating for pluralism raises some very basic philosophical and moral questions. Also, the concept of education for diversity, particularly in the locally controlled public school, may run directly counter to the purpose for which the local school exists as seen by the local school board and school administration. There are many areas concerning politics, sex, marriage, religion, family relationships, and war (to name but the most potentially controversial) that are considered "off limits" by many school boards, and even by many governing bodies of institutions of higher learning. In short, the imple-

Pluralism raises basic philosophical and moral questions

mentation of pluralism in foreign language education may require a degree of applied open-mindedness and a type of nonthreatening, nonauthoritarian atmosphere that may be difficult to establish within structured educational institutions as we now know them. (For example, the teacher who complains about a boy's long hair on Monday cannot expect him to be receptive to a unit on the values of diversity on Tuesday.) At the very least, the foreign language teacher who is to establish his "reason for being" around the concept of pluralism must be objective about divergent behaviors. Not only must he refrain from such absurdities as referring to foreign language syntax as "backwards" but, in addition, he must help students to develop a relativistic attitude toward other languages and other cultural patterns. Ideally, the student would also be encouraged to draw his own conclusions and make his own value judgments (hopefully by means of the target language). This process carries with it the possibility that the student may not draw the "right" conclusions concerning such things as social and economic systems, sexual mores, and religious beliefs. Furthermore, the attitudes that the student develops in the course of studying another language and another culture will supposedly lead him to transfer what he has learned and to apply it to his own surroundings. The result may be a tendency on the part of many students to question the validity of some of the constitutive rules by which the local community operates. This may be interpreted as "subversive" by groups within the community.

Implementation of pluralism has certain requirements for the teacher

Also, the development of linguistic and cultural relativism requires an open-ended, process-oriented type of education. It fits neither the frenetic activity of some of the "New Key" classrooms nor the currently popular, product-oriented curricular approach that is built on behavioral objectives and implemented by means of a "systems approach." Despite the humaneness with which many advocates of an educational systems approach may implement it, it is drawn by analogy from the input-output model of the industrial production line. Thus, there is the unavoidable implication that the end product is more important than the means used in reaching it. And the danger is that education will come to deal almost exclusively with a student "output" involving convergent thinking (that is, arriving at the one right answer that the teacher has determined for the student in advance). Thus, the problem is that, in developing attitudes of linguistic and cultural relativism, *divergent* rather than *conver-*

Development of linguistic and cultural relativism requires a process type of education

54

gent thinking is required. That is, the student must arrive at his own synthesis of the material that he has learned.

To attempt to predetermine (e.g., via behavioral objectives) that a student will end up with a given attitude (presumably positive) toward another culture is to opt for brainwashing rather than for education. If the effort is successful, it may be that the teacher has only succeeded in reversing the polarity of the student's prejudices (and perhaps only temporarily). That is, to find that a student or a group of students shows progress in developing positive attitudes toward another culture (as measured by an objective device of some kind) may only indicate the exchange of one set of specific stereotypes for another. It may do nothing whatever to help the student to cope with unanticipated "divergent" behaviors, which he may encounter throughout his life as he comes into contact with a third or a fourth or a fifth cultural group. In short, the student must learn the *process* of coping with any conceivable other-culture behavior rather than merely changing specific attitudes relative to the few specific items that a teacher is able to present by means of the local curriculum.

Predetermination of student attitudes toward another culture limits the process of dealing with other-culture behavior

All of this suggests a nonpressured learning atmosphere in which the student is encouraged to express his own ideas, using foreign language forms that may not always be accurate and precise. In the process he may express many ideas that are both ungrammatical and unpopular. It would appear that the various existing curricular approaches, whether based on personal or societal needs or upon literary or linguistic content, have built-in limitations that may prove inimical to the development of pluralistic attitudes. In short, implementing the concept of pluralism in foreign language education may require a complete restructuring of the existing practices and philosophies in curriculum, instruction, and administration. Therefore, if "pluralism in foreign language education" is to be—as the title of this chapter suggests—an important "reason for being," then the profession is faced with major changes that have implications for school curriculum specialists, teacher educators and, perhaps, deans of graduate schools.

Implementation of "pluralism in foreign language education"

References, Pluralism in foreign language education: A reason for being

1 Aarons, Alfred, Barbara Gordon, and William Stewart, eds. *Linguistic-Cultural Differences and American Education. Florida FL Reporter* 7,i(1969):1–175. [Special Anthology Issue.]

2 Andersson, Theodore, and Mildred Boyer,eds. *Bilingual Schooling in the United States*, Washington,D.C.: United States Government Printing Office, 1970.

3 Arendt, Jermaine D., and Percy Fearing,eds. *The Extended Foreign Language Sequence:With Emphasis on New Courses for Levels IV and V.* St. Paul: Minnesota State Department of Education, 1971.

4 Asrael, Jeremy R. "Soviet Union," 261–75 in James S. Coleman,ed., *Education and Political Development.* Princeton, New Jersey: Princeton Univ. Press, 1965.

5 Avery, Harry C. "Academic Reports:Conference on the Teaching of Latin in Inner City Schools." *Modern Language Journal* 54(1970):424–25.

6 Ballesteros, David. "Toward an Advantaged Society:Bilingual Education in the 70's." *The National Elementary Principal* 50,ii(1970):25–28.

7 Banathy, Bela H. "Current Trends in College Curriculum:A Systems Approach," 105–140 in Emma M. Birkmaier,ed., *Britannica Review of Foreign Language Education, Volume 1.* Chicago: Encyclopaedia Britannica, Inc., 1968 [1969].

8 Baron, Bruce G. "The Humanities and the Curriculum." *Educational Leadership* 27(1969): 287–95.

9 Bell, Terrel H. "Foreword." *The National Elementary Principal* 50,ii(1970):15.

10 Brooks, Nelson. "The Rung and the Ladder," 135–47 in Joseph A. Tursi,ed., *Foreign Languages and the "New" Student.* Reports of the Working Committees of the Northeast Conference on the Teaching of Foreign Languages. New York: Modern Language Association Materials Center, 1970.

11 Bruner, Jerome. "Bad Education." *Psychology Today* 4,vii(1970):51–70.

12 Bush, Maybell G. *The First School Days of the Non-English Child.* Madison, Wisconsin: State Department of Public Instruction, 1918.

13 Callahan, Raymond E. *Education and the Cult of Efficiency.* Chicago: Univ. of Chicago Press, 1962.

14 Carney, Helen K. "VOCAW and ECHO:Advertising Foreign Languages." *Foreign Language Annals* 4(1970):57–61.

15 Chomsky, Noam. "A Review of *Verbal Behavior* by B.F. Skinner." *Language* 35,i(1959):26–58.

16 ———— *Aspects of the Theory of Syntax.* Cambridge: Massachusetts Institute of Technology Press, 1965.

17 Christensen, J.A. "Education and the Delphic Oracles." *Media and Methods* 7,vi(1971):48–60.

18 Cullen, Arthur J. "A New Option for Foreign Language Students?" *Iowa Foreign Language Bulletin* 9,ii(1971):13–15.

19 Dewey, John. *Experience and Education.* New York: Macmillan, 1938.

20 Dodge, James,ed. *The Case for Foreign Language Study.* New York: Modern Language Association Materials Center, 1971.

21 Dow, James R. "On Advising Prospective Undergraduate Majors." *Die Unterrichtspraxis* 2,i(1969):64–68.

22 Ether, John A. "Cultural Pluralism and Self-Identity." *Educational Leadership* 27(1969): 232–34.

23 Fearing, Percy,ed. *Foreign Language in Elementary Schools:A Policy Statement.* St. Paul: Minnesota State Department of Education, 1969.

24 Fishman, Joshua A. *Language Loyalty in the United States.* The Hague: Mouton, 1966.

25 ———— "The Breadth and Depth of English in the United States," 41–43, 151 in Alfred Aarons, Barbara Gordon, and William Stewart,eds., *Linguistic-Cultural Differences and American Education. Florida FL Reporter* 7,i(1969):1–175.

26 Ford, Paul L. *The New England Primer.* New York: Dodd, Mead, 1897.

27 Frazier, Alexander. "The Larger Question:A New Sense of Common Identity." *Educational Leadership* 27(1969):215–17.

28 Gaarder, Bruce A. "Bilingualism and the Schools," 123–32 in Mildred R. Donoghue,ed., *Foreign Languages and the Schools:A Book of Readings.* Dubuque, Iowa: William C. Brown Company, 1967.

29 Glazer, Nathan, and Daniel P. Moynihan. *Beyond the Melting Pot.* Second edition. Cambridge: Massachusetts Institute of Technology Press, 1970.

30 Grittner, Frank M.,ed. "Course Content, Articulation, and Materials:A Committee Report to the National Symposium on the Advancement of German Teaching." *Die Unterrichtspraxis* 2,i(1969):53–72.

31 ———— *Teaching Foreign Languages.* New York: Harper and Row, 1969.

32 ———— "Why Study Foreign Languages?" New York: Modern Language Association Materials Center, 1969. [A tape-filmstrip presentation summarizing the values of foreign language study.]

33 Hagboldt, Peter. *The Teaching of German.* New York: D.C. Heath, 1940.

34 Harris, Earl G. A form letter sent to state foreign language supervisors. Jacksonville, Florida: The Duval County School Board, November 2, 1970.

35 Hechinger, Fred M. "Language and the Intellectual Crisis." *Foreign Language Annals* 4(1971): 272–77.

36 Hester, Ralph M.,ed. *Teaching a Living Language.* New York: Harper and Row, 1970.

37 Hogg, Thomas C., and Marlin R. McComb. "Cultural Pluralism:Its Implications for Education." *Educational Leadership* 27(1969):235–38.

38 Houts, Paul L. "Editorial." *The National Elementary Principal* 50,ii(1970):4–5.

39 Jackson, Mary. "Let's Make Foreign Language Study More Relevant." *Today's Education:NEA Journal* 60,iii(1971):18–20.

40 [Jakobovits, Leon A.] "Motivation in Foreign Language Learning," 62–75 in Joseph A. Tursi,ed., *Foreign Languages and the "New" Student.* Reports of the Working Committees of the Northeast Conference on the Teaching of Foreign Languages. New York: Modern Language Association Materials Center, 1970.

41 Joncich, Geraldine M.,ed. *Psychology and the Science of Education:Selected Writings of*

Edward L. Thorndike. New York: Teachers College, Columbia Univ., 1962.

42 Kai-yu Hsu. "The Teacher as an Architect of Learning." *Foreign Language Annals* 3(1970): 377–82.

43 Kelly, L.G. *25 Centuries of Language Teaching.* Rowley, Massachusetts: Newbury House, 1969.

44 Kliebard, Herbert M. "Bureaucracy and Curriculum Theory," 74–93 in Vernon F. Haubrich,ed., *Freedom, Bureaucracy, and Schooling.* Washington,D.C.:Association for Supervision and Curriculum Development, National Education Association, 1971.

45 ——— "Curriculum Differentiation for the Disadvantaged." *The Educational Forum* 32(1967): 47–54.

46 Krug, Edward A.,ed. *Charles W. Eliot and Popular Education.* New York: Teachers College, Columbia Univ., 1961.

47 Lado, Robert. "Language, Thought, and Memory in Language Teaching:A Thought View." *Modern Language Journal* 54(1970):580–85.

48 Lambert, Wallace E. "Psychological Approaches to the Study of Language," 215–50 in Joseph Michel,ed., *Foreign Language Teaching.* New York: Macmillan, 1967.

49 Leavitt, Sturgis E. *The Teaching of Spanish in the United States—A Historical Survey.* New York: Modern Language Association Materials Center, 1961.

50 Lee, Gordon C.,ed. *Crusade Against Ignorance: Thomas Jefferson on Education.* New York: Teachers College, Columbia Univ., 1961.

51 Lohnes, Walter F. "The Training of German Teachers in the United States." *Die Unterrichtspraxis* 2,ii(1969):69–76.

52 Mangers, Dennis H. "Education in the Grapes of Wrath." *The National Elementary Principal* 50,ii(1970):34–40.

53 McNeill, David. *Some Thoughts on First and Second Language Acquisition.* An unpublished paper presented to the Modern Foreign Language NDEA Title III Conference, Washington,D.C., 24 May 1965.

54 Mehl, Bernard. "Academic Colonialism—A New Look." *Educational Leadership* 27(1969):243–46.

55 Modiano, Nancy. "Where are the Children?" 93–170 in Alfred Aarons, Barbara Gordon, and William Stewart,eds., *Linguistic-Cultural Differences and American Education. Florida FL Reporter* 7,i(1969):1–175.

56 "NCTE Wins Award." *English Newsletter* 3,i(1970):1–2.

57 Neff, F.C. "Let Them Eat Cake." *Educational Forum* 28(1964):404–11.

58 Nelson, Robert J., and Leon A. Jakobovits,eds. "Motivation and Foreign Language Learning," 34–104 in Joseph A. Tursi,ed., *Foreign Languages and the "New" Student.* Reports of the Working Committees of the Northeast Conference on the Teaching of Foreign Languages. New York: Modern Language Association Materials Center, 1970.

59 *New York City Foreign Language Program for Secondary Schools:German Levels 1–4.* New York: Board of Education of the City of New York, 1967.

60 Oliva, Peter F. *The Teaching of Foreign Languages.* Englewood Cliffs, New Jersey: Prentice-Hall, 1969.

61 Penfield, Wilder. "The Uncommitted Cortex." *The Atlantic Monthly* 214,i(1964):77–81.

62 Peters, R.S. *Education as Initiation.* London: George G. Harrap, 1970.

63 Piaget, Jean. "On How Children Learn." *Psychology Today* 3,xii(1970):25–54.

64 Ramirez, Manuel,III. "Cultural Democracy:A New Philosophy for Educating the Mexican American Child." *The National Elementary Principal* 50,ii(1970:45–46.

65 Renoir, Alain. "The Treason of the Clerks:Parable for 1970." *Southern California Modern and Classical Language Association Forum* 8,iii(1970): 4–10.

66 Rippa, S. Alexander. *Education in A Free Society:An American History.* New York: David McKay, 1967.

67 Rodriguez, Armando. "The Challenge for Educators." *The National Elementary Principal* 50,ii(1970):18–19.

68 Roeming, Robert F. "Bilingualism and the National Interest." *The Modern Language Journal* 55(1971):73–81.

69 Rogers, Carl R. *The Interpersonal Relationship in the Facilitation of Learning.* Columbus, Ohio: Merrill, 1968. [A paper in the Virgil E. Herrick Memorial Lecture Series.]

70 Rosenzweig, Mark R. "Environmental Complexity, Cerebral Change, and Behavior." *American Psychologist* 21(1966):321–32.

71 Sandstrom, Eleanor L., and Paul Pimsleur,eds. "Foreign Languages for All Students?" 105–33 in Joseph A. Tursi,ed., *Foreign Languages and the "New" Student.* Reports of the Working Committees of the Northeast Conference on the Teaching of Foreign Languages. New York: Modern Language Association Materials Center, 1970.

72 Sizemore, Barbara A., and Anderson Thompson. "Separatism, Segregation, and Integration." *Educational Leadership* 27(1969):239–42.

73 Smith, B. Othanel, William O. Stanley, and J. Harlan Shores. *Fundamentals of Curriculum Development.* New York: Harcourt, Brace and World, 1957.

74 Spindler, George D. "The Transmission of American Culture," 1–12 in Alfred Aarons, Barbara Gordon, and William Stewart,eds., *Linguistic-Cultural Differences and American Education. Florida FL Reporter* 7,i(1969):1–175.

75 Steiner, Florence. "Behavioral Objectives and Evaluation," 35–78 in Dale L. Lange,ed., *Britannica Review of Foreign Language Education, Volume* 2. Chicago: Encyclopaedia Britannica, Inc., 1970.

76 Stephenson, Edward. "From Chomsky to Chafe—1957 to 1970." *The Arch* 18,ii(1971):1–7.

77 Strasheim, Lorraine A. "A Rationale for the Individualization and Personalization of Foreign-

Language Instruction," 15–34 in Dale L. Lange, ed., *Britannica Review of Foreign Language Education, Volume* 2. Chicago: Encyclopaedia Britannica, Inc., 1970.

78 ———— "The Anvil or the Hammer:A Guest Editorial." *Foreign Language Annals* 4(1970): 48–56.

79 Taylor, Harold. *Students without Teachers:The Crisis in the University.* New York: McGraw Hill, 1969.

80 [Torrey, Jane W.] "Motivation in Foreign Language Learning," 3–48 in Joseph A. Tursi,ed., *Foreign Languages and the "New" Student.* Reports of the Working Committees of the Northeast Conference on the Teaching of Foreign Languages. New York: Modern Language Association Materials Center, 1970.

81 Tursi, Joseph A., ed. *Foreign Languages and the "New" Student.* Reports of the Working Committees of the Northeast Conference on the Teaching of Foreign Languages. New York: Modern Language Association Materials Center, 1970.

82 Tyler, Fred T., and William A. Brownell. "Facts and Issues:A Concluding Statement," 316–20 in Henry B. Nelson,ed., *Individualizing Instruction:The Sixty-first Yearbook of the National Society for the Study of Education.* Chicago: Univ. of Chicago Press, 1962.

83 Van Doren, Mark. *Liberal Education.* Boston: Beacon Press, 1959.

84 Wachner, Clarence. *General Language:English and Its Foreign Relations.* New York: Holt, Rinehart and Winston, 1968.

85 Willis, Benjamin C.,ed. *The Central Purpose of American Education.* Washington,D.C.: Educational Policies Commission of the National Education Association, 1961.

86 Wilson, Charles E. "The Case for Black Studies." *Educational Leadership* 27(1969):218–21.

87 Wright, Louis B. *Culture on the Moving Frontier.* New York: Harper and Brothers, 1955.

88 Zeydel, Edwin H. *The Teaching of German in the United States—A Historical Survey.* New York: Modern Language Association Materials Center, 1961.

3

Cultural pluralism

Introduction

Genelle G. Morain

University of Georgia

There is something disturbing about linking the idea of the Great American Dream with a melting pot. In a melting pot, diverse elements are forced into cohesion. Individual identity is destroyed. What pours out of the pot at the end of the process is a new substance—a fusion with no discernible variation in texture, taste, color, or character. It seems ironic that the American, traditionally proud of his individualism, could have cherished this "melting pot" for so long.

The melting pot

The coming of the 1960s saw the development of a different concept—that of cultural pluralism. New analogies were used to convey the idea of parts retaining their identity while contributing to the whole: instruments in an orchestra; colors in the spectrum; threads in a tapestry. In the view of the cultural pluralist, each culture is recognized as possessing unique values; each contributes in its special way to the Family of Man. The phrase "Unity with diversity" has given a 20th-century slant to *e pluribus unum*.

"Unity with diversity"

What is the role of the foreign language teacher in an American society that is attaching new value to diversity? This chapter will discuss the problems facing the teacher who sees teaching for cross-cultural understanding as a necessity in a pluralistic society.

Purpose of the chapter

The attitude of the foreign language profession toward the teaching of culture has matured rapidly in the past 20 years. In the early fifties, teachers were still wondering if they should teach culture. By the Northeast Conference of 1960 they had come to an affirmative decision, but the problem remained of what culture to teach. The traditional view of the culture component—embracing history, literature, and the fine arts—was contrasted with the anthropological view of culture that included every aspect of man's life. Language teachers began to talk glibly of "Culture with a big C" (history-fine arts) and "culture with a small c" (the sum total of a way of life). Seelye's 1968 essay on the "Analysis and Teaching of the Cross-Cultural Context" (110)

Attitude of the profession toward the teaching of culture

pointed up the need to do more than talk. With the entrance of the seventies the profession was actively searching for ways to teach and test diverse aspects of culture.

Plural goals in teaching culture

The most frequently cited goal in discussions of language teaching is that of imparting to the student a kind of openness — in the sense of understanding himself, and in the sense of understanding others. The Northeast Conference of 1970 spoke of making the student aware of the "universality of human relationships" (Tursi, 129). Beaujour (9) defines the goal as ". . . real understanding. Understanding in order not to hate, not to despise, not to misunderstand." He stresses knowledge and self-knowledge rather than emotional empathy. Kirch (71) underscores the quest for openness by emphasizing that foreign language study has the potential to liberate the monocultural individual from his provincialism, thus giving him tolerance for other viewpoints, other beliefs, other ways of life. Reinert (104) contends that each time a person learns another language, he increases his power to understand the world. In an age in which artificial stimuli are too frequently used to expand the mind, Reinert sees language as the ". . . most powerful mind-expanding force." Edgerton (41) believes that an experience of language and culture enables the student to attain a richer self-development and a more compassionate understanding of others — a "real willingness to live and let live."

An often stated goal of foreign language study: understanding of self and others

Spokesmen for the profession agree on the culture-related goals of language study. But what of the students? Are students really concerned about acquiring an openness toward self and others? Martin's (82) study of American college students studying German abroad in the summer of 1969 revealed that the three primary interests expressed by the students were acquaintance with the German people, improvement of language skills, and a better understanding of themselves. These accord perfectly with the goals of the language teaching profession. Furthermore, Bolinger (14) reminds us that this is the age of the Peace Corps, of Vista, and of social action groups seeking people-to-people contact. Today's "new" student is eager for the opportunity to operate on multicultural levels.

Student-stated goals match those of the profession

If the goals of the profession and the expectations of the students mesh so closely, why are students disenchanted with languages? Why are so many universities dropping language requirements?—a trend morbidly heralded by some as "the death blow" to foreign language instruction (Bready, 20). The answer must be that the profession is not making good on its promises.

Motivation

Students enroll in foreign language courses for several reasons. The grimmest of these is because the study of foreign languages is required. Others volunteer for language study because they want something from it. Those who are "integratively" motivated want satisfaction. They are interested in the language itself, in the people who speak it, and in the way of life of the target country. Those who are "instrumentally" oriented want practical gains from language study, such as skills for their future profession. Regardless of the motive that impels the student to enroll, his ultimate achievement in the course correlates highly with the positive or negative feelings he holds about the course.

Why students enroll in foreign language courses

The importance of attitude as one of the factors explaining the degree of proficiency a student achieves in learning a second language was reaffirmed by Spolsky (117) and Cowan (34). In a 1970 attitudinal study, Mueller (86) administered a questionnaire to 375 students of basic French at the University of Kentucky. The poll questioned the student's attitudes toward many facets of foreign language study, including how he felt toward the French people after having studied their language. In all but one of the five courses involved, students were revealed to hold definitely negative attitudes. Those who were integratively or instrumentally motivated to take the courses made better grades than those who took them only to fulfill the requirements. But even the A and B students gave the course an unfavorable rating, perceiving it to be unimportant, boring, frustrating, and irrelevant.

Importance of student attitudes

Assessing the reasons for such negative attitudes, Mueller concludes that the unifunctional nature of the courses—their failure to take into account the varying interests and abilities of the students—is probably the major weakness. To the student walled in by ethnocentricity, it becomes a real imposition to have to learn another language, especially if he is forced to write it when he wants only to speak it, or speak it when he prefers to read it. The fast-spreading belief, so well articulated by Mueller (86), Jakobovits (62), Smith (116), and others, that curricular offerings should include plural learning approaches and a diversity of goals and content is brought into sharper focus by this

Reasons for negative attitudes

61

study. Under the present rigid structure of our courses, are we really able to teach language as a communicative facet of culture that opens the door to understanding of self and others?

The psychological factors related to ethnocentrism need further study. Attempts so far to change student attitudes toward the people whose language they are studying have met with only slight success. In an action research project at Parma High School, Cooke (31) provided experimental classes with learning experiences designed to foster positive attitudes toward native speakers of Spanish. The control classes were given a regular Spanish course containing only incidental cultural information. Tests revealed no appreciable differences in attitude change between experimental and control groups.

Psychological factors related t ethnocentrism: two studies

In a somewhat similar study involving students of German, Bals (6) wrote cultural material designed to parallel chapters in the textbook *Verstehen und Sprechen* (Holt). The experimental group received ten minutes of daily instruction on the cultural patterns of German teen-agers, while the control group was taught only from the textbook. Results of the Dufort Foreign Language Attitude Scale showed a very slight, but not statistically significant, improvement in attitude in the experimental group. Interestingly, there were no dropouts in the experimental group (three in the control group) and more grades went up over the ten-week period in the experimental group than in the control group.

Excellent suggestions for developing positive attitudes toward native speakers are given by Cooke in *Perspectives for Teachers of Latin American Culture* (32). Her point of departure is to make the students aware that differences exist within their own school and families as well as among other cultures; that being different is a neutral concept, which must be accepted for harmony within our own society as well as for international understanding. She provides specific techniques, such as role-playing and group discussion, which may be used to facilitate growth toward tolerance and compassion.

Suggestions for the development of positive stude attitudes

So far our discussion of motivation, attitudes, and cultural learning has centered on the student. What of the teacher? Sadly, many teachers find themselves confused when it comes to delineating their own role in the teaching of culture. They feel responsible to become the living embodiment of the spirit of France or the soul of Spain. No one ponders this with a deeper shudder than the participant at an overseas institute who has

What about the teacher?

watched an erstwhile sane American colleague effect a frantic overnight metamorphosis with the aid of French shoes, French cosmetics, a French hairdo and stylized French mannerisms. Beaujour (9) cites this type of cultural mimicry as one of the "non-goals" of language teaching.

Nor is it the duty of a language teacher to become a propagandist for the country whose language he teaches. His purpose is to impart understandings, insights, and awareness, not to create cultural converts.

Still another problem for the teacher is to be honest about his reasons for teaching culture. Although teachers have done enough reading in the journals to give lip service to such goals as "dissipating ethnocentrism," the real motive behind many a song and dance is self-preservation. A strategically inserted chorus of *Chevaliers de la table ronde* has averted more than one drill-inspired rebellion. Steiner (119) empathizes with this point of view: "When the pace lags, when the eyes droop, when the heat comes, the smart teacher will have the cultural unit ready." The value of the cultural insert for quick motivation is real. A teacher need not feel apologetic about this level of usage. The important thing is not to stop here. As Steiner (119) points out, cultural learnings not only encourage the student to pursue his studies but should supply a reason for doing so: contact with people and their way of life. Weiss (133) cautions that song-and-dance culture may give students a false sense of security, leading them to believe they have "studied culture" when really they have dabbled in stereotypes that have no relationship to reality. He insists that the teaching of culture should be done deliberately, not masked under the oompah of a German band. He would make sure the students understood the necessity of gaining cross-cultural awareness, and invite them to participate actively in the discovery of cultural insights. As a concrete example of such an approach, Weiss outlines a sequence that begins with the student cutting a picture of a refrigerator out of a German catalogue, moves through discussion of space, privacy, and distance concepts, and ends with students drawing inferences about the effect of climate on German art and literature. With the guidance of a skilled cultural interpreter, there is a beautiful logic in this progression from icebox to art.

It seems obvious that plural goals, including both formal and deep culture, are needed to provide the relevance that is the true motivating factor for today's "new" student.

Problems for the teacher

Culture should be a regular aspect of the curriculum

Subcultures in a pluralistic society

Americans have too long been reluctant to relinquish the melting pot. It is clear that our society is indeed a pluralistic one with a variety of cultural subgroups. Society has urged a type of conformism that motivated some groups—such as the French, the Germans, Italians, and Scandinavians—to merge into the mainstream. A recent article on name-changing practices among the French Canadians in the United States illustrates this process of gradual blend into the dominant society (Crane and Schulhof, 35). Other groups, however, including the Indians, the Blacks, Orientals, and Spanish-speaking Americans, have retained their ethnicity to a greater degree. Coexistence has not always been easy. At the points of cultural diversity, stereotypes have arisen that serve to perpetuate cross-cultural misunderstandings.

American society is pluralistic

That goal of foreign language study that deals with acquiring an openness to others—a sensitivity toward variation in language and life style—holds promise for the easing of tensions among subcultures. "The most relevant magic in our day," writes Marquardt, "is empathy—the habit of trying in time of conflict to see things the other person's way" (81). The language teacher who succeeds in helping a student to look objectively at another culture—to accept it on its own terms for what it means to its own members—is giving that student the tools and the insight to accept all cultures.

One goal of foreign language study has particular relevance

Those subcultures that have to a marked extent merged into the mainstream are being rediscovered by language teachers, who find that they provide new dimensions to the teaching of culture. Kuschmierz (75) describes the activities of the German Society at the University of Pittsburgh, Greensburg Campus. In addition to an array of other cultural activities, the Society sponsors excursions to the restored German communal settlement of the Harmony Society at Ambridge, and to the Spring Folk Festival of the Pennsylvania Dutch in the Appalachian Mountains. Students at Woodrow Wilson High School in Washington, D.C., also explore the Pennsylvania Dutch heritage and participate in the Georgetown Maifest as well (Thomison, 125). German influences on contemporary American architecture are studied by students at Penn Hills Township High School, who trace the influence of the Bauhaus school to their own West Pennsylvania (Rose, 108). Piehl & Bell (98) discuss a French cultural unit

Subcultures provide new dimensions for language teachers

64

based on the influence of the Basques in the American West. An in-depth study of the French in Delaware resulted from cooperation between the Eleutherian Mills Historical Library, the State Department of Education, and French teachers in the area (Low, 80). This study of the historical background of French immigrants to Delaware, combined with a perusal of old texts, letters, and manuscripts, provides an invaluable cross-cultural experience.

As for the subcultures that have retained their ethnicity, the current educational thrust is directed toward furthering their language skills, improving their self-image, and making others aware of the contribution made to a pluralistic culture by each member.

Furthering the language skills and other aspects of ethnic subcultural groups

Roeming (107) stresses that the primary goal of education for ethnically oriented non-speakers of English should be "achieving economic development through English proficiency." He warns that fostering a romantic attachment to an ambiguous cultural heritage cannot solve the immediate need for economic security. The role of the non-English language in the bilingual learning situation, he insists, is to supply love, compassion, and understanding during the transition from non-English to English. There is wisdom in this point of view, but experience is proving that a well-conceived bilingual program can also increase the student's bicultural assets.

Role of English

One example is the Calexico Intercultural Design (El Cid Project) in the Calexico Unified School District, California, where 87% of the students come from Spanish-speaking homes. Instructors in social studies and language arts have developed their own bilingual and bicultural Learning Achievement Packets (LAPS) that are structured on the behavioral objective format. The overriding emphasis of the project is a humanistic one: to enable the student to relate positively to two cultures, Mexican and American (Chetkovich, 28).

Examples of bilingual-bicultural programs: 1. Calexico

Another bilingual-bicultural program that is succeeding is located at Phoenix Union High School in Phoenix, Arizona. When the federally funded program began in 1969 under the direction of Marie L. Vega, 100 freshmen of Mexican-American background participated. The program has since expanded through the sophomore year, with extension into the junior year planned for 1971-72. The bilingual nature of classwork enables the students to improve their control of both English and Spanish. Equally important, they receive instruction in their

2. Phoenix

own culture, which gives them a new sense of dignity and worth (Weinhold, Plath, & Vega, 131). That the program is making a positive impact is seen in this quote from a student's questionnaire response:

The teachers here speak to in English and Spanish if you don't know Spanish they talk to you in English and the same for English they talk to you in Spanish . . . They should keep having this program for other students can learn about themselves were they came from and too be proud of what they are.

A course in Tlingit conversation and grammar is offered at Alaska Methodist University. A similar course, "Tlingit Culture," is offered as an elective in Juneau-Douglas High School, Juneau. A heavy component of culture, including dance, music, art, and legend, is built into the course with the intent of perpetuating the linguistic and artistic heritage of this Indian subculture (Harlow, 56).

3. Alaska Methodist University

Another subculture that has to a large extent retained its ethnicity is that of the Black American. Perhaps in no other area is there a greater urgency to develop understanding of cross-cultural variability, and a critical place to start is with the teachers in the American schools.

Black America: another cultural group

The new disciplines of psycholinguistics and sociolinguistics (Fishman, 44), with their stress on language as a form of cultural behavior, have made it safe to talk about the way Black children talk. Teachers have long been aware that many Black students from lower socioeconomic levels speak a kind of English that differs significantly from the English of the schools. Their conclusion, however, was that Black English was "substandard" in nature and that the children who spoke it were incompetent in the area of language skills. "They can't even speak English!" became the ethnocentric wail that excused much non-teaching in the public schools. Research has now shown that Black speech is a language system unto itself, highly developed and capable of expressing sophisticated linguistic nuances.

Recognition of Black speech

Kochman (73) points out that the communication style of the Black child is oral-aural. Expertise in the audiolingual realm is more highly valued in Black culture than in White middle-class culture. The prestige accorded men-of-words in the Black community reflects a rich oral tradition, the roots of which go back to Africa. The White community, on the other hand, attaches greater value to the printed page and the written document.

The oral tradition of the Black community

66

Scholastic achievement in the schools is measured almost completely through the written channel. Kochman sees an inconsistency in a society that depends upon oral ability for most socioeconomic relations, yet attaches greater value (reward) to written ability. Such an inconsistency strikes an old familiar chord with the foreign language teacher who has spent the last ten years encouraging test-makers to give importance to the oral channel as well as the written. Surely this same language teacher should take the lead in recognizing differences in communication styles across cultural lines, and in trying to teach receptiveness toward differences in values and life styles. The results of reducing ethnocentricity in the foreign language classroom may then spread throughout the school.

Inconsistency of the general society's language values

Indeed, evidence is available to show that positive reactions are already spreading beyond the school and into the community. German students from Tulsa Memorial High School have been visiting an elementary school in order to help German-speaking children learn English (Carney, 26). A child development program for cross-cultural children in one eastern metropolitan area involved special foreign language classes for the high school students who worked with non-English-speaking children (Zolar, 138). The "Proyecto Amistad" (Project Friendship) program conducted by American University takes Spanish majors out into the Spanish-speaking communities in Maryland to function as counselors, social workers, teachers, and interpreters (Beusch, 11). Programs such as these offer proof that language study *can* produce the openness toward other subcultures we so earnestly desire.

Programs offer proof that openness toward subcultures can be achieved

Culture across international boundaries

Perhaps the term "outreach" best expresses the philosophy mirrored currently in the teaching of culture. Concepts of time and space are changing as they relate to foreign language. "Culture with a capital C" had much to do with the past; "culture with a small c" invites a focus on contemporary life. Furthermore, the traditional limiting of culture to a study of the "mother country" has been replaced by a keen interest in expanding geographical frontiers. As Suzette Brace, French teacher at East Lansing High School, phrases it: "At this point, our students are more attracted to the exotic in French-speaking West Africa than to the magnificence in Louis XIV's court" (19). Consalvi's

The term "outreach" applied to cultural studies

(30) research in cross-cultural attitudes indicates that where values are concerned, students may be closer to each other internationally than they are to their parents.

Wheaton (134) suggests that students see their own striving toward individuality in the emerging nations' search for identity. She describes the steps taken by teacher and students to set up a course focusing on French spheres of influence outside of France. Each student chooses an area of specialization—Africa, Near or Middle East, Indochina, the Pacific, or the New World—and pursues an individualized, in-depth study of his topic.

Fontaine (46) also describes the intense involvement in cross-cultural studies that can come through foreign language study. Her fifth- and sixth-year French students spend one day a week in pursuit of an individual study project drawn from divergent French cultures. The following account of a cross-cultural experience illustrates the opportunity for new ideas that can come with language study.

Intense student involvement in cross-cultural studies

Five guest speakers from the Ivory Coast spoke to the entire class and then in smaller, informal conversation groups about the geography, history, economy, education, industry, sports, etc. of their country. They answered questions of the students, and a particularly lively interchange occurred on the subject of fetishism. They were all Catholics, yet they told how they reconciled their belief in certain fetishes with their religion. Their account of a sports favorite who had broken his leg in a soccer match was of special interest to the class. The leg had been x-rayed and there were two breaks. After the native healer had applied her special herbs and remedies, another x-ray showed no evidence of a break; the young soccer hero was able to continue to play for his team. A spirited exchange between our French AFS student, a member of the class whose father is a surgeon, and the Ivoiriens was valuable, not only for the French conversation, but also for the lesson in tolerance for the ideas of other nationalities and cultures (Fontaine, 46).

Such a practice of inviting native speakers into the classroom is one way to bring culture alive. Delaware has a vital exchange program with Panama, whereby 44 students and teachers from Panama spent this year in homes and schools in the state (Caldwell, 23). Brooks (22) tells of the visit of a Haitian surgeon to his fourth-year FLES (Foreign Language in the Elementary

Native speakers in the classroom

School) class in Cleveland, and of the delight the 11-year-olds took in plying their guest with questions in French. French teachers in Chicago (Cudecki, Kapsis, Schwartz & Woodson-Levey, 36) discuss ways of locating and working with native speakers in an urban area. Teachers interested in gaining maximum benefit from native informants should consult Caldwell & Abraham's article (24), "The Native as an Aide in the Classroom."

Evidence of the trend in French toward Canadian and African studies is seen in the colloquium sponsored by the Department of Romance Languages at the University of Vermont in June, 1971, entitled "La Littérature africaine et canadienne d'expression française, genèse et jeunesse." The colloquium featured an opening address by Léopold Sédar Senghor, President of the Republic of Senegal. *Canadian-African literary studies*

New language courses built around Black studies are being developed at a rapid pace. An interdisciplinary course at South Philadelphia High School deals with "The Role of Black People in Classical Antiquity"(Masciantonio, 83). The French Curriculum Guide for the Atlanta City Schools lists courses on "Traditional Family Life in Francophone Africa," "Life and Culture in the Francophone West Indies," and "The Contemporary African." Morehouse College in Atlanta offers "Historical Perspectives of Francophone Africa," as well as "Poetry of Negritude," "The Afro-French Novel," and "African Folk Literature." *Black studies*

Bostick's (15) excellent guide for the teacher of Afro-French literature and culture includes background information on African culture, a full discussion of African music and dance as they relate to literary expression, a study of the role of myth in African culture, a discussion of negritude, and a detailed presentation of methods and techniques for making African literature and culture a living experience in the classroom. Bostick believes that the study of African culture in the French class can stimulate renewed interest in learning French, especially among Black Americans. He cautions, however, that this phase of French study should be presented as a legitimate language learning experience and not as "a safari into some exotic world." *Black literature in the French language*

More suggestions for the teaching of Black literature in the language class are given by Deutsch (39). She suggests texts appropriate for second-level French students and more sophisticated prose and poetry suitable for advanced levels. The reader as yet unfamiliar with the literature of Francophone Africa would find Deutsch's treatment of the topic enlightening.

An innovative program combining French and African studies at the FLES level is described by Thom (124) and Keach (69). The project is a continuation on another dimension of the successful "Twinned Classroom" program that paired elementary school children in Ohio with their peers in France (Jonas, 67). The same children, now in fifth and sixth grades, are currently "twinned" with African counterparts in Upper Volta, a part of former French West Africa. The format of the original "Twinned Classroom" project is retained, with both the experimental and control groups receiving French instruction built on slide and tape units from Africa. The experimental group not only receives the culture units but responds in kind, communicating directly with their African peers via tapes and slides of their own making. The control group, on the other hand, benefits from the African units but does not share in the interpersonal, two-way exchange of cultural information. Sister Ruth Jonas, Director of the project, resides temporarily in Ouahigouya, a market town in Upper Volta where French is the official but not the native tongue. Here she uses tape recorder and camera to capture significant examples of Upper Voltaic culture. The slides are organized into sets of 15-20 pictures and an accompanying dialogue is taped in simple French by the children of the twin classes in the Ouahigouya schools. One example of a cultural unit is a sequence showing a little boy who turns to stare at the unusual sight of a car in his native village. He trips, dropping an earthenware jar which shatters on the ground. Painstakingly, he retrieves the pieces and carries them to his mother, who punishes him for his carelessness. Opportunities for discussion of socialization, interdependence, social control, change, and division of labor as they exist in Upper Voltaic culture are evident in this brief sequence. The children in Ohio who see and hear their African friends living such an experience acquire an awareness of what is universal and what is unique across cultures.

Combination of French and African studies at FLES level

An unusual feature of this project is that English-speaking children are communicating with native speakers of an African dialect through the shared medium of the French language. Although there is much of value in such a procedure, the aspect of language as bearer-of-culture is stripped away, since both groups of children are using a foreign language system to describe their native cultures. Final results of the two-year African phase of the twinned classroom project are awaited with interest by the profession.

Behind the classroom door: Strategies in action

In the realm of teaching for cross-cultural understanding, the language profession is finally starting to move from theory into practice. Leaders in the area are producing models and materials, and classroom teachers are developing productive techniques. Although the scope of this discussion will not permit a detailed presentation of materials and strategies, a survey of ongoing practices may open up channels for further investigation.

Textbook and other materials

An encouraging trend toward building cultural insights into commercially available texts is evident. The content of dialogues and reading passages is chosen to portray culturally significant events. Footnotes point out elements of "small c culture" which might otherwise escape both teacher and students. Multimedia approaches also place strong emphasis on culture. Georgia's four-year Spanish telecourse for elementary schools, "Viva Nuestra Amistad," uses over 140 native speakers to illuminate cultural differences due to age, sex, geographical distance, and social milieu (DeWright, 40).

Materials for the learning of cultural concepts

The Alameda County School Department, Hayward, California, has published a practical handbook for teachers of Spanish entitled *Cultural Understanding, Spanish, Level I* (37). Designed to accompany the instructional units in *Entender y Hablar* (Holt, Rinehart and Winston), the items are also cross-referenced for beginning Spanish texts published by Harcourt Brace Jovanovich and by Encyclopaedia Britannica Educational Corporation. Forty-two cultural concepts are presented, ranging in content from the formation of nicknames to the organization of Hispanic schools. Publication of a similar handbook for the teaching of French culture is planned for the near future.

In an introductory essay to *Cultural Understanding, Spanish, Level I* (37), Reid Scott discusses the problem faced by every language teacher: With class time so limited, how can one teach both a systematic culture course and a language course? His suggestion is to teach those aspects of the target culture that are essential to understanding the language itself. To clarify which aspects are essential, he forms an analogy with the linguistic concepts of the phoneme and the allophone. Just as the pho-

With limited time, how can the teacher include culture?

71

neme represents an abstract category of close but not identical sounds called allophones, so does the "culteme" include variations of cultural patterns that might be called "allocults." Phonemes and their boundaries must be learned if a speaker is to communicate accurately; a mastery of allophones, on the other hand, is desirable but not essential. A similar situation exists with "cultemes" and "allocults." Every culture has aspects that the foreigner must learn if he is to operate harmoniously within that culture. These are the "cultemes." And every culture has other aspects that a foreigner may violate without serious consequences—the "allocults." Scott warns that the major problem for anyone going from one culture to another is to identify cultemes and their boundaries. The situation is especially hazardous when a certain allocult belongs to one culteme in the traveler's culture and to another in the host culture. For example, whistling in a public theatre indicates approval in the United States, disapproval in Spain. It becomes obvious that cultemes must be presented at the same time as other elements of language, since many times the correct use of the language forms depends on the cultural circumstances.

Cultemes

Two publications of the State Department of Public Instruction, Springfield, Illinois, are recommended in their entirety to foreign language teachers: *Perspectives for Teachers of Latin American Culture*, edited by H. Ned Seelye (113) and *French Language Education. The Teaching of Culture in the Classroom*, edited by Charles Jay & Pat Castle (64). Each volume presents a collection of essays written by specialists actively involved in the teaching of culture. Their expressed purpose is not only to stimulate others to include the cultural component in foreign language teaching but to give direct and specific suggestions to help them do so.

Publications of Illinois State Department of Public Instruction

To the teacher hungry for specifics, Brooks (21) serves up a meaty article discussing nine techniques for teaching culture in the classroom. Representative of these is the "inquiry technique," which recognizes that a young American becomes what he is because of his contact with a long list of cultural elements: Mother Goose, baby sitter, school bus, braces on teeth, etc. The inquiry method consists of ferreting out a similar list for the youthful counterpart in another culture.

Nine techniques for teaching culture

The reader who has not had the opportunity to explore the superb four-volume publication *Background Data for the Teaching of French* (91) will benefit from Nostrand & Nostrand's essay in *French Language Education: The Teaching of Culture in the Classroom* (93). The authors present a system for analyzing culture that enables the observer to see how patterns become meaningful in the context of the total life-style. This "emergent model" of culture is a kind of structured inventory in which some 30 topics are subsumed under the four headings: "The Culture," "The Society," "The Individual," and "The Ecology." Such a model helps the student to understand ". . . what values the culture-bearers are pursuing and what assumptions guide the pursuit."

Emergent cultural model

A different model for analyzing culture through language study is seen in *Japanese in Action: An Unorthodox Approach to the Spoken Language and the People Who Speak It* (Seward, 114). Seward lists 13 areas dealing with "common civilities" in which the student of Japanese should be able to operate with poise and control: (*1*) meeting an acquaintance; (*2*) entering a home or ship; (*3*) as a guest, before eating; (*4*) as a guest, after eating; (*5*) as a host, serving guests; (*6*) returning home; (*7*) parting; (*8*) expressing appreciation; (*9*) asking pardon; (*10*) calling attention to yourself (when kept waiting at counters, etc.); (*11*) as a guest, departing; (*12*) seeing off guests; (*13*) the bow and bowing. Guidelines such as these might well serve as a checklist for students of any language. For instance, how many alloculuts of the "expressing appreciation" culteme does the student know?

"Common civilities" as a list of cultemes

Culture and curricular pluralism

Examples of curricular pluralism, in which the foreign language is brought into juxtaposition with another discipline for the mutual enrichment of both, are presented in detail by Ort & Smith (94). For an even more accessible discussion of current interdisciplinary programs the reader is referred to Chapter 5 of this volume (Warriner).

Interdisciplinary programs and methods

The content of many interdisciplinary courses lies within the realm of the social sciences. Techniques developed by social scientists offer possibilities for adoption by foreign language teachers. Ort & Smith (94) suggest that the case-study method, for instance, could be used in language classes to show how cultural differences are translated into behavioral patterns. Murphy (87) gives excellent examples of other techniques borrowed from the social sciences that could be used to enhance the teaching of culture. Working with a selection from Laurence Wylie's *Village*

The case-study method

73

en Vaucluse, he shows how the student can be led step by step to analyze a text, formulate culturally valid concepts, and translate them into dramatic action through role-playing. Wheaton (134) urges that English and social studies teachers encourage their students to do research for papers in whatever languages the students can handle. Such "comparison point of view" research would supply cross-cultural perspective.

At least two language courses have been developed for high school students that focus explicitly on cross-cultural comparison. A course for seniors in a fifth-year French class at Upper Arlington High School (Ohio) utilizes cultural materials collected by the instructor in France during the summer of 1971. Slides of French teen-agers are accompanied by taped conversations on topics relevant to their interests. The new film series *Toute la Bande* (Scholastic Magazines) is used to provide further audiovisual depiction of themes and value systems, and magazines and textbooks provide reading experiences to trigger discussion and debate. The goal of the course is the development of openness toward other cultures, with the resultant diminishing of prejudice and stereotyping (Allen, 4).

Using cross-cultural comparison and media

Another multimedia course that focuses on cross-cultural understanding is offered to French, Spanish, and German classes in San Leandro, California (Torres, 127). Torres & Scott (128) have developed a model for teaching culture that emphasizes everything that is related to youth, using the target language to move from concrete culture items to more abstract concepts. In one unit, the purpose of which is to link vocabulary to culture, the behavioral objectives include the student's ability to demonstrate knowledge of the following cultural aspects of the Spanish language:

Cross-cultural understanding: emphasis on youth

> Polite expressions; taboo words; slang words; use of foreign words in common vocabulary; use and historical facts about *olé* and *vale*; voice inflection, intonation and vocabulary that express command, imitation, surprise, indignation, pleasure, sorrow, coaxing, admiration, approval, menace, reassurance, cussing words, and the use of the name of the Lord.

The teaching unit presents the related concepts that must be developed, their method of presentation, suggested class activities to insure correct body and facial movements, and suggestions for evaluation. The Torres and Scott units, which illuminate culture aspect-by-aspect in systematic fashion, exemplify the kind of materials teachers need to improve the presentation of culture.

Some interdisciplinary courses relate language to the arts, such as the "French Drama" course at Walt Whitman High School, Bethesda, Maryland, in which students read, discuss, and enact scenes from the dramas of each period (Stone, 121). Whiteside (136) combines the methods of ethnomusicology with those of cultural anthropology to bring insights from these disciplines to the study of music in the French classroom. An interdisciplinary approach to culture involving art, music, and literature coordinated with language study is offered at Milford Mill High School, Baltimore (Rivkin, 105). A stereo player with speakers mounted in the classroom wall brings classical and popular music to the students, who use the target language to learn the vocabulary of music appreciation and to discuss instruments, themes, and plots. Slides from the National Gallery of Art are coordinated with musical presentations. Students write their own dramatic skits to illustrate relationships among characters in operas studied. Rivkin has used this approach with students from both high and low socioeconomic backgrounds. Students in both categories have responded with intense interest.

Language related to culture of an artistic nature

Curricular pluralism can become another channel through which cultural goals are realized.

Grammar used to teach culture

Grammar is considered an important adjunct to the teaching of culture in many classrooms. Bourgeacq (16) asserts that our tendency to lump many expressions that differ from English into the category of "idioms" conveys to the student the impression that the foreign language is made up of illogical structures. An "illogical" construction by English standards becomes logical, Bourgeacq insists, when seen from the foreign perspective. He recommends that the cultural foundation for grammar be presented simultaneously with structure to give the student the necessary insight. Johnson (66) links the task of learning personal pronouns in Spanish with the "feelings" that are culturally associated with each pronoun (politeness, groupness, the ego, etc.). Kleeman (72) finds operatic texts in German an excellent source of grammatical illustrations and reports success in drilling everything from adjective endings to relative clauses while analyzing Wagnerian texts. Eppert (42) describes an interesting strategy

Aspects of culture in grammar

75

involving the use of results from recent polls in Germany to kindle discussion, impart cultural insights, and drill grammatical structures.

Literature as a reflection of culture

For many years literature was the most important means of bringing culture into the language classroom. The advent of the anthropological approach does not diminish the need for literary study. Instead it gives teachers new ways to enrich literary analysis. Seelye (112) demonstrates how sensitive literary analysis can reveal insights into cross-cultural antagonisms that make for misunderstanding. His article on the "banana trilogy" of Miguel Asturias points out the ambivalence that the Central American feels toward the *yanqui* and shows how literary works can give the American student an awareness of the attitudes of others. Nostrand (92) discusses the link between literature and social behavior in an article entitled "Theme Analysis in the Study of Literature." An unusual French seminar at Saint Joseph College (Flinton, 45) gives the students opportunity to discuss literary, psychological, and sociological problems suggested by their study of French authors. In individual presentations of selected topics, students make creative use of transparencies, films, art slides, records, and tapes to bring in cultural aspects. One student introduced Samuel Beckett by an original "garbage heap" prepared in the middle of a small lounge. Concealed under it was a recording by her friends of human wails, sighs, baby cries, gasping, and moans: a mood-creating approach the originality of which there is no denying.

Some examples of literature a culture

Culture and the mass media

Sten-Gunnar (120) insists that the study of language is linked more closely to the study of culture than to the study of literature. Even the books especially designed to teach culture are inadequate, he maintains, pointing out that of all the culture experts who organized French civilization into books for foreigners, not one wrote a single paragraph prophetic of the May, 1968, revolts. He urges that authentic texts of interviews, press extracts, and radio broadcast be made accessible to the language teacher to provide linguistically and culturally diversified materials that can be used immediately and discarded as they become outdated. Koepke (74) gives excellent examples of how contemporary texts — a propaganda speech delivered by Goebbels

Media provide most authentic cultural materials

76

in 1933; today's editorial from *Zeit* — can be analyzed stylistically and historically to provide insights into German culture. Lange (76) emphasizes that magazines and newspapers reflect the most current aspects of attitudes and cultural themes. James (63) cites examples to show that the new German advertising reveals aspects of language and humor. An ad of the Federal Railways, for instance, shows two trains on a switching yard beneath a canopy of high-tension wires. The legend: "Our locomotives are giving up smoking." Another approach to humor and culture is proposed by Hall & Lafourcade (55), who see cartoons and comic books as an aid to societal understanding. Cartoons depict visual aspects of culture as well as situational cues that alert the native to produce appropriate responses (a sneeze to elicit "Health!"). They portray paralinguistic and onomatopoeic features of language and reveal popular attitudes on social, moral, and political problems. The natural speech of cartoons, sometimes criticized by literary purists, adds the dimension of real life too often lacking in the classroom. Bouygues (18) echoes the cry for texts that are alive, texts that will surprise, intrigue, even shock the student. As illustration he uses a text dealing with *Occitan,* the language of the south of France. He suggests that as the problems between *Langue d'oc* and the rest of France are discussed, certain similarities might be noted between the problems of the North and the South in the United States.

Printed matter

Radio is another aspect of mass communication that is being used with effect by language teachers. Students of Spanish at Van Horn High School, Independence, Missouri, are using shortwave radio as part of their independent study programs (Clapper, 29). Nelson (89) gives suggestions for those interested in using radio to help students maintain listening skills while expanding cultural awareness.

Radio

Commercial film as a means of portraying culture is discussed with enthusiasm by Decock (38). He insists that there is no justification for the guilt complex harbored by teachers when they "lose an hour" showing a film. Time is enriched, not lost, if the film is skillfully used to analyze psychological, social, and cultural manifestations. Hocking (59) points out that film can bring the foreign experience into the classroom so directly that it becomes immediate and personal, not vicarious. The magic of TV and films, he states, is that experience is "reproduced rather than described, shared rather than observed." Unfortunately,

Commercial film

teachers are still reluctant to make full use of film. The expense
and the technical procedures discourage them. The whir of the
projector arouses a vague sense of disquiet. Far too many still
perceive the printed page as the One, the True, the Only culture-
bearer. Films should make an increasingly important contribution to the study of culture.

Kinesics and culture

McLuhan (84) asserts that the new mass media—radio, TV,
film—have helped 20th-century man recover his awareness of
facial language and bodily gesture. Although a person can stop
talking, Goffman (53) reminds us, he cannot stop communicating through body idiom. The teacher desirous of placing language in its cultural matrix must be concerned with the latest
findings of kinesic research. Birdwhistell's new book, *Kinesics*
and Context, (13) is a valuable aid for the serious student of
gesture. He debunks the assumption that there are universal
movement patterns characteristic of all men. Research has
failed to uncover a single gesture, stance, or facial expression
that has the same social meaning in all societies. Gestures, says
Birdwhistell, are really bound morphs—incapable of standing
alone. As with other stem forms, prefixual, suffixual, transfixual,
or infixual behavior must be attached to them to give meaning to
the whole. Research with English, American, and German kinesic systems suggests that their body motion languages may vary
to the same degree as their spoken languages. Future research
may enable scholars to speak confidently of national kinesic systems, but at present it is safest to say that observable cross-cultural differences exist.

Facial language and body
gesture as cultural elements

Seward (114) lists 28 ways in which the Japanese employ sign
language and discusses their cross-cultural significance. Poyatos (102) writes of national character and individual personality
as possibly reflected in gesture, and relates kinesic activity to
classroom presentation. Canfield's (25) collection of Spanish
gestures, postures, and facial expressions is available to classroom teachers in a packet containing slides and tapes. French
gestures are described by Nostrand (91, Section I,G,2,a-b-c). The
"Audio-Motor Unit," a listening comprehension technique developed by Kalivoda, Morain, & Elkins (68), recognizes the
importance of kinesic involvement in language learning. Each
unit, composed of a series of oral commands, elicits physical
responses from the students that demonstrate their comprehen-

The teaching of facial language
and body gestures

sion. The unit might teach the vocabulary of kinesics ("Shrug your shoulders," "Shake hands," "Jump rope") or it might illustrate a gesture or sequence of movements that carries special meaning to members of the target culture. The authors give a sample unit based on eating a meal in a Spanish restaurant that calls for at least four culturally determined kinesic patterns. Such a link between kinesics and culture adds one more dimension to language learning.

Culture and the classics

Paradoxically, the so-called dead languages, Latin and classical Greek, are pumping lifeblood into the study of culture. Or perhaps culture is pumping new life into the classics. At any rate, when a Junior Classical League's annual state convention attracts over 600 high school students (Colorado, April, 1971), one can scarcely start the obsequies. Creative new programs like the Latin FLES offerings in the District of Columbia (LeBovit, 77) and the Latin and Greek FLES courses in Philadelphia (Masciantonio, 83) may account for the quickened pulse of the classics. These multimedia courses for inner city children are designed to strengthen communication in English while opening new channels for cultural enrichment. Dimensional mock-ups of Rome and Pompeii, films, maps, charts, filmstrips, taped songs and dramas are used to give the students a feeling of direct involvement with the culture of ancient Rome and Greece. An imaginative attempt at the secondary level to involve the student with the "life of the times" is Latin teacher Bernard Barcio's catapult construction project at North Central High, Indianapolis, Indiana. The struggle to rediscover the secret of the Romans' catapult bow for use on a life-scale model has led his students to intensive research and a feeling of rapport with the ancients that could never come from translating the Gallic Wars (Barcio, 7). A survey of Greek civilization in an advanced Latin class led to a course in classical Greek at Menlo-Atherton High School, California (Allan, 2). The approach—cultural, multisensory, fully integrated with language—is a good example of the new vigor in the classics.

Classical languages give lifeblood to study of culture

Folklore and culture

With relevancy the rallying cry of the day, it might seem paradoxical that articles on folklore are finding their way into contemporary journals. The answer is that folklore, far from being a moribund aspect of culture, can do much to breathe life into the study of foreign languages.

Morain (85) enumerates some 35 different forms of folklore as evidence that folklore makes up an important component of the total culture. She suggests that folklore can illuminate cultural themes and help to clarify value systems. Weiss (132) expands this approach to apply to the study of contrasting national cultures and regional subcultures. Both authors give examples that are directly applicable to the foreign language classroom.

Folklore lends much to culture study

Lord & Farner (79) include folkloristic content in their conversation class because it offers subject matter that the student can discuss freely rather than parrot, and because students find it helpful in their own literary studies. The adult native speaker of German has a background of exposure to traditional oral materials that is usually missing from the American student's training. The authors find that tapes based on children's rhymes and games, the Grimm's *Kinder und Hausmärchen*, and the Till Eulenspiegel materials not only stimulate conversation but help fill a real gap in cultural preparation.

Francke (49) proposes that the technique of the *Nacherzählung* be used as a means of testing the student's ability to express himself in the language. He believes that the Grimm tales are ideal for the *Nacherzählung* because they represent one of the original forms of oral literature. Their simple style, short form, and repetitive action combine to make an ideal vehicle for oral exercises.

The "Nacherzählung" as both language and cultural exercise

In a sophisticated treatment of folkloristic materials, Gershman (51) relates children's taunts, jeers, and rhymes to modern French poetry.

Of the many genres of folklore, the proverb seems to be especially popular with language teachers. Seward (114), previously cited for his work with Japanese language and culture, discusses the values of *kotowaza-otoshi* (proverb-dropping) for the nonnative speaker. The correct use of proverbs gives a favorable impression of linguistic ability and familiarity with the target culture, he maintains. They also provide excellent guideposts to the study of social psychology, history, and traditional attitudes. This attribute of proverbs is discussed by Foster (47), who presents a total of 107 proverbs, most of immediate Spanish origin, grouped under such thematic headings as "Fate Overrides Man's Best-laid Plans," and "Human Character Is Flexible." Ways in which proverbs may be used to study stereotyping are presented

The proverb as used in foreign language instruction

by Zenner (137). He lists many examples to show how religious groups, ethnic groups, ecological groups, and local groups express their attitudes, hostilities, and amusement through proverbs. He also suggests that proverb collections can be used to reveal aspects of the structure of thought for the people studied.

Rysan (109) points out that traditional folklore in all its variations is flourishing in the 20th century. He distinguishes between traditional folklore (individual-oriented, conservative) and "mass-lore," which reflects the state of the mass man who has been *de*-individualized. The masses as well as folk-groups continue to generate lore, Rysan maintains. He urges further study of the phenomenon of mass-lore, especially as it is directed against present-day minorities who serve as scapegoats.

Student-produced materials

Involvement of students in the creation of their own cultural materials is strongly supported by Bourque (17) who tells of student successes in making films and slide presentations to illustrate stories read by the class. At Bishop Scully High School, Latin students create sets of transparencies in color to accompany teacher-made tapes. The sets relate topics such as "Oratory," "Communication," and "Astronomy" to the study of Latin (Sister Anna Roberta, 106). Students at CONVAL Regional School in Peterboro, New Hampshire, produce their own slide-tape, video tape, Super-8 film programs (Fournier, 48). Carney (27) relates the success experienced by students in Tulsa, Oklahoma, under the ECHO project (Echoes of Classical Heritage in Oklahoma) and the VOCAW program (Voices of Children Around the World). Latin, French, German, Spanish, and Russian students visit elementary social studies classes and teach aspects of language and culture to rapt audiences. Advanced French students at Toccoa High School, Toccoa, Georgia, (Sims & Hite, 115) armed with class roll books and a list of review commands created personalized audiomotor units on tape for beginning students. Graduate students in Foreign Language Education at Wayne State University formed their own cultural research teams and investigated teen-age patterns in Europe and Mexico (Pindur, 100). They developed written and oral questionnaires designed to reveal sociocultural attitudes and trends among adolescents (Jenks, 65). Such activities, involving students in research, preparation, and teaching of cultural materials, make participation in languages truly dimensional.

Student-created materials: slide, film, tape

Intensive language experiences

The principle of total immersion in the language has led to the development of intensive language experiences outside the school context. Programs of this type range from the large-scale, multilingual program with rich curricular offerings and solid academic orientation, such as the Southeastern Language Center at the University of Georgia, to small-scale, informal camps of the type sponsored by the Jefferson County, Colorado, language teachers (Preller, 103). Haukebo (58) presents an overview of such innovative language programs, all of which place heavy emphasis on the cultural content.

Total immersion programs in the U.S.

Field trips abroad

A gratifying number of schools make the effort to transport their students to the foreign country for total cultural immersion. In a monumental climax to a pen pal letter exchange, Tittle (126) took his FLES students to visit their pen pals in Niederstetten, Germany. Plans were made for German elementary students to return the visit in 1971. Students from Dillingham High School, Alaska, spent two months in Japan studying culture and language under the tutelage of Japanese students from Alaska Methodist University, Anchorage, (Harlow, 56). French III students at Dreher High School, Columbia, South Carolina, live for ten days with a French family during the summer, complete culturally oriented assignments, and return to a special follow-up class in the fall (Palyok, 95). A two-week tour to Mexico enables Spanish students at Box Elder High School, Brigham City, Utah, to profit from four days of study with private tutors before setting out on a tour of culturally significant areas (Bingham, 12). A trip to Italy in the summer brings the winter's academic studies to life for Latin students at Bishop Scully High School, Amsterdam, New York, (Sister Anna Roberta, 106). Students of French in New Hampshire are representative of eastern area students who have ready access to Quebec Province as a source of cross-cultural insights (Fournier, 48).

Immersion in the foreign culture

Pen pals

Farkas (43) points out the motivating effects of student-to-student correspondence and lists eight organizations that can serve as sources for starting exchanges of letters or tapes. Hopulele (60) calls for research on the effects of such exchanges, and reports on his own efforts to secure data. The method of selecting pen pals, described by Becker (10), is challenged by Stafford (118) who cautions that French postal employees may not always be able to cooperate. Becker has students address their letters to the Maître de Postes of a specific city, asking him to forward them to the English teacher in that city's lycée.

Measuring cross-cultural understanding

In a hard-hitting communique to the teachers of New York State on the subject of testing and culture, Paul M. Glaude (52) states: "There are no satisfactory culture tests anywhere in existence today." It is hard to quarrel with this statement. The encouraging thing is that as a profession we are finally coming to realize that it is true.

The testing of cross-cultural understanding

As recently as 1968 the Modern Language Association published *A Handbook on Foreign Language Classroom Testing*, compiled by outstanding foreign language teachers from all levels of instruction with the blessing of both the MLA Test Advisory Committee and the Educational Testing Service. The treatment of the testing of culture in this handbook is disappointing. Although it repeatedly emphasizes that culture should be taught, and that culture may be considered either in a narrow (literary-artistic) sense or an extended sense (the whole way of life), the handbook provides no leadership in the construction of "whole way of life" items. The examples of ideal test items include the following fugitives from the 19th century:

German:	Approximately what dates delimit the period of Old High German?
Italian:	Match the operas with the names of their composers.
Spanish:	Match the region with the product associated with it.
French:	La Seine se jette dans _____.
Russian:	(No sample test items even given in the area of culture.)

Fortunately for those interested in measuring more sensitive cultural insights, help is available from such prime movers in the area as H. Ned Seelye and the Nostrands.

The best introduction to the new approach to testing culture remains Seelye's discussion on measuring cultural achievement

83

in Volume 1 of the *Britannica Review of Foreign Language Education* (110). Seelye also (111) gives concrete help for teachers struggling to write performance objectives in the area of culture. He identifies the components of a performance objective as purpose, terminal behavior, conditions or constraints, and criterion of acceptable performance. To clarify the meaning of "purpose," Seelye outlines seven cultural purposes that can be taught in the classroom through culture-oriented activities. These include not only those purposes that show that a culture is an interrelated system of patterns but also those that concern student skill in analyzing another culture and in evaluating statements made by fellow Americans about other cultures. The seventh purpose concerns cultural attitudes the teacher hopes will develop during foreign language study. Seelye gives examples of specific activities that may be used to achieve the stated purposes. He also supplies a column of commentary coordinated with each purpose that helps to sharpen the reader's focus. Although he feels strongly that precisely stated performance objectives are essential to the teaching and learning of culture, Seelye cautions that they form but one part of the total learning process.

Testing linked to cultural objectives

Seven cultural purposes

Frances and Howard L. Nostrand (90) have isolated nine kinds of understandings that form valid cross-cultural objectives in foreign language teaching. A few examples of the "understandings" and the techniques for testing them suggested by the authors will illustrate that this type of testing calls for more than factual retention.

Nine kinds of cultural understandings: some examples of test items

1 *Understanding*: The ability to recognize a pattern when it is illustrated. This includes the ability to select from a context the theme expressions that will be emotionally charged for a culture-bearer.

Technique (type ba): Cloze procedure: a literary text or news item (or telegram or partly legible handwriting) is presented, with blanks or scrawls replacing some words or phrases which the examinee will be able to fill in if he is familiar with the aspect of the culture or of the language that is illustrated.

Technique (type ac): The professor began to read a book with a knife in his hand. What was the purpose of the knife?

  A To peel a banana
*B To cut the pages
  C To commit suicide
  D None of the above

2 *Understanding*: The ability to predict how a pattern is likely to apply in a given situation.

Technique (type a): Two middle-class Frenchmen are arguing heatedly across a café table. They gesticulate with increasing emotion. How may you expect the tension to end?

   A They are probably drunk and capable of any sort of violence.

   B They are probably insulting each other's honor and will be lifelong enemies.

 *C They will probably grow calm as they turn to another subject.

Seward (114) offers suggestions for testing linguistic ability while surrounded by the foreign culture, in this case, Japan. A few examples will illustrate the pragmatic orientation of the items:

Testing for linguistic ability in the foreign culture

Translate a newspaper article; speak in Japanese on the telephone; write a letter; interpret a taped conversation between two Japanese; comprehend a newscast; identify five major dialects; read a letter; take a dictation; walk down the street and read the first 20 signs to be sighted; give a ten-minute, impromptu talk about an everyday topic of conversation; give the meanings of 100 technical words or phrases (20 each from the fields of medicine, law, economy, science, and the arts), to be selected by the testing committee as being readily understood by the average Japanese college graduate.

Although Seward was thinking of a test for professional interpreters, many of the items would be appropriate for high school and college students.

Impact on national tests

Realistically, what are the chances that items testing the interrelation of cultural patterns and the capability of functioning effectively within a culture will make an impact on major national tests in the near future? One optimistic sign is the decision of the Bureau of Foreign Language Education in New York State to work for a drastic revision of the cultural component of the Regents examination. The Bureau has criticized the Regents exam for including questions that confirm teachers in their belief that culture is an accumulation of facts. It is requesting a change in focus that will test the ability to relate a cultural item in one area to the fabric of the total culture. In sum, "The entire Regents examination in any and each modern foreign language could constitute a kind of culture question, at least through impregnation of every question with cultural considerations in varying degrees of focus" (Glaude, 52). Such a description could well serve as the desired goal for all foreign language testing.

Preparation for teaching culture: The shaky foundation

Seelye observed in 1968 that most language teachers have had such inadequate training in cross-cultural understanding themselves that they cannot hope to do an effective job of teaching it (110). The learning about another culture has therefore been haphazard and incomplete. In the two years following this glum pronouncement the situation has had time to improve. Is there evidence to show that it has?

Martin (82) administered a questionnaire to American students who had studied in Germany in programs sponsored by American colleges. He analyzed the type of cultural preparation they had received in their stateside studies in relation to their cultural experience abroad. The question, "Did you find the German people to be different from that which you had been prepared to expect?" elicited a majority of "Yes" replies. This would indicate that information received by the students through formal courses had been either inaccurate, or inadequate to counteract the stereotypes of the German people they had already absorbed. Questions designed to show what pre-program training the student had received in techniques of cross-cultural analysis revealed that the majority of participants had been forced by inadequate training at home to acquire cultural information in hit-or-miss fashion abroad.

Cultural preparation for an intensive program abroad

While only the most stagnant backwaters of academe reject the teaching of culture completely, most language departments feel vindicated if they offer one course in "capital C" culture. A poll of German departments by Von Hofe, Hill, Koepke, Øksenholt, Reichmann, & Steinhauer (130) confirms that when culture is offered to undergraduate German students, the emphasis is almost invariably on the artistic-intellectual aspect of German history. If the examples seem to be pointing a negative finger at German studies, it should be remembered that German teachers themselves are the ones who have cared enough to make the studies. The blunt fact is that although the profession continues to exhort its members to teach culture, it gives them grossly inadequate preparation to do so. The most dedicated teacher in the

Cultural emphasis in college language departments

classroom cannot acquire anthropological expertise through osmosis.

In April, 1971, the Seattle Symposium on the Training of Foreign Language Teachers recommended to the profession that any program of studies for language teachers leading to the masters degree should contain course work *equally divided* among the areas of culture, language training, linguistics, and methodology (Altman, 5). "Equally divided" does not mean one five-hour course on fine arts and history.

Fortunately, some institutions are taking positive steps to strengthen cultural training. Usually, although not always, it is the Department of Foreign Language Education that assumes the initiative for curricular innovation in this area. At Florida State the Department of Foreign Language Education requires all graduate students to take a seminar entitled "The Teaching of Cultural Aspects." As part of their work, students prepare supplementary cultural units for major foreign language texts (Frechette, 50). Training in cultural analysis is incorporated into three graduate courses for teachers at the State University of New York at Buffalo (Papalia, 96). An exceptionally rich offering is provided by the School of Education of New York University where the Division of Foreign Languages and International Education offers such graduate courses as "French Civilization for Teachers," "Spain and Latin America During the 20th Century," "Spanish Life Through the Spanish Press," "The People and Culture of Puerto Rico," "Caracteres de la Civilización Hispánica," and "Hispanoamérica y España en el Mundo de Hoy" (Guerra, 54). Purdue University offers two courses for prospective teachers of French, one oriented toward formal culture, the other toward the anthropological approach (Hatfield, 57). The foreign language methods class at Brigham Young University includes a strong cultural component in which students receive intensive training in the techniques of the "cultural aside," the "slice of life," and the "culture capsule" described by Taylor (122). Graduate courses at Brigham Young University include "Contemporary Hispanic Life," and "Seminar in the Teaching of Culture in Language Classes" (Taylor, 123, and Jackson, 61). Although culture courses at Stanford are primarily of the "capital C" type, the German Department offers a course in "Germany Today" and one on "German Newspapers" (Politzer, 101). Students in an undergraduate methods course in FLES and secondary foreign languages at Ohio State University took half

Steps to strengthen cultural training in teacher preparation

87

the course on campus, then journeyed to Puebla, Mexico, for on-the-spot culture training the second half of the quarter (Allen, 4). In Puebla the students taught FLES (English) in the Mexican elementary schools and Spanish in a bilingual high school. The College of Education at the University of Georgia transplants the Spanish Methods class to Valencia, Spain, for one quarter, where strategies for cross-cultural analysis are built into the total program.

In-service training programs with an emphasis on cultural acquisitions are also beginning to appear. A summer workshop in Lyons, France, for French teachers who wish intensive cultural training is offered by the Foreign Language Education Department at Ohio State (Allen, 3). Participants live with French families and collect data in the community for future use in the classroom. The Foreign Language Department of the Nashville Metropolitan Schools sponsors summer cultural workshops for teachers of French and Spanish in cooperation with Trevecca College (1). The Georgia State Department of Education holds an annual Cultural Island Language Retreat for teachers of French, Spanish, and German, who spend two days in isolation, studying culture as presented by native speakers and practicing techniques for teaching it (Keaton, 70).

In-service training programs with cultural emphasis

Barrutia advocates that two semesters of study abroad be required of all foreign language teachers (8). He contends that well-conceived foreign study centers, designed to increase cultural understanding, could provide the answer to the negative reaction toward language learning in the United States today. One such program was initiated in 1970 by the Council on International Educational Exchange (CIEE) (33). Under this "Cooperative International Program for Teacher Education," American students who plan careers as high school teachers of foreign languages may incorporate a semester (two quarters) of study abroad into their pre-service education. The undergraduate French program is at the University of Rennes, the graduate program at the University of Paris. The University of Seville is the site of the undergraduate Spanish center. A graduate Spanish section and German division are planned. Study of culture and society forms a vital part of the curriculum. Students meet with community leaders to discuss the problems of unions, political parties, agricultural groups, and student movements. Lectures on educational institutions are followed by visits to the schools at all levels, from elementary through the Univer-

Cultural study abroad: CIEE

sity faculties and advanced technical institutes. Courses such as "Popular Media and Contemporary Literature," "Language and Society," "Social and Political Institutions," "Music," and "Folklore," increase the dimensional approach to cultural training.

Allen's (4) insistence that students abroad should participate in the life of the speech community because ". . . it is that life which gives the language its meaning" seems to be well served by the new programs currently under development. There is, then, some evidence to indicate that the profession is trying to overcome its failure to prepare future teachers to do the very thing they are asked to do: teach cross-cultural understanding.

Forecast for the future

A seer with even a cloudy crystal ball could predict that the future will hold increased emphasis on teaching for cross-cultural understanding. Today's "new" student is people-oriented. He wants to use language to come closer to people; to their way of thinking; to their way of life. In learning about others he hopes to come to an understanding of himself. The goals of our students are as simple as that: To reach outward and to look inward.

This means that the foreign language profession must itself become more open — more pluralistic in its approach to cultural instruction. The "capital C" aspect of culture requires knowledge of music, art, literature, history, and philosophy. The "small c" component demands insights into linguistics, psychology, sociology, geography, and anthropology. Future teachers must know how to analyze a culture, how to compare cultures, and how to teach and test cross-cultural understanding. The cultural preparation for language teachers must become infinitely more dimensional if such varied competencies are to be acquired.

Needs of future teachers

Nelson (88) envisions the establishment of an "Institut d'études françaises" at the University of Illinois. This center would continue to prepare students interested in belletristic research, and students desirous of becoming language teachers. In addition, it would offer foreign language majors in history, the fine arts, and anthropological culture. The faculty would include specialists in history, the behavioral sciences, fine arts, literature, and the creative arts (writers, actors, etc.). A number of associate faculty members from related disciplines would contribute on a visiting basis. University students at the institute

"Institut d'études françaises" at University of Illinois

would be joined by teachers in the field, expanding their skills and understandings under any of several flexible plans for continuing education.

Lohnes (78) calls for establishing training centers abroad and suggests, for example, that the AATG (American Association of Teachers of German) administer a German area center in the Federal Republic of Germany. The curriculum should be based specifically on the needs of future German teachers in the United States, and would include culture and area studies as well as a work program under which students would spend weeks or months working and living independently in Germany.

Training centers abroad

A few programs now in effect contain some of the strengths suggested by Nelson and Lohnes. A coordinated professional effort is needed to explore the possibility of establishing centers for language and culture studies, whether at home or abroad or in combination of the two.

Pillet (99) calls for another type of professional cooperation: establishment of a central clearinghouse for the collecting, selecting, and disseminating of teacher-created materials and of guidelines for instructional strategies. He insists that the need for such an agency is as important to the profession as the currently existing organization for the dissemination of theory and research. Practical, classroom-tested strategies and materials would become readily available under the proposed system.

A cultural clearinghouse

Conclusions

1 Today's student sees language study as more than the study of language. It is also a means of reaching out and a way of looking within. Although some very encouraging activities are taking place behind classroom doors, many teachers still regard the use of culture as a surface motivating device. Culture study *is* an excellent motivator, but on a potentially far deeper level than teachers seem to realize. An understanding of culture – anthropological and traditional – can provide the missing component in the language student's search for relevancy.

2 The tolerance for disparate modes of thought and expression and the acceptance of other life-styles, acquired in the foreign language classroom, could prove to be important factors in the reduction of ethnocentricity across subcultural as well as international boundaries.

3 Techniques for measuring cross-cultural understandings are still in their infancy. Only a few scholars are devoting serious effort to the testing of culture. A good start has been made in setting forth behavioral objectives that reflect overt and measurable cultural acquisitions. The area of attitudes toward other cultures lends itself less readily to measurement strategies. The profession needs to turn its attention to the development of sound cultural testing. The product of such development must be reflected in local, state, and national testing instruments if we seriously look upon cultural understanding as the "fifth skill."

4 The pressuring of teachers to "Teach culture!" without providing them with the knowledge and materials to do so amounts to a professional disgrace. Departments of Foreign Languages and Foreign Language Education must cooperate immediately to provide training in cross-cultural understanding and in techniques of analyzing, teaching, and testing culture. The further establishment of centers for intensive study of language and culture at home and abroad has been suggested. Also suggested is the organization of a central clearinghouse of the collection and dissemination of teacher-created cultural materials. One thing is clear: the profession must move rapidly from exhortation to action if the goal of increased understanding across cultures is to be realized.

References, Cultural pluralism

1 *Accent on ACTFL* 1, iii(1971):9.
2 Allan, Edward V. "Classical Greek at Menlo-Atherton." *American Foreign Language Teacher* 1, iv(1971):35–36,41.
3 Allen, Edward D. to author. Personal communication, 9 April 1971.
4 Allen, Virginia F. "Understanding the Cultural Context." *Modern Language Journal* 53(1969): 324–26.
5 Altman, Howard B. "The Seattle Symposium on the Training of Foreign Language Teachers." *Modern Language Journal* 55(1971):229–32.

6 Bals, Hildegard. "The Effects of Adding Content in Culture to the German Curriculum:A Method of Study." Unpublished Ed.D. Dissertation. Athens, Georgia: Univ. of Georgia, 1971.

7 Barcio, Bernard to Alan Garfinkel to author. Personal communication, 5 May 1971.

8 Barrutia, Richard. "Study Abroad." *Modern Language Journal* 55 (1971):232–34.

9 Beaujour, Michel. "Teaching Culture in the Foreign Environment–Goals and Non-Goals." *Modern Language Journal* 53 (1969):317–20.

10 Becker, James E. "Pen Pals in France." *Accent on ACTFL* 1,ii(1971):7–8.

11 Beusch, Ann A. to author. Personal communication, 17 March 1971. [Director of Proyecto Amistad: Jessica Goldin.]

12 Bingham, Vernon A. to author. Personal communication, 1 April 1971.

13 Birdwhistell, Ray L. *Kinesics and Context:Essays on Body Motion Communication.* Philadelphia: Univ. of Pennsylvania Press, 1970.

14 Bolinger, Dwight. "Let's Change Our Base of Operations." *Modern Language Journal* 55(1971):148–56.

15 Bostick, Herman. "Introduction of Afro-French Literature and Culture in the Secondary School Curriculum:A Teacher's Guide." Unpublished Ph.D. Dissertation. Columbus, Ohio: The Ohio State University, 1971.

16 Bourgeacq, Jacques A. "De la langue à la tolérance." *French Review* 44(1970):341–48.

17 Bourque, Jane M. "Sound and Substance." *American Foreign Language Teacher* 1,ii(1970):12–13.

18 Bouygues, C. "Civilisation–Culture ou apprentissage d'une lecture." *French Review* 44(1970):51–62.

19 Brace, Suzette to author. Personal communication, 20 April 1971.

20 Bready, James H. "Signs of Retreat From the Hard Foreign Languages." *Accent on ACTFL* 1,iii(1971):7. [From the *Baltimore Evening Sun.* 24 December 1970.]

21 Brooks, Nelson. "Teaching Culture Abroad:From Concept to Classroom Techniques." *Modern Language Journal* 53(1969):320–24.

22 Brooks, Robert. "Letter to editor of Professional Notes." *French Review* 43(1970):496–97.

23 Caldwell, Genelle to author. Personal communication, 10 March 1971.

24 —— and J. Abraham. "The Native as an Aide in the Classroom." *Department of Foreign Languages Bulletin* 6,iv(1967):11–12. [ERIC Document Reproduction Service: ED 012 567.]

25 Canfield, C. Lincoln. *Spanish with a Flourish.* American Association of Teachers of Spanish and Portuguese. Cultural Unit I, 1968. [See current *Hispanica* for ordering information.]

26 Carney, Helen to author. Personal communication, March 1971. [Teacher: Jim Brown.]

27 —— "VOCAW and ECHO:Advertising Foreign Languages." *Foreign Language Annals* 4(1970):57–61. [VOCAW-Voices of Children Around the World; ECHO-Echoes of Classical Heritage in Oklahoma.]

28 Chetkovich, Delon. "Calexico Makes News." *Newsletter of the Foreign Language Association of Northern California* 19(1971):5.

29 Clapper, William to author. Personal communication, March 1971. [Teacher: Miss Willella Curnutt, Van Horn High School, Independence, Missouri.]

30 Consalvi, Conrad. "Some Cross and Intracultural Comparisons of Expressed Values of Arab and American College Students." *Journal of Cross-Cultural Psychology* 2(1971):95–107.

31 Cooke, Madeline A. "A Study of the Development of Positive Attitudes Toward Native Speakers of Spanish." Unpublished Ph.D. Dissertation. Columbus, Ohio: The Ohio State University, 1969.

32 —— "Suggestions for Developing More Positive Attitudes Toward Native Speakers of Spanish," 118–39 in H. Ned Seelye,ed., *Perspectives for Teachers of Latin American Culture.* Springfield, Illinois: State Department of Public Instruction, 1970.

33 *Cooperative International Program for Teacher Education.* Brochure. New York: The Council on International Educational Exchange. [777 United Nations Plaza, New York 10017.]

34 Cowan, Susie. "English Proficiency and Bicultural Attitudes of Japanese Students." *The English Teachers' Magazine* 17(1968):38–44.

35 Crane, Martha, and Tom Schulhof. "Name-Changing Patterns Among French Canadians in Waterville, Maine." *French Review* 43(1970):459–66.

36 Cudecki, Edwin, Anita Kapsis, Arthur S. Schwartz, and Roy A. Woodson-Levey. "Teaching of French Culture in the Classroom," 11–20 in Charles Jay and Pat Castle,eds., *French Language Education:The Teaching of Culture in the Classroom.* Springfield, Illinois: State Department of Public Instruction, 1971.

37 *Cultural Understanding:Spanish Level I.* Hayward, California: The Alameda County School Department, 1969.

38 Decock, Jean. "L'utilisation du film commercial dans l'enseignement des langues." *French Review* 43(1970):467–73.

39 Deutsch, Rachel F. "Suggestions for the Teaching of Negro Literature of French Expression." *French Review* 42(1969):706–17.

40 DeWright, Yvonne, "Telecourse Title Calls for Cultural Outreach." *Foreign Language Beacon* 5,ii(1970):20–21.

41 Edgerton, Mills F.,Jr. "A Philosophy for the Teaching of Foreign Languages." *Modern Language Journal* 55(1971):5–15.

42 Eppert, Franz. "Deutschlandkunde–aber wie?" *Die Unterrichtspraxis* 4,i(1971):69–73.

43 Farkas, Z.J. "Motivation through Pen Pals." *Die Unterrichtspraxis* 2,i(1969):49.

44 Fishman, Joshua A. *Sociolinguistics:A Brief Introduction.* Rowley Mass.: Newberry House Publishers, 1970.

45 Flinton, Sister Margaret to author. Personal communication, 25 March 1971.

46 Fontaine, Lyrace F. *Why Canadian and African Studies in French?* Burlington, Vermont: Bur-

lington High School, 1971. [Mimeograph.]

47 Foster, George M. "Character and Personal Relationships Seen Through Proverbs in Tzintzuntzan, Mexico." *Journal of American Folklore* 83(1970):304–17.

48 Fournier, Robert R. to author. Personal communication, 12 March 1971.

49 Francke, Walter K. "Put a Grimm in your Oral Nacherzählung," *Die Unterrichtspraxis* 2,i (1969):34–37.

50 Frechette, Ernest A. to author. Personal communication, 30 March 1971.

51 Gershman, Herbert S. "Children's Rhymes and Modern Poetry." *French Review* 44(1971):539–48.

52 Glaude, Paul M. "The Culture Question." Supervisory letter. Albany, New York: Bureau of Foreign Language Education, The State Education Department, 30 April 1970.

53 Goffman, Erving. *Behavior in Public Places.* New York: The Free Press, 1963.

54 Guerra, Emilio L. to author. Personal communication, 7 April 1971.

55 Hall, Wendell, and Enrique Lafourcade. "Teaching Aspects of the Foreign Culture Through Comic Strips," 51–61 in H. Ned Seelye,ed., *Perspectives for Teachers of Latin American Culture.* Springfield, Illinois: State Department of Public Instruction, 1970.

56 Harlow, Jean W. to author. Personal communication, 23 March 1971.

57 Hatfield, William to author. Personal communication, 23 April 1971.

58 Haukebo, Gerhard K. *Summer Foreign Language Programs for School Students.* MLA/ERIC Focus Report 10. New York: Modern Language Association Materials Center, 1969.

59 Hocking, Elton, "Culture, Relevance and Survival." *Modern Language Journal* 54(1970):585–88.

60 Hopulele, Mihai. "La correspondance scolaire internationale vue par les élèves." *Le français dans le monde* 74(1970):36–39.

61 Jackson, T. Wendell to author. Personal communication, 9 April 1971.

62 Jakobovits, Leon A. *Psycholinguistic Analysis of Second Language Learning and Bilingualism.* Urbana, Illinois: Univ. of Illinois, 1969.

63 James, Carl. "Notes and News." *Modern Language Journal* 54(1970):149.

64 Jay, Charles, and Pat Castle,eds. *French Language Education:The Teaching of Culture in the Classroom.* Springfield, Illinois: State Department of Public Instruction, 1971.

65 Jenks, Frederick L. "Mexico's New Generation Speaks Out:Trends in Urban Society." *American Foreign Language Teacher* 1,iv(1971):32–33,41.

66 Johnson, Mary to author. Personal communication, March 1971.

67 Jonas, Sister Ruth Adelaide. "The Twinned Classroom Approach in FLES." *Modern Language Journal* 53(1969):342–46.

68 Kalivoda, Theodore G., Genelle Morain, and Robert J. Elkins. "The Audio-Motor Unit:A Listening Comprehension Strategy that Works." *Foreign Language Annals* 4(1971):392–400.

69 Keach, Everett T.,Jr. to author. Personal communication, March, 1971.

70 Keaton, Ruth. "Best Meeting I Ever Attended: Cultural Retreat Wins Praise." *The Foreign Language Beacon* 5,iii(1970):12–15.

71 Kirch, Max S. "Relevance in Language and Culture." *Modern Language Journal* 54(1970):413–15.

72 Kleeman, Frances A. to author. Personal communication, 28 March, 1971.

73 Kochman, Thomas. "Culture and Communication:Implications for Black English in the Classroom," 172–74 in Alfred C. Aarons, Barbara Y. Gordon, and William A. Steward,eds., *Linguistic and Cultural Differences and American Education. The Florida Foreign Language Reporter* 7,i(1969).

74 Koepke, Wulf. "Kulturkunde und Textlektüre." *Die Unterrichtspraxis* 4,i(1971):59–69.

75 Kuschmierz, Ruth L. "The German Society at the University of Pittsburgh, Greensburg Campus." *Die Unterrichtspraxis* 3,i(1970):179–81.

76 Lange, Dale L. "Methodische Rundschau: The American Scene:The Use of Newspapers and Magazines in the Classroom." *Die Unterrichtspraxis* 2,ii(1969):148–53.

77 LeBovit, Judith. "Latin FLES Stirs National Interest." *Foreign Language Beacon* 6,ii(1971):23–24. [Reprint of paper originally presented at the 1970 Northeast Conference on the Teaching of Foreign Languages.]

78 Lohnes, Walter F.W. "The Training of German Teachers in the United States." *Die Unterrichtspraxis* 2,ii(1969):69–76.

79 Lord, Elizabeth Grunbaum, and Dorothy Copps Farner. "Not Small Talk, But Something Solid to Talk About." *Die Unterrichtspraxis* 2,ii(1969):25–30.

80 Low, Betty-Bright P. to author. Personal communication, 2 April 1971.

81 Marquardt, William F. "Creating Empathy Through Literature Between Members of the Mainstream Culture and Disadvantaged Learners of the Minority Culture," 133–41 in Alfred C. Aarons, Barbara Y. Gordon, and William A. Steward,eds., *Linguistic and Cultural Differences and American Education. The Florida Foreign Language Reporter* 7,i(1969).

82 Martin, Robert L., Jr. "An Investigation of Selected Student Variables and their Associations in Participants of Summer Study Abroad Programs." Unpublished Ed.D. Dissertation. Athens, Georgia: The Univ. of Georgia, 1971.

83 Masciantonio, Rudolph. "Innovative Classical Programs in the School District of Philadelphia." *Foreign Language Annals* 3(1970):592–95.

84 McLuhan, Marshall. "Classroom Without Walls," 1–3 in Edmund Carpenter and Marshall McLuhan,eds., *Exploration in Communication.* Boston: Beacon Press, 1968.

85 Morain, Genelle. *French Culture:The Folklore Facet.* MLA/ERIC Focus Report 9. New York: Modern Language Association Materials Center,

1969.

86 Mueller, Theodore H. "Student Attitudes in the Basic French Courses at the University of Kentucky." *Modern Language Journal* 55(1971): 290–98.

87 Murphy, Joseph A. "The Contributions of Social Studies Methodology to Foreign Language Teaching." Unpublished Ph.D. Dissertation. Columbus, Ohio: The Ohio State University, 1968. [See especially Chapter 5, "Techniques and Strategies:Application," 104–81.]

88 Nelson, Robert J. "A Modern Curriculum in French Studies," 64–73 in Charles Jay and Pat Castle,eds., *French Language Education:The Teaching of Culture in the Classroom*. Springfield, Illinois: State Department of Public Instruction, 1971.

89 ——— *Using Radio to Develop and Maintain Competence in a Foreign Language*. MLA/ERIC Focus Report 11. New York: Modern Language Association Materials Center, 1969.

90 Nostrand, Frances B. and Howard L. "Testing Understanding of the Foreign Culture," 161–70 in H. Ned Seelye,ed., *Perspectives for Teachers of Latin American Culture*. Springfield, Illinois: State Department of Public Instruction, 1970.

91 Nostrand, Howard L. *Background Data for the Teaching of French:Final Report of Project OE-6-14-005*. Part A: La culture et la société françaises au XXe siècle, 2 vols.; Part B: Exemples littéraires: Part C: Contemporary Culture and Society of the United States. Seattle: Department of Romance Languages and Literature, Univ. of Washington, 1967.

92 ——— "Theme Analysis in the Study of Literature," 182–97 in Joseph Strelka,ed., *Problems of Literary Revolution:Yearbook of Comparative Criticism*. University Park: Pennsylvania State Univ. Press, 1969.

93 ——— and Frances B. "Culture-Wide Values and Assumptions as Essential Content for Levels I to III," 48–63 in Charles Jay and Pat Castle,eds., *French Language Education:The Teaching of Culture in the Classroom*. Springfield, Illinois: State Department of Public Instruction, 1971.

94 Ort, Barbara A., and Dwight R. Smith,comps. "The Language Teacher Tours the Curriculum: New Horizons for Foreign Language Education." *Foreign Language Annals* 3(1969):28–74.

95 Palyok, Jeanne to author. Personal communication, 22 March 1971.

96 Papalia, Anthony to author. Personal communication, 31 March 1971.

97 Paquette, F. André, and Suzanne Tollinger. *A Handbook on Foreign Language Classroom Testing: French, German, Italian, Russian, Spanish*. New York: Modern Language Association, 1968. [1970.]

98 Piehl, Helen, and Anne Bell. "'Oh Say Can you See'—Hear, Taste, and Even Dance in Your Foreign Language Classes?" 88–95 in Charles Jay and Pat Castle,eds., *French Language Education:The Teaching of Culture in the Classroom*.

Springfield, Illinois: State Department of Public Instruction, 1971.

99 Pillet, Roger A., "Culture in FLES:French," 21–28 in Charles Jay and Pat Castle,eds., *French Language Education:The Teaching of Culture in the Classroom*. Springfield, Illinois: State Department of Public Instruction, 1971.

100 Pindur, Nancy. "Dating Patterns—German." *American Foreign Language Teacher* 1,iv(1971): 34,41,44.

101 Politzer, Robert to author. Personal communication, 31 March 1971.

102 Poyatos, Fernando. "Kinésica del Espanol Actual." *Hispanica* 53(1970):444–52.

103 Preller, Arnold G. to author. Personal communication, 7 April 1971.

104 Reinert, Harry. "Student Attitudes Toward Foreign Languages—No Sale." *Modern Language Journal* 54(1970):107–112.

105 Rivkin, Robert to author. Personal communication, March 1971.

106 Roberta, Sister Anna to author. Personal communication, 20 March 1971.

107 Roeming, Robert F. "Bilingualism and the National Interest." *Modern Language Journal* 55(1971):73–81.

108 Rose, Martha. "Use of Supplementary Teaching Materials." Speech given at the Pennsylvania Modern Language Association Conference, Fall, 1969.

109 Rysan, Joseph. "Folklore and Mass-Lore." *South Atlantic Bulletin* 36,i(1971):3–9.

110 Seelye, H. Ned. "Analysis and Teaching of the Cross-Cultural Context," 37–81 in Emma Birkmaier,ed., *Britannica Review of Foreign Language Education, Volume 1*. Chicago: Encyclopaedia Britannica, Inc., 1968 [1969].

111 ——— "Performance Objectives for Teaching Cultural Concepts." *Foreign Language Annals* 3(1970):566–78.

112 ——— "The Yanqui in the Banana Trilogy of Miguel Angel Asturias," 95–103 in H. Ned Seelye,ed., *Perspectives for Teachers of Latin American Culture*. Springfield, Illinois: State Department of Public Instruction, 1970.

113 ———,ed. *Perspectives for Teachers of Latin American Culture*. Springfield, Illinois: State Department of Public Instruction, 1970.

114 Seward, Jack. *Japanese in Action:An Unorthodox Approach to the Spoken Language and the People Who Speak It*. New York: Walker and Company, 1969.

115 Sims, Lida, and Rachel Hite to author. Personal communication, 25 May 1971.

116 Smith, Alfred N. "The Importance of Attitude in Foreign Language Learning." *Modern Language Journal* 55(1971):82–88.

117 Spolsky, Bernard. "Attitudinal Aspects of Second Language Learning." 19(1969):271–83.

118 Stafford, Jane H. "Letter to editor." *French Review* 43(1970):496.

119 Steiner, Florence. "Culture:A Motivating Factor in the French Classroom," 28–35 in Charles Jay and Pat Castle,eds., *French Language Education:The Teaching of Culture in the Classroom*.

Springfield, Illinois: State Department of Public Instruction, 1971.

120 Sten-Gunnar, Hellstrom. "S.O.S. civilisation française." *Le français dans le monde* 72(1970): 7-8.

121 Stone, Estelle to author. Personal communication, 23 March 1971.

122 Taylor, James S. "Direct Classroom Teaching of Cultural Concepts," 42-50 in H. Ned Seelye,ed., *Perspectives for Teachers of Latin American Culture.* Springfield, Illinois: State Department of Public Instruction, 1970.

123 —— to author. Personal communication, 25 May 1971.

124 Thom, Stanley G. to author. Personal communication, March 1971.

125 Thomison, Raquel to author. Personal communication, March 1971.

126 Tittle, Jackson. *Elementary Students' Field Trip—to Germany.* Project Report. Akron, Ohio: Akron City Schools, 1970. [Mimeograph.]

127 Torres, Eduardo E. to author. Personal communication, 25 March 1971.

128 —— and Reid Scott. "Teaching For Cross-Cultural Understanding." San Leandro, California: Public Schools, 1970. [Mimeograph.]

129 Tursi, Joseph A.,ed. *Foreign Languages and the "New" Student.* Reports of the Working Committees of the Northeast Conference on the Teaching of Foreign Languages. New York: Modern Language Association Materials Center, 1970.

130 Von Hofe, Harold, Claude Hill, Wulf Koepke, Svein Øksenholt, Eberhard Reichmann, and Harry Steinhauer. "The German Culture and Civilization Course at American Colleges and Universities:A TAP Survey for the Year 1967-1968." *Die Unterrichtspraxis* 2,i(1969):91-98. [TAP-Teaching Aid Project.]

131 Weinhold, E. Raymond, Paul J. Plath, and Marie Vega. *Final Evaluation Report, Phoenix Union Bilingual Program.* Phoenix: Union High School System, 1970.

132 Weiss, Gerhard H. *Folktale and Folklore—Useful Cultural Tools for Teachers of German.* MLA/ ERIC Focus Report 6. New York: Modern Language Association Materials Center, 1969.

133 —— "The Language Teacher—An Interpreter of Culture." *Die Unterrichtspraxis* 4,i(1971): 36-42.

134 Wheaton, Marjorie. " 'Brainwashing' Anyone?" *French Review* 43(1970):805-11.

135 —— to author. Personal communication, 17 March 1971.

136 Whiteside, Dale. "French Music Past and Present:Mini-Lessons in Culture," 36-43 in Charles Jay and Pat Castle,eds., *French Language Education:The Teaching of Culture in the Classroom.* Springfield, Illinois: State Department of Public Instruction, 1971.

137 Zenner, Walter P. "Ethnic Stereotyping in Arabic Proverbs." *Journal of American Folklore* 83(1970):417-529.

138 Zolar, William to author. Personal communication, 25 March 1971. [Janice Galetka, Child Development Teacher.]

4

Approaches to bilingualism: Recognition of a multilingual society

Introduction

Manuel T. Pacheco

University of Colorado

Bilingualism continues to be a confusing term in spite of the many attempts to produce an exact definition of it. Most users of the term agree that it refers to the knowledge and use of two languages by the same person. Some writers, such as Brooks (12), emphasize the *use* of two languages while others contend that it is possible to be bilingual without using one of the two languages. Jakobovits (34) sees no particular advantage in attempting to determine when a person is bilingual or in setting arbitrary limits for a definition. He prefers to consider bilingualism as a relative rather than as an absolute concept. Mackey (41) and Fishman (24) assert that the effort should be to determine how bilingual a person is from a sociolinguistic point of view. This means that the native language must be analyzed in terms of who uses it when, with whom, under what circumstances, and for what purposes.

Bilingualism, a confusing term

Bilinguals may thus be classified according to their skill in two languages along a continuum in the receptive skills and the productive skills according to domain, formality, and level. Within this framework, it can be stated that approximately half of the children in the world are bilingual. According to Saville & Troike (54) about one-fourth of the people in the United States can communicate in more than one language and one of every ten people speaks a language other than English natively. Gaarder (27) estimates that there are 34 or more languages represented by these twenty million people.

How bilinguals may be classified

Even though the United States is clearly a multilingual nation, the society in general has not encouraged the maintenance and cultivation of languages other than English until recently. Reasons for this trend include: the feeling that speaking another language hinders progress in English, superior ethnocentric attitudes among native speakers of English, the clash of cultural values, the promulgation of the "melting pot" concept for all minority groups, and the association of bilingualism with low intelligence.

Why bilingualism is not encouraged in the U.S.

Approaches to bilingualism / Pacheco

Many educational psychologists have found a positive correlation between bilingualism and low socioeconomic status, lack of refinement in the home, poor school achievement, disciplinary problems, and poor sanitation conditions. This positive correlation has often been attributed to: (*1*) the bilingual status of the child rather than to the school's inability to provide programs of education that recognize the linguistic and cultural differences of these children, (2) an economy which is geared toward the native speaker of English, and (3) differing social aspirations and values among non-English-speaking groups.

Bilingualism and low socioeconomic status

Since English is not the native language of thousands of children who enter school every year, the concept of America as a "melting pot" has not materialized. The parents of some children have chosen to preserve their ethnic identity through their native language; other children who were supposed to undergo the "melting" have not ceased being what they were except in very superficial ways; and some children now in school arrived in this country only recently.

The "melting pot" has not materialized

Thus, as Saville & Troike (54) point out, the educational idea that only English should be used as a medium of instruction has left thousands of children illiterate in their native language and has fostered low achievement in English. Since education begins in infancy, when a child reaches school he has already developed a conceptual structure, which is rooted in the language that he uses. Yet, while English-speaking children in the United States begin their formal education in their mother tongue from carefully prepared reading-readiness and reading programs, many children who are native speakers of their languages are not encouraged to begin *their* formal schooling in *their* mother tongue and are required to function in English as the sole language of instruction and to read in English before they are ready (Perales & Howard, 45).

The implications of English as the only language of instruction

The recognition of this problem by some educators, political figures, and concerned individuals in many groups has led to the establishment of bilingual education programs funded primarily under the 1967-added Title VII of the Elementary and Secondary Education Act of 1965. (Title VII is commonly known as the "Bilingual Education Act.") An axiom of bilingual education as it exists now is that the best medium for teaching and learning is the mother tongue of the student, at least until the national or majority language has been mastered to the extent that students can learn through the second language. This allows the educa-

"Bilingual Education Act"

tion of the child to continue uninterrupted from home to school, permitting continuous progress in concept development rather than waiting until a new language has been acquired. This differs from foreign language instruction in the sense that in foreign language instruction language is a subject to be studied with one of several aims, which may include preparation for studying the literature, gaining cultural awareness, travel abroad, or occupational advantage.

With this background, the remainder of this chapter will present the efforts made in the past year to provide a rationale for bilingual education both for minority sociolinguistic groups and for native speakers of English; a characterization of current attempts to provide equal educational opportunities for all linguistic segments of the society in the form of bilingual education, including problems in materials production and identification, personnel development, evaluation, identification of research needs and accomplishments; and a section which will suggest the direction in which bilingual education is headed.

Rationale for bilingual education

While much of the attention directed toward bilingual education in the United States is a result of the vocal demands of minority linguistic and sociocultural groups to be allowed to maintain their ethnic identities, there are psychological, educational, sociological, linguistic, and economic reasons for it as well. Gaarder (27) summarizes them as follows:

A rationale for bilingual education

1 The bilingual child's conceptual development and acquisition of experiences and information proceed at a normal rate if the child's native language is used as a medium of instruction, whereas retardation in school work is almost inevitable if the student's native language is not used for instruction.

2 In order to provide a mutually reinforcing bond between the home and the school, the child's native language should be used by teachers and as a school language, especially where a substantial number of non-English speakers exists in the community.

3 Rejection of the mother tongue of a large group of children in our schools will adversely affect those children's concept of themselves, their parents, and of their homes. Such an

effect is to be expected, since language is the most important medium for the expression of the self.

4 Unless a bilingual adult has achieved reasonable literacy in his mother tongue, he will not be able to use his unique potential career advantage—his competence in two languages—for a technical or professional career where language matters.

5 Competence in a native language other than English and the cultural heritage conveyed by each are a badly needed national resource that should be conserved.

In a more elaborated rationale, Andersson & Boyer (2) support Gaarder's argument, noting that American schooling has not met the needs of children coming from homes where non-English languages are spoken and citing the need for improvements in which the sense of identity of children from such homes can be maintained and strengthened through programs of studies that use the children's native language as a medium of instruction. They also point out the need for bicultural education, which Ulibarri et al. (61) define as schooling that will allow children to participate and function effectively in two contrasting sociocultures. This requires that the bilingual/bicultural education program give children a firsthand knowledge of the roles he is expected to play in the two sociocultures in addition to being proficient in both languages.

Bilingual/bicultural education

In a book devoted to early childhood bilingual education, John and Horner (35) summarize the evidence that supports the pedagogical soundness of a bilingual approach in educating the child who is not a native speaker of the national language. They note that according to current views, a great deal of a child's early learning consists of ordering the world around him and that language plays a critical role in the young child's ordering process. Between the ages of five and seven, the child's use of language accelerates and words become a medium of learning and problem solving. It is precisely at this age that the non-English-speaking child is forced to learn in English in most schools.

Childhood bilingual education

Additional justification for bilingual education has begun to appear in the literature in the form of research findings such as Paulston (44), Treviño (57), and the Paterson (New Jersey) Inner-City Committee for Action (15), which indicate that when one of the languages used for instruction is the mother tongue, children who learn through two languages tend to learn as well as or better than those who learn only through one. Riley (52) found similar justification for encouraging bilingualism, while Landry (38) found a correlation between bilingualism and creative ability among girls.

Conversely, that minority-language students do not succeed under the traditional curricular organization becomes clear when one studies the Congressional hearings on bilingual education, which reveal that in the 1960 census, Mexican-Americans had an average of only 7.1 years of schooling as compared to 12.1 years for Anglo-Americans. In Texas, the statistics are even more sobering. The median number of school years completed by people with Spanish surnames was 4.7 as compared to 9.7 years for Anglo-Americans. These same Congressional hearings also noted that 75% of adult American Indians on reservations cannot speak, read, or write English. Statistics also indicate that 29% of the Puerto Rican students in New York City public schools were in vocational schools in 1964 as compared to 10% of other high school pupils. Similar to the Texas situation was that in Maine—French-speaking children in parts of the state were an average of three years below national norms for reading in English and only 2% of these children went on to higher education. Although the present condition may be somewhat improved, there is no evidence that it has been significantly changed. Statistics provided in proposals for funding of bilingual education programs reveal that in many geographical areas the problem is even more acute than the above figures indicate. The Santa Fe Public Schools Bilingual Education Program proposal (7) and Bebo (5) indicate that in a recent survey in New Mexico it was found that over 6½% of the adult Mexican-American population had never attended school, about 15% had completed only eight years of schooling, only 4% had completed high school, and about 2% had a college education.

Soriano & McClafferty (55) indicate that similar educational problems exist among the Spanish-speaking population of the Midwest, even though the linguistic problems are different due to factors such as isolation from a Spanish-speaking milieu. They call attention to the fact that little research or special effort has been made on their behalf, since concern is mainly directed toward the larger Mexican-American population of the Southwest.

Ulibarri (59) adds another dimension to the rationale for bilingual education programs when he characterizes minority-lan-

Minority-language students and the traditional curriculum

101

Approaches to bilingualism / Pacheco

guage group members as usually coming from an impoverished socioeconomic environment. He speaks of the child from such a situation as being *microculturalized* because of the extremely narrow cultural diversification he experiences in his daily existence. In addition, the impoverished child comes from an overcrowded home in which learning and mental growth are hampered by the noise and disturbance in the home. Furthermore, the child has become acquainted with and accustomed to a concept of cultural norms and values that are in many ways different from those he encounters in the typical, middle-class-oriented school. Thus, when such a child reaches school, he is apt to experience frustration, bewilderment, and failure.

Bilingual education and the "microculturalized" child

It is reasonable to conclude that a child who starts school with frustration and failure may not ever catch up to his English-speaking peers. The problem is often compounded by the low expectation that teachers, parents, and classmates have for those who don't speak the majority language.

Writing from still another perspective, Walsh (63) sees the desirability of bilingual education programs for the much larger group of children whose first and only language is English. He contends that bilingual schooling offers the means to give monolingual English-speaking children a fluent and naturally acquired command of a second language, because the youngster's learning comes not just from foreign language classes but from the use of this language as a medium for taking part in all of the other school activities. He cites schools in West Berlin and in Dade County in Florida where successful programs have been in operation for several years where the goal of the programs is either to bring the students' command of his second language up to the level of his control of the native language or to maintain and develop the native language of the student in an environment where the national language and the native language are not the same.

Bilingual education for the monolingual majority

A little-publicized bilingual program in Johnstown, Colorado (64), has as one of its express purposes the development of bilingual skills not only for the native speakers of Spanish but also for native speakers of English. In this program, equal instructional time in both languages for all subject matter areas for both Mexican-Americans and Anglo-Americans is provided. Independent evaluators have called this program an exemplary model.

Recent findings by Lambert et al. (37) in Canada provide additional evidence that such programs can be a successful way of acquiring a new language without any adverse effects in conceptual or native language development.

It can be concluded, then, that the child who enters the traditional school with foreign language skills often leaves with more limited prospects than many of his English-speaking classmates. He has not been allowed or encouraged to maintain and develop his native language, and he has not had the proper schooling to allow the development of English language skills that would give him even the limited oral and literate skills available to the inadequately educated monolingual.

On the other hand, a bilingual and bicultural approach to education can encourage and aid the student to ultimately participate fully and equally in an open society while at the same time preserving and rediscovering his cultural identity without being isolated from the majority sociocultural group. English speakers in such a program can overcome the isolation of a monolingual and monocultural education by being exposed to instruction in other languages and cultures. As John and Horner (35) write: "The schools have it within their power to insure that our bilingual citizens are welcome assets, not uneducated and unproductive liabilities."

Some conclusions

Efforts to promote and recognize bilingualism

In the past few years the need for bilingual education has been increasing in most nations of the world. In some countries the status of regionally used languages has risen while the need to maintain the national language for political and educational reasons has continued. In other nations, ethnic groups using a language other than the national language have been allowed to support and organize educational programs that use their own language. In their invaluable, monumental effort to characterize bilingual education in this country, Andersson & Boyer (2) describe the national efforts of some 20 bilingual or plurilingual nations to provide bilingual education for their citizens. Although they emerge with more questions than answers concerning the universal aspects of bilingualism, they uncover some useful information regarding the roles that sociolinguistics, economics, psychology, education, sociology, and politics can play in determining the desirability or the success of a national effort to encourage and support bilingualism.

The need for bilingualism and efforts to provide it

Approaches to bilingualism / Pacheco

As a result of the "Bilingual Education Act" of 1967 there are 164 federally funded bilingual education projects currently under way in the United States involving 17 different languages (including Chinese, French, Japanese, Portuguese, Russian, Spanish, and 9 different American Indian languages) in at least 22 states. An uncounted number of bilingual education programs receive no federal funds. According to Albar A. Peña in the National Conference on Bilingual Education (43), the number of proposals for funding far exceeds the number that can be funded with the money available under the Act. Of the more than 300 proposals for the first year of operation, only 76 could be funded.

"Bilingual Education Act" programs

In administering funds for the Act, the Office of Education is supporting projects that provide bilingual education programs designed to meet the special needs of children 3 to 18 years of age who have a limited English-speaking ability and who come from environments where the dominant language is not English. There are basically five purposes involved, according to the Draft Guidelines to the Bilingual Education Program (Andersson & Boyer, 2). They are:

Five purposes for bilingual education programs

1 to insure that children in such programs become more proficient in the use of two languages, and do not lose any of the common school learnings by providing adequate curriculums, materials, and teaching techniques;
2 to integrate the study of the history and culture associated with the children's native language;
3 to insure that bilingual education programs prepare, develop, or adapt proper materials for teaching and provide equipment necessary to implement the curriculum;
4 to insure the proper training of persons who participate in bilingual education programs;
5 to insure the development and effective use of evaluation.

Models of bilingualism

In spite of the many attempts to provide bilingual education throughout the world, knowledge about advantages and disadvantages of bilingual schooling, the kind of bilingualism that is appropriate for a country, and the conditions under which it is harmful or useful has been lacking. Mackey (41) writes that there have been neither stable references to the many kinds of bilingual schooling nor standard measures for the many variables involved. For example, in the United Kingdom, schools in which half the school subjects are taught in English are called bilingual schools, as are schools in Canada where all subjects are taught in English to French-Canadian children. In the Soviet Union, schools in which all subjects except Russian are taught in English are bilingual schools, as are schools in which some of the subjects are taught in Georgian and the rest in Russian.

In an attempt to remedy the confusing situation, Mackey developed a typology of bilingualism (41) that permits more meaningful comparisons to be made between various studies of bilingual education because of the greater precision that can be given the term *bilingual education* (Spolsky, 56). His model considers the various combinations of language use at home, in school, in the community, and in the nation. Within the school the curriculum may use one or two languages for instruction, with the aim of maintaining both languages or transferring from one medium of instruction to another. The change is characterized as being either gradual or abrupt. Where maintenance of both languages is the aim, the languages may be in differentiated or equal roles.

A typology of bilingualism that permits comparison of bilingual education studies

In another model, Fishman & Lovas (26) propose that realistic educational goals based on realistic societal information be established for bilingual education programs. To do this, the sociolinguistic characteristics and the linguistic and cultural preferences of the community have to be determined before initiating a project. Their model identifies four types of programs that could be implemented—each with different objectives and corresponding to the functional needs of the community being served.

A model which is based on realistic societal information

Four types of resulting programs

1 The *transitional bilingualism* program uses the students' native language in the early grades to the extent necessary to allow pupils to adjust to school or to master subject matter until skills in English have been developed to allow using it as the language of instruction.

2 *Monoliterate bilingualism* programs indicate goals of development in both languages for the audiolingual skills but do not concern themselves with the reading and writing skills in the native language. Such programs emphasize the development of fluency in the students' native language as a link between home and school. Programs for American Indians often fall into this category, since often there is no body of written material for the child to learn in his native language.

3 *Partial bilingualism* programs seek fluency and literacy in

105

both languages, but literacy in the mother tongue is restricted to certain subject matter, generally that related to the ethnic group and its cultural heritage. In such programs, the literate skills in the native language are commonly developed in the social studies, literature, and the arts, while mathematics and science are restricted to English. Language and cultural maintenance are the ultimate objectives in such programs.

4 *Full bilingualism* programs propose that students develop all skills in both languages in all domains. In such programs both languages are ordinarily used for instruction in all subjects. This kind of program is directed at language maintenance and development of the minority language.

Transitional bilingualism programs such as the one in Eskimo and English in Alaska (9) and that in Gary, Indiana, (29) are criticized by Gaarder (28) and Ulibarri (60) on the grounds that such programs are simply a "bridge to English" with the basic purpose of socializing the child into the majority-language environment with little regard for the inherent value of the child's linguistic and cultural background. This point of view does not consider that some language communities are in the process of language shift to English and do not support a language maintenance concept.

Transitional bilingual programs

Monoliterate bilingualism programs such as the one in Navajo in San Juan in Utah (8) and in Pico Rivera in California (McDonald, 40) are only superficially different from transitional bilingualism programs, since the end result of such programs in a society that stresses literacy probably leads to shift. As Fishman & Lovas (26) point out, the intellectual imbalance between English literacy and mother-tongue illiteracy poses a difficult problem for any language-maintenance-oriented community.

Monoliterate bilingual programs

Partial bilingualism programs such as the Redwood City (Cohen, 14) and San Francisco (53) projects in California and the English-Russian-Spanish project in Woodburn, Oregon, (65) are the most numerous in the United States although full bilingualism programs are generally considered to be ideal. Ulibarri (59) takes issue with full bilingualism projects that teach subject matter twice to develop skills in all domains in both languages, while Fishman & Lovas (26) question their value as ideal models because they do not always meet the functional needs of the community.

Partial bilingual programs

An examination of bilingual project proposals reveals that

there are several programs that seem to fulfill a community need and specify the desired aim of equal proficiency in two languages. Among them are programs in Texas at Abernathy (31), Corpus Christi (3), El Paso (47), and Fort Worth (48), and the Spanish-Ute-Navajo program in southwestern Colorado (49).

Full bilingual programs

Instructional personnel in the bilingual program

One of the biggest problems facing bilingual education programs is the shortage of suitable trained instructional personnel. Few teacher education programs direct their efforts to this end and few helpful books and guidelines regarding teacher practices and qualifications are available. The roles of the English-medium teacher, the teacher of English as a second language, the other-language-medium teacher, and the special role of the teacher aide (in addition to the qualifications, in-service and pre-service training, recruitment and selection of teachers, and the use of foreign teachers) all need to be considered.

A shortage of trained personnel

The role of the teacher aide is still ill-defined. The Bilingual Education Act does not state any specific requirements. Consequently the duties of the aide in the classroom have varied from relieving the classroom teacher of "housekeeping chores" to becoming deeply involved in the instructional process. Ulibarri (59) suggests that with proper in-service training, the bicultural aide can bridge the gap between the bicultural children and the monocultural teacher. Gaarder (28) notes, however, that aides are sometimes expected to be better qualified than the classroom teacher and are often required to perform tasks that are beyond their level of expertise and training.

The role of the teacher aide

There is general agreement that a training program for teachers and aides should include courses in the history and culture of the non-English-speaking community to be served, language and linguistics, second-language teaching methodology, and curriculum (Guerra, 30; John & Horner, 35; Saville & Troike, 54; Ulibarri, 59). In addition, Guerra (30) would include evaluation and research techniques, instructional technology, and the administration and supervision of the bilingual program, while Saville & Troike (54) see a need for training in the selection and production of instructional materials.

Contents of a bilingual teacher/teacher aide training program

Ulibarri (59) proposes that in-service training would fill gaps in the training that teachers bring to the bilingual program. He and Bordie (11) suggest that a program in cultural sensitivity

In-service training

107

training should also be made a part of the training program.

From a special conference on teacher qualifications for teachers of English as a second language held in Washington came eight broad guidelines which Marckwardt (42) characterizes as emphasizing personal qualities, attitudes, skills, experience, and knowledge rather than courses and credit hours. Similar recommendations are set forth by Andersson & Boyer (2) and Andersson (1) for all bilingual program personnel.

Teacher qualifications

Teacher recruitment and training programs

Since the implementation of bilingual programs is often hindered because of the lack of a teaching staff, elaborate programs of recruitment of personnel have been instituted in some locales. John & Horner (35) relate that members of the New York City Board of Education regularly travel to Puerto Rico on recruitment trips for their programs.

The San Antonio Conference on Bilingual/Bicultural Education (6) produced some guidelines for the recruitment and retention of personnel for bilingual programs, taking note of the urgent need for information dissemination campaigns, high-intensity language programs in colleges and universities, retraining bilingual professionals as bilingual teachers, more use of "floating teachers," improved and accelerated use of teacher aides, use of community parents in planning and instruction, use of differentiated staffing, adequate compensation commensurate with the tasks performed, teacher involvement in planning bilingual programs, and acceptance of varying proficiency levels of teachers to be improved through teacher-training programs.

Guidelines for recruitment and retention of personnel

To date, a majority of the bilingual teacher-training programs that exist in this country are still mainly designed to meet the most critical certification requirements and consist of special summer sessions supplemented by in-service training programs. There are, however, some colleges and universities that are beginning to offer courses and programs designed to alleviate the critical shortage of trained personnel. They appear in the form of TESOL programs with bilingual and bicultural elements, bilingual summer training programs with or without in-service follow-up, undergraduate and graduate bilingual education training programs, and special undergraduate or graduate courses in bilingual education.

Present certification requirements are met minimally

Among recently funded full-year teacher-training projects in support of bilingual education are those at: Navajo Community College in Many Farms, Arizona, which is aimed at materials development and teacher training; D.C. Teacher's College in Washington, which is aimed at fully certifying 15 teachers educated and with experience in Latin-American countries; the University of New Mexico, which is involving ten specialists in curriculum development and materials production; New Mexico State Department of Education, which is training Spanish-medium teachers for New Mexico and Colorado; the Philadelphia Public Schools, which (with Temple University) is training 40 teachers with teaching experience and education in Latin America as Spanish-medium teachers; and the Edgewood Independent School District in Texas, which is giving intensive summer and part-time academic year training to Spanish-speaking persons employed as Spanish-medium teachers in the bilingual schools of Texas.

Full-year teacher training projects for experienced teachers

In some projects, the area colleges participate in the training of personnel for teaching, materials development, or both. For example, the Brown University Bilingual Institute (13) developed curricular materials for the Providence (50) bilingual education program. In Oklahoma, the Southeastern State College provided the pre-service training for the Choctaw Bilingual Education Program (Littlejohn, 39) in early fiscal 1970. The University of Alaska continues to provide the training sessions for the Bilingual Education Project in Eskimo and English (9), while in New York City, the Board of Education, Hunter College and Lehman College, and five City School Districts are participating in Project BEST (Condon, 16), which represents an attempt by these agencies to provide trained teachers, relevant materials, and involvement of community members in an ongoing program of bilingual education.

The first full-scale undergraduate-level bilingual education training program was developed at Our Lady of the Lake College in San Antonio, Texas, and just recently the college itself has become bilingual. John & Horner (35) report that the training program offers a double major in elementary education and sociology, stressing the culture and heritage of minority groups, Spanish literature and history, and the language and behavior of bilingual children. A similar program of teacher preparation is in operation at Chapman College in California.

Undergraduate teacher training programs

A promising development is the availability of special graduate and undergraduate courses in bilingual education in numerous colleges and universities, including the University of Michigan, UCLA, Georgetown University, the University of Texas, and the University of New Mexico.

Curriculum materials

Very few materials for bilingual education programs are available. An examination of currently funded proposals reveals that in all cases new materials have had to be created for the projects. In many instances the teaching personnel is neither qualified to develop appropriate materials nor has time allotted for it (Gaarder, 28).

Bilingual curricular materials are lacking

The three main sources of curriculum materials are those imported from foreign countries in which the non-English language is spoken, materials published in the United States, and materials created for use in a specific bilingual program by teachers, administrators, and other professionals.

Sources of bilingual curricular materials

However instructional materials are provided, there seems to be a general consensus in the literature that they must reflect respect for the minority group culture; comprise a full representation of the values, history, and traditions of the students for whom they are intended; and be linguistically appropriate for the student's age and educational level.

Necessary qualities of instructional materials

John & Horner (35) and Ulibarri (59) agree that although some imported materials might be quite appropriate for a bilingual education program, they are generally not relevant to the socioculture of the area being served or to the curriculums and methodology used in the school, since these texts often require a background knowledge of the social values and education practices of the countries providing the materials. On the other hand, Andersson & Boyer (2) suggest that bilingual educators have not even "scratched the surface" in evaluating and experimenting with imported materials, and they identify sources for finding such materials.

Imported programs are not necessarily relevant

Materials available in the United States are generally language materials designed to teach the non-English language to speakers of English. Unfortunately, they are often used in the language development aspects of the program for native speakers of that language. Such materials have serious limitations for the non-English speaker, since they concentrate on those aspects of the non-English language that English-speakers need most and that non-English speakers need most in English.

Materials that are designed to teach the subject matter areas and that have been developed in the United States are usually translations of English originals. Ulibarri (60) notes that some of these are very good, especially for mathematics and the sciences. However, others are not appropriate for the socioculture in which they are used. One of the major problems in creating materials commercially is making them adaptable to the many types of bilingual curricula, to the dialect and environmental background of the student, and the kind of bilingual program being conducted.

Subject matter materials are generally translations

Although teacher-made materials can have the advantage of being tailored to fit the language and special needs of the program, they often result in what John & Horner (35) have called a "duplication of effort," with separate teachers working on the same basic program. They recommend a regional effort to develop materials, either through regional centers (such as the Southwestern Cooperative Educational Laboratory in Albuquerque, New Mexico, and the Southwest Educational Development Laboratory in Austin, Texas) or in association with universities.

Teacher-made material

In addition, some state education agencies have recently started to support the development of bilingual educational materials. For example, the Texas Education Agency is developing instructional materials for grades kindergarten to 2 and is working on literacy and social studies materials in Spanish, while the State Department of Education in New Mexico and the University of New Mexico have a fellowship program that is aimed at developing instructional materials for bilingual programs.

Specially designed materials

While the problems of developing curriculum materials for bilingual programs in languages with written forms are troublesome, the problems in materials development for American Indian programs are staggering because of the lack of written forms in many Indian languages. Bauer (4) writes that Navajo has been the chief area of concentration and that some materials exist for the Hopi, Sioux, and Eskimo; but texts for other groups can be developed only after extensive descriptive language work and the development of a suitable orthography have been completed.

Production of materials for American Indian programs

In spite of the difficulties involved in materials production for Indian languages, there exists an impressive collection of curriculum materials that are available commercially for bilingual programs. John & Horner (35) provide sources for these materials and tell of the activities of the Bureau of Indian Affairs and bilingual education projects in developing additional courses of study.

Other sources for instructional materials for many language groups according to subject area, interest area, age level, and difficulty are provided by Andersson & Boyer (2), John & Horner (35), and Ulibarri (59). Many state education departments such as those in New York, Texas, and California also provide lists of materials that can be used for bilingual education programs. In addition, the Center for Applied Linguistics, the Modern Language Association, the American Council on the Teaching of Foreign Languages, TESOL, and foreign governmental services can be useful sources for materials and professional services.

Sources for materials

Community involvement

That community cooperation is essential to the success of bilingual education programs is a generally accepted premise because of the effect the attitude of the community can have on the learning of the child. Saville & Troike (54) see a great need for communication between the schools and the community at all stages of planning and implementation. Evidence of such communication is seen in the proposals for funding in the form of open school-board meetings, newspaper articles, feature items on radio and television in both languages, special speakers, encouragement of community leaders and parents to visit their children's programs, and parental involvement in the instructional process. Ulibarri (59) finds that an extremely efficient and effective method of fulfilling the stated aims of a bilingual project is to involve parents, "old timers," and community leaders as human resources. They are often able to furnish their expertise in such areas as folklore, traditions, and cultural values. Hoffman (33) writes of such involvement in the Rough Rock Demonstration School in Arizona, where Navajo mothers, fathers, and grandparents are often in evidence, either helping with the instruction in manual arts or simply observing the instruction that is taking place. A description of a bilingual/bicultural program in Tucson (Ulibarri, 60) reveals that mothers and children are involved in Home Task Schemes in which the mother goes to school with the child—to be helped by the teacher and aide with materials and techniques for certain tasks that the mother is to teach the child at home. The following week, the mother reports the progress made and receives

Community cooperation base on communication

more instruction for another task. The process then continues.

A common method that is used to communicate with the community is the use of a community newsletter. It is distributed by the school authorities to reach all segments of the target community to disseminate information about the purposes, plans, and activities in the bilingual program. Examples of such newsletters are in Edinburg (22) and El Paso (47) in Texas and in the San Juan School District in Utah (8).

A community newspaper

In spite of the elaborate plans and effective public relations programs used to keep the community and parents involved, uncontrollable problems can and do arise. Picchiotti (46) describes a bilingual program located in a Puerto Rican community but designed to serve several ethnic groups. While the Puerto Rican community is generally enthusiastic about the program, the Mexican-American community resents that a second center is not located in their community. The non-Spanish-speaking community, however, is "indifferent, resentful, or hostile," because bilingual centers had not been provided for their parents or grandparents, who were under pressure to assimilate with the majority culture. Although the program has apparently not been seriously affected, this instance demonstrates that administrators need to stress constantly the necessity for total community acceptance of a new approach to the education of children.

Problems arise in spite of communication successes

Evaluation

A most necessary aspect of any bilingual program is testing and evaluating the student's linguistic, conceptual, and attitudinal status; achievement in specific content areas in the appropriate language; and the effectiveness and interaction of materials, program design, and instruction.

The identification, annotation, and evaluation of testing instruments for each aspect of the evaluation component is clearly beyond the scope of this chapter. Andersson & Boyer (2) offer some thoughts on the nature of an effective testing program and John & Horner (35) identify and discuss several kinds of instruments that are currently available for early childhood bilingual education.

In testing the general language competence of children, bilinguals have traditionally been compared with each other or with monolinguals on the basis of scores on intelligence tests or scores of scholastic attainment. There has been little concern

How bilinguals have been tested in general language competence

with the proficiency of the bilingual in each of his two languages and even less attention has been given to a description of the situations in which each language was used. Recent work on "domains" by Cooper (17) has led to the realization that comprehension and speaking skills involve different abilities and that they are apt to vary within the same individual in different social contexts and spheres of activity.

Using the concept of domain as a basis for description, Cooper & Greenfield (18,19) devised a word-frequency estimation test to find out how often particular words are heard or used. In this way a usage rating scale was developed as a measure of language usage. Other instruments that can be used to measure language usage are identified in *Bilingualism in the Barrio* (Fishman et al., 25).

A new approach: a usage rating scale

John & Horner (35) relate that there is much more literature on the development of instruments to measure language proficiency than on measurements of language usage. For example, rating scales in which bilinguals rate their skills in each language (Fishman et al., 25), fluency tests to measure speed of verbal production or verbal response tests to measure quality rather than strength or speed, dominance tests to determine which of the bilingual's two languages is dominant, and tests to determine native language competence are all used (John & Horner, 35).

The literature on the language testing of bilinguals

A promising technique, still in the experimental stage, is story retelling (John & Horner, 35), which is used to collect representative samples of sequential speech for comparison of children from significantly different sociolinguistic and economic backgrounds. The child looks at corresponding pictures while a rather long story is read to him. Then, while looking at the pictures in sequence, the child is asked to retell the story. He is then evaluated on whether he uses one-word labels and occasional short phrases; short phrases that give some evidence of sequencing, including new elements that did not appear in the original; or retells the story accurately and concisely.

A promising technique: story retelling

Andersson & Boyer (2) recommend that language diagnostic tests should be given at the beginning of the school year to determine the relative strength of the children's two languages, which might be followed by periodic proficiency tests to record the factor of language balance each year.

Diagnostic tests

In the area of general ability and conceptual development tests, problems of a more urgent nature than for language tests arise. For the most part, presently available tests have been designed for native-English speakers and the test scores of all children have been compared to national norms. Since most tests scores reflect previous experience and education and since the bilingual child has grown up under poverty conditions and in a *microculturalized* world (Ulibarri, 59) with little knowledge of the language used in the test, poor results are inevitable (Ulibarri, 59). There is some evidence that bilingual programs are attempting to remedy the situation by adapting available tests or developing new ones. Discernible practices are to translate some of the more commonly known tests, to develop tests specifically for the target-language group, or to develop tests for use in specific bilingual programs (John & Horner, 35).

How can the bilingual's general ability and conceptual development be tested?

Instruments for measuring specific subject matter skills present the same kinds of difficulty that general ability and conceptual development instruments do. If an instrument has been designed for and standardized on English-speaking, middle-class student populations, its validity can be questioned for children whose language or social background is considerably different.

How to measure skill in specific subject areas

Soriano & McClafferty (55) describe the attempts to produce both appropriate instructional materials and testing devices in the Foreign Language Innovative Curricula Studies (FLICS) project in Michigan. John & Horner (35), who tell of other such activities at the Southwest Educational Development Laboratory in Austin, Texas, at the Good Samaritan Center in San Antonio, and at the Applied Language Research Center in El Paso, identify other tests that can be used to measure skills development in language arts.

Attempts to produce both materials and testing devices

Andersson & Boyer (2) consider evaluation in the affective areas more important than evaluation in cognitive learning, since successful cognitive learning depends to a large extent on the motivation and attitude of children. A review of the literature reveals little research activity in the development of satisfactory instruments. Since tests are not available in many cases or not entirely satisfactory, many bilingual programs have contracted the services of education service centers, regional educational laboratories, national testing organizations, and universities. The fact that the United States Office of Education suggests that every federally funded bilingual project have an educational audit has spurred serious efforts to have an effective program evaluation component in the proposals for funding.

The concept of accountability difficult to apply to bilingual programs

Thus experimental and control groups, student's pre- and post-intervention performance tests, comparisons of records in entire schools or districts with past records, and annual reports from school authorities are used by an impartial evaluator or team of evaluators when they visit the program. The written report of such evaluations can be a "token of accountability" to the public (Andersson & Boyer, 2).

Effectiveness of bilingual education

Since bilingual education is still in its infancy, it is premature to determine the complete extent of its successes and failures. Interim evaluations of programs that are requesting funds for continuation (8, 10, 31, 48) indicate that objectives are being met but not to the high degree that was originally expected. Since most bilingual projects will continue to be funded for periods of at least five years with final evaluations at the end of each year, more empirical data will become available within the next few years and will indicate areas of strength, weaknesses, and uncertainty.

Evaluation of effectiveness of bilingual programs in an interim state

Some objective evaluations have already been provided from programs that have been operating for several years. If the results can be projected to ongoing programs, a successful future for the concept of bilingual education can be predicted. In Dade County, Florida, (20) the public schools have not only prepared special materials to teach English to Spanish-speakers but have also made a program of language maintenance and development possible for Cuban refugee children. In some schools, first- and second-grade students have an activity period conducted in Spanish, with storytelling, music, games, and role-playing. More significantly, however, three elementary schools aim to teach monolingual students of Spanish and English to understand, speak, read, and write the two languages well enough to use them both as vehicles for learning other subjects. Results show that achievement in language and arithmetic has not been impaired even though each member of the bilingual group had only half of his instruction in his own language and added the acquisition of a second language to his study load.

Some "objective" evaluations of bilingual programs

Pryor (51) reports that in Harlandale, Texas, in a one-year project, Mexican-American first graders taught in Spanish and English did as well in reading English as the classes instructed in English only and made more progress in communicative

Specific examples

116

skills, conceptual development, and social and personal adjustment than classes taught in English only.

Valencia (62) in determining the relative effects of early Spanish language instruction on English and Spanish language development among Mexican-Americans, found that students improved in Spanish vocabulary, spelling, and reading comprehension in addition to developing their language skills in English. Also, independent evaluators noted overwhelming interest and support for the program by parents.

Tucker et al. (58) write of the effectiveness and practicability of an alternate-days bilingual approach to education in the Philippines that is showing some positive and exciting results. In this program the bilingually instructed classes follow all subjects, using Tagalog as the language of instruction one day and English the next day to continue the previous day's lesson. The switching has caused no appreciable or continuing difficulty to students or teachers. After one year of instruction, the bilingually instructed students seemed to be developing language and content skills comparable to their control counterparts. This program would seem to interest educators in diverse settings who are contemplating changes in language policy.

Evaluation of an alternate-day program

In a different but highly relevant study, d'Anglejan & Tucker (21) and Lambert et al. (37) describe a bilingual school project in the Montreal area at St. Lambert's School, where English-speaking children followed the first three years of formal instruction entirely or principally in French, upon the request of the community to conduct such a program. The results to date show that this type of bilingual training is much more effective than was originally expected. The children involved demonstrated a very high level of skill in both the receptive and productive aspects of French, the major language of instruction. They also showed generally excellent command of all aspects of English, the native language of the children, and a high level of achievement in subject matter taught through the foreign language only. In addition, there were no indications of cognitive retardation that could be attributed to the experimental program.

Evaluation of a Canadian bilingual program

Although this kind of bilingual program is excluded for funding under the "Bilingual Education Act" because it does not meet the poverty criterion and the instruction in two languages requirement, it seems reasonable to consider such a project as a possible alternative to current language programs in the elementary school.

117

If the results of the St. Lambert's program are interpreted as evidence that bilingual education as it exists today in the United States is unnecessary, then the observations that Ervin-Tripp (23) makes must be taken into account. She points out that in the Montreal area, English-speaking children have no sense of inferiority in school; teachers do not have low expectations for their achievement; their social group has economic and social power in the community; their native language is respected, since it is the dominant one and will be used for instruction in later years. In the classroom, children are not expected to compete with native speakers of French in a milieu that simultaneously expects failure, blames them for their failures, and does not allow them an opportunity to excel in their own language.

Problems and areas in need of research

In spite of the recorded successes of bilingual education programs in this country and in others, the number of problems and areas in dire need of research is staggering. The statement that "bilingual educators are more dedicated than they are sophisticated" (Ulibarri, 60) is still true. Gaarder (28), in calling for formative evaluation by knowledgeable outside observers, calls for assistance from research-oriented scholars and investigators to answer questions such as:

Questions that need answer from research

1 How can the degree of scholarly competence of prospective teachers and/or aides in the non-English medium be quickly and fairly determined?

2 Should teachers be required to be bilingual and teach in both languages or should there be a separate teacher for each medium?

3 How can the relative merits of keeping languages separate (or mixing them) with respect to time, place, and teacher in the school be determined?

4 How can materials be produced for teaching American Indians their own languages and through their own languages?

5 How can the extent to which children know their mother tongue be determined when the mother tongue is not English?

The National Conference on Bilingual Education (43) made recommendations for basic research in the area of first- and

118

second-language learning. The recommendations called for a national system for collection and dissemination of information on bilingualism and bilingual education, research in the areas of attitude and motivation and their effect on language learning, identification of successful bilingual programs for replication, and bilingual research to be performed in an operational setting.

The National Conference on Bilingual Education and recommended research

The Conference offered suggestions for over 60 research activities in the areas of basic research, language acquisition, teacher preparation, methods and materials for teaching the two languages, curriculum content, and evaluation. Recognizing the limited number of persons capable of research who are also interested in bilingual education, it was suggested that available and interested persons be identified and have them train others. Kloss (36) and Ulibarri (60) identify and examine the problems involved in researching bilingualism and make suggestions for research projects and related case studies.

Mackey (41) calls for an overall research policy with a framework of interrelated projects into the problems of bilingual education. Andersson & Boyer (2) endorse his statement and call for research and action at a national level to ensure as broad a base as possible and to prevent unnecessary duplication and atomization of effort. John & Horner (35) add that if research on bilingualism is to be effective it must go beyond the narrow confines of purely linguistic or psychological studies. In developing their sociolinguistic models, Fishman & Lovas (26) and Mackey (41) make it possible to integrate the linguistic, psychological, and social aspects of bilingualism.

Many organizations have an interest in the research aspects of bilingualism. Among them are the Center for Applied Linguistics, the American Council on the Teaching of Foreign Languages, the Teachers of English to Speakers of Other Languages, the Bureau of Indian Affairs, the Southwest Council for Bilingual Education, many state departments of education, and the International Center for Research on Bilingualism at Laval University in Quebec.

Organizations which could sponsor research in bilingualism

Among the regional educational development laboratories engaged in bilingual research and development are the Southwest Educational Cooperative Laboratory of Albuquerque and the Southwest Educational Development Laboratory of Austin. There are also several regional education service centers that are active in preparing teaching and testing materials.

Summary and conclusions

1 Although knowledge about all aspects of bilingual education is limited, it is heartening to note that definite progress has been made during the period under review. Among the significant developments are:

(a) There are numerous bilingual education programs being implemented in many parts of the United States.

(b) There is evidence of pilot and experimental research being conducted and reported so that a major body of knowledge is developing.

(c) There are now several sources to which the bilingual educator can turn for direction (Andersson & Boyer, 2; John & Horner, 35; Saville & Troike, 54; Ulibarri, 59; Zintz, 66).

(d) Models for bilingual education are now available that incorporate social factors as well as linguistic and psychological factors (Andersson & Boyer, 2; Fishman & Lovas, 26; Mackey, 41).

(e) There is evidence that the problems of minority-language groups are being recognized by different segments of the educational world.

2 The "Bilingual Education Act" of 1967 represents an attempt to provide an adequate education for children in economically depressed environments who enter school with a limited knowledge of English: they are allowed to continue their cognitive and linguistic growth in their first language while acquiring English as a second one.

3 The available evidence suggests, however, that bilingual education need not be limited to those for whom English is not a native language. It is reasonable to expect, as Fishman (24) does, that the day is coming when more and more genuine bilingual education, for all those who want it, regardless of income, mother tongue, or language dominance, will be part of American education.

4 Based on the available evidence, it can be expected that if the quality of bilingual programs matches its promise, many educational and societal benefits will result. The non-English-speaking child in such a program will build a healthy and confident self-image; he will be able to learn all of the curriculum through his native language until he is able to do so in a second language with no loss of cognitive or language skills; he will

acquire cultural awareness and a sympathetic cross-cultural understanding and be free to participate in the majority culture and in his ancestral culture. The English-speaking child who participates in a bilingual program will learn a second language; he will acquire cultural awareness and cross-cultural understanding by studying his and the other ethnic group's culture and history; and he will also feel comfortable associating with representatives of the other cultural group.

5 If bilingual programs are successful, it can also be expected that the community will decide to support their continuance with or without federal support. Andersson & Boyer (2) state that it is to be hoped that the "Bilingual Education Act" will clearly demonstrate not only its benefits for the lower income strata of our society but also its effectiveness in maintaining and cultivating valuable language and cultural resources of all socioeconomic levels, and that as a result of this demonstration, Congress will be moved to broaden the Act in order to help conserve the language resources in the national interest. Such actions might include appropriating monies at least equal to the authorization made by Congress and removing the poverty criterion that now makes the Act primarily an antipoverty measure and only secondarily supports educational innovation.

6 Although the situation continues to improve, bilingual education in the United States still suffers from three serious deficiencies: a lack of funds to operate the number of programs that are needed, a lack of even partially trained personnel, and a lack of evaluated curriculums, materials, and methods. As current programs are evaluated and modified, future programs will benefit from the information gleaned from them, and in this manner make bilingual education live up to its promise of an effective and equal education for all segments of our multilingual society.

References, Approaches to bilingualism: Recognition of a multilingual society

1 Andersson, Theodore. "Bilingual Elementary Schooling:A Report to Texas Educators." *Florida Foreign Language Reporter* 7,i(1969):37–40.

2 ———— and Mildred Boyer. *Bilingual Schooling in the United States.* 2 Volumes. Washington, D.C.: United States Government Printing Office, 1970.

3 *Aprendemos en dos idiomas.* Initial Plan for the Implementation of a Bilingual Education Program under the Provisions of Title VII, Public Law 89–10, as amended in 1967. Corpus Christi: Corpus Christi Independent School District, 1970. [Mimeograph.]

4 Bauer, Evelyn. "Bilingual Education in BIA Schools." *TESOL Quarterly* 4(1970):223–29.

5 Bebo, Phillip. Superintendent, Santa Fe Public Schools, Santa Fe, New Mexico. Personal Correspondence, 23 March 1971.

6 Bernal, Ernest M., Jr. *The San Antonio Conference. Bilingual-Bicultural Education. Where Do We Go From Here? (March 28–29, 1969)*. San Antonio: Saint Mary's Univ., 1969. [ERIC Document Reproduction Service: ED 033 777.]

7 *Bilingual-Bicultural Education Program*. Formal Project Application for Funding of Bilingual Education Program under the Provisions of Title VII, Public Law 89–10, as amended in 1967. Santa Fe: Santa Fe Public Schools, 1970. [Mimeograph.]

8 *Bilingual Education for Navajo*. Application for Continuation of a Bilingual Education Program under the Provisions of Title VII, Public Law 89–10, as amended in 1967. Monticello, Utah: San Juan School District, 1970. [Mimeograph.]

9 *Bilingual Education Project in Eskimo and English*. Initial Plan for the Implementation of a Bilingual Education Program under the Provisions of Title VII, Public Law 89–10, as amended in 1967. Anchorage: Alaska State Department of Education, District 1, State Operated Schools, 1970. [Mimeograph.]

10 *Bilingual Project, OENSU*. Application for Continuation of a Bilingual Education Program under the Provisions of Title VII, Public Law 89–10, as amended in 1967. Derby, Vermont: Orleans-Essex North Supervisory Union, 1971. [Mimeograph.]

11 Bordie, John. "Cultural Sensitivity Training for the Teacher of Spanish-Speaking Children." *TESOL Quarterly* 4(1970):337–42.

12 Brooks, Nelson. "The Meaning of Bilingualism Today." *Foreign Language Annals* 2(1969): 304–09.

13 *The Brown University Bilingual Institute (Summer, 1970). A Report*. A Bilingual Program under the Provisions of Title VII, Public Law 89–10, as amended in 1967. Providence, Rhode Island: Brown University, 1970. [Mimeograph.]

14 Cohen, Andrew D. *A Sociolinguistic Approach to Bilingual Education*. Stanford, California, 1970. [Mimeograph by author.]

15 *Complete INCCA Report:A Bi-lingual Pilot Project for Foreign Speaking Children with Language and Cultural Conflicts to Evaluate Present Teaching Methods and Materials Under a Controlled Educational Situation*. Paterson, New Jersey: Inner-City Community for Action, 1969. [ERIC Document Reproduction Service: ED 041 062.]

16 Condon, E.C. *Project BEST:A Brief Description of the Project*. New York: New York Consortium on Bilingual Education, 1970. [Mimeograph.]

17 Cooper, Robert L. "Two Contextual Measures of Bilingualism." *Modern Language Journal* 53 (1969):172–78.

18 —— and Lawrence Greenfield. "Language Use in a Bilingual Community." *Modern Language Journal* 53(1969):166–72.

19 —— "Word Frequency Estimation as a Measure of Degree of Bilingualism." *Modern Language Journal* 53(1969):163–66.

20 *Dade County Public Schools Program in Bilingual Education*. Miami: Dade County Public Schools, 1970. [Mimeograph.]

21 D'Anglejan, Alison, and G. Richard Tucker. "Academic Report:The St. Lambert Program of Home-School Language Switch." *Modern Language Journal* 55(1971):99–101.

22 *ECISD Bilingual Project Newsletter* 1,i–v(1969–1971):n. pag. [Edinburg, Texas: Consolidated Independent School District; Mimeograph.]

23 Ervin-Tripp, Susan. "Structure and Process in Language Acquisition," 313–44 in James E. Alatis,ed., *Report of the Twenty-First Annual Round Table Meeting on Linguistics and Language Study*. Georgetown Univ. Monograph Series on Languages and Linguistics, Volume 23. Washington, D.C.: Georgetown Univ. Press, 1970.

24 Fishman, Joshua A. "The Politics of Bilingual Education," 47–54 in James E. Alatis,ed., *Report of the Twenty-First Annual Round Table Meeting on Linguistics and Language Study*. Georgetown Univ. Monograph Series on Languages and Linguistics, Volume 23. Washington, D.C.: Georgetown Univ. Press, 1970.

25 —— et al. *Bilingualism in the Barrio*. 2 Volumes. Washington, D.C.: United States Office of Education, 1968.

26 —— and John Lovas. "Bilingual Education in Sociolinguistic Perspective." *TESOL Quarterly* 4(1970):215–22.

27 Gaarder, A. Bruce. "Bilingualism," 149–69 in Donald D. Walsh, ed., *A Handbook for Teachers of Spanish and Portuguese*. Lexington, Massachusetts: D.C. Heath, 1969.

28 —— "The First Seventy-Six Bilingual Education Projects," 163–75 in James E. Alatis,ed., *Report of the Twenty-First Annual Round Table Meeting on Linguistics and Language Study*. Georgetown Univ. Monograph Series on Languages and Linguistics, Volume 23. Washington, D.C.: Georgetown Univ. Press, 1970.

29 *Gary Oral Language Program*. Application for an Operating Grant under the Provisions of Title VII, Public Law 89–10, as amended in 1967. Gary, Indiana: School City of Gary, 1969.

30 Guerra, Emilio L. "Training Teachers for Spanish-Speaking Children on the Mainland." *American Foreign Language Teacher* 1,iii(1971): In Press.

31 *HABLA–Helping Advance Bilingual Learning in Abernathy*. Application for Continuation of a Bilingual Education Program under the provisions of Title VII, Public Law 89–10, as amended in 1967. Abernathy, Texas: Abernathy Independent School District, 1970. [Mimeograph.]

32 *Helpful Hints for New BIA Teachers*. Window Rock, Arizona: Bureau of Indian Affairs, 1970. [ERIC Document Reproduction Service: ED 040 959.]

33 Hoffman, Virginia. "Language Learning at Rough Rock." *Childhood Education* 46(1969): 139–45.

34 Jakobovits, Leon A. *Foreign Language Learning:A Psycholinguistic Analysis of the Issues.* Rowley, Massachusetts: Newbury House Publishers, 1970.

35 John, Vera P., and Vivian M. Horner. *Early Bilingual Education.* New York: The Modern Language Association of America, 1971. [Available from the MLA Materials Center, 62 Fifth Avenue, New York, N.Y. 10011.]

36 Kloss, Heinz. *Research Possibilities on Group Bilingualism:A Report.* Quebec: International Center for Research on Bilingualism, 1969. [ERIC Document Reproduction Service: ED 037 728.]

37 Lambert, Wallace E., et al. "Some Cognitive Consequences of Following the Curricula of the Early School Grades in a Foreign Language," 229–74 in James E. Alatis,ed., *Report of the Twenty-First Annual Round Table Meeting on Linguistics and Language Study.* Georgetown Univ. Monograph Series on Languages and Linguistics, Volume 23. Washington, D.C.: Georgetown Univ. Press, 1970.

38 Landry, Richard G. *Bilingualism and Creative Abilities.* Fargo: North Dakota State Univ., 1968. [ERIC Document Reproduction Service: ED 039 602.]

39 Littlejohn, Joseph E. *An Interim Evaluation of the Choctaw Bilingual Education Program.* McCurtain County and Durant, Oklahoma: Choctaw Bilingual Education Program, 1970. [Mimeograph.]

40 McDonald, Christina. *Bilingual Bicultural Education para los estudiantes de El Rancho.* Pico Rivera, California: El Rancho Unified School District, n.d. [Mimeograph.]

41 Mackey, William F. "A Typology of Bilingual Education." *Foreign Language Annals* 3(1970): 596–608.

42 Marckwardt, Albert. "Statements of Qualifications and Guidelines for Preparation of Teachers of English to Speakers of Other Languages." *TESOL Newsletter* 4,ii–iii(1970):4–5.

43 *National Conference on Bilingual Education: Language Skills.* Final Report. Washington, D.C.: United States Office of Education, 1969. [ERIC Document Reproduction Service: ED 033 256.]

44 Paulston, Christine B. *Las Escuelas Bilingües: The Peruvian Experience.* Paper presented at the Third Annual TESOL Convention, Chicago, 1969. [ERIC Document Reproduction Service: ED 030 876.]

45 Perales, Alonso M., and Lester B. Howard. *On Teaching the Disciplines to Disadvantaged Mexican-Americans:A Linguistic Approach.* Paper presented at the Third Annual TESOL Convention, Chicago, 1969. [ERIC Document Reproduction Service: ED 031 689.]

46 Picchiotti, Natalie. *Community Involvement in the Bilingual Center.* Paper given at the Third Annual TESOL Convention, Chicago, 1969. [ERIC Document Reproduction Service: ED 031 690.]

47 *Programa Bilingüe–ALMA:Adelante los México-Americanos.* Initial Plan for the Implementation of a Bilingual Education Program under the Provisions of Title VII, Public Law 89–10, as amended in 1967. El Paso: El Paso Independent School District, 1970. [Mimeograph.]

48 *Programa en dos lenguas.* Application for Continuation of Bilingual Education Program under the Provisions of Title VII, Public Law 89–10, as amended in 1967. Fort Worth: Fort Worth Independent School District, 1970. [Mimeograph.]

49 *Project SUN.* Initial Plan for the Implementation of a Bilingual Education Program under the Provisions of Title VII, Public Law 89–10, as amended in 1967. Cortez, Colorado: Southwest Board of Cooperative Services, 1969. [Mimeograph.]

50 *Providence Title VII Bilingual Education Program.* Final Report. Kingston, Rhode Island: Curriculum Research and Development Center, 1970. [Mimeograph.]

51 Pryor, Guy C. *Evaluation of the Bi-Lingual Project of Harlandale Independent School District, San Antonio, Texas, in the First Grades of Four Elementary Schools during 1966–67 School Year.* San Antonio: Harlandale Independent School District, 1967. [ERIC Document Reproduction Service: ED 023 508.]

52 Riley, John E. *The Influence of Bilingualism on Tested Verbal Ability in Spanish and English.* Final Report. United States Office of Education Grant 7-80000390016-(010). Washington, D.C.: United States Office of Education, 1968. [ERIC Document Reproduction Service: ED 026 935.]

53 *San Francisco Bilingual-Bicultural Project for Spanish/English Speaking Children.* Initial Plan for the Implementation of a Bilingual Education Program under the provisions of Title VII, Public Law 89–10, as amended in 1967. San Francisco: Unified School District, 1970. [Mimeograph.]

54 Saville, Muriel R., and Rudolph C. Troike. *A Handbook of Bilingual Education.* Washington, D.C.: Center for Applied Linguistics, 1970. [ERIC Document Reproduction Service: ED 035 877.]

55 Soriano, Jesse M., and James McClafferty. "Spanish Speakers of the Midwest:They are Americans Too." *Foreign Language Annals* 2(1969):316–24.

56 Spolsky, Bernard. "TESOL," 323–40 in Dale L. Lange, ed., *Britannica Review of Foreign Language Education, Volume 2.* Chicago: Encyclopaedia Britannica, Inc., 1970.

57 Treviño, Bertha G. "Bilingual Instruction in the Primary Grades." *Modern Language Journal* 54(1970):255–56.

58 Tucker, G. Richard, et al. "An Alternate Days Approach to Bilingual Education," 281–95 in James E. Alatis, ed., *Report of the Twenty-First Annual Round Table Meeting on Linguistics and Language Study.* Georgetown Univ. Monograph Series on Languages and Linguistics, Volume 23. Washington, D.C.: Georgetown Univ. Press, 1970.

59 Ulibarri, Horacio. *Bilingual Education:A Handbook for Educators.* Albuquerque: Univ. of New Mexico, 1970. [ERIC Document Reproduction

Service: ED 038 078.]

60 ——, ed. *Interpretive Studies on Bilingual Education.* Albuquerque: Univ. of New Mexico, 1970. [ERIC Document Reproduction Service: ED 038 079.]

61 —— et al. *Bilingual Education:PREP VI.* Washington, D.C.: United States Office of Education, 1970. [ERIC Document Reproduction Service: ED 034 082.]

62 Valencia, Atilano A. *The Relative Effects of Early Spanish Language Instruction on Spanish and English Linguistic Development. An Evaluation Report of the Pecos Language Arts Program for the Western States Small School Project.* Albuquerque: Southwestern Cooperative Educational Laboratory, 1970. [ERIC Document Reproduction Service: ED 036 382.]

63 Walsh, Donald D. "Bilingualism and Bilingual Education:A Guest Editorial." *Foreign Language Annals* 2(1969):298–303.

64 *Weld County Bilingual/Bicultural Program.* Initial Plan for the Implementation of a Bilingual Education Program under the Provisions of Title VII, Public Law 89–10, as amended in 1967. Johnstown, Colorado: Colorado School District RE-5J, 1969. [Mimeograph.]

65 *Woodburn English/Russian/Spanish Education Project.* Initial Plan for the Implementation of a Bilingual Education Program under the Provisions of Title VII, Public Law 89–10, as amended in 1967. Woodburn, Oregon: Woodburn School District #103c, 1970. [Mimeograph.]

66 Zintz, Miles V. *What Classroom Teachers Should Know about Bilingual Education.* Albuquerque: Univ. of New Mexico, 1969. [ERIC Document Reproduction Service: ED 028 427.]

5

Foreign language interdisciplinary programs and activities

Introduction

The purpose of this chapter will be to review the foreign language curriculum to determine the nature and extent of interdisciplinary activities and programs. Significant literature related to this topic will be cited, and valuable information from it will be reported. The results of a nationwide survey to identify such activities and programs will also be reported. There were two phases to the survey. The author first wrote to all foreign language supervisors in state departments of education throughout the country to enlist their assistance in the identification of programs. Information was received from approximately one-half of the states. A questionnaire was subsequently directed to the individuals or institutions named by the supervisors. The following information was sought in that questionnaire:

Helen P. Warriner

*Virginia State Department
of Education*

*Purpose of chapter
and questionnaire*

1 The objectives of the course or activity.
2 The language(s) used in conducting the program.
3 The extent of target language usage.
4 The identification of those who initiated the interdisciplinary program or activity.
5 Their reasons for initiating it.
6 The number of students enrolled.
7 The criteria for enrolling students.
8 The amount of credit assigned and the field in which it is awarded.
9 The characteristics of the teacher that qualify him for interdisciplinary instruction.
10 The nature and sources of the instructional materials.
11 The problems encountered in planning and conducting activities of an interdisciplinary nature.
12 The solutions for them.
13 The changes that will or would be made to refine the program.
14 The evaluation of the effectiveness of the program.

In addition to these topics, the approximately 50 respondents supplied much valuable unsolicited information, which will be reported as is appropriate. (See item 34 in list of references for this chapter.)

Obviously not all programs prevalent throughout the country were identified, but it is possible that representative types of them were reported to the writer.

Two fields that are closely related to foreign language study are not included in this investigation: bilingual and area studies programs. Bilingual programs do make extensive use of interdisciplinary material and approaches but they are treated in another chapter in this volume. Area studies programs, the second field, are often not directed primarily to the learning of a foreign language. They are therefore considered too far removed from foreign language programs to be of much significance here.

A review of the literature and a survey of practices relating to foreign language interdisciplinary activities and programs reveal that different interpretations are being made of the term *interdisciplinary* and that such activities and programs vary sharply in the degree to which they are interdisciplinary. For accurate communication, therefore, a definition is essential as an introduction to the study of this aspect of foreign language education.

Different interpretations of the term

The definition should be approached by defining *discipline* as this term is used in curricular references. Phenix (44) describes a discipline as knowledge that is organized for instruction and appropriate for teaching and learning. Its analytic characteristics enable it to simplify understanding and economize thought because it provides schemes for explaining disparate elements of related knowledge. Synthetically a discipline reveals patterns and relationships among those disparate elements, orders them hierarchically, and thus gives meaning to details. A discipline is dynamic because it is capable of growth and development by the discovery of new knowledge and susceptible to change by the disavowal of previously accepted truths.

Definition of discipline

Phenix goes on to explain that there is no definitive line separating a discipline from an area of study. The distinction is basically one of degree. Those subjects such as linguistics are more purely disciplines than are those such as foreign languages, which, as they are conventionally taught, circumscribe various combinations of language, history, geography, literature, and other related fields.

In everyday scholastic usage, the term *discipline* refers to many subjects in the curriculum even though they might not be pure disciplines. For purposes of this study, the word *discipline* is used in its curricular frame of reference—*as an area of study.*

With this usage in mind, an understanding of *interdisciplinary* can be approached. In the simplest terms, Secrest (49) suggests that an interdisciplinary endeavor is a crossing of intellectual, organizational curricular boundaries occasioned by the desire or necessity to achieve an objective or to solve a problem prevalent in the everyday, real-life world. His own words are worthy of consideration: "Polydisciplinary efforts are the natural adaptive response of intellectual man to the challenge presented by problems of the real world as contrasted with the simplified models or representations in use within academe at any one point in history. Such efforts either begin as coalitions of individuals of varying skills but with at least one unifying purpose or intellectual interest, or with that rare individual who is able to master several disciplines and bring them together in a novel and unified fashion."

The meaning of *interdisciplinary* in reference to foreign languages is obscured by the fact that a foreign language is more appropriately an area of study comprising components of various disciplines than it is a pure discipline. The examination of almost any foreign language course of study, however specialized it might be, usually reveals material from the belletristic field and from one or more of the social sciences. Activities and programs now being characterized by the term *interdisciplinary* therefore often represent more of an increase in degree or a shift in focus than they do a total change in classification of the content of foreign language classes.

What is considered interdisciplinary is more obvious in some instances than in others. A course in the History of Russia taught in French to students of Wakefield High School in Arlington, Virginia, in 1970 (38) is unique because it probably has not been offered in many other schools of any type or during any period of education in the United States. On the other hand, the course in Latin American Civilization at Central High School in Macon, Georgia, (38) might not be quite so unique. The difference lies in the fact that Spanish and Latin-American studies naturally are closely related whereas Russian history and the French language are not usually dealt with in the same departments of American schools. And yet the content of both classes is drawn largely from the social sciences, and the medium of communication is a foreign language. Another kind of interdisciplinary program is exemplified by Highland Park Senior High School in St. Paul, Minnesota, (38) which does not claim to offer an interdisciplinary program in foreign languages, but where French students select topics on which to give oral, demonstrative projects in the target language. The teacher indicates that the students often delve into other disciplines in their choices. Representative topics include the making of French bread, the demonstration and description of holds in wrestling, the use of makeup in the theatre, how a volcano works, and the making of pottery. One might even go a step further and ponder whether or not the use of addition and subtraction in a sixth-grade French class is an interdisciplinary activity. Or what of the singing of "Guantanamera" in third-level Spanish?

It can be readily seen that interdisciplinary activities and classes in foreign language programs cannot be identified easily. The term *discipline* in its curricular frame of reference is not clearly definable simply because no clear lines separate one discipline from another. Therefore no foreign language program, however conventional it may be, is purely unidisciplinary. Furthermore, programs generally referred to as being interdisciplinary vary in the degree to which they differ from foreign language activities considered conventional and in the amount of time devoted to the interdisciplinary aspect of those programs.

Interdisciplinary programs not easily identified

Therefore there will be no attempt to judge which foreign language classes can be described as interdisciplinary and which cannot. Instead, this review will attempt to focus on those classes and activities which seem to possess interdisciplinary characteristics worthy of consideration because they are either typically or uniquely representative of this type of instruction. Such an investigation should contribute to a better understanding of the curricular changes in foreign languages which are clearly in progress at the present time.

Curricular trends provide a rationale for interdisciplinary activities and programs

Curricular changes do not occur in a vacuum. They develop within a framework of trends resulting from fluctuating patterns of the society that shape the school. So it is with interdisciplinary activities in foreign language programs. Some of the factors that make it feasible or even advisable to link foreign languages with the content from other disciplines or areas of study will now be examined.

Factors which link foreign languages to other disciplines

(1) The modern student shares a voice in curriculum planning and demands that it be relevant to his immediate needs and interests.

Students who grew up in a ten-easy-lesson approach to everything, enjoy-now, pay-later society, are not prone to accept readily promises that what they are asked to study will eventually be for their own good. Kersten & Ott (28) propose that the material to be studied and the way in which it is presented must be applicable to the students' immediate needs and interests and that it appeal to their intellectual curiosity. Seelye (51) holds a similar point of view. He suggests that foreign language teachers first strive to capitalize on student interests that are already functioning and that, once the motivational factor is thus provided for, the instructor then must lead him to new interests. Lawson (31) calls for the use of language in fields of interest outside of the conventional language classroom choices and suggests such topics as cooking, contemporary music, war, poverty, and foreign cars as examples. The history courses taught in French in several Virginia schools include as a primary objective the application of language skills to an immediately practical purpose—the study of another discipline (56).

Students demand relevancy

(2) Student influence on the curriculum is now being forced upon the teachers in some instances, and in others student opinion is being actively sought.

Student opinion

Strasheim (53) thinks that it is essential to enlist student opinion in order to broaden the curriculum beyond the conventional offerings. In fact, she sees a need for the shift of emphasis from one that places a premium upon the teacher and teaching to one in which the student and learning are central. Stratemeyer, Forkner, McKim, & Passow (55) also suggest that the learner and his individual patterns of learning be considered in curricular planning. One of the Northeast Conference committees of 1971 (23) advocated the consideration of student opinion in making content choices for foreign language classes. This committee suggests that there is no longer a need for the teacher to be a disseminator of information. The student has access to many sources which can fulfill this function for him. Instead the teacher must serve as a stimulus for learning and as a guide to the sources which the student will use.

(3) A student population more heterogeneous in interests and

abilities now is enrolled in foreign languages, and these students need a more diversified curriculum.

Heterogeneous student interests and abilities

Hocking (22) asserts that there are two major obsolete assumptions of higher education that have limited the development of foreign language programs. One is that all foreign language study is directed ultimately towards literature. The other is that high school foreign language instruction exists primarily for college-preparatory purposes. Strasheim (53) goes on to elaborate that as a result of this elitist philosophy, elementary and secondary foreign language teachers have felt more closely aligned with college professors than with their colleagues in the schools in which they teach. They have, therefore, not participated to much of an extent in curricular innovations that have been going on in the schools.

Change is under way, however. Students in foreign languages today are not necessarily members of the minority group of intellectually and socially privileged youngsters that once populated the classes; and with their new voice in curriculum formation, they are no longer willing to accept the one-way approach to the study of foreign languages. Many foreign language curriculum reformers advocate the diversification of the curriculum to serve the varied needs, interests, and abilities of all the students (Nelson & Jakobovits, 41; Sandstrom & Pimsleur, 48). Remak (46) advocates that foreign language teachers seek a more competitive role in the new free-market curriculum and that foreign languages earn for themselves a position of higher prominence in the curriculum. Grittner (21) suggests that the profession abandon the notion of directing foreign language study at the high school level exclusively to college preparation. Strasheim (53) thinks that the diverse nature of foreign language students today requires many new approaches, including interdisciplinary programs.

(4) The erosion of degree requirements in foreign languages in higher education has precipitated a swing towards subject matter different from, and in addition to, literature in order to attract and hold students.

Effect of changes in degree requirements

In foreign language circles, it is a much discussed fact that the diverse attacks on the undergraduate and graduate college curriculum during the past several years have resulted in a decrease in foreign language requirements at those levels of education. Although Alden (1) reports that the tensions of department chairmen of a year or so ago may have abated, he observes that the ". . . pendulum is still swinging in the same direction and shows no signs of engaging in a return course." Many react to the demise or diminishing of requirements with a new sense of freedom to seek out the content which is most appropriate to the many individual students in the classes. No longer are students in many institutions forced to accept the fare that their instructors choose to place before them. That fare has most often been a generous if not an exclusive portion of literature. Professors are now being forced to change methods and content to silence the cry of irrelevance and to attract students to their classes. Keller (27) believes that one of the changes most desired by students is the opportunity to see relationships between the various aspects of their education. He criticizes the present curriculum for fostering subject-centered, course-centered, class-centered education. Alden (1) discovered that many departments are broadening the base of their programs to include content from the social sciences. Bryn Mawr College, for example, is considering an interdepartmental major in French studies. American University reports no problems with the survival of foreign languages even though they are not protected by requirements. This institution attributes part of its success in the struggle to attract students to such courses as the Semantics of Communism (graduate Russian), History of Art (undergraduate French), and Social Science in Latin America (undergraduate Spanish).

(5) Efforts are now being made to individualize instruction in order to provide multiple alternatives for the students within the same class or group.

Individualization of instruction

No longer in some schools do all students have to study the same things in the same way. Strasheim (54) suggests that there is room in American education for many different foreign language programs to suit the many individual backgrounds and interests represented in the classes. She advocates interdisciplinary programs as one means of achieving individualization. Logan (33) reports that at Live Oak High School in Morgan Hill, California, students may study mini-courses in German on a contractual basis. To date, students have pursued topics in science, philosophy, and home economics; and greater diversification is anticipated. With the help of the instructional staff, the student decides upon the topic which he wishes to investigate and then works independently most of the time. Keitel (25), in providing a rationale for teaching World History in German, notes that no longer can everybody be taught alike. Alden's sur-

131

vey of changes in college foreign language programs (1) discovered much support for the individualization of instruction at that level.

(6) Longer sequences of foreign language study have produced many students with a significant degree of fluency, and they are therefore more capable of using language as a tool with which to study other disciplines.

Effect of long sequence of study

During the last decade, students have tended to start foreign language study earlier and pursue it for a longer period of time than they used to. Therefore, they develop a greater degree of linguistic skill which enables them to use language more effectively as a tool for the study of content. This has previously not been typical of the foreign language classroom.

(7) The curriculum at all levels is badly fragmented and in need of unification.

Need for curricular unity

In 1966 Goodlad (20) observed that the emphasis was on a separated rather than on a fused curriculum. He predicted, however, that curricular efforts would soon be directed to the total curriculum instead of to the bits and pieces characteristic of a discipline-centered approach. It seems that these efforts have already begun. Miel (40) also believed, in 1964, that efforts at that time to unify the curriculum might prove more effective than previous ones because of increased knowledge of the structure of individual disciplines. The shortcomings of the discipline-centered curriculum lead Stratemeyer and her colleagues (55) to a plea for a more unified one. Among those shortcomings they note: (*a*) that it is difficult in real life to unify knowledge from disparate disciplines in the solution of problems; (*b*) that isolated knowledge is not purposeful; (*c*) that education organized by disciplines does not lend itself to the recognition of individual differences in students; (*d*) that the discipline-centered curriculum is easily proliferated by new areas of study, some of which are of only transitory value; and (*e*) that education organized by disciplines places a high premium on the mastery of facts. Seelye (50) also recognizes the danger of separating academic disciplines, and he makes a plea for cooperative and complementary endeavors between the foreign language and social studies departments in the teaching about culture. Behmer (2) suggests for the high school student a curriculum which permits him "to perceive how the individual subjects which fill his school day are actually bound together in the history, philosophy, and value systems of Western man." The humanities program for third-, fourth-, and fifth-year students in Gary, Indiana, (43) indeed seems to have precisely that kind of unity and emphasis. Its objectives include the interrelating of subject areas in order to create a learning environment oriented towards people, their needs, and problems.

(8) The pressure on students to pursue studies in many differ- *Pressure on students* ent fields has generally increased student and faculty interest in *to pursue many fields* some schools in interdisciplinary programs as a timesaving expediency.

Greenham, in Ort & Smith (42) indicates that a program in American history was initiated at Canton, Ohio, because many college-bound students did not have the time for advanced language classes even though they were interested in further study. Warriner (56) lists as a benefit to be derived from the study of history in French or Spanish the conservation of time made possible by the students' pursuit of two subjects simultaneously.

(9) The federal government often indirectly encouraged the *Indirect federal* development of interdisciplinary programs to help meet national *influence* needs.

Secrest (49) views the development of interdisciplinary programs as an inevitability caused by a natural and evolutionary process. He indicates, for example, that international affairs and especially World War II led to the area studies program. The federal government, too, he thinks, has played a role in that it has utilized the organized research unit to unify the many areas of academic expertise in the solution of the nation's problems.

The literature related to interdisciplinary activities and programs

In this section those references from the bibliography that relate specifically to interdisciplinary programs in foreign languages will be summarized, and an interpretative commentary will be offered for many of them.

The advocation of interdisciplinary studies

Since the interest in interdisciplinary studies in foreign languages seems to be increasing, it is perhaps appropriate to review chronologically the literature supporting them.

A Northeast Conference Committee in 1966 whose report was edited by Corrin (10) prepared one of the earliest articles dealing extensively with the interdisciplinary approach in foreign languages. Viewing language as a utilitarian subject, the committee urged the rearrangement of curricular priorities in order to embrace other material in addition to literature. The report treated briefly some of the problems of designing interdisciplinary programs and concluded with a review of programs in operation or being planned at that time. The chief value of this article resides in its historical significance, for it helped to focus regional if not national attention on the issue. Although the advice to the designers of interdisciplinary programs is somewhat limited in this article, if judged by later standards, it made an important contribution at that time.

A Northeast Conference Report on interdisciplinary studies

In 1969, Seelye (50) in his analysis of the teaching of culture in foreign language classes, suggested that social studies and foreign language teachers have much to learn from each other, that team planning and teaching should be a profitable curricular venture, that language is a means to an end; and that it should be applied to the development of skills and attitudes through the integration of disciplines.

Integration of social studies and foreign languages

A significant essay by Secrest (49) that same year provided a rationale from the generalist's point of view for *polydisciplinary* programs, a term which he used synonymously with *interdisciplinary*. In his opinion, forces outside of the schools helped to ignite the present interest in interdisciplinary programs. He suggested that many scientific and technological developments would not have been possible without the contribution of various disciplines, that developments in the field of international affairs had led to the establishment of area studies programs, and that the organized research unit that employed contributors from several disciplines in the solution of the nation's societal problems had encouraged and paved the way for educators to embrace interdisciplinary approaches. Perhaps Secrest's most significant analysis was that interdisciplinary efforts are at the cutting edge of the current intellectual revolution in that they attempt to apply academic knowledge to the solution of problems. He advocated that these efforts be employed more extensively in the classroom.

Polydisciplinary studies

Among other recommendations in reference to foreign language teaching, Benardo (3) proposed the lowering of the barriers between the disciplines in the compartmentalized curriculum. He expressed the opinion that teachers as well as students stand to profit from a more integrated program of studies.

Meyer (39) saw the curriculum as being badly out of balance. He also suggested that because of the compartmentalization that characterizes it, some things are left out of the students' education that should not be omitted. He advocated team teaching as a step in the direction towards unification.

Unification and integration of curriculum

Strasheim (53,54) helped to set the stage for interdisciplinary activities by proposing that the curriculum should be integrated and by suggesting that the student is an individual capable of helping to determine what he should study. Among other means of altering the curriculum to adapt it to individual needs and interests, Strasheim suggested that foreign language teachers work together with those in other subject areas in planning for instruction and that interdisciplinary activities be increased.

Nelson & Jakobovits (41) reaffirmed the recommendations of the 1966 Northeast Committee Report (Corrin, 10), which advocated interdisciplinary programs.

Logan (33), in his chapter on individualized instruction in Volume 2 of *The Britannica Review of Foreign Language Education*, described curricular trends that have led to the individualization of programs. He pointed to interdisciplinary activities as one means of achieving individualization, and he helped to build a rationale for them.

Interdisciplinary activities and individualization

Keller (27), also writing in 1970, suggested that integration, not fragmentation, of the curriculum was essential for the schools. His solution to the problem of fragmentation is the humanities program, which unites disciplines and elucidates the relationships between fields of knowledge.

Egginton (16) saw the social sciences and foreign languages as having natural curricular relationships; and he proposed that these relationships be exploited by adopting a conceptual approach (*fatalismo* and *analfabetismo*, for example) to Latin-American studies programs.

In 1971, Lawson (31), a school superintendent from Shaker Heights, Ohio, asserted that school administrators have difficulty justifying a discipline that is restricted by the nature of its instruction to a small, select segment of the school population. He was entirely sympathetic toward language study, however, and he asked that the profession set as a goal for itself the teaching of 75–100% of the student population by the end of the 1970s. He thinks that more youngsters must be attracted into foreign language programs and kept longer. Among numerous proposals that Lawson made in order to achieve the more attrac-

An interdisciplinary program in a small school

tive and relevant curriculum, he included the need to correlate foreign languages with other disciplines.

A Northeast Conference Committee in 1971 (Hugot, 23) also made reference to interdisciplinary programs. In its summary of innovative trends, it described humanities classes in French (Foreign Language Innovative Curricula Studies) and a special unit of study in Delaware French classes on the French heritage in that state (18). It also lent support to the idea advanced in 1966 by a similar Northeast Conference Committee (10) that interdisciplinary programs could enhance the teaching of foreign languages.

In summary, it should be pointed out that few articles advocating foreign language interdisciplinary programs and activities could be found in the contemporary literature prior to 1965. By 1970, numerous proponents of interdisciplinary studies were writing. The increase in the number of individuals and committees addressing themselves to this topic therefore appears to represent a growing recognition of the need for such studies.

Literature on interdisciplinary programs increases

Review of the literature and description of programs: Modern languages

One of the more widely publicized interdisciplinary programs in which foreign languages have been engaged is the Humanities in French course, a part of the Foreign Language Innovative Curricula Studies Project (FLICS) that was developed in Michigan. A readable yet detailed account of this program appears in Ort & Smith's article (42) in *Foreign Language Annals*. The humanities course was designed for students who had completed at least two years of French; and art, literature, and music are integrated with the foreign language. The stress is on contemporary French life. The units provide an overview of French culture treated anthropologically, a treatment of the problems of youth today, an analysis of the French value system, an acquaintance with French literature, (placing emphasis on what authors chose to write about, why they wrote, and for whom they intended their material), a study of the field of communication, and a review of technology in France and the United States. The last unit takes an area studies approach. A one-year version of the course was designed for fourth-year high school French students, and a two-year course of study was prepared for those beginning in French III.

Humanities in French: Michigan

Two other publications describing the FLICS humanities in

French programs became available in 1969: the summary (17) and the end-of-grant reports (34). The end-of-grant report indicated that the humanities class helped to make the foreign language program more flexible, that students' enthusiasm was high due to their opportunity to form concepts on the basis of a wide range of resources available to them, and that participation in the free exchange of opinions and ideas was extensive. Sample tests were provided in the end-of-grant report. The summary report asserted that a lack of appropriate materials for the advanced French student helped to generate the development of the humanities in French program.

The *Foreign Language Annals* article by Ort & Smith (42) that appeared in 1969 is a compendium of descriptions of interdisciplinary programs in practice or planned at that time. The Humanities in French program (FLICS) just described was one of them. Other programs were also explained in the article. The first two program descriptions are important because of their student viewpoint.

A compendium of descriptions

The government class taught in French at Gunn High School in Palo Alto, California, was discussed by a student in the Ort & Smith article (42). Students in this program spent three periods a day in a French, English, social studies block of time with a three-member teaching team in which the teachers in English and social studies each had some background in French. The student described how the three courses were integrated. He also related the benefits of using the foreign language in such a program. Students and faculty were satisfied with the results of the program, both in terms of progress in French and understanding of concepts in government.

A government course in French

Students in the Canton, Ohio, schools became so interested in the American history course taught in French at Lincoln High School that the course had to be opened up to qualified students from two other high schools in the district during the following year. To qualify, students had to have finished three years of French. Furthermore, the course was chosen by students, at least to some degree, because they did not wish to participate in the Advanced Placement Program in levels four and five. As a result, those students that did take both French and history did better in history than in literature.

American history in French

Three programs in the Ort & Smith article (42) were used to provide insights into the nature and extent of planning in interdisciplinary programs. The Jefferson County, Colorado, schools

planning memorandum for an interdisciplinary program indi- *Spanish and Latin-American*
cates the range of content topics to be dealt with in a program of *studies: three programs*
Spanish and Latin-American studies: contemporary literature
to psychology and philosophy of the Latin-American to Spanish
music. Residence in Mexico, letter and tape exchanges, weekend
camps, teacher exchanges, and a foreign language resource center were structures that were to be planned as integral parts of
the program.

The description of the Spanish Five course in Bethesda-Chevy
Chase High School in Maryland, which was scheduled to begin
in 1968–69, related the broad range of curricular considerations
that had taken place in terms of planning the course. Similarly,
the German social studies course designed for students at Mc-
Kean High School at Wilmington, Delaware, exemplifies the
detailed course planning that is necessary to make such a program of interdisciplinary studies successful.

Interdepartmental cooperation in an interdisciplinary program
is outlined in the Jameville-Dewitt High School in New York.
The semester course in Latin-American civilization was successful because of cooperation between departments. This element may be the key to the success or failure of such programs.

Two programs described in the Ort & Smith article (42) relate
the importance of materials development to interdisciplinary *Importance of materials*
programs. The description of the semester course in Latin- *development*
American History at Boulder High School in Boulder, Colorado,
details the range of knowledge for which materials must be chosen. Another Latin-American Studies program at Brandywine
High School in Wilmington, Delaware, reported not only a rather
extensive and useful bibliography of materials on Latin America, but also related information concerning research in such a
program. In a design using a control group of 20 students and
two experimental groups of approximately 25 fourth-year students of Spanish in each group, results of classroom tests indicated that students in the experimental groups could successfully study a regular curricular subject and learn as much about
Latin-American studies as the control group that studied the
same concepts in English.

Another research project planned to evaluate the contribution of interdisciplinary approaches to the learning of both
language and some content in another discipline is that of Keitel
(in Ort & Smith, 42) at Hamilton High School in Sussex, Wisconsin. In this school a course titled *German and World Cultures*

was offered. In order to evaluate the course, a design of control and experimental group achievement contrasts was indicated. Three groups were used; two were designated control groups and one as experimental. One control group was composed of regular German-level-three students who served as a language control group; another included students who had not studied German. This group was used to check achievement in history against the experimental group that, of course, was composed of students who took the interdisciplinary course. Standardized testing was to be administered to compare the progress of the three groups, but the results were not available for inclusion in the article. In another publication, however, Keitel (26) indicates that the results of the testing program showed that students in the experimental treatment or interdisciplinary course learned both German and history at about the same level as the control groups in each area. Keitel also has evidence that indicates that this interdisciplinary program helped retain some students who might have otherwise terminated their study of German.

Evaluation of an interdisciplinary program

Intensive interdisciplinary programs are also reviewed in the Ort & Smith (42) article. The Academic Center for Latin-American Studies, begun in 1967, has provided an opportunity for secondary school students who have completed three years of Spanish to begin an in-depth study of the many aspects of Latin-American culture through the medium of the Spanish language during a six-week summer period. A total immersion program for the Commack, New York, schools was also described in this category. The students in the program used Spanish for one-half of the school day for the study of language, social studies, humanities, and the lunch-recreation period. These students achieved significantly high scores on the Regents Examinations in Spanish and social studies, the Modern Language Association Cooperative Tests, and the College Entrance Examination Boards.

General evaluation of participants in interdisciplinary programs

Different kinds of administrative structures also seem to be beneficial to the development of interdisciplinary programs. In Seattle, teachers of social studies, art, math, music, language arts, physical education, and foreign languages were described as working together as an interdisciplinary team. Within this framework a tour abroad was simulated and a multilingual, cultural event was sponsored. In a freer structure, French students in Bloomfield, Michigan, were reported to have pursued their own interests as long as they also satisfied basic requirements

Administrative structures

for individual skill acquisition in the language. Their studies extended to other areas of the curriculum and into the community. Representative of their investigations were a comparison of ski areas in the United States and France, planning a trip as French exchange students, examination of current events as presented in the foreign journalistic media, and ordering Christmas gifts and cards from French sources.

The Ort & Smith article (42) provides the most comprehensive review available in the literature in reference to interdisciplinary activities involving foreign languages. Both commonality and diversity can be seen in the programs reviewed. Social studies content obviously dominates, but is not exclusive. The article provides much valuable information for the interdisciplinary curriculum planner.

The publication that comprehensively describes an interdisciplinary program from the origin of the idea through the evaluation stage is that by Warriner (56). A similar report is found in the article by Ort & Smith (42). The report describes 11 social studies courses taught in French or Spanish in 10 different high schools in Virginia in 1965-66 and 1966-67. All but one of the courses were taught in French; that one was in Spanish. Extensive evaluation techniques were employed. Control classes in both history and language were designated where possible, and standardized tests were administered. Student, teacher, and consultant evaluations were reported. This information as well as the statistical data indicated that the students who had three levels of language study prior to the social studies course could use their language as a tool to pursue another discipline.

Interdisciplinary programs: from origin to evaluation

An article appearing in a recent issue of the *American Foreign Language Teacher* (43) indicates that students in Gary, Indiana, provided the stimulus to initiate an interdisciplinary program there. They wanted to apply their foreign language skills to a practical purpose. Four areas of study—language, art, music, and history—are included in the humanities course that is taught by a team of five teachers. The course is offered in a magnet school that draws third-, fourth-, and fifth-year students from all parts of the city. They spend one-half of the school day in this program.

A student-stimulated interdisciplinary program

Jennings (24) provided four units on the French economy that were developed for third- and fourth-year French students in the Minneapolis, Minnesota, schools. A bibliography and sample tests are included in her report.

Lange (30) advocated the use of foreign newspapers and magazines to broaden the scope of content in foreign language classes. He also suggested strategies for using this material.

Review of the literature and description of programs:
The classics

Masciantonio is a major spokesman for the interdisciplinary theme in the classics. In his *Annals* article (37), he described the entire Philadelphia classics program in the elementary and secondary schools. At the time of the preparation of that paper, two interdisciplinary programs were being taught at the city's magnet school — The Role of Black People in Classical Antiquity and Classical Humanities Through Films. Numerous other courses such as Greek and Latin in Scientific Terminology, Great Books of Greece and Rome, and Ethnomusicology were being planned.

The Philadelphia classics program

In another article (36) Masciantonio pondered the impact that FLES classical studies would have on the secondary school program. He foresaw, among other things, the need for interdisciplinary courses.

Behmer (2) advocated an approach that he calls "Bridges to Understanding." It is a variation of a humanities program. He saw the Latin course as being nurtured by other disciplines, and he proposed that the classics instructor serve as a resource person for teachers of other disciplines. He even advocated that Latin be removed from language departments or wherever it is found and that it stand alone in a coordinating role for other curricular disciplines. Perhaps his most practical recommendation was that classics teachers need to be more adequately trained for their role, a role that most writers recognize is expanding. An interdisciplinary approach is needed to provide them with the breadth that is needed in teaching the broad field of the classics.

"Bridges to Understanding"

Lazzatti (32) observed that in one state only one out of a total of 550 Latin teachers had participated in planning or conducting a humanities program. He indicated that more students are now reading the classics, frequently in translation, but that paradoxically Latin teachers have little to do with this and are concurrently diminishing in numbers. Lazzatti concluded that a major cause for this paradox is the inadequacy of the training of Latin teachers. He suggested that the question of the survival of Latin in the curriculum will be answered during the 1970s. He advocated that Latin teachers assume a role in teaching the classics

Latin teachers poorly trained in meeting student needs

in translation and that they decrease their stress on the analysis of language in favor of increasing the emphasis on culture. Lazzatti proposed that teacher-preparation programs be broadened to include the study of Greek; a course in Western Arts and Ideas; practice-teaching in humanities as well as in Latin; and study of ancient philosophy, archeology, and other fields related to classical studies. Lazzatti's essay suggested that the problems of the classics are largely traceable to the teachers and subsequently to the schools that prepared them.

Connor (9) also proposed that the classicists move along the continuum away from language and in the direction of the humanities. He endorsed courses in the classics in translation. Connor, like Lazzatti, pointed to the need for improved preparation of the classics instructor. He advocated a close relationship between the classics teacher in the schools and the colleges, and he proposed that the classics be directed in the form of liberal education to citizens as well as to scholars.

Champlin (8) offered a description of a Latin program at North Kingstown High School in New York in which classical plays are read in translation as early as the first year. *Antigone* and *Amphitryon* are staged in English by the students. Comparisons are made of plays such as Aeschylus' *Orestia* and O'Neill's *Mourning Becomes Electra*. The art teachers in the school assist with the course by teaching the art and architecture of Pompeii. This class also studies the influence of the Greek tragedy on the opera. *The classics, drama, and art*

The classics and astronomy are linked in a program at Brablec High School in Roseville, Michigan, described by Young (57). The science and Latin teachers there work together in presenting a planetarium program in which mythology is used. Originally designed to show Latin students how mythology is the basis for the names of various constellations, the science instructor then used the program in his classes to show the influence of Greek culture on modern science. *The classics and astronomy*

Sadler (47) provided ideas for the Latin teacher interested in establishing a link between botany and Latin. He offered a listing of horticultural (generic) names in Latin.

The colleges and universities

A brief report was given in a recent issue of the *Association of Departments of Foreign Languages Bulletin* (12) of an experimental course in intermediate French at the University of Cali-

142

fornia at Santa Barbara. Three full-length films are used each quarter. Student reading material is provided by the film scripts. The same article reports that the language instructors in the French and Italian departments at the University of California at Riverside select their material from contemporary books, magazines, and newspapers. Topics such as revolution, sex, drugs, and war are representative of the content of the classes.

Film and contemporary problems

Ladd (29) reported that at Clackamas Community College the German professors are attempting to make that language more attractive to the students now that foreign languages are under attack in the colleges. They do so by relating German to the students' major fields. Several times each semester the students give oral reports on topics which they select from their own area of specialization, and in doing so they use German as a tool.

German related to the major

Cullen (11) described the program at Elbert Covell College of the University of the Pacific in Stockton, California, in which all instruction is in Spanish. Many of the students are Latin Americans; however, American students seeking to learn Spanish fluently also study there. Cullen criticizes the exclusive teaching of literature in advanced language classes for its lack of appeal to all students. He believes that this approach attributes to the tendency of male students to drop foreign languages as soon as possible. Cullen believes that the teaching of literature will eventually succumb to interdisciplinary studies providing students with wider choices in content.

The Massachusetts Institute of Technology has had a humanities course in French since 1953. Bottiglia (5) described that program in his article in the *Modern Language Journal*. Entering freshmen are tested, and if they possess enough competency they may choose the humanities program in French. A second-year program is available if they desire to continue. The Greek and Judaeo-Christian traditions and the rise of science are studied as a basis for modern Western ideas.

Humanities in French

Stansfield (38) reports that at the University of Colorado readings in social studies were introduced into third-semester Spanish classes to make the study of Spanish more relevant and to acquaint students with the jargon of the social scientist so as to permit them to be able to read Spanish works in this field. It was intended especially for students of the social sciences, but a more general population enrolled. Mimeographed selections from books, magazines, and newspapers provided the textual material for these third-semester students. Evaluation showed

Third-semester introduction of social science materials in Spanish

143

that the students preferred this kind of content over studies in Hispanic culture. This approach did not, however, seem to cause more students to continue their study of Spanish. Stansfield cautioned against looking upon classes of this type as a panacea for alleviating the complaints about language courses.

Berg (4) reported that the nature of the entire curriculum at Marymount College in Virginia is interdisciplinary. A Spanish class, for example, studies the history and cultural ambience of Spain through the drama of the country. Students do many interdisciplinary research projects. The college operates a study-abroad program whereby students spend a semester studying in Spain or France. Their studies abroad are necessarily interdisciplinary.

Entire curriculum is interdisciplinary

Alden's survey (1) reviewed the curricular changes that have taken place since many colleges deleted or decreased their foreign language requirements within various degree programs. A number of interdisciplinary activities resulted from these changes. Exemplary of them are Creative Writing and Black Literature in French at Wellesley. American University offers courses for undergraduates in History of Art (French), Social Science in Latin America (Spanish), and Manners and Customs (German) among other similar titles. At the graduate level students can take, for example, Semantics of Communism (Russian), Foreign Policy (French), and the Socio-Political Scene (German).

Curricular changes related to deleted language requirement

Several writers addressed themselves to the need for interdisciplinary graduate and undergraduate programs for teachers. The papers from the Seminar in Language and Language Learning (52) evaluated the interdisciplinary needs of doctoral candidates who will subsequently be responsible for the organization of foreign language programs in the schools and colleges. The several authors proposed that these students need to pursue studies in linguistics, psychology, programmed instruction, anthropology, and the cultural context of language teaching in order to be adequately equipped for their responsibilities.

Interdisciplinary programs for teachers

Four articles that discuss the doctor of arts degree that is currently being developed in several graduate schools have appeared in recent issues of the *Association of Departments of Foreign Languages Bulletin* (6,13,14,15). It is being designed as an interdisciplinary degree for teachers, and the emphasis on research that characterizes the doctor of philosophy degree is not to be found in this program. It is proposed, however, to be on

144

a level of achievement with the doctor of philosophy degree, and the efforts to develop it are endorsed by the Council of Graduate Schools. The Carnegie Corporation has awarded grants to several universities to develop the degree that is proposed to help unify for the potential teacher the disciplines that he will need in his future occupation. The Claremont Graduate School is developing such a degree in French, Spanish, and German (15). Five areas of study are pursued—humanities, creative arts, social sciences, linguistics, and a second foreign language—as a backdrop for the study of the candidate's major language. Each student is required to serve a teaching internship that is designed to give him broad experience, and a research project having to do with the teaching of languages culminates the degree.

Doctor of arts degree

Remak (46) suggested that, in order to make foreign language programs appealing enough to combat student apathy, teachers need broader training in disciplines related to languages.

Powers' committee in its recent Northeast Conference report (45) concurred with the seminar writers (52) and Remak (46). The report described three of the available interdisciplinary graduate programs in foreign language education at the doctoral level—those at Ohio State University, Florida State University, and the University of Texas.

Graduate programs in foreign language education

It can readily be seen from the literature that the interest in, and efforts on behalf of, interdisciplinary approaches to the teaching of foreign languages are prevalent in all levels of instruction and in all languages. Less is said in the literature about foreign language programs in the elementary schools; however, it is perhaps true that they have always had to be more interdisciplinary than foreign language instruction at higher levels. If, however, foreign languages are to become a component of basic education in the United States, as many leaders would have them become, then there is little doubt that FLES would have to develop as even more of an integral part of the elementary school curriculum.

The results of a survey

The nationwide survey conducted by the author, which was previously described, revealed that a number of interdisciplinary programs on the secondary school and college levels—about which nothing has appeared in the literature—are being conducted.

A nationwide survey

145

All of the programs uncovered in this survey involved modern languages rather than the classics. Almost all of them were in progress at the conclusion of the survey in May, 1971.

The material from which the information in this section was compiled is taken from the files of the Foreign Language Service of the Virginia State Department of Education (38).

French

Libertyville High School, Libertyville, Illinois — French History and Civilization. This course is taught to students who have previously had four years of French. Particular emphasis is placed on art, music, and literature in addition to the history; and efforts are made to relate this material to today's world. Students established the general objectives of the course. They had previously studied grammar exhaustively, and only one of them wanted literature. (His preference is fulfilled by an independent study program.) The unit of credit is awarded in French.

Emphasis on art, music, and literature

Northwestern Senior High School, Hyattsville, Maryland — French Culture and Cooking. This course is described as essentially an enrichment course taught mostly in English although most of the students enrolled have had three years of study in French. Credit, however, is awarded in French. Four times as many students wish to take the class as the facilities can accommodate. Many field trips are taken, for example, to a supermarket, the French market in Washington, D.C., specialty food shops, and a French kitchen supplier. The students hear a lecture by a French *sommelier*, go to the French church in Washington, and attend French films. They actually prepare foods twice a week, and they hold quarterly gourmet lunches for the faculty in order to help finance their cooking. On those occasions, students dress in the provincial costume of the region whose food is featured, and they simulate the setting of a French café. Some of the students instigated a trip to France. The teacher indicates that the students from this class were more culturally curious and aware than other French students in the group from the same school.

An enrichment course with field trips

Albert Einstein High School, Kensington, Maryland — European History in French. The purpose of this course was to provide students with an opportunity to use their language skills as a tool for acquiring knowledge in a content area and to accommodate students who are interested in both the social sciences and French but who would have difficulty finding time for both. It is an elective for students who have had at least four years of French with a grade of B or better. The credit may be assigned to either language or history, according to the wishes of the student. French is used exclusively.

Randallstown Senior High School, Randallstown, Maryland — Interdisciplinary activities integrated into regular classes. Short units about architecture, music, and other subjects are included in the regular French classes. Some language classes study an opera such as "Carmen," "La Vida Breve," "Das Rhinegold," "Die Walküre," "Die Dreigroschenoper," and "Die Fledermaus." German students study the *lieder* of Schubert, Schumann, Beethoven, Brahms, and others and relate them to the study of poetry.

Burlington High School, Burlington, Vermont — Interdisciplinary activities made possible through independent study. Stress is placed in some cases on areas of the world that speak French other than France. The students relate their study of French drama to their conventional drama class taught in English. Also, a course in French cuisine is being jointly planned with the home economics department.

Integrated activities and independent study

Arlington and Fairfax Counties and the City of Alexandria, Virginia — History of France, World History, and History of Russia. Several high schools in these districts offer social studies courses taught in French. They are described jointly, for they have much in common since they all originated from the same planning that was coordinated through the State Department of Education. Most of the courses have been offered since 1966-67. They are taught almost exclusively in French to students who have had three or four levels previously. At Wakefield High School in Arlington, History of Russia taught in French was offered for the first time in 1970–71. This was done at the request of students who had had World History in French in 1969–70 and preferred another interdisciplinary course over the conventional French sequence.

Social studies in French

Walt Whitman High School, Bethesda, Maryland — French Drama. French is used most of the time in this class comprising fifth-year French students. They see films as well as read plays. Student interest warrants that the course be continued.

Milford High School, Baltimore, Maryland — Interdisciplinary activities integrated into regular fourth- and fifth-year French classes. In this program French is taught through the humani-

147

ties. Particular stress is placed on music. The reasons for this approach are to maintain interest in French and to teach culture. French is used most of the time according to the instructor.

Eleutherian Mills Historical Library, Greenville, Delaware – The French in Delaware, a unit of study for Advanced French Classes. This unit of study (18) was initiated by the state foreign language supervisor to develop in the students an awareness of the French culture's influence on local history. It was also designed to provide a change of pace for advanced French classes. To date it has been used in fifth-year classes in which French is spoken most of the time.

Influence of French on local history

Waltham, Massachusetts – Conversational and Workable French for Industrial Arts Students. This class developed when a scheduling error occurred and 35 industrial arts students erroneously signed up for French. (The course was not continued after the first year because of financial problems in the school.) The students were beginners in French, but the target language is reported to have been used all of the time. The credit was assigned in French. No texts were used, and all instructional materials were teacher-originated. The instructor reports that there was much student enthusiasm for the course and suggests that additional specialized language courses should be offered to students in business and vocational curricula.

French and industrial arts

Bloomington Public Schools, Bloomington, Minnesota – Social Studies in French. This course is currently being planned for the academic year 1971–1972.

Walden Middle School, Atlanta, Georgia – Interdisciplinary activities in French language arts and social studies. This program will be conducted on the basis of learning packets in order to individualize instruction.

Spanish

Orono High School, Orono, Maine – Focus on Latin America. The orientation of this program is different from others being reviewed in that it is a social studies course that leads to language study. Students pursue individualized units in the social studies, art, music, folklore, and language.

Latin-American studies

Central High School, Macon, Georgia – Latin-American Civilization. Spanish is used approximately 75% of the time in this course, which is designed to provide students who have had elementary school Spanish with alternative content to that of the regular high school program at the intermediate level. They must have completed the FLES program and Levels I and II at the high school before enrolling. Credit is assigned to social studies even though Spanish is the principal language used in conducting the class.

Van Horn High School, Independence, Missouri — Interdisciplinary activities integrated into the regular advanced Spanish classes. The teacher and a consultant originated this course to try to interest more students in continuing the study of Spanish at the fourth- and fifth-year levels. Students formulate the list of topics. There are no alternatives to the course; students who are continuing the study of Spanish at this level enroll in this one. The target language is used all the time. Exemplary of the topics chosen by the students are "Contemporary Issues in Spain and Latin America," "Spanish Shorthand," "The Spanish Detective Story," "Man and Revolution in Latin America," "Early American Civilization (Inca, Maya, Aztec)," and "The Dictator — Where? How? Why?"

An advanced course with an interdisciplinary element

Fargo South High School, Fargo, North Dakota — Unit of Study on Peru. One of the reasons for the teacher's initiating this unit was to motivate students. According to the respondent they, indeed, welcomed the change. They first select topics from a list given them by the teacher. They then work in groups to prepare written and oral reports. Some of these topics lead students to other disciplines.

A specific country

Tucson Public Schools, Tucson, Arizona — Interdisciplinary activities integrated into other courses. Language is considered as a means to an end, and either Spanish or English is used as is necessary in this program which seeks an amalgam of language, sociology, geography, and other related fields. The teaching materials are locally developed to take advantage of the intercultural environment (Indian-Mexican-Anglo) of the community. The program is for all language learners, however, and credit is awarded in Spanish.

Brandywine High School, Wilmington, Delaware — History and Culture of Latin America. This course was initiated by a Fulbright curriculum specialist who worked in the school several years ago. The students have had three previous years of Spanish, and this course follows as the next level of sequence. Spanish is used exclusively. Uniquely, one-half of the credit is awarded in Spanish, and one-half is given in social studies. A one-semester course on the History and Culture of Spain is available to students who complete the course on Latin America.

149

Interdisciplinary programs and activities/Warriner

Skelly Junior High School, Tulsa, Oklahoma — South of the Border Science. This course is planned for students who have completed three years of Spanish. General science will be offered, and the students may elect to take their credit in either language or science.

Planned programs

Walden Middle School, Atlanta, Georgia — Interdisciplinary activities in Spanish, language arts, and social studies. The coordinators of foreign languages, language arts, and social studies are preparing the plans for this course to be initiated in the fall of 1971. Workshops for the teachers will be held prior to the initiation of the course.

German

Ridgefield High School, Ridgefield, Connecticut — A mini-course curriculum for German IV and V. German is used nearly all of the time in this course, which is designed to provide students with some voice in the selection of material to be studied; to help them acquire practical linguistic skills needed for travel in Germany; to allow them to engage in the study of relevant subject matter while continuing to pursue important traditional values; and to supplement and enhance the students' studies in other departments, particularly in English, history, music, and art. Each student selects four of six mini-courses offered, and the credit is given in German. The facilities and staff of other departments are used in the instruction. The six topics are German for Travelers; The German-Speaking Lands and America; Introduction to Scientific German; The German-Speaking World — Its History and Culture; Survey of German Literature; and Recent German, Swiss, and American Literature.

Hanover High School, Hanover, New Hampshire — Electives in geography, history, music, and cooking. The elective system was designed to provide students with a choice of material to be studied in order to motivate them to study German. The language is used much of the time, and one-quarter of a unit of credit is given in German for each course. Plans for the future, if consummated, will allow dual credit to be assigned to both German and the discipline being studied. The instructor indicates that these courses are a step towards more truly interdisciplinary programs. He reports that in addition to these electives, students in individual study sometimes pursue interdisciplinary projects linking other subjects with the foreign language.

Elective programs

Bloomington Public Schools, Bloomington, Minnesota — Social

Studies in German. This course is currently being planned for the academic year 1971–72.

The University of Georgia – Survey of German History Since the Reformation. This course is open to history majors as well as upper level undergraduate and graduate German students. The target language is used most of the time, and students may assign the credit to either German or history.

College-level programs

Virginia Polytechnic Institute and State University – German for Architectural Application. The foreign language chairman and architecture professor initiated a course in German for architecture students. It was designed to prepare these students linguistically for a summer program in which they study in Germany. The instructor is the wife of a professor from the School of Architecture. The husband-and-wife team collaborate in the planning of the course, but many architecture professors assist by keeping the instructor informed of design projects that are assigned to the students. She then plans the instruction to accommodate the individual architecture assignments. The students may take as many as six quarters of German for Architectural Application. They begin using the language extensively from the first quarter. It is an elective, and approximately 50 students are enrolled each quarter. The credit is awarded in German. Not all students who take the course go to Germany.

Some pertinent questions related to interdisciplinary programs and activities

What follows is essentially a summary of the information about interdisciplinary programs and activities condensed from the literature and the survey results.

Who initiates interdisciplinary programs?

Usually it is the teacher who takes the initiative in starting interdisciplinary programs. Frequently a curriculum supervisor or coordinator assists the teacher, and in fact this individual sometimes originates the idea. On such occasions, the program is sometimes a part of a federally funded project. In at least three states (Delaware, Michigan, and Virginia), the state foreign language supervisor has had a major role in initiating or helping to plan interdisciplinary programs. One course was identified that had been started by a Fulbright curriculum specialist from South America. No evidence was discovered to indicate

Programs are teacher-stimulated

that students, without provocation, request interdisciplinary programs; but this perhaps does happen in some instances. Teachers occasionally ask students what they would like to study, and then the students play a major role in planning the course.

Who are the students?

Students engaged in interdisciplinary activities are found at every level of education, from the elementary school through the graduate school. At any level below the third year of high school modern language programs, however, interdisciplinary ventures are more likely to take the form of activities or lessons within more conventional courses of study. At that level or above, the trend seems to be in the direction of interdisciplinary courses or units of study within courses.

Students are found at all levels

More is being written about the upper-level programs. Perhaps this is because the change has been more abrupt at that level, in that interdisciplinary programs represent a more radical departure from the somewhat specialized literature programs characteristic of that level. At the lower levels of language instruction the content traditionally taught is broader in scope, and the changes are therefore perhaps more subtle.

Upper-level programs prevalent

The field of the classics is different from the modern languages in that several of its most innovative interdisciplinary programs are in the elementary school.

There appears to be no particular pattern as to the types of schools employing the interdisciplinary approach. The key as to which students have an opportunity to study a foreign language by the interdisciplinary system seems closely related to the presence of an alert, creative teacher sensitive to the need for curricular change and the interests of the students.

Key is the teacher

In approximately one-half of the courses reviewed in the literature and discovered through the survey, the students could select either the interdisciplinary program or a more conventional one. In the other instances, they had to pursue the interdisciplinary program if they were to continue in the sequence of language study.

What is studied?

In the modern languages, the social sciences seem to predominate. This is perhaps due to several factors. There is a natural affinity between the two disciplines. Both are humanistically oriented, and both are related to the cultural patterns and development of man. And perhaps language teachers are more likely to have pursued advanced studies in the social sciences than in mathematics, chemistry, or even art and music.

Variety, however, abounds. Architecture, the sciences, industrial arts, the fine arts, contemporary topics such as black literature, cooking, or virtually anything else found in the curriculum in English is being taught in foreign language classes.

The content of interdisciplinary Latin programs is somewhat more likely to be oriented towards humanistic studies although it is not restricted to this field.

What kinds of teaching materials are used in interdisciplinary programs and activities?

This has not been an easy problem for even the teachers planning courses to answer. Significantly, several of the survey respondents indicated that securing the appropriate teaching materials was their biggest difficulty. They often have to search widely to secure multiple items, which then have to be adapted, combined, and supplemented to suit the students and the course of study. Literary and civilization books still predominate in the textbook world, and few publishers have addressed themselves seriously to a market more comprehensive in scope but more limited in sales potential. Rarely, therefore, does one text seem to serve as the guide for the class. A variety of materials, many of which are teacher-made, is often used. College libraries, foreign publishers, importers of foreign books, and embassies are sometimes sources of materials for the interdisciplinary programs.

Materials are the biggest difficulty

It might seem easy to simply use texts from abroad. But often either the level of language proficiency or the level of development of the content or both are not compatible with American students' skills in the language and with their intellectual sophistication in the discipline to be studied.

What are some of the problems encountered in planning and conducting interdisciplinary programs and activities and how are they solved?

This question was addressed to the recipients of the survey, and much valuable information was submitted in response.

The problem of finding materials was mentioned with overwhelming frequency. To overcome this difficulty, it is usually necessary for the teacher to spend time seeking, adapting, and preparing a wide variety of materials from different fields which all are related to specific classroom objectives. That this task is a time-consuming one is understood. But the result of such a search may lead to more stimulating learning.

Simply breaking through the barriers of tradition was another difficulty pointed out. Administrators sometimes met the innovative teacher's ideas with skepticism. The teacher's persistence with a well-formulated plan seems to have been the answer in most cases, but it is impossible to estimate how many teachers did not succeed in arguing for the interdisciplinary class. The state foreign language supervisor helped in one case.

The barriers of tradition

On the other side of the coin, a supervisor respondent reported that overcoming the apathy of the teachers towards the need for interdisciplinary programs was a source of frustration. He indicated that patience and the strength of a good idea helped to win that battle.

Teacher apathy

Professional jealousy was identified as another cause of frustration by one teacher who needed to use equipment and facilities in another department. Whether or not jealousy was the most accurate choice of words might be open to question, but that it is difficult for teachers to begin working together after many years of being separated in the departmentalized curriculum is quite conceivable. The solution in this case was that another teacher from the other discipline came to the rescue of the foreign language teacher and served as a mediator between him and his adversary. Another individual with a similar problem sought to remove any possible professional threat that her program might have presented for the other department.

Professional jealousy

Some problems were reported concerning the assignment of credit. Generally these kinds of problems are more easily resolved than others.

Credit

One respondent to the questionnaire, a teacher, indicated that increasing students' comprehension and oral and written production of the foreign language was no particular problem but that improving *accuracy* in producing language was more demanding. He reinforced his basic classroom instruction with special laboratory exercises and started the practice of using the first five minutes of every class to have the students do oral and written exercises.

Student accuracy

The respondents, most of whom were teachers, would perhaps not be sensitive to the problem of identifying instructors with preparation adequate for work in more than one department. But in programs that are not initiated by teacher volition, this can be a task requiring much effort before solution. Often not only the competency of the instructor is of concern, but once the competent teacher is found, certification sometimes arises as another facet of the same problem (56).

What has been learned from the experience that has improved the program or will lead to changes in the future?

Taking general information from the results of the questionnaire, it is possible to make some useful generalizations. A French history teacher reported that she has learned to get the students to take an increasingly active part in class. Individual and group projects were done, reports were made to the class, and much discussion took place. The text became more of a background tool, and corollary readings that helped the students probe deeply have assumed more of their time.

Teacher reaction to interdisciplinary programs

Other history teachers indicated that originally the scope of the course was too ambitious. They proposed that less material be presented in order to permit more thoroughness of investigation.

Several respondents indicated that more time was needed for planning. Often it seems that the impetus of a good idea precipitated teachers headlong into an ambitious undertaking, and they then almost became overwhelmed by problems that they had not foreseen.

Some teachers are seeking more individualization within these programs.

Significantly, approximately a third of the respondents indicated that they saw no need for making significant changes in their present interdisciplinary programs in the future. One can only conjecture that numerous factors, both valid and unjustifiable, might contribute to this assessment.

Who is the teacher in an interdisciplinary program?

In almost every case, the interdisciplinary program was initiated and conducted by a foreign language teacher who had had training or experience in another subject to be integrated with the foreign language being taught. Many such teachers have gained at least a part of their language proficiency by extra-scholastic experience such as residence abroad. A few are natives.

Foreign language teacher with training in another subject

If enthusiasm and motivation help to qualify one for his job,

155

the interdisciplinary teachers perhaps possess an important advantage, for it is this enthusiasm that causes many of them to exert the considerable extra effort needed to plan and sustain them in conducting a challenging undertaking.

Occasionally in-service sessions have been held for teachers about to engage in interdisciplinary courses (Warriner, 56). These sessions were directed to the approaches and techniques of teaching a discipline, other than foreign language, in which the instructors had had little or no previous professional experience.

In-service sessions

Have interdisciplinary programs been evaluated?

Several of the courses in the studies reviewed were evaluated by experimental and control-group testing (Keitel, 25 and 26; Warriner, 56). No significant differences were discovered in most instances between experimental and control groups in either history or foreign languages. In other words, students in the interdisciplinary course gained as much as their peers in both history and the foreign language while expending essentially the time and effort needed for one course. On this basis, some have argued that credit should be awarded in both the foreign language and in the content area to students who are successful in interdisciplinary programs.

Objective evaluation

Subjective evaluation also seems favorable to interdisciplinary efforts. One teacher thought that the students could express themselves orally and in written form much better as a result of this kind of instruction. Another indicated that students displayed "heightened" interest in language study and the French people. She also thought that as a result they took their responsibilities toward the course willingly and seriously. Many teachers had sought student evaluations and had been highly encouraged by the results. Several teachers reported that the course objectives, such as developing a more positive attitude toward the peoples being studied, were achieved.

Subjective evaluation

One of the most convincing bits of evidence favoring interdisciplinary teaching comes from a school in which the students requested a second such course in preference to returning to the more conventional program in which they could have continued to study with the same instructor.

Some convincing evidence

College Entrance Examination Board scores were studied in one case in which students took these examinations during two consecutive years. The results were favorable.

Enrollment in some interdisciplinary courses increased voluntarily during the second year. This could indicate that students' attitude toward the class was favorable.

In the final analysis, it must be recognized that far too little is known about the true effectiveness of interdisciplinary programs. Much research needs to be done to assure students of quality instruction.

Conclusions and implications

1 It is evident that interdisciplinary activities and programs are not new to foreign language instruction. They are logical and inevitable, for language itself is primarily a tool that man uses to communicate with his peers about anything and everything that concerns him or gives him pleasure. Thus foreign language students have always been singing in German, telling time in Spanish, reading Virgil in Latin, and studying art in French.

2 It is apparent, however, to those acquainted with curricular trends in foreign languages that interdisciplinary activities and programs are becoming more numerous. Research confirms this trend.

3 The foreign language professor is being forced to change by his own recognition that instruction needs to be improved as well by the cry of the students and of the public for relevance.

4 Even though students currently exercise more influence over the curriculum than ever before, this review of interdisciplinary activities and programs suggests that the instructor still is assuming the lion's share of the initiative in deciding what is to be studied in foreign languages.

5 Proportionately more is appearing in the literature to advocate interdisciplinary activities and programs than is available to describe programs that are already functioning. This perhaps indicates that efforts to unite or interrelate portions of the fragmented curriculum are in the embryonic stages. A further assumption might be that today's proponents of interdisciplinary efforts are paving the way for increased studies of this type in the future.

6 At the present time, most interdisciplinary efforts appear to be found at the intermediate and advanced stages of language learning. More emphasis placed on this type of

learning at the early stages of instruction would perhaps enhance language learning at those levels. Carney (7) indicates that even ". . . FLES gained strength from being secondary, from attaching itself to the ongoing social studies activities of the elementary school." (The efforts, however, need not be confined to the social sciences.)

7 McMurrin (35) indicates that educators in recent years have been too concerned with methods and too little concerned with content. He proposes that more attention now be given to the substance of education.

8 Teachers are inclined to teach as they have been taught. Their own undergraduate and graduate foreign language education needs to be broadened in scope and unified in purpose to enable them to focus a coalition of resources on the problems of living that enter into their classroom instruction.

9 Appropriate instructional materials are lacking, a fact that, in many cases, impedes the efforts of the interdisciplinary curriculum planner. Materials that do exist are not readily accessible to the foreign language teacher and planner. As a result, time, effort, and money will have to be spent bringing such materials together.

10 Important questions need to be answered. For example, more needs to be known about the short- and long-term effects of interdisciplinary programs and activities upon students. Do they learn as much language? Do they learn as much of the discipline being studied? How does an interdisciplinary program affect their attitude towards foreign language study?

11 Efforts on behalf of interdisciplinary programs and activities are now being expended by too few foreign language teachers. The majority of students can benefit from such programs only when all teachers realize that any subject matter worthy of academic consideration is potentially a medium of and an incentive for foreign language instruction.

12 Any area of study or discipline worthy of consideration in one's native language is worthy of being studied in a foreign language.

13 Interdisciplinary activities and programs move foreign language instruction closer to bilingualism—its ultimate goal.

14 Interdisciplinary activities in foreign languages and in other fields suggest a healthy, vital sign for education, for they propel the fragmented academic world a step closer to the everyday world of problems needing solutions.

15 Interdisciplinary programs and activities are no panacea to the problems of language learning. They represent one small step in a positive direction towards making foreign language study more meaningful to more students.

References, Foreign language interdisciplinary programs and activities

1 Alden, Douglas W. "Report from Cassandra." *Association of Departments of Foreign Languages Bulletin* 2,iii(1971):25-27.
2 Behmer, Daniel E. "Many Languages—Many Voices; The BTU Program." *American Foreign Language Teacher* 1,ii(1970):47-48.[BTU-Bridges to Understanding.]
3 Benardo, Leo. *What It's All About:A Foreign Language Supervisor's Report*. Speech to the Secondary School Foreign Language Symposium, Bloomington, Indiana, 7 October 1969. [ERIC Document Reproduction Service: ED 039 822.]
4 Berg, M. Majella. *The First Five Years. A 1967 Recollection of the Experimental Liberal Arts Enrichment Program at Marymont College of Virginia*. [ERIC Document Reproduction Service: ED 039 822.]
5 Bottiglia, William F. "Humanities in French at M.I.T." *Modern Language Journal* 49(1965):354-58.
6 Brennan, Michael J. "On the Doctor of Arts Degree." *Association of Departments of Foreign Languages Bulletin* 1,iii(1970):52-55.
7 Carney, Helen K. "VOCAW and ECHO:Advertising Foreign Languages." *Foreign Language Annals* 4(1970):57-61.
8 Champlin, Marjorie W. *Classical Humanities for High School Students*. Speech at the Classical Institute, State University College at Buffalo, New York, 26 June 1970. [ERIC Document Reproduction Service: ED 042 384.]
9 Connor, W. Robert. "The New Classical Profession." *Association of Departments of Foreign Languages Bulletin* 2,iii(1971):25-27.
10 Corrin, Brownlee Sands,ed. "Content and Cross-roads:Wider Uses for Foreign Languages,"59-81 in Robert G. Mead,ed., *Language Teaching: Broader Contexts*. Reports of the Working Committees of the Northeast Conference on the Teaching of Foreign Languages. New York: Modern Language Association Materials Center, 1966.
11 Cullen, Arthur J. "A New Option for Foreign Language Students." *Association of Departments of Foreign Languages Bulletin* 3, ii(1970): 10-12.
12 "Curricular Innovations." *Association of Departments of Foreign Languages Bulletin* 2,i(1970): 37-42.

13 "The Doctor of Arts." *Association of Departments of Foreign Languages Bulletin* 2,iv(1970): 31-33.

14 "The Doctor of Arts Degree." *Association of Departments of Foreign Languages Bulletin* 2,i(1970):27-32.

15 "The Doctor of Arts in Modern Languages at Claremont Graduate School." *Association of Departments of Foreign Languages Bulletin* 2,iii(1971):25-27.

16 Egginton, Everett. "Inquiry and Foreign Language Teaching." *American Foreign Language Teacher* 1,ii(1970):21-23.

17 *Foreign Language Innovative Curricula Studies.* Summary Report, USOE 3-7-704431. Lansing, Michigan: Ann Arbor Public Schools, 1969. [ERIC Document Reproduction Service: ED 032 538.]

18 "The French in Delaware." Dover, Delaware: State Department of Public Instruction, 1971.

19 *German Curriculum Guide and Catalogue of Courses, 1971-1972.* Morgan Hill, California: Live Oak Union High School, n.d.

20 Goodlad, John I. "Directions of Curriculum Change," 162-66 in Edmund C. Short and George D. Marconnit,eds., *Contemporary Thought on Public School Curriculum.* Dubuque, Iowa: William C. Brown Company, 1968.

21 Grittner, Frank M. "A Critical Re-Examination of Methods and Materials." *Modern Language Journal* 53(1969):467-77.

22 Hocking, Elton. "The Schools Take Over Foreign Languages." *Journal of Secondary Education* 39(1964):243-50.

23 Hugot, François,ed. "Innovative Trends in Foreign Language Teaching," 90-141 in James W. Dodge,ed., *Leadership for Continuing Development.* Reports of the Working Committees of the Northeast Conference on the Teaching of Foreign Languages. New York: Modern Language Association Materials Center, 1971.

24 Jennings, Carol,et al. *L'Economie Française. Units in Economics for French Classes:Intermediate Level.* Minneapolis: Minneapolis Public Schools, 1967.

25 Keitel, Helmut A. "Development and Dissemination of Materials for the Teaching of World History in Foreign Language (German)." *Modern Language Journal* 54(1970):112-15.

26 —— *Development and Dissemination of Materials for the Teaching of World History in a Foreign Language (German).* Final Report. OEC 3-7-070210-2703. Sussex, Wisconsin: Hamilton School District 16. [ERIC Document Reproduction Service: ED 035 332.]

27 Keller, Charles. "A Case for the Humanities." Speech at the Humanities Day Project IMPACT of Southwest Iowa, Council Bluffs, Iowa, 8 June 1970.

28 Kersten, Caesar S., and Vesperella E. Ott. "How Relevant Is Your Foreign Language Program." *Modern Language Journal* 54(1970):9-13.

29 Ladd, Magdalena M. "Motivation Through Major Interests in Intermediate Foreign Language Learning." *Modern Language Journal* 54(1970):578-79.

30 Lange, Dale L. "Methodische Rundschau:The American Scene:The Use of Newspapers and Magazines in the Classroom." *Die Unterrichtspraxis* 2,ii(1969):148-53.

31 Lawson, John H. "Should Foreign Language Be Eliminated from the Curriculum?" 3-7 in James W. Dodge,ed., *The Case for Foreign Language Study.* New York: Modern Language Association Materials Center, 1971.

32 Lazzatti, John J. "Classics in the Humanities Movement." *American Foreign Language Teacher* 1,ii(1970):37-38.

33 Logan, Gerald E. "Curricula for Individualized Instruction," 133-155 in Dale L. Lange,ed., *Brittannica Review of Foreign Language Education, Volume 2.* Chicago: Encyclopaedia Britannica, Inc., 1970.

34 McClafferty, James,et al. *Foreign Language Innovative Curricula Studies.* End of Grant Report. Title III, ESEA, 1968-1969. OEG-3-7-704431-(056). Ann Arbor, Michigan: Ann Arbor Board of Education, 1969. [ERIC Document Reproduction Service: ED 035 327.]

35 McMurrin, Sterling M. "What Tasks for the Schools?" 79-83 in Edmund C. Short and George D. Marconnit,eds., *Contemporary Thought in Public School Curriculum.* Dubuque, Iowa: William C. Brown Company, 1968.

36 Masciantonio, Rudolph. "FLES Latin and Its Necessary Consequences on the Secondary School Program." *Bulletin of the Pennsylvania Classical Association* 27,iv(1969):11-12. [ERIC Document Reproduction Service: ED 030 354.]

37 —— "Innovative Classical Programs in the School District of Philadelphia." *Foreign Language Annals* 3(1970):592-95.

38 Material and Information from the Files of the Foreign Language Service of the State Department of Education, Richmond, Virginia. Information compiled in 1971 basically from the Questionnaire mentioned in the introduction to this chapter.

39 Meyer, James A. "Teaming a First Step for Interdisciplinary Teaching." *Clearing House* 43(1969):406-10.

40 Miel, Alice. "Reassessment of the Curriculum—Why?" 9-23 in Dwayne Huebner,ed., *A Reassessment of the Curriculum.* New York: Teachers College Press, 1964.

41 Nelson, Robert J., and Leon A. Jakobovits,eds. "Motivation in Modern Language Learning," 31-104 in Joseph A. Tursi,ed., *Foreign Languages and the "New" Student.* Reports of the Working Committees of the Northeast Conference. New York: Modern Language Association Materials Center, 1970.

42 Ort, Barbara A., and Dwight R. Smith,comps. "The Language Teacher Tours the Curriculum." *Foreign Language Annals* 3(1969):28-74.

43 "Outstanding Foreign Language Program." *American Foreign Language Teacher* 1,ii(1970): 14-17.

44 Phenix, Philip H. "The Disciplines as Curriculum Content," 59-65 in A. Harry Passow,ed.,

Curriculum Crossroads. New York: Teachers College Press, 1962.

45 Powers, James R.,ed. "Professional Responsibilities," 15-51 in James W. Dodge,ed., *Leadership for Continuing Development*. Reports of the Working Committees of the Northeast Conference on the Teaching of Foreign Languages. New York: Modern Language Association Materials Center, 1971.

46 Remak, Henry H.H. "Foreign Languages and Literatures in the Free Market Curriculum." *Association of Departments of Foreign Languages Bulletin*. 2,iii(1971):18-23.

47 Sadler, J.D. "Horticultural Classics." *The Classical Journal* 65(1970):267-69.

48 Sandstrom, Eleanor L., and Paul Pimsleur,eds. "Foreign Languages for All Students?" 105-33 in Joseph A. Tursi,ed., *Foreign Languages and the "New" Student*. Reports of the Working Committees of the Northeast Conference on the Teaching of Foreign Languages. New York: Modern Language Association Materials Center, 1970.

49 Secrest, Leigh. *The Rationale for Polydisciplinary Programs*. Address to the Ninth Annual Meeting of the Council of Graduate Schools in the U.S., Washington,D.C., 4-6 December 1969. [ERIC Document Reproduction Service: ED 037 151.]

50 Seelye, H. Ned. "Analysis and Teaching of the Cross-Cultural Context," 37-81 in Emma M. Birkmaier,ed., *Britannica Review of Foreign Language Education, Volume 1*. Chicago: Encyclopaedia Britannica, Inc., 1968[1969].

51 —— "Pertinency in Latin America Studies," 6-14 in *A Handbook on Latin America for Teachers:Methodology and Annotated Bibliography*. Springfield, Illinois: Office of the Superintendent of Public Instruction, 1968.

52 *Seminar in Language and Language Learning*. Papers presented at a Seminar in Language and Language Learning. Final Report. Seattle: Univ. of Washington, 1962. [ERIC Document Reproduction Service: ED 025 181.]

53 Strasheim, Lorraine A. "A Rationale for the Individualization and Personalization of Foreign Language Instruction," 15-34 in Dale L. Lange, ed., *Britannica Review of Foreign Language Education, Volume 2*. Chicago: Encyclopaedia Britannica, Inc., 1970.

54 —— "The Anvil or the Hammer:A Guest Editorial." *Foreign Language Annals* 4(1970):48-56.

55 Stratemeyer, Florence B., Hamden L. Forkner, Margaret G. McKim, and A. Harry Passow. "Varied Proposals of Scope, Sequence, and Organization," 297-306 in Edmund C. Short and George D. Marconnit,eds., *Contemporary Thought in Public School Curriculum Design*. Dubuque, Iowa: William C. Brown Company, 1968.

56 Warriner, Helen P. *The Effectiveness of the Use of Foreign Languages in Teaching Academic Subjects*. Richmond: Virginia State Department of Education, 1968.

57 Young, Nick. "Connecting Mythology and Astronomy." *American Foreign Language Teacher* 1,iii(1971):37-38.

6

Language learning processes

G. Richard Tucker
and
Alison d'Anglejan
McGill University

In this chapter, which has been written from a psychological rather than a pedagogical perspective, we focus our attention on the individual, and view the language learning process as an interaction between this individual, his genetic endowment, and instructional and sociocultural factors. We discuss current views of native-language acquisition, the similarities and differences between native and second (foreign) language learning; and then review, in more detail, recent research relevant to the language learning process. Finally, we describe briefly several areas for future research.

A psycholinguistic view of native-language acquisition

During the past 18 months, several introductory textbooks in psycholinguistics have appeared. This development is noteworthy, and we specifically wish to call these books to the attention of the reader because previously no comprehensive textbook had existed for this area – although several anthologies had appeared earlier. Blumenthal (6) and, to a lesser extent, Hörmann (33) provide a very useful historical perspective within which to read and evaluate the current psycholinguistic literature. Carol Chomsky (14) and Menyuk (47) describe in detail the results of their empirical studies of language acquisition by young English-speaking children; while Deese (20), Herriot (32), McNeill (46), and (most recently) Menyuk (48) attempt to present integrated accounts of the process of language acquisition and language behavior. Either McNeill (46) or Menyuk (48) would probably provide the most comprehensive and thorough introduction to the field for the language teacher.

Textbooks in psycholinguistics

The question of how a child acquires the ability to speak and understand his native language continues to be a central issue in the study of psycholinguistics. Until a decade ago researchers thought that the learning of language could be accounted for by

Child language development

the same principles that apply to any other learning situation. The major role in the child's language development was attributed to the mother, whose selective reinforcement of utterances appropriate to her own language was seen to bring about the emergence of the child's phonological, syntactic, and semantic systems. Child language was viewed as an impoverished or incomplete form of adult speech, which gradually emerged through a process of training or selective reinforcement into the "correct," systematic speech characteristic of the adult members of a given linguistic community. Such a theory seemed logical enough in view of the fact that the child's speech comes to resemble closely that of his immediate family and the sociocultural group in which he grows up. Thus, the single most important process involved in language acquisition was thought to be learning, with environmental factors providing the linguistic stimulus and shaping the child's responses.

Until recently environmental factors thought to be of utmost importance in child language

The authors of several recent textbooks in psycholinguistics present a contrasting theory of language acquisition. They shift the focus of attention away from learning and emphasize instead the concept of an innate biologically determined mechanism (Lenneberg, 44). During the last decade, Noam Chomsky's theory of transformational grammar (Chomsky, 15) has drawn the attention of researchers and language teachers to the highly creative nature of language and to the inability of learning theory to account for the fact that, by the age of five or six, children are able to produce and comprehend utterances that they have not previously encountered. He showed that there is an important distinction to be made between the child's linguistic performance and his linguistic competence (i.e., his inborn knowledge of the abstract universal aspects of language or deep structure). In fact, McNeill (46) proposes that the concept of a sentence may be a part of man's innate mental capacity and that it serves as the main guiding principle in a child's attempt to process the linguistic information to which he is exposed.

New approach to child language looks at biological factors

Both Shipley, Smith, & Gleitman (64) and Snow (66), however, present empirical evidence that suggests that parents provide their children with a more simplified sample of speech than was previously suspected. Their speech, biased toward simplicity, may provide them with a tractable input, which can serve as a basis for the hypothesis testing that will ultimately result in the development of more sophisticated linguistic skills. Macnamara (45) suggests that the role of meaning in language learning has

164

been neglected. He proposes that infants learn language initially by guessing, independent of language, the meaning that a speaker intends to convey to them and by working out the relationship between the meaning and the language.

The reexamination of child language in the light of transformational grammar has shown that it is highly systematic and that there is a natural order in the emergence of grammar. Certain rules that are shared by all languages are the first to emerge (e.g., all languages employ syllabic structure; all are characterized by grammatical categories such as noun, verb, and adjective). These are linguistic universals and arise from the child's innate knowledge of language. Other rules requiring more exposure to linguistic information emerge at later stages in the child's development. These developmental stages reflect changes in the child's method of expressing the underlying structure of language. Their onset is predictable and not immediately related to the linguistic input from the environment.

Child language highly systematic and natural

The extreme nativistic position that attributes an insignificant role to learning in the language acquisition process is challenged by Hebb, Lambert, & Tucker (31), who propose a more moderate view in which learning cooperates with heredity in the child's mastery of language. They stress the fact that it is inappropriate to attempt to classify language as either learned or innate. Like most other forms of human behavior, language is determined as much by the learner's heredity as it is by his environment. Experience plays an essential part in the development of any such cognitive process, but this in no way decreases the overriding importance of hereditary predispositions. Clearly the human child is born with a predisposition to talk and an innate capacity for auditory analysis. Certain consistencies and similarities in the early environment of children across cultures may account for much of the regularity of verbal development.

The nativistic position in regard to the development of child language is challenged

The relationship between language and cognition is reviewed in a monograph edited by Hayes (30) in which the language learning process is studied in relation to other facets of cognitive development. In his contribution to this monograph, Bever (5) draws a parallel between the child's ability to perform certain Piaget-type tasks and his ability to comprehend certain grammatical structures. He proposes that some aspects of linguistic structure that appear to be language universals may, in fact, be reflections of more general cognitive universals.

Although we will not attempt to review the rapidly expanding body of literature that deals with the acquisition of language by children from disadvantaged backgrounds, the recent work by Houston (34) and Williams (76) provides an excellent introduction to this area.

In conclusion, no definitive answer has yet been found to the question of how the child learns to speak and understand his native language. The extreme nativistic position that language is innate is unacceptable to the cognitive psychologists who attribute an important role to learning or environment in the language-acquisition process, and they suggest that language development must be examined in relationship to other areas of cognitive growth rather than in isolation.

No definitive answer as to how the child learns native language

Native-language acquisition and second (foreign) language learning: Analogous or different?

The language learning process, which we have described in the previous section, involves an interaction between various environmental and hereditary factors. As a starting point for the discussion to follow, consider the implications of two facts: (1) nearly all children, from diverse backgrounds, with different IQ's, and with various physiological limitations, do become fluent speakers of some code, and (2) nearly all children who first acquire one code but then move to a location where another is used very quickly become fluent speakers of the second (although, in fact, their parents may not). Observations such as these, together with recent developments in psycholinguistic research and theorizing, have led investigators to examine critically once again the nature of the relationship between the process of acquiring a native language and the process of second-language learning.

Language learning process

As one of their goals, many foreign- or second-language teaching programs during the past fifteen years have attempted to develop a functional communicative competence in their pupils. These programs have been characterized by an attempt to replicate, as closely as possible in the classroom, the conditions and environmental supports thought to be conducive to native-language acquisition. One of the implicit guiding principles seems to have been the tenet that the more closely foreign language pedagogy can be made to approach the natural conditions under which children acquire their mother tongue, the more successful the instruction will be. In all probability, this tenet is basical-

A goal of foreign language learning

166

ly correct. However, as we know, many language programs have achieved only limited success. This may be attributed, in part, to two factors: (1) our very limited (and in the early 1950s, probably incorrect) understanding of the way in which children learn to talk, and (2) the even more unsatisfactory attempts to reproduce in the classroom natural conditions conducive to language acquisition.

The results of empirical evidence and systematic observation during the last five years lead us to conclude that the processes of native-language acquisition and second- or foreign-language learning are essentially analogous; but that language teaching methodologies fail to exploit and, in fact, frequently ignore these similarities completely.

Native and foreign language learning processes are essentially analogous

This position has been discussed by Bocaz de Arriagada (7), Cook (17), Cooper (19), and Stern (68). Cook (17), in particular, argues cogently that there appears to be very little similarity between the process of first-language acquisition as we understand it today and the process of second-language learning that is implicit in today's teaching. As mentioned previously, recent research by developmental psycholinguists has suggested that there are regular patterns in a young child's speech that may be different from those that are found in the language of the adults in his community, and that the child, by formulating and testing a series of increasingly complex hypotheses, comes gradually to acquire both receptive and productive control of the language(s) to which he is exposed. Cook argues that present foreign language teaching relegates the goal of developing successful communication skills to a position subservient to the goal of immediately acquiring adult native-speaker syntactic and phonological competence in the target language. The student is usually not permitted to formulate and test gradually his own hypotheses regarding the target language. He is asked to learn language *qua* language and is not permitted to incidentally acquire a code during the normal process of growth or development.

The similarity is not apparent in foreign language teaching

As Cooper (19) has suggested, the processes of first- and second-language learning are probably analogous, although first- and second-language learners are by no means identical. He reiterates the position that language learning does not occur through habit formation, but argues that it could be facilitated by developing within the classroom various communicative contexts similar to those in nature that exploit the language learn-

Second-language learning could be facilitated by the development of communicative contexts

167

ing abilities of the student. This general argument is more completely developed by Fuller (27).

Bocaz de Arriagada (7) urges that teaching materials, particularly those dealing with phonology, should reflect the basic similarities between first- and second-language learning. Likewise, James (38) discusses the relationship between native- and second-language learning and assesses the role of the dialogue as a potential language-teaching device. The dialogue is viewed as important in that it can involve the learner in a variety of realistic social situations comparable to those experienced by the child acquiring his native language.

Teaching materials: teaching phonology and use of the dialogue

Stern (68), however, rightly cautions that all subsequent languages that are learned must be filtered, in part, "through the language acquisition device of an individual, [and] modified by his first language" (p. 64). This caution is also emphasized by Jakobovits (37), who notes that students are more advanced cognitively when they study a second language than when they acquire their first, and that they have already learned *how* to communicate via speech when they begin their second-language study.

Some cautions

By way of summary, Stern (68) suggests that we cannot expect prescriptive guidelines for second-language teaching from studies of native-language acquisition; but that attention should be directed toward the development of a general theory of language acquisition that takes into account problems of second-language learning as well as the other more traditional observations of native-language acquisition, verbal behavior, or speech pathology.

Bearing these ideas in mind, we have been impressed by recent developments in the area of "error analysis," and particularly with the work done by Richards (60,61). His work appears to complement and extend the more traditional "contrastive analysis" research that has recently been reviewed by Nemser & Slama-Cazacu (53) and by Wardhaugh (75). Richards (60,61) draws attention to the similarities between the "errors" (in the traditional pre-Chomsky view of language acquisition) made by young mother-tongue speakers of English and the errors made by adults from various ethnolinguistic backgrounds who are studying English as a second language. He distinguishes between *interlingual* errors (e.g., the difficulty that a native speaker of English studying Tagalog would be expected to encounter when he attempted to produce /ŋ/ in an initial position or that a

Error analysis and extending contrastive analysis

speaker of Cebuano might encounter when required to distinguish and use productively simple past, present, or future verb forms in English), which are predicted by contrastive analysis, and *intralingual* or developmental errors, which appear to be common to students of English as a foreign language sampled from many different backgrounds. He argues convincingly that the investigation of these developmental errors, such as overgeneralization, incomplete rule application, and the hypothesizing of false concepts, helps to illustrate some of the general characteristics of language acquisition and suggests a strategy for investigating the language learning process. Buteau (10) has applied these ideas and used this technique to investigate the study of French by English-speaking high school students. She found that errors could not be attributed to a single source, such as interference from English. Certain errors made by English-speaking students were also found to be made frequently by native speakers of French. Buteau suggests that there might be difficulties inherent in the language.

Hunt (35) suggests an intriguing research strategy to study empirically whether a child's control of second-language syntactic patterns develops in the same manner as his control of the patterns in his native language. For example, he observes that a native speaker of English presented with the information that:

A technique to study the development of second-language syntactic patterns

    1 aluminum comes from bauxite
    2 it is a metal
    3 it is an ore
    4 it looks like clay
    5 it is abundant
    6 it has many uses

will, at a certain stage, be able to combine the elements to produce the sentence, "Aluminum, an abundant metal with many uses, comes from bauxite, a clay-like ore." He suggests that this paradigm may be a useful research tool to examine the relationship between control of native- and second-language syntactic patterns, and wonders whether students from various language backgrounds would produce similar constructions at comparable periods in their training.

A project now being conducted by Swain (70) to investigate the simultaneous acquisition of French and English by a group of young children being raised bilingually in Quebec represents the most exciting and relevant research in this general area of the relationship between first- and second-language learning.

Simultaneous acquisition of French and English

She is asking whether their acquisition of English follows the normal pattern for that of monolingual English speakers and their acquisition of French that of monolingual French speakers, or whether there are developmental patterns and, by inference, processes that are unique to the child being raised bilingually. She plans to extend this basic study with an intensive longitudinal evaluation of first- and second-language development of children participating in bilingual education programs in Ontario. Systematic, controlled research of this type simply has not been carried out previously and should be given high priority.

In summary, we can argue that the processes of native- and second-language learning are similar; but that the teaching profession has not yet been able to take maximum advantage of these similarities in their teaching. We shall now review briefly some of the recent empirical research relevant to the process of second-language learning and teaching.

A psycholinguistic view of foreign language learning

We shall adopt as our working hypothesis for the discussion to follow the view that the goal for the student studying a foreign language should be to acquire "communicative competence" – a view that has been developed in detail by Campbell (11), Cooper (19), DiPietro (22), Edgerton (23), and Jakobovits (37). They stress the necessity for the individual to acquire both linguistic and sociolinguistic rules of the target language and culture, and they discuss the benefits that can accrue to someone who has mastered a second language.

Foreign language study for "communicative competence

Successful second-language learning results from the interaction among individual (or learner), instructional, and sociocultural factors. We will now review briefly the current research relevant to each of these three factors. With regard to individual characteristics, two demonstrably independent sources of influence affect language study: (1) aptitude and intellectual potential (e.g., a language-related measure such as IQ or the ability to perceive and mimic novel sound sequences), and (2) attitudes and motivational orientation toward the other group and their culture (e.g., an interest in sociocultural phenomena apart from language). Jakobovits (37), Lambert & Gardner (42), and Nelson & Jakobovits (52) discuss, in detail, and from slightly different

Interactive factors in second-language learning

perspectives, the relative contribution made by each variable to foreign language mastery.

The pioneering and most comprehensive research in this area has been carried out by Wallace E. Lambert and Robert C. Gardner. We are delighted to report that the book summarizing their work will be published before the end of this year (42). They have examined the roles of aptitude and attitude in predicting successful language learning in diverse settings where the language to be learned, French, was a second language, as in Quebec, or a foreign language, as in Maine and Louisiana. Their subjects were pupils at various stages in their formal language training. They found that a pupil's foreign language achievement could not be accurately predicted from knowledge of his linguistic aptitude, but that a more accurate prediction could be made by using information concerning his attitude toward the target language and its native speakers. The attitudinal component shows itself in at least two forms, an instrumental as well as an integrative orientation; and it is crucial for the language teacher to realize that various sociocultural factors can and do affect this attitudinal component. In addition, they replicated their North American research in the Philippines by using this same technique to examine the acquisition of English by Tagalog-speaking students.

The roles of aptitude and attitude

Complementary research carried out by Feenstra (24) documents the importance of the attitudes held by parents and teachers as well as by the students themselves in predicting second-language achievement. In a comprehensive series of studies, he examined pupils' aptitudes, their reasons for studying the language in question, the degree of effort that they spent in learning the language, their skill in various aspects of language achievement, and finally the attitudes of students, teachers, and parents towards the French-speaking community. Support for these findings, together with many practical illustrative examples from the classroom, has been provided by Smith (65).

Attitudes of parents, teachers, and students

Likewise, Spolsky (67) has examined the relationship among method of instruction, age of student, aptitude, and attitude toward the language being studied, and its native speakers in predicting the language proficiency of foreign students attending American universities. He found that their desire to identify with speakers of English rather than with speakers of their own native language was significantly related to their level of proficiency in English.

Interaction of several factors

Learning processes/Tucker and d'Anglejan

A recent and probably representative survey by Reinert (59) revealed that a majority of the foreign language students in Edmonds, Washington, were not at all integratively motivated to study a foreign language. They did so merely to fulfill a requirement. In view of the demonstrated importance of attitudinal factors on language success and the apparent ease of generalizing of Reinert's findings to other areas of North America, researchers and educators must begin to consider to what extent the attitudinal component can be modified once a student has acquired the prevailing stereotypes or expectations of his parents and his community.

Taylor, Guiora, Catford, & Lane (71,72) have examined the role of selected personality variables in language learning. They *Personality variables* have demonstrated that a student's ability to speak a second language authentically is related to his sensitivity to various cues in interpersonal situations. In separate studies, they asked university undergraduates and Defense Language Institute students to watch silent film clips and to note changes in people's facial expressions. All students then studied Japanese, a totally unfamiliar language to them, for four one-hour sessions. The investigators found that information about factors along what they called an "empathy dimension" enabled them to best predict accuracy of pronunciation. Their study represents one of the first attempts to predict quantitatively the influence of subtle variables such as sensitivity toward others and tolerance for anxiety.

The research related to the influences of aptitude and intellectual potential on language learning has already been summarized by Jakobovits (37), and by Nelson & Jakobovits (52). They discuss the importance of the following factors as predictors of *Important predictors of* success in foreign language learning: (*1*) IQ, which is reported *success in foreign language* to account for 15–20% of the variance; (2) aptitude, which con- *learning* tributes about 33%; (3) perseverance and motivation, contributing about 33%; and (4) instructional variables, which contribute less than 15%.

The evidence regarding the influence of sociocultural factors *Composition of the linguistic* on language mastery complements and extends that reported *community can affect langua* above. Previous research summarized by Jacobson (36), Lam- *study* bert & Gardner (42), and by Nelson & Jakobovits (52) has demonstrated that a student's orientation to language study can be affected by the ethnolinguistic composition of the larger linguistic community of which he is a member. Of even more relevance

172

for the present review, however, may be the demonstrated effects on pupils' performance of teachers' attitudes and expectations. Several recent investigations have directed the attention of educators toward the relationship between teachers' subjective biases and their evaluations of pupils (e.g., Frender, Brown, & Lambert, 26; Rosenthal & Jacobson, 62; and Seligman, Tucker, & Lambert, 63). The findings of these studies suggest that a teacher who is insensitive to local varieties of important world languages may reveal her personal bias first by denigrating the local variety actually used by certain of her pupils and also by evaluating negatively even the nonverbal performance of these pupils.

Teachers' attitudes and their relationship to evaluation of pupils

These findings and the demonstrated relationship between attitudinal factors and aptitude in predicting language success suggest that we again raise the question, To what extent can the attitudinal component be modified once the student has acquired the prevailing stereotypes or expectations of his parents and his community? There appear to be two alternative strategies: (1) intensive study of the target language, and (2) vicarious preparation. The first might take the form of an immersion program of instruction conducted mainly via the target language. Lambert, Just, & Segalowitz (41) and Tucker, Lambert, d'Anglejan, & Silny (74) suggest that English-Canadian children following a "home-school language switch" program of French instruction learn to read, write, speak, and understand English as well as carefully selected English counterparts who are schooled via English and that, in addition and at no apparent cost, they learn to read, write, speak, and understand French in a way that students of French as a second language never do. They also develop a more positive outlook toward French Canadians than do their peers in the community who have not had the benefit of this educational innovation.

How can prevailing student attitudes be modified?

The first alternative: an immersion program

The second alternative, that of vicarious preparation, could take the form of a systematic introduction to the other culture, its people and its values, before any formal language training is started. The immense potential of such a program remains to be tested. There are risks inherent, however, in setting up "vicarious preparation" programs. Two types of possible negative reactions are "secondary anomie" and the "echh phenomenon." The term *secondary anomie* refers to a student's dissatisfaction when he discovers, after having thoroughly prepared himself to study a language by prior vicarious immersion in the other cul-

The second alternative: vicarious preparation

173

ture, that he lacks even the most rudimentary skills needed for communication with members of the target group. For those planning language programs, there is a delicate balance involved; the inability to express himself may become a strong motivating force for one student, whereas for another it may result in a sense of despair and in rejection of language study altogether.

The *echh phenomenon* is a term to describe a student's disgust or shock when he is exposed, without adequate preparation, to certain novel values, traditions, or customs associated with a foreign people. For example, a group of elementary school pupils studying French in the U.S. exchanged letters, tape recordings, and slides with another group of French-speaking youngsters in Upper Volta (Jonas, 39). They learned through this exchange that many of the African children ate and even enjoyed eating grasshoppers; they also saw that the African youngsters typically had dirty feet. Their *first* reactions were negative not only toward those people whose language they were studying but also to blacks here in North America. In this example, American middle-class eating habits and values of cleanliness threw the attitudinal switch. It takes a gifted teacher to capitalize on such incidents and use them to advantage.

The basic research examining the interaction between individual and instructional factors has been adequately summarized by Jakobovits (37) and Nelson & Jakobovits (52, specifically pp. 36–62). For our purposes, the recent articles by Anthony (2) and Chastain (12) provide useful summary introductions to the main issues.

There appear to be *two major directions* to the recent research in this area: one line questions the theoretical framework within which language research has been carried out, and the other line evaluates the effects of various strategies for language teaching. In the former vein, O'Donnell (54) and Lamendella (43) both argue that pure linguistic research may be irrelevant to the process of language learning or teaching. They suggest that it is a mistake to expect transformational grammar or any other formal linguistic theory to provide practical suggestions for the language teacher; but that such research does have important implications for curriculum planners and specialists preparing materials (e.g., in suggesting sequencing of materials, the order of introduction of various grammatical structures, etc.). On the other hand, Kandiah (40) argues that the transforma-

The echh phenomenon *and an exchange program*

Directions for research concerning the interaction of the individual and instructional factors

tional model provides the teacher with an insightful way of looking at language, and possibly restores intellectual activity to a position of respectability in the classroom.

The important theoretical and practical issues are summarized in articles by Bosco (8) and Bosco & DiPietro (9), who state that there is a need for instructional tasks that are productive as well as informative and that are represented in the concrete experiences of the students. They argue that the language classroom should be an excellent laboratory in which to test various theories, but caution that the important everyday problems encountered by the classroom teacher are often not amenable to experimental manipulation. They draw attention to the fact that the teacher must maximize all instances of positive transfer between the native and target languages, present language in a multisensory manner, and stress the purposive character of language behavior. The proposals of these language teachers coincide extremely well with the ideas expressed by researchers Cooper (19) and Fuller (27), mentioned earlier in this chapter.

A need for productive and informative instructional tasks

Although Belasco (4) argues that the pedagogical philosophy of acquiring a foreign language in a monocultural American setting must, of necessity, emanate from the undergraduate foreign language classroom, we disagree with this position. In view of the demonstrated persistence of language maintenance efforts by many immigrant groups and the rapid spread of bilingual education programs described by Andersson & Boyer (1), we believe that the focus of attention regarding the processes of language learning and teaching will rapidly shift away from the university classroom.

Focus of attention away from the undergraduate foreign language classroom?

In a more pragmatic vein, Cooke (18), Desselmann (21), and Guthrie & Baldwin (29) examine the effects of different instructional techniques in language teaching. They contrast the effects of inductive versus deductive strategies, and the influence of verbalization on the internalization of correct hypotheses regarding appropriate language behavior. In general, concept formation appears to be facilitated by training on the application of verbalized rules rather than by simply discrimination or verbalization training alone. Politzer (57) introduced a novel approach to examining the characteristics of teaching behavior that seem to be related to good student performance. He found that the imaginative use of free-response drills and of teacher-prepared visual aids are related to high student achievement.

Effects of different instructional techniques

With regard to specific language teaching strategies, Chastain

(13) suggests that programmed materials can be prepared which better correspond to cognitive interpretations of learning, and Miller (49) has demonstrated that, contrary to many educators' predictions, programmed language instruction does not have a negative effect on student attitudes. Two slightly less conventional approaches have been described by Asher (3) and by Gauthier (28). Asher reports a series of studies examining the effectiveness of incorporating motor learning techniques into second-language teaching. He finds that motor learning has enormous resistance to extinction and that the combination of total physical response with language training can accelerate learning. Gauthier, on the other hand, reports success by dividing the language learning process into an extended comprehension period before he requires any type of formal oral production. He finds that optimal results are achieved by first encouraging passive aural comprehension, then conducting dual-language conversations, with the student answering in his mother tongue questions posed by the teacher in the target language, and finally encouraging spontaneous oral expression in the target language.

Specific language teaching strategies

As this brief review of the interaction between individual and instructional factors suggests, there is still little consensus regarding optimal classroom techniques.

Thus far, we have attempted to describe briefly the nature of the first- and second-language learning process, and we have suggested that foreign language learning results from an interaction between individual, instructional, and sociocultural factors. We believe that the product of a successful interaction will be an individual who can and *does* communicate in the target language. Furthermore, we agree with Campbell (11) that the individual who has truly learned to speak and understand a foreign language will have acquired the "competence of a native speaker" in that language. This statement, of course, implies that the student must be provided by the teacher with rules that will permit him to produce and interpret an infinite number of grammatical utterances that he has never before seen or heard in the classroom or in textbooks.

As social science researchers, we have been particularly interested to note, however, that educators no longer describe the acquisition of a language code in isolation as being a sufficient sign of successful language learning. Rather, they now appear to place emphasis on the acquisition by the student of "communicative competence" (cf., Cooper, 19; Jakobovits, 37; Oller,

Second-language learning emphasis is becoming more complete

55,56). By this they mean that the individual must also acquire the appropriate contextual or sociolinguistic cues to accompany his mastery of linguistic forms. This new emphasis, we feel, represents an important new dimension in language teaching—an emphasis that should generate a great deal of psycholinguistic and sociolinguistic research during the coming years.

This view of successful foreign language learning as involving the mastery of linguistic forms as well as the sociolinguistic rules of the target community raises for us the important question of whether successful foreign language learning can occur in the absence of a network of target-language speakers with whom to interact. Here it may be important to distinguish operationally the terms *foreign* and *second-language* learning. To us, the term *second language* implies that the code is a functional and viable one in the community where it is taught. Thus, the study of French by Anglophones in Quebec represents the attempt to acquire a second language; the study of Spanish in Quebec, a foreign language. In situations when a network of target-language speakers with whom students *could* interact does exist, the goal of complete language mastery is a realistic one. As Lambert, Just, & Segalowitz (41) have suggested, the questions that have typically been asked, "At what age should the second language be introduced? How many periods per week should be devoted to the study of the second language?" etc., have perhaps biased the thinking and planning of educators for too long. They suggest that in settings such as Montreal the new question, "How can we make our children bilingual?" is both relevant and answerable.

In settings where a network of target-language speakers does not exist, however, this same question becomes more urgent and the general answer *would appear* that we cannot make children bilingual; but imaginative solutions are being attempted. One of the most intriguing studies that we have examined is that described by Jonas (39). She began an intensive French foreign language program for elementary school pupils from Ohio. These pupils, who had essentially no native speakers of French in their community with whom to interact, exchanged letters, tape recordings, and slides with groups of French-speaking youngsters from France and from Upper Volta. The French language achievement of these children is now being compared with that of a control group of American students following the same French program who have not had the benefit of this

Successful foreign language learning

An imaginative solution to the question of bilingualism for children

unique experience. Should this innovative program succeed, the language learning activities of many thousands of American students could easily and inexpensively be made much more meaningful, resulting in far greater levels of achievement than with present techniques. Clearly, this represents an important area for future research.

Directions for future research

Finally, we would like to mention very briefly a few relatively unexplored, but potentially important, research areas. Moeser (50,51), in extending the earlier research by Reber (58) and Foss (25), has been investigating the acquisition by adults of minia- *Miniature linguistic systems* ture linguistic systems, commonly referred to as artificial languages. Using a miniature linguistic system, the researcher can control completely, or eliminate, effects attributable to type of instructional strategy, previous experience with the vocabulary and syntax, attitudes toward a language's native speakers, etc. Although the relevance of this technique for studying the acquisition of natural language remains to be demonstrated, the paradigm may be an attractive one.

During the decade of the 1960s, language researchers de- *Implications of recent* veloped a set of very precise and powerful descriptive and pre- *advances in linguistic theory* dictive tools. As psychologists looking in from outside, we view *for language learning* the recent advances in linguistic theory as similar in their potential impact to the development of the ideas of correlation and analysis of variance in psychology. We believe that one of the important new research directions will be the simultaneous study of the development of linguistic and other cognitive skills. The monograph by Hayes (30) contains the most recent and comprehensive collection of papers in this area. We recommend particularly the contributions by Clark (16) and Bever (5) to that volume.

The implications of such research will be extremely important *Implications of such research* for the language teacher. As Jakobovits (37) has pointed out, the *for the teacher* typical foreign language student brings a well-developed set of linguistic and cognitive skills with him to the classroom. The successful teacher must take maximum advantage of this existing framework. Streiff (69) describes a comprehensive English-language training program that has been developed for use with Navajo children. The program includes intensive and systematic development of the auditory, visual, and tactile modalities

178

through which linguistically sound language patterns are introduced and practised. We believe that this type of program represents an important but, as yet, relatively unexplored area for future research.

In conclusion, we suggest that members of the language teaching profession examine carefully the strengths and weaknesses of programs that make language learning an incidental by-product of regular classroom activity. Apparently successful immersion-type or bilingual education programs have been described by Andersson & Boyer (1); Lambert, Just, & Segalowitz (41); Terwilliger (73); and Tucker, Lambert, d'Anglejan, & Silny (74). In our view, these programs represent the most significant challenge of the decade to the language teaching profession.

Summary and conclusions

1 The question of how a child acquires the ability to speak and understand his native language continues to be a central issue in psycholinguistics.

2 This question cannot be answered with exclusive reference to traditional learning theory.

3 Some researchers have shifted the focus of attention away from learning, and emphasize the concept of an innate, biologically determined mechanism.

4 Recently, a more moderate view has been proposed in which learning is seen to cooperate with heredity in the child's acquisition of language.

5 The processes of native-language acquisition and second or foreign language learning are essentially analogous.

6 Language teaching methodologies often fail to exploit these similarities.

7 Two independent sources of influence affect success in language learning: aptitude and attitude.

8 Intensive language study or vicarious preparation are suggested as methods for modifying the student's attitude toward the target language or its native speakers.

9 Foreign language mastery involves the acquisition of communicative competence.

10 The student must acquire the appropriate contextual or sociolinguistic cues to acompany his mastery of linguistic forms.

11 The simultaneous study of the development of linguistic

179

and other cognitive skills represents an important new research direction.

12 The apparent success of immersion-type language teaching programs poses a significant challenge to the foreign language teaching profession.

References, Language learning processes

1 Andersson, Theodore, and Mildred Boyer, eds. *Bilingual Schooling in the United States.* Washington,D.C.: Government Printing Office, 1970.

2 Anthony, Edward M. "A 'Traditional' Linguistic Basis for Language Teaching." *TESOL Quarterly* 4(1970):3–16.

3 Asher, James J. "The Total Physical Response Technique of Learning." *Journal of Special Education* 3(1969):253–62.

4 Belasco, Simon. "C'est la guerre? Or Can Cognition and Verbal Behavior Co-Exist in Second-Language Learning." *Modern Language Journal* 54(1970):395–412.

5 Bever, Thomas G. "The Cognitive Basis for Linguistic Structures," 279–362 in John R. Hayes,ed., *Cognition and the Development of Language* New York: John Wiley and Sons, 1970.

6 Blumenthal, Arthur L. *Language and Psychology.* New York: John Wiley and Sons, 1970.

7 Bocaz de Arriagada, Aura. "Teaching English as a Foreign Language and Language Ontogeny." *English Teaching* (May 1970):n.p. [ERIC Document Reproduction Service: ED 040 395.] [*English Teaching* is a regular bulletin for teachers of English in Brazil.]

8 Bosco, Frederick J. "The Relevance of Recent Psychological Studies to TESOL." *TESOL Quarterly* 4(1970):73–88.

9 —— and Robert J. DiPietro. "Instructional Strategies:Their Psychological and Linguistic Bases." *International Review of Applied Linguistics in Language Teaching* 8(1970):1–19.

10 Buteau, Magdelhayne F. "Student's Errors and the Learning of French as a Second Language: A Pilot Study." *International Review of Applied Linguistics in Language Teaching* 8(1970): 133–45.

11 Campbell, Russell N. "An Evaluation and Comparison of Present Methods for Teaching English Grammar to Speakers of Other Languages." *TESOL Quarterly* 4(1970):37–48.

12 Chastain, Kenneth. "The Audiolingual Habit Theory Versus the Cognitive Code-Learning Theory:Some Theoretical Considerations." *International Review of Applied Linguistics in Language Teaching* 7(1969):97–106.

13 —— "Behavioristic and Cognitive Approaches in Programmed Instruction." *Language Learning* 20(1970):223–35.

14 Chomsky, Carol. *The Acquisition of Syntax in Children from 5 to 10.* Cambridge, Massachusetts: Massachusetts Institute of Technology Press, 1969.

15 Chomsky, Noam. *Syntactic Structures.* The Hague: Mouton, 1957.

16 Clark, Herbert H. "The Primitive Nature of Children's Relational Concepts," 269–78 in John R. Hayes,ed., *Cognition and the Development of Language.* New York: John Wiley and Sons, 1970.

17 Cook, Vivian J. "The Analogy Between First and Second Language Learning." *International Review of Applied Linguistics in Language Teaching* 7(1969):207–16.

18 Cooke, David A. "The Role of Explanation in Foreign Language Teaching." Research in progress. Toronto: Ontario Institute for Studies in Education, 1971.

19 Cooper, Robert L. "What Do We Learn When We Learn A Language?" *TESOL Quarterly* 4(1970): 303–14.

20 Deese, James. *Psycholinguistics.* Boston: Allyn and Bacon, 1970.

21 Desselmann, Günther. "The Consolidation of Grammatical Structures with the Help of Language Models." *Jezyki Szkole* 13(1969):209–19.

22 DiPietro, Robert J. "Student Competence and Performance in ESL." *TESOL Quarterly* 4(1970): 49–62.

23 Edgerton, Mills F. "A Philosophy for the Teacher of Foreign Languages." *Modern Language Journal* 15(1971):5–15.

24 Feenstra, Henry J. "Parent and Teacher At-

titudes:Their Role in Second-Language Acquisition." *Canadian Modern Language Review* 26(1969):5–13.

25 Foss, D.J. "An Analysis of Learning in a Miniature Linguistic System." *Journal of Experimental Psychology* 76(1968):450–59.

26 Frender, Robert, Bruce Brown, and Wallace E. Lambert. "The Role of Speech Characteristics in Scholastic Success." *Canadian Journal of Behavioral Science* 2(1970):229–306.

27 Fuller, Georgia W. "Classroom Application of Recent Linguistic Theory and Research." Unpublished manuscript, 22 May 1970.

28 Gauthier, Robert. "Tan-Gau–A Natural Method for Learning a Second Language." *Education* 4(n.d.):33–36.

29 Guthrie, John T., and Thelma L. Baldwin. "Effects of Discrimination, Grammatical Rules, and Application of Grammatical Concepts." *Journal of Educational Psychology* 61(1970):358–64.

30 Hayes, John R.,ed. *Cognition and the Development of Language.* New York: John Wiley and Sons, 1970.

31 Hebb, Donald O., Wallace E. Lambert, and G. Richard Tucker. "Language, Thought and Experience." *Modern Language Journal* 55(1971):212–22.

32 Herriot, Peter. *Introduction to the Psychology of Language.* London: Methuen, 1970.

33 Hörmann, Heinz. *Psycholinguistics:An Introduction to Research and Theory.* Berlin: Springer-Verlag, 1971.

34 Houston, Susan H. "A Reexamination of Some Assumptions About the Language of Disadvantaged Children." *Child Development* 41(1970):947–63.

35 Hunt, Kellogg W. "Do Sentences in the Second Language Grow Like Those in the First?" *TESOL Quarterly* 4(1970):195–202.

36 Jacobson, Rodolfo. "The Teaching of English to Speakers of Other Languages and/or Dialects—An Oversimplification." *TESOL Quarterly* 4(1970):241–53.

37 Jakobovits, Leon A. *Foreign Language Learning:A Psycholinguistic Analysis of the Issues.* Rowley, Massachusetts: Newbury House, 1970.

38 James, Carl. "The Applied Linguistics of Pedagogic Dialogues." *Language Learning* 20(1970):45–54.

39 Jonas, Sister Ruth. *A Matched Classroom Approach to the Teaching of French in the Elementary Grades.* U.S. Office of Education, Contract OEC-3-061944-1891, continuing 1971. Cincinnati: College of Mount St. Joseph on the Ohio, 1966–71. [A five year project.]

40 Kandiah, T. "The Transformational Challenge and the Teacher of English." *Language Learning* 20(1970):151–82.

41 Lambert, Wallace E., Marcel Just, and Norman Segalowitz. "Some Cognitive Consequences of Following the Curricula of Grades One and Two in a Foreign Language," 229–79 in James A. Alatis,ed., *Report of the 21st Annual Round Table Meeting on Linguistics and Language Study.* Georgetown Univ. Monograph Series on Languages and Linguistics, Volume 23. Washington,D.C.: Georgetown Univ. Press, 1970.

42 Lambert, Wallace E., and Robert C. Gardner. *Attitudes and Motivation in Second Language Learning.* Rowley, Massachusetts: Newbury House, 1971. [In press.]

43 Lamendella, John T. "On the Irrelevance of Transformational Grammar to Second Language Pedagogy." *Language Learning* 19(1969):255–70.

44 Lenneberg, Eric. *Biological Foundations of Language.* New York: John Wiley and Sons, 1967.

45 Macnamara, John. *The Primacy of Semantics in Language Learning Among Infants.* Montreal: McGill University, 1970. [Mimeograph.]

46 McNeill, David. *The Acquisition of Language:A Study of Developmental Psycholinguistics.* New York: Harper & Row, 1970.

47 Menyuk, Paula. *Sentences Children Use.* Cambridge, Massachusetts: Massachusetts Institute of Technology Press, 1969.

48 ——— *The Acquisition and Development of Language.* Englewood Cliffs, New Jersey: Prentice-Hall, 1971.

49 Miller, Richard I. "A Study of Student Attitudes and Motivation in a Collegiate French Course Using Programmed Language Instruction." *International Review of Applied Linguistics in Language Teaching* (1971):In press.

50 Moeser, Shannon. "Learning of a Miniature Linguistic System:Effects of External Referents and Order of Word Classes." Unpublished M.A. thesis. Montreal: McGill University, 1969.

51 ——— "The Effects of Semantic Referents on the Learning of Syntax." Ph.D. dissertation in progress. Montreal: McGill University, 1971.

52 Nelson, Robert J., and Leon A. Jakobovits,eds. "Motivation in Foreign Language Learning," 31–104 in Joseph A. Tursi,ed., *Foreign Languages and the "New" Student.* Reports of the Working Committees of the Northeast Conference on the Teaching of Foreign Languages. New York: Modern Language Association Materials Center, 1970.

53 Nemser, William, and Tatiana Slama-Cazacu. "A Contribution to Contrastive Linguistics." *Revue Roumaine de Linguistique* 15(1970):101–28.

54 O'Donnell, R.C. "Does Research in Linguistics Have Practical Applications?" *English Journal* 59(1970):410–12, 420.

55 Oller, John W. "Language Communication and Second Language Learning." Paper presented at the Second International Congress of Applied Linguistics. Cambridge, England, 1969.

56 ——— "Transformational Theory and Pragmatics." *Modern Language Journal* 54(1970):504–07.

57 Politzer, Robert L. "Some Reflections on Good and Bad Language Teaching Behavior." *Language Learning* 20(1970):31–43.

58 Reber, Arthur S. "Implicit Learning of Artificial Grammars." *Journal of Verbal Learning and Verbal Behavior* 6(1967):855–63.

59 Reinert, Harry. "Student Attitudes Toward Foreign Language—No Sale." *Modern Language Journal* 54(1970):107–12.

60 Richards, Jack C. "A Non-Contrastive Approach to Error Analysis." Paper presented at the TESOL Convention. San Francisco, 1970.

61 ——— "Error Analysis and Second Language Strategies." *Language Sciences* (1971):In press.

62 Rosenthal, Robert, and Lenore Jacobson. *Pygmalion in the Classroom.* New York: Holt, Rinehart and Winston, 1968.

63 Seligman, Clive R., G. Richard Tucker, and Wallace E. Lambert. "The Effects of Speech Style and Other Attributes on Teachers' Attitudes Toward Pupils." *Language in Society* (1971):In press.

64 Shipley, Elizabeth F., Carlota S. Smith, and Lila R. Gleitman. "A Study of the Acquisition of Language:Free Responses to Commands." *Language* 45(1969):322–42.

65 Smith, Alfred N. "The Importance of Attitude in Foreign Language Teaching." *Modern Language Journal* 55(1971):82–88.

66 Snow, Catherine E. "Language Acquisition and Mothers' Speech." Unpublished Ph.D. Dissertation. Montreal: McGill University, 1971.

67 Spolsky, Bernard. "Attitudinal Aspects of Second Language Learning." *Language Learning* 19(1969):271–85.

68 Stern, H.H. "First and Second Language Acquisition," 57–66 in H.H. Stern,ed., *Perspectives on Second Language Teaching.* Modern Language Center Publications, Number 1. Toronto: The Ontario Institute for Studies in Education, 1970.

69 Streiff, Paul. *The CITE Curriculum Rationale.* Presentation at New Schools Using CITE Materials on the Navajo Reservation. Los Angeles: University of California at Los Angeles, 1970. [Mimeograph.] [CITE-Consultants in Total Education.]

70 Swain, Merrill. "Bilingualism as a First Language." Ph.D. dissertation in progress. Irvine: University of California, 1971.

71 Taylor, Linda L., Alexander Z. Guiora, J.C. Catford, and Harlan L. Lane. "The Role of Personality Variables in Second Language Behavior." *Comprehensive Psychiatry* 10(1969):463–74.

72 ——— "Psychological Variables and Ability to Pronounce a Second Language." *Language and Speech* (1970):In press.

73 Terwilliger, Ronald I. "Multi-grade Proficiency Groupings for Foreign Language Instruction." *Modern Language Journal* 54(1970):331–33.

74 Tucker, G. Richard, Wallace E. Lambert, Alison d'Anglejan, and F. Silny. "Cognitive and Attitudinal Consequences of Following the Curricula of the First Four Grades in a Second Language." Paper presented at TESOL Convention. New Orleans, 1971.

75 Wardhaugh, Ronald. "The Contrastive Analysis Hypothesis." *TESOL Quarterly* 4(1970):123–130.

76 Williams, Frederick,ed. *Language and Poverty: Perspectives on a Theme.* Chicago: Markham, 1970.

7

Instructional strategies in foreign language learning and teaching

Introduction

Alan Garfinkel

Oklahoma State University

Considerable time and effort has gone into the development of a specific definition of *instructional strategies* for the purpose of research in education. Seifman (177) quotes a curriculum guide written by Taba that defines an instructional strategy as "a pattern and a sequence of teacher behaviors designed to accommodate all important variables consciously and systematically." The reader may prefer Lange's (114) more succinct phraseology that describes them as "classroom procedures or techniques." By whatever definition, the subject at hand is that which teachers and foreign language curriculum specialists do in the classroom to enhance student achievement in the study of a second language.

Definition of instructional strategies

The purpose of this chapter is to examine foreign language education in terms of four elements related to classroom instruction: the public image of language instruction, texts and teaching materials, instructional strategies, and professional resources. It is the writer's intention to provide a significant amount of practical information that will be of use to as large a number of teachers as possible.

Purpose of the chapter

In accordance with the theme of this volume, it will be the teacher's responsibility to accept any of the ideas presented here. As Harnack (86) points out, the teacher is the final decision-maker with regard to which instructional strategies he will employ. Pluralism in language teaching advises the teacher that there is no panacea for language learning problems, that each teacher is different as surely as each student is different, and that any instructional strategy may be the one suited to a particular academic situation.

The coverage of the present chapter is limited almost exclusively to items appearing in 1970. Exceptions have been made for several foreign items, which are, of necessity, slower in coming to the reader's attention. The reader who is interested in earlier materials is referred to the works of Smith (184), Jarvis (100), and Lange (114). More recent materials can be found in

183

current issues of the journals listed in the Master List of the ACTFL Bibliography (Lange, 115). Other sources include Carroll's chapters in the *Encyclopedia of Educational Research* (40) and the *Handbook of Research on Teaching* (39), as well as the Nostrand bibliography (143), Chastain's chapter in *The Teacher's Handbook* (43), *Language-Teaching Abstracts* (117), *CIJE* (48), and the lists of selected ERIC documents (Mildenberger & Mazzeo, 133; Monka, 137) that appear in *Foreign Language Annals*. (See *Foreign Language Annals* 4(1970):203, 306–11 for a complete explanation of ERIC.)

The public image of language instruction

Since any profession is dependent, to a certain extent, on its public image for an indication of its success and failure, it seems appropriate to begin this examination of the state of the art with some indication of the kind of public image that foreign language instruction has generated during the past year. The medium selected for this investigation is the *New York Times*, a meticulously indexed newspaper of sufficient comprehensiveness, frequency of publication, and range of distribution to be considered a national publication. The stories that appeared in it as the year ran its course are a sampling of the press notices the profession received during 1970.

Public image: New York Times

A professional group, the American Association for the Advancement of Slavic Studies, received the first *Times* coverage of the year in the context of a speech before that group by Shulman (145). In opposition to budget cuts in federal programs for Slavic studies, he called attention to the difference between the cost of the entire federally funded Slavic studies program ($18 million) and of only 2 of the 547 F-111 fighter planes ($32 million). The public needs to have comparisons like this brought to its attention, especially under the auspices of a professional language teachers' association.

Opposition to budget cuts for Slavic studies

Language teaching received unexpected support from the Presidential Commission on the Bicentennial of the American Revolution, which urged that "all Americans start now to learn at least one foreign language, looking forward to many more visitors from abroad" (22).

A discouraging article appeared on August 23 (Malcolm, 123) in the *Times*. In a most unsympathetic context, it spoke of language learning as irrelevant, of sagging enrollments, and of inflexible methodologies. One was left with the impression that the language teaching profession is in a sorely depressed shape and that its leading professional associations are powerless to help. Even the most confirmed pessimists of our field might find it difficult to have a drearier outlook. Brooks (31) came to the rescue with a letter to the editor. He replied to an earlier editorial that had lamented the "facts" presented on August 23 but had ended with the following statement: "To call irrelevant what is merely difficult is the road to intellectual as well as national decay" (61). Brooks thanked the *Times* for its kind words and pointed out some things that were overlooked in the *Times* editorial and the article on which it was based. Brooks is to be commended for standing up in defense of the profession. However, it is unfortunate that, journalistically speaking, he stood alone.

Foreign language learning irrelevant?

The teaching of English as a second language received favorable publicity on August 28 (97) in an article that described the use of cameras to enable Havasupai Indian children to make their own conversation stimuli by taking pictures of things they wanted to talk about.

English as a second language

The year of *New York Times* coverage closed with the beginning of another series of articles and counter-articles on whether or not the New School for Social Research of New York should teach a nonstandard dialect of Spanish (along with standard ones) under the name of Spanglish (186).

The public image of foreign language instruction is by no means entirely negative. But the profession does face some problems in making the relevance of language study more widely understood and appreciated. There is a discrepancy between the enthusiasm reflected in the great number of innovative programs of instruction reported below and the reporting by the media on the progress in language instruction. Teachers, leaders in the field, and professional language teachers' associations would be well-advised to attempt to remedy this situation.

Problems of image

Texts and teaching materials

The purpose of this section is to identify and evaluate some of the year's texts and teaching materials that appear to have a strong potential for affecting instructional strategies. This limited approach to a review of the year's materials may be explained by the fact that the information explosion, evident in all fields in recent years, is undiminished in our own. Thus, it is improbable

Identify and evaluate materials

185

that a single language teacher would be aware of all materials produced for all levels and languages in even a single year. Two problems complicate the situation: (1) it is difficult for the teacher to be aware of materials at levels other than the one he may teach, and (2) no single source exists that classifies and evaluates language teaching materials. So, no claim of completeness is made for this section. The reader who requires a more comprehensive presentation of materials is referred to the long-out-of-date MLA *Selective List of Materials* (Ollman 144), to Smith's discussion of 1969 materials (184), and to the advertising and review columns of recent issues of language-teaching journals.

French materials with a potential for affecting instructional strategies seem to have been the most numerous in 1970. We turn first to them and subsequently to materials for other languages.

C'est la vie: Lectures d' aujourd'hui is the title of a fascinating second-language reader by Pimsleur (153). The book's 37 readings are short and of strictly controlled difficulty. The length of each reading passage ranges from 65 to 656 words. Here the student has materials that put Scherer's (174) description of progressive second-language reading into classroom practice. The readings come from newspapers, magazines, and other sources. Their subjects range from advice to the lovelorn to camping, and from horoscopes to Napoleon, literature, and smoking. English is avoided in the text. Meaning is made clear by various devices, ranging from marginal drawings to French synonyms. There is a French-to-English glossary, unusual in that it lists conjugated forms of verbs and irregular noun plurals. Exercises with each reading are superior models for methodology courses because they utilize a variety of tasks, including definitions and transformations.

Of similar style and interest is *La dynamite* (Campbell & Bauer, 36), which presents new vocabulary by means of French definitions and drawings, and which provides for reentry of the items in the exercises following the reading selection.

The teacher in search of inventive materials will also be impressed by a current series of books dealing with the day-to-day life of Frenchmen in various occupations. One of them details the life of an automobile salesman (Roe, 163).

A series of thirteen 16-mm. color films entitled *Toute la bande* (200) is the latest addition to the Scholastic Publications cata-

French materials

Outstanding readers

logue. The films are supported by printed materials and are sure to be of intense interest to young French students. The films' soundtracks include music with an attractive, modern beat, and the plots are "slices of life," acted by what appear to be real students. Boys, girls, and their various flirtations are given ample attention. *Toute la bande* is a charming supplement. Unfortunately, films are an expensive medium, and not all schools will be able to own this set. It is hoped that enough university audiovisual libraries will acquire the set of films to make it available by rental to a large number of high school classes.

Film series supplements

Another multimedia set, *En avant* (64), was recently released in the United States. It is well-known in Britain as the materials used in experiments funded by the Nuffield Foundation (Kellerman, 105).

Smith (184) discussed the methodology associated with Lenard's new materials *Jeunes voix, jeunes visages* (118). The reader's attention is being called here to the excellent teacher's edition (Lenard, 119) and other elements supplied with these materials. Among these are workbooks and text pamphlets. A visual element is provided by means of filmstrips, which have not been distributed as of this writing. An examination of the teacher's edition is indicative of the author's classroom expertise. Notes placed between the exercises anticipate likely errors and show ways to prevent them while, at the same time, facilitating comprehension. By varying the commonly accepted order of reading before writing (while preserving that of listening before speaking), the "verbal-active method" espoused by the author is unusual. The profession would be well-advised to experiment with these materials. They may have strong potential for affecting classroom instructional strategies.

New materials using the "verbal-active method"

Encyclopaedia Britannica Films (Rosselot, Wood, Favrod, & Wilgocki, 165) has released a new edition of its multimedia text, *Je Parle Français*. New films were made to update the visual elements of the series, and rewriting of the printed segments has also been completed. The films are the basic presentation mode of the text, and they are, therefore, the medium through which French is understood. Filmstrips are also used to support classroom drills. A few years ago, this series and perhaps one other were the only ones to use the visual element extensively. Now, other publishers are using the visual element and the next several years will probably see many more publishers developing this vital element of language instruction.

A film-text course

The outlook for French materials in the future is even brighter. It is likely that, among others already released, *La clef* (de Petra & de Petra, 52) and *La France en direct* (Capelle & Capelle, 37) will attract considerable attention.

Spanish materials

The year's production of Spanish materials was less innovative than that of French. Unfortunately, too many of the year's Spanish texts bring to mind a stereotype that includes a visual element limited to a single photograph that does double duty as a cultural element and a single vehicle for comprehension (usually translation alone) and a long reading section of uncontrolled difficulty and low interest, accompanied by a series of unvaried exercises.

One of the exceptions to this stereotype is a book by Lado & Woodford (111). Although it has long and difficult reading selections that lack visual support, the grammatical drills are exceptionally fine because they focus on usage as well as on form. This is clearly one of the more usable Spanish texts published in 1970.

Smith (184) has reviewed other exceptions to the stereotype, including A-LM Materials (Kaminar de Mujica & Segreda, 103) and Wolfe's book, *Curso básico de español* (215) for the first-year college course. Some new materials in preparation possess potential for being successful. *Spanish for Communication* (Dellacio et al., 51), for one, promises to be a text with attention paid to cognitive theory and individualization, without ignoring communication.

German materials

Among the many interesting German materials published in 1970 are some imported directly from Germany. A multimedia set entitled *Auf Deutsch, bitte* was published in Munich by Hueber (Schulz, Griesbach, & Lund, 176). Circulars describing the text indicate that it has a strong visual element.

Also published in Germany is *Deutsch als Fremdsprache* (Braun, Nieder, & Schmöe, 30). Published by Klett in Stuttgart, their series has three levels. The medium for the visual element at each level is a set of slides.

A number of interesting readers are also being made available. Since classes with interdisciplinary elements are becoming more and more widely accepted, *Mensch und Welt: An Elementary Science Reader* (Dyck & Schwarz, 60) will probably meet with enthusiastic acceptance. *Was wollen die Deutschen? 21 Zeitgenossen* (Drath, 58) features interviews with contemporary Germans such as Chancellor Willy Brandt.

Logan (122) is now writing what may be the coming year's most exciting German materials. They are the types of materials used in his own individualized classes.

The Southwest Cooperative Educational Laboratory (SWCEL) (188) published its materials for the teaching of English as a second language in 1970. Each segment has specific behavioral objectives and a systematic program for achieving them. An extensive in-service teacher-training program is part of the materials. Such a program reflects confidence in the materials and assures one that teachers will understand the author's intentions.

Materials for English as a second language

Commercially published materials in Latin and Russian were not numerous during 1970. The reader's attention is called to the teacher-made materials reported in the following section.

Classroom strategies

This section provides descriptions of instructional strategies reported in 1970. The reports of strategies presented came from several sources: (*1*) manual and computerized searches of the ERIC files; (2) library materials devoted to language teaching; (3) a questionnaire (Figure 1) to approximately 1200 state coordinators, local supervisors, and department heads to uncover reports of programs not mentioned in the literature.

The following limiting criteria were used to make a report of manageable size:

Criteria for inclusion

1 Each item cited refers directly to some aspect of teacher or coordinator classroom behavior.
2 The discussion presented below is generally limited to instructional strategies reported during 1970.
3 An effort was made to avoid repetition. Where two or more very similar strategies were reported, only one was listed. On the other hand, special attention was given to those that seemed particularly innovative, in order that they might receive wider recognition.
4 While a few programs involving interdisciplinary activities and individualization are cited, the reader is referred to the chapters in this volume by Warriner (Chapter 5) and Gougher (Chapter 8) for more numerous and detailed descriptions of such activities.

Four subsections in this part of the chapter are assigned to instructional strategies aimed at the development of the stu-

```
┌─────────────────────────────────────────────────────────────┐
│              REPORT FORM – BRITANNICA REVIEW                  │
│                       (BRFLE 3)                              │
│                                                              │
│              SECTION ON METHODS AS REFLECTED                  │
│                  IN CLASSROOM PRACTICES                       │
│                                                              │
│                   Deadline: April 1, 1971                    │
│                                                              │
│     (Please use this form and/or an expendable copy of your report.) │
│                                                              │
│    I. Title of your project:                                 │
│                                                              │
│   II. Objectives (What purposes did it have?):               │
│                                                              │
│                                                              │
│                                                              │
│  III. Materials (What kinds of materials were involved?):    │
│                                                              │
│                                                              │
│   IV. Methods (What procedures were involved?):              │
│                                                              │
│                                                              │
│                                                              │
│    V. Evaluation (Was there any kind of evaluation – empirical or other – │
│       involved? What conclusions were reached?):             │
│                                                              │
│                                                              │
│                                                              │
│  Source of Information (name of person                       │
│  who did the above work) _____     │
│                                                              │
│  School _____ Address _____    │
│                                                              │
│  Are copies of your work available? _____ Please list address │
│  if different from above.                                    │
└─────────────────────────────────────────────────────────────┘
```

Figure 1. Report form

dent's ability to listen, speak, read, and write a foreign language. A fifth subsection presents reports that deal with more than one skill and with curriculum improvement of a somewhat more general nature.

Listening

A recent news article (Wagner, 208) described the work of Nelson and others at the University of Illinois who have arranged to make shortwave radio newscasts in French readily available to college students of French. By having recordings fed into their remote dial-access language laboratory equipment, the students may listen to a newscast that is only six hours old, Mondays through Fridays on a 24-hour basis. Since the equip-

Shortwave radio

190

ment may be dialed from any telephone anywhere, a French teacher, lacking his own shortwave equipment, could arrange to record the broadcast from his telephone during the school year for the price of a long distance call to 217-333-6301. Since phone rates are low at night, this might prove to be an inexpensive source for some exciting new listening material.

Garnier (73) reports having given "the student an eye and an ear in foreign language class" with the use of a flannel board, while Mengler (130) provides step-by-step recipes for use of the flannel board. Tucker (201) has found that the felt-backed flannel board pictures will adhere to a piece of styrofoam which measures approximately $18 \times 24 \times \frac{1}{2}$ in. The styrofoam is very light in weight and is easily carried around a classroom. *Flannel board*

Films are increasingly being used as media for showing cultural patterns as they present listening materials, according to Decock (50), who mentions films and film sources for the French class. English (65) describes the work of Richard J. Blakely, a French instructor at the University of California at Santa Barbara. Blakely shows an entire film, then repeats isolated scenes for work with listening and speaking. According to *Audio-Visual Language Journal* (168), the Russian section of the Language Center at the University of Essex (Colchester, Essex, United Kingdom) offers free loan of two short elementary Russian films, along with scripts and suggestions for use. The films were made in the U.S.S.R. Michalski (132) is another who has reported on the use of films for listening and as a vehicle for culturally oriented lessons. He uses television news film from Germany. *Films*

Anyone who has observed FLES or junior high school language teachers at work knows that they frequently make several presentations per day. Stough et al. (194) report having made video tapes of basic presentations in order to allow each class during the day to get the same quality of listening material. Presumably, the tapes free the teacher to do a better job of listening to student responses. *Video tapes*

Graduate assistants at Duke University help in basic French courses by conversing in class with the teacher. Tate (198) reports that this arrangement gives classes a chance to listen to a native-like conversation.

Walker (209) in creating her own materials in Russian has especially concentrated on the development of materials for listening. She says: "Listening is our first priority in teaching."

Bockman (24, 25) compared achievement in listening in

191

groups using programmed materials on an independent study basis and those using conventional materials in class study. There were no significant differences between the groups given equal exposure to the different strategies. The results, therefore, indicate that programmed materials for listening may be as effective as conventional materials used in a classroom to develop listening comprehension.

Listening in independent study

Speaking

The literature for 1970 seems to indicate less concentration on the development of the listening skill than in the development of the speaking skill. Generally, the learning of a second language requires an American teacher of foreign language to do what he can to create an environment in which the student will be motivated to speak. It is not often that foreign language teachers and learners have the advantage of being but minutes away from an area where the second language is spoken as a matter of course. Yet there are opportunities where such situations exist. Silberman (181) makes special note of the parkway project in Philadelphia where he reports that Spanish classes are two and one half hours long and that, during part of each class, students are free to go to the Spanish-speaking area of town and converse with storekeepers and other Spanish-speaking citizens. Another example of direct language contact is noted by Hinojosa-Smith (93) of Texas A & I University, who reports having worked successfully with large numbers of native speakers as small-group drill leaders. The group leaders are advanced Spanish students who speak with native fluency because of their Mexican-American heritage. They have, in effect, replaced machines for practice in Spanish.

Opportunities to use the spoken language

The language laboratory, however, has not been displaced as an aid in the development of the speaking skill. In 1968, Hamson (83) described a closed-booth laboratory at the University of Michigan that gives each student an air-cooled isolation booth in which he can hear without earphones and speak without fear of disturbing or being disturbed by other students. According to a subsequent report (84), the arrangement is still giving satisfactory service. Hamson notes that lab work more closely approximates a real conversation when it is heard without earphones.

Language laboratory

Other audiovisual aids, including machines, continue to provide stimuli for developing the speaking skill. Bourque (28) notes that visual aids for language classes made by students are

often very effective. She describes how two mediocre language
students were motivated to take a more active part in class
when photographs they made themselves were used to stimulate
speaking. She describes other student-made elements such as
games of "Concentration" and "Jeopardy." Berwald (21) suggests having students become actors by doing readings and
other presentations before a videotape camera, which Molepske
(136) reports having done with appreciable success. Matthews
(128) has done much the same thing with audio recordings. The
students went to great lengths to prepare French programs with
suitable music and sound effects, and the programs were later
broadcast by the French National Radio Network. French teachers who would like to implement a similar strategy will find
Slack's (182) radio and television vocabulary list useful. Remington (161) had students put their homeroom period to good
use by making marionettes and using them to encourage speaking in class.

In at least one case, the audio and visual senses were aug-
mented by the sense of smell. Engler (63) has students do research projects that include a spoken presentation before the
class. They include such interesting materials as the basic
scents that might be used by a French perfumer in his trade.

Teacher-made materials of various kinds are also in wide use.
Stockton (193) asks students to be able to speak within the limits
of "basic sentences." For each of the sentences, a set of questions, whose answers form the sentence to be spoken, was written. One such set of questions is provided below to illustrate the
technique.

Basic sentence to be learned:
   Il paraît que le marchand de bois a découvert une grotte
   dans la forêt.
Possible questions to be asked and answered orally:
   1 Où est-ce que le marchand de bois a découvert une grotte?
      (dans la forêt)
   2 Qui a découvert une grotte dans la forêt?
      (le marchand de bois)
   3 Qu'est-ce que le marchand de bois a découvert dans la
      forêt?
      (une grotte)
   4 Qu'est-ce que le marchand de bois a fait?
      (Il a découvert une grotte dans la forêt.)

5 Comment est-ce qu'il paraît?

(Il paraît que le marchand de bois a découvert une grotte dans la forêt.)

Hill (92*)[1] stimulates conversation in Russian by talking about baseball and basketball. He has developed a list of "Russian Baseball and Basketball Terminology" that he is willing to share. Berlin (20*) helps students develop their speaking skill by using visual cards as stimuli. Since some cards require a more complex utterance than others, they are color-coded according to difficulty, making an oral presentation easier to score. Anderson (7) links speaking goals to evaluation by numbering certain of the spoken exercises done in class. He then devotes a portion of each class to a quick review of one of the numbered exercises in accordance with a revolving schedule. The schedule is structured to repeat a given exercise several times per semester (for example, on the 3d, 4th, 27th, and 81st days of the semester).

Specific teacher "techniques"

Many reports stress the use of speaking topics that suit the students' interests. Agatstein (1) reports having used French magazine articles about the youth movement in France. His report contains a "generation gap" vocabulary list. Klin (108) recommends cutting down on the amount of literature used in a conversation class. He suggests the use of visually oriented materials like *L'art de la conversation* (Hester & Lenard, 90). Schuh (175) discusses a system for teaching German speaking skills to the very young. One of the techniques Schuh has called "Selbständiges Erzählen." It is in effect the use of the monologue to develop "freies Sprechen." Schuh is very insistent that the curriculum of the "kindergarten" foreign language program be solidly based.

Student-interest speaking topics

Language teachers are placing more and more emphasis on the value of using samples of the target language within real-life contexts for the development of speaking. Buckby (34) presents some visually cued drills whose visuals are likely to cue the very response that is to be practiced. For example, an unidentifiable object cues "What is it?" Spears & Lottinville (189) have written to a large number of American companies (including Del Monte, Libby McNeill & Libby, Campbell, and Kellogg) to get French labels from the companies' export divisions. They paste these labels on old cans and bottles and put the

Use of real-life contexts

---

1 Editor's note: Asterisks with reference numbers indicate that materials or further information may be obtained from the address given with that entry in the list of references.

new French products on the shelves of a "grocery store." A number of contexts for speaking suggest themselves, including naming, buying, selling, and exchanging the projects. Logan (121) has gone a step further, for his "store" includes only German brands. Chuikov (45) also stresses the importance of context. His article contains examples for teaching English. Sosenko (187) notes that commands of various kinds form a context of their own. He provides tables of examples of three kinds of dialogue. Chilelli (44) stresses the use of a meaningful context in teaching the Spanish verb *gustar*. Pollei (157) reports having prepared "total physical response" units. His use of the quote indicates an application of Asher's (13) work. Palmer (147) and Minn (134) both demonstrate the value of contextually oriented exercises.

Research on instructional strategies for speaking was reported during 1970 by Brown (32), of Ball State University, who evaluated an experimental device called the "Tok-Bak." It is a plastic headpiece that reflects the student's voice back to him when he speaks. Brown used one instrument for pronunciation mimicry and another for phonetic discrimination. Results in the latter group were not significant, but those in the former group significantly favored the device. Subjective reactions of the students were mixed.

Research: a speaking device

Rothfarb (166) discusses the importance of knowing how much speaking the students do and how much the teacher does in the target language. Using a modified Flanders interaction analysis scale, she found that there was a great deal of teacher-talk in the FLES classes she observed. Furthermore, she found that native-speaking teachers use more English than those who were not native speakers. Gagnon (72) found that a high level of interaction in French between student and teacher correlates with high student achievement, but that it is not possible to correlate specific teacher behavior with student achievement on a reliable basis.

Who speaks?

Hammerly (81) asked 35 students to record imitations of Spanish sounds before seeing them in their written forms. Then he let the writing be seen and asked for a rerecording. He noted phonetic deterioration from one recording to another. Locke (120), working in a speech clinic and not in a classroom, gave unfamiliar German and Swedish sounds to 100 children, ages 4 to 12. He asked the children to mimic the sounds, allowing ten repetitions. His measures (which he judged high in reliability)

Using repetition

indicated that more than two repetitions does not help a child to mimic any better than two repetitions alone.

Jenkins (101) compared classes receiving explanation before, after, and between pattern drills to those not receiving any explanation. The group receiving explanation before the drill had significantly (P > .025 level) higher scores.

Explanation before the pattern drill

Reading

There was relatively little specific research attention to second-language reading skills in 1970. Most of the literature refers to applications of the Scherer (174) framework for gradual progress in reading from the point at which one reads only what has been aurally and orally mastered to the stage of free reading of unedited material. It seems clear that the profession is strongly opposed to the kind of teaching of reading that involves no more than making literature available to the student, talking to him (or at him) about it, and testing his ability to repeat lectures and translate chapters. To the extent that the tasks involved in reading a second language are analyzed and strategies are proposed to insure success in those tasks, progress in the teaching of reading is being made.

Literature refers to Scherer's framework

Donati (57) suggests a procedure used by a number of teachers. He selects quotations that place the word or phrase being presented in a well-known context. The context provides a hint at the meaning of the word. He also recognizes the value of rhyme, rhythm, synonyms, and antonyms in the development of reading from context.

Use of context

Mortenson & Rhoads (140) reported having field-tested visuals and other materials devised by Scanlan to enhance the reading skill in Latin classes. Each student has a copy of the visuals shown in class that he may take home to help him prepare his assignments.

Visuals

Smith (185) discusses an analytical "crutch" to enable beginning students to read the modified adjective construction in German. He leads the student through a series of examples in English that eventually lead to the German phrase structure using the modified adjective construction, which is then further exploited. Aronson (12) lists specific examples of ways of using vocabulary for the development of reading Russian, and Eskey (68) presents a strategy for reading English as a second language that focuses on words rather than structures.

Development of structure and vocabulary

Ladd (110) reports that magazine articles about topics in

which individual students have a special interest make good reading materials for her classes. *Magazines*

Mathieu (127) lists procedures for listening to and reading poetry in early language instruction. His contribution gives specific ways to teach students to savor the musical quality of a poem, as well as to understand its lexical meaning. Here the language teacher has an opportunity to have a genuine effect on the life-style of his student as an adult by providing him with a sensitivity to poetry he might never otherwise acquire. Furthermore, the methods suggested by Mathieu can be used by a teacher who is, to coin a term, "poem-deaf" himself and wishes to develop his own sensibilities as well as those of his students. *Reading poetry*

Mueller (142) describes research in progress on reading at two levels. One experiment deals with beginning reading and features new roles for the teaching of grammar. The other involves reading for meaning in classes with some previous instruction in grammar.

Research reported by Parent (149) indicates that parallel bilingual reading columns are effective devices for lower-ability students, yet do not impair the progress of higher-ability students. In further study of these results, Parent & Belasco (150) point out a need for further research on the part parallel-column material might be expected to play in the forging of a post-audiolingual methodological theory, concentrating on what Belasco (18) calls the coexistence of cognition and verbal behavior. *Bilingual reading columns*

Writing

Clay (46) suggests that specific Latin passages from the works of famous authors be given to students so that they may copy certain of the structures and styles they observe. Bilingual dictionaries are not used with the passages and no new vocabulary is introduced. Dinter (55) describes procedures in teaching composition. He uses topics based on contemporary German newspapers and films. Pill (151) employs a type of guided composition to include "continuous, coherent, and correct French writing" in a program that places emphasis on all the basic skills. Shepherd (180) describes the personal journals or diaries that students write in his individualized French program. *Developmental techniques*

Bucklin (35) relates a simplified system of morphological analysis for teaching the writing of French verbs. He proposes a system of three "slots" into which a verb stem and as many as two bound morphemes may be added. He has made a group of color-coded slot cards to accompany his strategy. Goodman (78) employs a series of diagrams to make generalizations on written French verb tense sequence. Turner (205) uses student-made posters to generate writing in her first-year Latin classes. She encourages students to select, mount, and label interesting pictures from newspapers and magazines and finds that one student's work tends to stimulate another's. Orfali (146) presents a written German word game that combines nouns and adjectives in varied contexts. Arapoff (8) advises that, in the interest of avoiding direct translation, contexts used for writing should be drawn from second-language reading experiences rather than from a student's own life experiences. Erk (66,67) discusses the use of a graphemic system to aid writing in German classes, while Diem (54) does likewise for French classes.

Teaching of grammar

Electronic equipment has been used to enhance writing skills. Turner (204) describes computer-assisted instruction in Spanish at Dartmouth College, and Sandberg (173) discusses electronically presented writing drills. For classes located in isolated areas that are unable to employ language teachers, Prather (158) describes the Victor Electronic Remote Blackboard which enables a language specialist 50 miles away from a class to send written messages to a class for use with a nonspecialist.

Use of electronic equipment

Translation, per se, is more important to teachers of Latin than to teachers of modern languages. Strasheim (195) had identified strategies for teaching translations in Latin classes on phonetic, lexical, structural, and cultural levels. She includes specific examples.

Translation

Curricular change

The last group of strategies presented in this chapter are those dealing with more than one skill or with the entire language teaching curriculum. It is often appropriate and desirable to consider strategies for enhancing the entire curriculum. When both published and unpublished sources are considered, fully half of the year's work is widely focused.

Teaching strategies for all skills are presented in a booklet edited by Hammond & Garfinkel (82). The strategies are some of those used by Oklahoma teachers. In a similar publication Heymans (91) lists 20 "do's" and "don'ts" for successful teaching and classroom management. He closes the article with outlines for several lesson plans. Pimsleur (152) enumerates some of the more unsettling problems facing language teachers, such as

Strategies for more than one skill

dropouts, negative attitudes, poor discipline, and underachievement. He advises that combining clearly stated goals with an appropriately designed testing program can help solve these problems. Examples of tests for specific goals are included. Wright (216) makes suggestions for designing tests for first-level French classes.

Ross (164) presents ideas for improving the effectiveness of language lab work in listening and speaking. His article, based on experience with *A-LM* Russian materials, stresses the importance of exercises using indirect quotes. Taylor (199) has written one of the chapters dealing with teaching techniques that appear in *Perspectives for Teachers of Latin American Culture.* The entire volume is a noteworthy contribution. *Language laboratory with listening and speaking*

Hehr (87) suggests that German teachers plan extracurricular trips to seek out elements of German culture that are to be found in many American cities. She mentions a trip to see a concert by the Vienna Choir Boys as an example. Fagin (69) coordinated the activities of high school French students in Oklahoma who financed a trip to New Orleans with bake sales and similar activities. Mementos of the trip stimulated French conversation for months afterward. *Field trips*

Semke (178) suggests a lively game that could be used in connection with a "total physical response" strategy. Archibeque (9) notes the value of having advanced students function as tutors. He lists selection criteria as well. Davidson & Geake (49) present specific techniques for evaluating achievement in listening and speaking skills. *Total physical response*

Morton (141) describes the college-level curriculum at the College of Artesia (Artesia, New Mexico). There is no language requirement other than one for demonstrated proficiency, as a percentage of junior and senior classes in several subjects must be taken in Spanish. The curriculum features programmed instruction to help the student acquire proficiency, becoming in its own words, "the first college to promise instruction to suit stated goals." Morel (138,139) has devised a curriculum called "total immersion." It makes use of three daily classes (foreign language, social studies, and advanced placement) in the second language. Summer travel is also featured in this program for high school juniors and seniors. Morel notes that "total immersion" students far exceed average scores on national examinations in listening, reading, and writing. Goetz (77*) has written an activity resource unit for teaching culture in the language class. *Programmed learning*

Total immersion

Instructional strategies/Garfinkel

The Minnesota Department of Education has produced a new guide that lists resources and makes suggestions for activities and projects in Level IV and V language classes (Arendt & Fearing, 11). The Stillwater, Oklahoma, city schools have produced video tapes for the teaching of first-year conversational Russian under the auspices of a federal grant. Anderson (6) reports that other districts can acquire copies of the tapes. Bergen (19*) describes a group of audiovisual strategies, designed to contextualize French dialogues on a personal basis, that she calls "the Bridge Technique." Bourque (27) notes that the FLES curriculum "is very much alive at Fairfield [Connecticut]." He reports that tests show significantly higher achievement for FLES students over those not taking FLES.

Resources and curriculum

Horodowich (95) suggests a type of ability grouping in Spanish classes. The criterion is achievement in Spanish rather than intelligence quotients. Nonetheless, the teacher considering ability grouping should be aware of such discussions as those presented by Silberman (181). Steiner (191) presents a rationale for stating curricular objectives in terms of specific behaviors. She provides lesson plans and discusses those objectives that are most readily individualized. Masciantonio (126) reports new courses in the Philadelphia classics curriculum. Classes in Latin and Greek and special interdisciplinary courses are made possible by the curriculum of a "magnet school" that specializes in languages. Alonso (3*) reports a new curriculum for languages that fits her district's plans to operate on a 12-month basis. Courses have been redesigned into self-contained nine-week units or "courses." A student may branch from the regular sequential curriculum to elect up to 34 language "courses" in a four-year program. A new numbering system aids articulation.

Curricular innovations

Teachers and curriculum specialists made numerous efforts during the year to get public notice for language teaching or to otherwise increase enrollments by advertising of one kind or another. Meyer (131) describes a one-day visit to the University of Wisconsin Whitewater campus where high school students saw the ACTFL filmstrip *Why Study Foreign Languages?*, enjoyed language-oriented entertainment, and took a campus tour. The article identified Grittner and Durette as planners of the event.

Efforts at public notice

The twinning of two cities, York, Pennsylvania, and Arles, France, (71*) in 1955 has led to exchanges of teachers between the two towns. The twinning process involves many institutions and activities of both communities, including the respective chambers of commerce and extending even to the printing of a French comic strip in the York daily newspaper. Of course, the program is to be commended for uniting world citizens as well as for producing an immediate, practical justification for taking French in York, Pennsylvania.

Other instances of community involvement in language teaching were reported. At El Paso, Texas, Dickson (53*) reports that the city planetarium has aided Spanish students in charting stars and designing Spanish horoscopes. French students have written French reports on the Apollo missions, using planetarium equipment to learn about them. Walker (210) discovered that several of her students' families were planning Mexican summer vacations. She brought some Mexican money to class to stimulate conversation and found the students wanted their own for their forthcoming trips. She mentioned this to the local bank, which then bought a supply of pesos and used Spanish advertisements in the local paper to sell them. For a while, the Spanish classes were almost as well-known as the football team, and they had no losing streak. Barcio (16) and his students of Latin read about Roman catapults and decided to find out how to build one. They found that catapult construction is a lost art and that the writings of the Ancients could give them only indirect information. Nevertheless, they used this to build several catapults (Figure 2), held and won contests with other schools, and received national publicity on three television shows. Barcio notes that "there is always present the haunting feeling of respect for the Ancients and an intensely rewarding sense that one is experiencing an aspect of history overlooked by others. . . . (accompanied by) the feeling that you are silently working with the minds of the past." His efforts to publicize this study as he pursues it are noteworthy.

Carney (38) reports having advanced junior and senior high school language students go to elementary schools to supplement units about children around the world studied there. Her program for injecting modern foreign languages into the elementary curriculum is called VOCAW (Voices of Children Around the World). Her similar program for Latin is ECHO (Echoes of Classical Heritage in Oklahoma). A program in Danville, Illinois, (Wilson, 213) sent Mexican-American high school students to elementary schools to give elementary school children a taste of learning Spanish. Rundell (167) reports a single

Community involvement

Use of advanced students in elementary programs

201

Figure 2. Catapult constructed by Barcio's students

six-week junior high school course that gives a sample unit of each of several languages, accompanied by a unit on the nature of language. These programs are designed to stimulate interest in bringing foreign languages to the elementary and junior high school where they do not yet exist.

Interdisciplinary courses with foreign languages do exist. *Interdisciplinary programs* Warriner (Chapter 5) has provided a comprehensive treatment of the topic. The purpose here is to mention only a few in order to make note of the trend. Marton (125) reports having taught European history in French, using the same materials used in France. Tamarkin (197) has prepared video tapes for training paramedical assistants and people in other fields who must communicate in Spanish. Her videotaped units deal with stores, hospitals, offices, and other lifelike situations. The tapes are available for loan from Manchester Community College, Manchester, Connecticut.

Keitel (104) found that an experimental group without previous exposure to world history courses that took its first world history course in German was able to enhance achievement in all four German skills without affecting achievement in history. Haile (80) reports having exposed beginning students of German to certain principles of linguistics and language analysis. Seward (179) reports having used French as a medium for teaching basic German.

Individualized programs are thoroughly discussed in Gougher's *Individualized programs* chapter of the present volume, Chapter 8. A few are mentioned here because such programs represent a new orientation toward instructional strategies. Birulin (23*) describes objectives, materials, procedures, and evaluation in a tutorialized situation. Wood (214) describes a school in Missouri that has applied all of several recent educational innovations (team teaching, differentiated staffing, flexible schedule, etc.) to the language curriculum. Logan (121) provides a short description of what may be presently one of the country's most completely individualized programs. He shows how a wide range of choices makes it possible for German to be one of the most popular classes in a school that has a low percentage of college-preparatory students. Steiner & White (192) describe a learning activities center they put together themselves. LaLeike (112*) describes another of the more widely known individualized programs. Funded under a federal grant, one of its objectives is to act as an information center on individualized instruction. Gascoigne (74) and Aldridge (2) are two of many teachers who have written specific behavioral objectives for their Spanish classes, which permit students to function individually. Koch (109*) has done likewise for her French classes. Ryberg (170) makes suggestions for involving students in individualizing a program, and McClennan (129) describes his individualized German program at Mountain View, California. Wells (212*) reports a program involving differentiated staffing. A new periodical report on individualization (98) is an excellent source of further information.

Instructional strategies are always enhanced by well-coordinated programs. Further, a district need have only a few language teachers to coordinate a program. Arendt (10) describes the coordination of the language curriculum in the Minneapolis Public Schools. Bartlesville, Oklahoma, teachers, under the leadership of ACTFL board member Lois Ellsworth (62), have formed the highly effective Bartlesville Language Council to make curricular needs and achievements known to administrators and the public alike.

Coordination of a foreign language program

Service centers to help local language teachers become more aware of new instructional strategies are sorely needed. A notable example is the German Center at Bowling Green State University (76).

Two studies designed to compare instructional strategies appeared in 1970. Probst (159) compared audio-lingual-visual classes to cognitive-code classes and found the audio-lingual-visual classes significantly superior (P > .05 level). Chastain (42) reported no significant difference between "audiolingual habit theory" classes and "cognitive-code learning theory" classes in his second continuous year of experimentation. He concludes that neither method is best for all students.

Research in instructional strategies

Horne (94) has experimented with varying class sizes and found that groups of five to nine students are ideal for intensive language instruction.

Papalia (148) studied reasons that cause students to drop out of the foreign language class sequences. He found that classes in agricultural and heavily industrialized areas begin language study late and have the highest attrition levels, while classes in areas of high socioeconomic status (neither agricultural nor industrial) showed the most extended sequences of language study combined with lowest attrition rates. Papalia further notes that he found a great deal of "teacher-talk" and "direct behaviors" in classes he observed.

Smart, Elton, & Burnett (183) urge the use of personality scales and other measures in addition to intellectual instruments for predicting language success.

Professional resource materials

New materials of professional interest to both pre-service and in-service teachers have been plentiful in the past year. Although it is not possible to include an exhaustive list of such materials here, several of the American and foreign publications that have apparent potential for affecting instructional strategies have been selected for presentation.

Hester (89) has edited a collection of four essays that deal with a methodology referred to as the "verbal-active method." It should be read by the profession, for it is an interesting discussion of the accepted order of presentation for language skills. The verbal-active method seems to owe a great deal to the natural and direct methods. It advocates the presentation of listening before speaking, but calls for writing to precede reading. No research data are provided to justify the position, but a look at the classroom-wise ways of a teacher's edition written by one of the contributors, Lenard (119), leaves one with the impression that her position deserves serious attention in the form of discussion and research.

The "verbal-active method"

Allen & Seifman have edited a collection of articles on several areas of the curriculum entitled *The Teacher's Handbook*, and Chastain's (43) chapter in that volume is a remarkable distillation of the problems and issues that face the language-teaching profession.

A chapter by Valette (207) appears in a recent text by Bloom and Madeus. Here she has made another important contribution to the area of evaluating language learning by outlining the objectives of language teaching and suggesting specific ways to evaluate them. The fact that administrators in pre-service training will be exposed to the goals and strategies for evaluation considered important by members of our profession adds to the value of this chapter.

Evaluating language learning

The National Society for the Study of Education yearbooks for 1970 included one on *Linguistics in School Programs* (Marckwardt, 124). Edited by Marckwardt, the volume contains chapters by Moulton and Bowen among others. It does not deal directly with second-language learning.

205

Two new journals made their appearance in 1970. *Ziel-sprache Deutsch* (217), an all-German publication on language teaching printed in West Germany, brings to at least three the number of West German journals of special interest to the foreign language teacher. This places those language teachers who read German in an enviable position. They can build both German reading and pedagogical skills at once. *The American Foreign Language Teacher* (5) is intended for classroom teachers. It includes practical hints and items to be duplicated and handed out to classes as conversation stimuli. The publication's first year indicates that it has real potential for filling a pressing need for specific examples of instructional strategies a teacher may employ. Most language teachers will find helpful material in this new publication.

New journals

Newbury House Publishers of Rowley, Massachusetts, has recently begun a series of books on foreign language education. These include volumes by Kelly and Jakobovits. Kelly's work, *25 Centuries of Language Teaching: 500 B.C.–1969* (106) is sure to be regarded as the definitive work on the history of language teaching. One can safely forecast that few, if any, subsequent works on foreign language education that contain historical chapters will be without reference to this fascinating book. Jakobovits' *Foreign Language Learning: A Psycholinguistic Analysis of the Issues* (99) is valuable both to the theoretician and the classroom teacher. Jakobovits examines the psycholinguistic theories underlying "the habit-skill approach" and "the rule-governed grammar approach." He finds the habit-skill approach to be "theoretically untenable" because, among other reasons, it pays insufficient attention to communicative competence as opposed to mastery of mechanical manipulation. However, the theoretical analysis of language teaching is only the first value of this publication. It also includes scales for measuring student attitude toward the study of language. These scales, which are copyrighted by the Northeast Conference and are available in quantities from the Modern Language Association Materials Center, have potential for increasing the validity and reliability of future research by replacing the improvised scales so often used. Furthermore, they are of real value to the classroom teacher who is interested in the attitudes of students in his classes. One can easily forecast that the coming year will see extended discussion of Jakobovits' recent work.

A new series of books on foreign language education

Green (79) has written a programmed introduction to Spanish

phonology which will aid the teacher in learning to analyze the points of phonetic interference between English and Spanish. The book's structure is not unlike Buchanan's (33) programmed introduction to English phonology, which is also a most useful publication. One would hope that some tape recordings might become available to enable the student to have recorded illustrations of the frames and that a second edition would include self-evaluation tests in addition to the review frames already included. Nevertheless, the program forms an important addition to the year's progress in foreign language education.

A programmed introduction to Spanish phonology

Language and the Teacher: A Series in Applied Linguistics is the title of a new series of inexpensive paperbacks published by the Center for Curriculum Development, Inc. The series makes reprints of recent research and writing in foreign language education readily available at a low cost. Lugton edited the series, which has seven titles presently available, with several others forthcoming. Those released include *The Successful Foreign Language Teacher* (156) and *Improving Achievement in Foreign Language* (155), both by Politzer & Weiss, and *Language Learning and Machine Teaching* (17) by Barrutia.

Paperbacks in foreign language education

The 1970 *Reports of the Working Committees of the Northeast Conference on the Teaching of Foreign Languages* (Tursi, 206) is entitled *Foreign Languages and the "New" Student*. The reports present the Jakobovits attitude scales mentioned above, accompanied by two other committee reports entitled "Motivation in Foreign Language Learning" and "Foreign Languages for All Students?" The report on motivation includes a statement by Jakobovits and reactions to it by some members of the committee. The report on whether or not language should be taught to all students strongly advocates that language offerings be as broad as possible. The report states the following:

1970 Northeast Conference Report

1 We do not know whom to exclude from language classes.
2 We cannot predict who will need foreign languages in later life.
3 Foreign lands are more accessible.
4 Foreign language study is educationally beneficial.
5 There are new educational and career opportunities which require foreign language expertise.
6 Studying language tends to make the student more receptive to the different cultural patterns in our multi-ethnic society.
7 Exclusion may be psychologically damaging.

Instructional strategies/Garfinkel

The reasons are each discussed and supported, often by research data. The "on the floor" general sessions of the Northeast Conference are available on tapes (Dodge, 56).

The appearance of Volume 2 of the *Britannica Review of Foreign Language Education* (BRFLE) (Lange, 116) provides the profession with a continuing review of its work. The compilation of the writing and research in Foreign Language Education shows what is happening in the field. For more details on the contents of BRFLE 2, see Chapter 8 in this volume.

BRFLE 2

The Teaching of German: Problems and Methods (Reichmann, 160) is a collection of over 200 journal articles on the teaching of German. It is *not* of limited appeal, however, because many of the articles are applicable to other languages. Collaborators include Brooks, Jakobovits, Lange, Leamon, Stack, Strasheim, Valette, and others. The book is supplemented with resource information and is the second publication of its kind to be sponsored by one of the AAT's. It was preceded by one written under the auspices of the AATSP (American Association of Teachers of Spanish and Portuguese) (Walsh, 211). The other AAT's might well consider the development of such handbooks for their own languages and, perhaps, making them into premiums to be distributed with a "comprehensive" membership much like the one used by ACTFL.

Other collections of essays

Kadler (102) has written a most useful presentation of the basic principles of linguistics and their application to language teaching. Of special interest are the chapters calling attention to points of interference between English and French, German, Russian, and Spanish. They deal with phonemic, phonetic, and morphophonemic problems. There is a good selective bibliography, which carries references specifically for each of the languages mentioned above, along with general ones. Kadler's book should certainly be considered for use in an applied linguistics course.

Principles of linguistics applied to language teaching

Similarly valuable is the definitive edition of Politzer's *Foreign Language Learning: A Linguistic Introduction* (154). This book has been field-tested through the issuance of preliminary editions.

Teachers who are frequently called upon to advise their students will be interested in hearing of Casewit's *How to Get a Job Overseas* (41), a book that names the names and lists the addresses of potential employers, while discussing the possibilities of jobs in 22 different fields. Foreign language requirements for some positions are mentioned. This inexpensive paperback is an excellent addition to the teacher's professional library.

The Educational Testing Service (135) has released a filmstrip and record combination accompanied by a set of 25 prepared ditto masters to help teachers deal with classroom testing. Some of the masters are work sheets designed to accompany film Number 5 of the series entitled *Principles and Methods of Teaching Second Languages* (Ferguson et al., 70). The others are sample test items that put into practice the theory presented in the filmstrip and record. The cost of the set is quite reasonable.

Another resource of low cost and high value is the filmstrip and record combination produced by the National Audiovisual Center to help people become more familiar with ERIC (General Services Administration, 75). There are three filmstrips and one record in the series. They are entitled "Introduction to ERIC," "How to Use ERIC," and "ERIC Advanced Training Program." The viewer will note that these filmstrips frequently feature ERIC documents on foreign language as illustrations. While this may be coincidental, the possibility also exists that our profession may be making more efficient use of the system than others. True or not, it is a pleasant thought. In any case, all school districts having access to an ERIC collection (whether within their systems or in a nearby library) should offer their teachers a chance to see this excellent introduction to what may be the most important single reference tool available to the teacher.

Information about ERIC

Conference reports, however useful they may be, usually do not have a great deal of entertainment value along with their more scholarly products. That trend has been most refreshingly broken by *New Teachers for New Students* (Hanzeli & Love, 85), a report on the proceedings of the Seattle Symposium on the Training of Foreign Language Teachers. The report sparkles with engagingly written presentations. Two of its high points are the papers by Strasheim (196) and Ryberg (170). Strasheim, in the keynote paper, pleads for honesty in explaining the rationale of language learning to "new students." Ryberg, a proponent of "change—now," ends his paper with a model for teacher preparation.

A useful conference report

Sadler (172) claims to have discovered a valid instrument for separating "recommendable" from "non-recommendable" teachers. This writer remains skeptical of its value.

Professional resource materials for language teachers emanate from all the world's industrialized nations. Few of them are imported to these shores, and fewer yet get the readership they deserve. It is the purpose of the following section to call attention to recent foreign sources that seem worthy of special note. Items whose publishers maintain American sales and distribution offices are not included below, nor are those appearing before 1966. Let us begin with some British sources.

Professional resource material

Longmans has a new paperback series entitled "Education Today: Language Teaching." There are four excellent books in the series. Perhaps the most valuable of them is the first, S. Pit Corder's *The Visual Element in Language Teaching* (47). He discusses some of the principles of visual literacy and analyzes the capabilities of various media for the visual element. There is no bibliography, but this remains an important book that does not have an American counterpart.

Professional materials from England

The Incorporated Association of Assistant Masters in Secondary Schools (96) is a professional group of what we might call assistant principals or, perhaps, curriculum directors. They have produced a handbook entitled *The Teaching of Modern Languages*. This handbook has a great deal of material unduplicated by American sources. There are some sage administrative tips for those managing a travel program. There is a chapter on classroom management as well as a good chapter on the rationale for language study. The bibliography lists several other books and the addresses of several British book stores.

While we have no shortage of language laboratory manuals here, it is always interesting to get an idea of how the lab is dealt with elsewhere. Turner's *Programming for the Language Laboratory* (203) is a collection of readings on how the lab may be used in teaching English as a second language, and French, German, Russian, and Spanish. Since no one ever has enough drill material, the specific drills and examples listed in these chapters may be useful, even to those who are already familiar with much of our writing on the topic.

Naturally, there are a great many more fine British books that the reader can get with a minimum of perseverance. Two journals are especially deserving of the reader's attention: *Language-Teaching Abstracts* (117) and *Audio-Visual Language Journal* (14*). They are excellent for those interested in keeping track of British developments in language teaching.

A recent French publication is by Bouton (29). It discusses some theoretical aspects of language acquisition by adults.

France

Many French publications are readily available in this country. Journals such as the *French Review* list many sources.

Sweden

English is widely taught in Swedish schools. Dunlop (59) provides a description of techniques used by teachers at the British Center in Stockholm, which would be useful to teachers of English as a second language.

Germany

West German publishers provide their language teachers with an array of titles at least as long as our own. Two recent releases are by Helmers (88) and Rutt (169).

Other countries

Many other countries produce a number of professional resources for language teachers. Among these are Australia and the Republic of the Philippines. A good source book to lead one to the world's more productive language teaching departments and institutions is a list compiled by Lane & Capelle (113). It lists major teaching departments, as well as the journals read and contributed to by the faculty of each. It is an invaluable reference.

In summary, although we have seen that America produces a large assortment of professional resources, there is no reason for language teachers, of all people, to be ethnocentric. It is important to get other opinions to enrich our own. These, of course, will be all the more valuable for having come from many sources and for including many viewpoints.

Conclusions and recommendations

This chapter has combined a presentation of sources of information about instructional strategies with an examination of classroom practices employed in schools throughout the nation as described in published and unpublished reports. The purpose has been to provide the classroom teacher with current, useful ideas that he may adopt for his own use or investigation.

The following are conclusions and recommendations based on the materials examined for this report:

1 Bosco & Di Pietro (26) have made a valid point in presenting their classification of methodologies. There seems to be a limited number of basic instructional strategies, subject to a large number of changes and variations, which, as Jarvis (100) also notes, do not seem to be *directly* related to any theory of how language is learned.

2 Since the reviews of strategies by Jarvis (100) and Smith (184) there appears to have been a significant increase in

attention to individualization and interdisciplinary activities. To the extent that such activities are not subject to excessive dependence on the native language and other dangers enumerated by Rivers et al. (162), these explorations are to be warmly commended. In addition, efforts such as those of Altman (4) to define individualization are valuable so long as they continue to stress the differences as well as the similarities between programs.

3 The *MLA Selective List of Materials* (Ollman, 144) should be updated and published on an annual or semiannual subscription basis. The MLA materials selection criteria will need study in view of recent developments in language learning and instruction.

4 The need for local organization of language teachers has never been greater (Spolsky, 190). Some states have strong local organizations that adequately promote the interests of language teachers in public and governmental circles (Tuel, 202). Local newsletters are in need of the support of individual teachers to supply them with material to create an interchange of information on instructional strategies. Area service centers like the one started at Bowling Green State University (76) are important developments.

5 National journals should follow the examples of the *Modern Language Journal* and the *American Foreign Language Teacher*, among others, by allowing for teacher input via a column for that purpose. By encouraging classroom teachers to contribute more articles and reports, the journals will focus on practical application as well as on presentation of theory.

6 Although such programs are not yet perfected and even if it is necessary to seek donations from the profession to finance them, the ERIC Clearinghouse on Languages and Linguistics, located at the Modern Language Association, should be urged to continue its progress toward computerized access to ERIC documents. The entire ERIC collection grows at the rate of over 800 documents per month, and it will soon be unmanageable and useless without such help.

7 Many ideas are being tried with little formal evaluation. While Bosco & Di Pietro (26) note that classroom activities have "so many facets that the strict controls necessary for experimentation are not readily established or maintained," it does not seem reasonable to depend solely on

intuition to determine the value of an idea. Teachers should learn to combine intuition with evaluative measures of a more formal nature.

8 Many of the pilot studies and even some of the more strictly controlled research reports issued during the year deal with all four language skills, in addition to other factors. While such all-inclusiveness does not necessarily render invalid either the strategy involved or the research designed to evaluate it, teachers and researchers alike might be well-advised to avoid what is known as "vacuum cleaner research" (i.e., research whose objectives are so numerous that sufficiently intensive study of any one of them becomes impossible).

9 Special attention should be given to the public image of language teaching. This writer maintains that we should frequently take public pride in what has been accomplished, at the same time that we work to accomplish more.

1970 began what appears to be a decade of search for flexible strategies to deal with new students and new responsibilities in language teaching. While we continue to generate such information, we must also focus on better ways to evaluate and to disseminate it, making our newfound knowledge ever more relevant and available to the classroom teacher.

References, Instructional strategies in foreign language learning and teaching

1 Agatstein, Michael. "La revolte des jeunes or An Experiment in Relevancy." *Modern Language Journal* 43(1970):637–40.
2 Aldridge, Rebecca. Unpublished report. Tonkawa, Oklahoma: Tonkawa High School,n.d. [Mimeograph.]
3* Alonso, Elizabeth B. "Reorganization of Foreign Language Curriculum." Survey response. Foreign Language Department, Lindsey Hopkins Building, 1410 North East Second Street, Miami, Florida 33132.
4 Altman, Howard B. "Toward A Definition of Individualized Foreign Language Instruction." *The American Foreign Language Teacher* 1,iii(1970)12–13.
5 *The American Foreign Language Teacher.*

Editor's note: Asterisks with reference numbers indicate that materials or further information may be obtained from the address given in the entry.

Frederick Jenks,ed. Detroit: Advancement Press of America. [Available from Box 7800, Detroit, Michigan.]

6   Anderson, Cathy. "Conversational Russian, Semester II Under Title III Supervision." Survey response. C.E. Donart High School, Stillwater, Oklahoma.

7   Anderson, J. to author. Personal communication. 1971.

8   Arapoff, Nancy. "Writing a Thinking Process." *English Teaching Forum* 8,iii(1970):4–8.

9   Archibeque, Joe D. "Utilizing the Advanced Spanish Student As a Classroom Tutor." *Hispania* 53(1970):70–72.

10 Arendt, Jermaine D. "Annual Report Foreign Language Department." Minneapolis: Minneapolis Public Schools, 1970. [Mimeograph.]

11 —— and Percy Fearing. *The Extended Foreign Language Sequence*. St. Paul: Minnesota State Department of Education, 1971.

12 Aronson, Howard I. "On Teaching Russian Vocabulary." *Slavic and Eastern European Journal* 14(1970)475–83.

13 Asher, James J. "The Total Physical Response Approach to Second Language Learning." *Modern Language Journal* 53(1969):3–17.

14* *Audio-Visual Language Journal*. D.E. Ager,ed. London: Audio-Visual Language Association. [Available from J. Warburton, 102 Margaret Road, New Barnet, Herts, United Kingdom. Check also with W. H. Everett & Son, Ltd., 10 Friar Street, Carter Lane, London, EC4 5 DU, United Kingdom, for other materials.]

15 Ballard, Virginia S. "Cooperative Teaching in Level I Spanish." Survey response. Anne Arundel County Public Schools, Annapolis, Maryland.

16 Barcio, Bernard to author. Personal communication, 1971.

17 Barrutia, Richard. *Language Learning and Machine Teaching*. Philadelphia: Center for Curriculum Development, 1970.

18 Belasco, Simon. "C'est la guerre? Or Can Cognition and Verbal Behavior Co-exist in Second Language Learning." *Modern Language Journal* 54(1970):395–412.

19* Bergen, Marylyn F. "The Bridge Technique." Survey response. French Department, Bellarmine-Ursuline College, 2000 Norris Place, Louisville, Kentucky.

20* Berlin, E. Clair. "Oral Grade Card Scoring." Survey response. Pacifica High School, 6851 Lampson Avenue, Garden Grove, California 92641.

21 Berwald, John P. "The Video Tape Recorder as a Teaching Aid." *French Review* 53(1970):923–27.

22 "Bicentennial Commission Urges Language Study." *New York Times* 4 July(1970):n. pag.

23* Birulin, Solomon L. "Tutorializing Foreign Language Studies." Seattle, Washington: Chief Sealth High School, 1970. [Mimeograph.] [2600 Southwest Thistle, Seattle, Washington.]

24 Bockman, John F. "An Experiment in Independent Foreign Language Study." *Arizona Foreign Language Teachers Forum* 17,ii(1970):8–11. [ERIC Document Reproduction Service: ED 037 135.]

25 —— *Townsend Junior High School Independent Foreign Language Study Project:A Second Evaluation and Program Report*. Tucson, Arizona: Tucson Public Schools, 1970. [ERIC Document Reproduction Service: ED 040 642.]

26 Bosco, Frederick J., and Robert J. Di Pietro. "Bases for Instructional Strategies." *International Review of Applied Linguistics* 8(1970):3–19.

27 Bourque, Edward H. "FLES is Very Much Alive in Fairfield." *Hispania* 53(1970):82–85.

28 Bourque, Jane M. "Sound and Substance." *The American Foreign Language Teacher* 1,ii(1970)12–13.

29 Bouton, Charles P. *Les mécanismes d'acquisition du français:Langue étranger chez l'adulte*. Paris: C. Klincksiek, 1969.

30 Braun, K., L. Nieder, and F. Schmöe,eds. *Deutsch als Fremdsprache*. Stuttgart: Klett Verlag, 1970.

31 Brooks, Nelson. "Foreign Language Studies." *New York Times* 2 October(1970):34.

32 Brown, James W. to author. Personal communication, 1971.

33 Buchanan, Cynthia. *A Programmed Introduction to Linguistics*. Boston: D.C. Heath, 1965.

34 Buckby, Michael. "Another Look at Drills." *Audio-Visual Language Journal* 8(1970):111–17.

35 Bucklin, Lincoln B. "Slot Cards for the Teaching of French Verbs," 146–47 in Jerrold L. Mordaunt,ed., *Proceedings:Pacific Northwest Conference on Foreign Languages, Twentieth Annual Meeting, April 11–12, 1969*. Volume 20. Victoria, B.C.: Univ. of Victoria, 1969. [ERIC Document Reproduction Service: ED 036 224.]

36 Campbell, Hugh, and Camille Bauer. *La dynamite*. Boston: Houghton Mifflin, 1970.

37 Capelle, Janine, and Guy Capelle. *La France en direct*. Waltham, Massachusetts: Ginn, 1970.

38 Carney, Helen K. "VOCAW and ECHO:Advertising Foreign Languages." *Foreign Language Annals* 4(1970):57–61.

39 Carroll, John B. "Research on Teaching Foreign Languages," 1060–1100 in N.L. Gage,ed., *Handbook of Research on Teaching*. Chicago: Rand McNally, 1963.

40 —— "Modern Languages," 866–78 in Robert Ebel,ed., *Encyclopedia of Educational Research*. 4th Edition. New York: Macmillan, 1969.

41 Casewit, Curtis. *How to Get a Job Overseas*. New York: ARC Books, 1970. [Available: Arco Publishing Company, 219 Park Avenue South, New York.]

42 Chastain, Kenneth D. "A Methodological Study Comparing Audio-Lingual Habit Theory and the Cognitive Code Learning Theory:A Continuation." *Modern Language Journal* 54(1970):257–66.

43 —— "Modern Languages," 319–29 in Dwight Allen and Eli Seifman,eds., *The Teacher's*

Handbook. Glenview, Illinois: Scott-Foresman, 1971.

44 Chilelli, Jeffrey. "Another Technique for Teaching *Gustar*." *Hispania* 53(1970):458–59.

45 Chuikov, B.T. "One Way of Encouraging the Link Between Written and Oral Work." *Inostrannye Jazyki v Škole* 4(1970):92–96.

46 Clay, Jenny. "Suggestions for the Teaching of Latin Composition," 171–77 in Jerrold L. Mordaunt,ed., *Proceedings:Northwest Conference on Foreign Languages, Twentieth Annual Meeting, April 11–12, 1969*. Volume 20. Victoria, B.C.: Univ. of Victoria, 1969. [ERIC Document Reproduction Service: ED 036 223.]

47 Corder, S. Pit. *The Visual Element in Language Teaching*. London: Longmans, 1966.

48 *Current Index to Journals in Education*. New York: CCM Information Corporation.

49 Davidson, J.M., and P.M. Geake. "An Assessment of Oral Testing Methods in Modern Languages." *Modern Languages* 51(1970):116–23.

50 Decock, Jean. "L'utilisation du film commercial dans l'enseignement des langues." *French Review* 53(1970):467–73.

51 Dellacio, Carl,et al. *Spanish for Communication*. Boston: Houghton Mifflin, in preparation.

52 de Petra, Yvette, and Dedini de Petra. *La clef*. New York: Holt, Rinehart and Winston, 1970.

53* Dickson, Margaret. "Planetarium Program and Other Projects." El Paso, Texas: El Paso Indian School District, 1970. [Mimeograph.] [P.O. Box 1710, 100 West Rio Grande, El Paso, Texas 79902.]

54 Diem, Jean-Marie. "Les techniques d'enseignement de l'orthographie." *Pédagogie* 25(1970):209–18.

55 Dinter, Wolfgang. "Der Precis:Ein Weg zur Einführung in das Schreiben von Aufsätzen." *Die Unterrichtspraxis* 3,ii(1970):33–40.

56 Dodge, James W.,ed. *Northeast Conference Tapes*. Middlebury, Vermont: Northeast Conference on the Teaching of Foreign Languages, 1971. [Available from editor at Middlebury College.]

57 Donati, Richard. "Using Quotations to Encourage Careful Reading." *French Review* 43(1970):630–34.

58 Drath, Viola Herms. *Was wollen die Deutschen? 21 Zeitgenossen*. New York: Macmillan, 1970.

59 Dunlop, Ian. *Practical Techniques in the Teaching of Oral English*. Volume 2. Stockholm: Almquist and Wiksell, 1970.

60 Dyck, J.W., and W.J. Schwarz. *Mensch und Welt:An Elementary Science Reader*. Waltham, Massachusetts: Ginn, 1970.

61 "Educational Isolationism." *New York Times*. 12 September(1970):n. pag.

62 Ellsworth, Lois to author. Personal communication, n.d.

63 Engler, Janice. "Independent Study." Boise, Idaho: Boise High School, n.d. [Mimeograph.]

64 *En avant*. Boston: Houghton Mifflin, 1970.

65 English, Bob. "Language Class Clicks with French Flicks." Santa Barbara, California:

Univ. of California at Santa Barbara, Office of Public Information, 1970. [Press release.] [Mimeograph.]

66 Erk, Heinrich. "Unterrichtsproblem Orthographie." *Zielsprache Deutsch* 1(1970):64–77.

67 ———. "Unterrichtsproblem Orthographie." *Zielsprache Deutsch* 1(1970):123–32.

68 Eskey, David E. *A New Technique for Teaching of Reading to Advanced Students*. Paper presented at Fourth Annual TESOL Convention, San Francisco, 18–21 March 1970. [ERIC Document Reproduction Service: ED 038 649.]

69 Fagin, Della to author. Personal communication, 1 April 1971.

70 Ferguson, Charles,et al. *Principles and Methods of Teaching Second Languages*. New York: Teaching Film Custodians, 1965.

71* *Fifteen Years—York-Arles Friendship*. York, Pennsylvania: York-Arles Twinning Committee, 1970. [Marguerite Erikson, 170 East Springettsbury Avenue, York, Pennsylvania 17403.]

72 Gagnon, Marc. "Relation Between Systematic Observance of Verbal Interaction and Pupil Success in Foreign Language Classes." *Dissertation Abstracts International* 30(1970):3346A (Stanford).

73 Garnier, Marthe G. "The Flannelboard for Foreign Language Teaching." *Die Unterrichtspraxis* 3,iii(1970):138–39.

74 Gascoigne, Katherine A. "Wisconsin Consortium Report." Madison, Wisconsin: James Madison Memorial High School, n.d. [Mimeograph.]

75 General Services Administration. *ERIC Training Filmstrips*. Washington,D.C.: National Audiovisual Center, 1970. [Zipcode 20409.]

76 "The German Center." *Foreign Language Annals* 3(1970):557.

77* Goetz, Dorothy F. "Activity Resource Unit for Teaching Culture in Foreign Language." Survey response. Bergenfield High School, 80 South Prospect, Bergenfield, New Jersey.

78 Goodman, Patricia. "Visual Generalizations." Ponca City, Oklahoma: Ponca City High School, n.d. [Mimeograph.] [Zipcode 74601.]

79 Green, Jerald R. *Spanish Phonology for Teachers:A Programmed Introduction*. Philadelphia: Center for Curriculum Development, 1970.

80 Haile, H.G. "Learning About Language." *Modern Language Journal* 54(1970):120–25.

81 Hammerly, Hector. "And Then They Disbelieved Their Ears." *Hispania* 53(1970):72–75.

82 Hammond, Patricia, and Alan Garfinkel,eds. *Recipes for Teaching Foreign Languages in Oklahoma*. Oklahoma City: Oklahoma Curriculum Improvement Commission, 1970.

83 Hamson, Erwin M. "The Closed Booth Laboratory." *Audio-Visual Language Journal* 6(1968):74–77.

84 ——— to author. Personal communication, n.d.

85 Hanzeli, Victor E., and William D. Love,eds. *New Teachers for New Students*. Seattle and New York: Washington Foreign Language Program and the American Council on the Teaching of Foreign Languages, 1970. [Available: Modern Language Association Materials Cen-

ter, 62 Fifth Avenue, New York 10011.]

86 Harnack, Robert S. *The Teacher:Decision Maker and Curriculum Planner*. Scranton, Pennsylvania: International Textbook Company, 1968.

87 Hehr, Edith S. "More Suggestions for German Club." *Die Unterrichtspraxis* 3,i(1970):181.

88 Helmers, Hermann. *Didaktik der Deutschen Sprache*. Stuttgart: Klett Verlag, 1970.

89 Hester, Ralph M.,ed. *Teaching a Living Language*. New York: Harper & Row, 1970.

90 —— and Yvonne Lenard. *L'art de la conversation*. New York: Harper & Row, 1970.

91 Heymans, G.C. "Audio-Lingual Teaching:Some Practical Suggestions." *Canadian Modern Language Review* 26,iii(1970):24–28.

92* Hill, Steven P. "Russian Baseball and Basketball Terminology." *University of Illinois Modern Foreign Language Newsletter* February (1970):n. pag. [List of terms available from Department of Slavic Languages, Univ. of Illinois, Urbana, Illinois 61801.]

93 Hinojosa-Smith, Rolando. "'Live' Language Laboratory." Kingsville, Texas: Texas A & I Univ., n.d. [Mimeograph.]

94 Horne, Kibbey M. "Optimum Class Size for Intensive Language Instruction." *Modern Language Journal* 54(1970):189–95.

95 Horodowich, Peggy L. "Levels of Language Success." *Hispania* 53(1970):260–62.

96 Incorporated Association of Assistant Masters in Secondary Schools. *The Teaching of Modern Languages*. London: Univ. of London Press, 1967.

97 "Indian Children Find Words by Taking Pictures." *New York Times* 28 August(1970):33.

98 *Individualization of Foreign Language Learning in America*. John F. Bockman and Ronald L. Gougher,eds. West Chester State College: West Chester, Pennsylvania. [Available: Foreign Language Department; zipcode 19380.]

99 Jakobovits, Leon A. *Foreign Language Learning:A Psycholinguistic Analysis of the Issues*. Rowley, Massachusetts: Newbury House, 1970.

100 Jarvis, Gilbert A. "Strategies of Instruction for Listening and Reading," 79–111 in Dale L. Lange,ed., *The Britannica Review of Foreign Language Education, Volume 2*. Chicago: Encyclopaedia Britannica, Inc., 1970.

101 Jenkins, Jacinto C. "The Effects of Explanation with Spanish Pattern Drills." *Dissertation Abstracts* 30(1970):3193A(Stanford).

102 Kadler, Eric H. *Linguistics and Teaching Foreign Languages*. New York: Van Nostrand Reinhold, 1970.

103 Kaminar de Mujica, Barbara, and Guillermo Segreda. *A-LM Spanish, Level II*. Second edition. New York: Harcourt Brace Jovanovich, 1970.

104 Keitel, Helmut A. "Development and Dissemination of Materials for Teaching World History in a Foreign Language(German)." *Modern Language Journal* 54(1970):112–15.

105 Kellermann, Marcelle. *Two Experiments on Language Teaching in Primary Schools in Leeds*. London: The Nuffield Foundation, 1964.

106 Kelly, Louis G. *25 Centuries of Language Teaching*. Rowley, Massachusetts: Newbury House, 1970.

107 Kennedy, Dora F. to author. Personal communication, n.d.

108 Klin, George. "Content and Methods in Conversation Courses." *French Review* 53(1970):641–47.

109* Koch, Judy. "French Program at Pullman High School." Pullman, Washington: Pullman High School, n.d. [Mimeograph.] [Zipcode 99163.]

110 Ladd, Magdalena. "Motivation Through Major Interest in Intermediate Foreign Language Learning." *Modern Language Journal* 54(1970):578–79.

111 Lado, Robert, and Protase Woodford. *Español: Lengua y letra*. New York: McGraw-Hill, 1970.

112* LaLeike, Fred H. "Individualized Foreign Language Program." Survey response. Joint School District #1, 710 South Main Street, West Bend, Wisconsin.

113 Lane, Harlan, and Guy C. Capelle. *The World's Research in Language Learning*. Ann Arbor, Michigan: Center for Research on Language and Language Behavior, 1969.

114 Lange, Dale L. "Methods," 281–310 in Emma Marie Birkmaier,ed., *The Britannica Review of Foreign Language Education, Volume 1*. Chicago: Encyclopaedia Britannica, Inc., 1968 [1969].

115 ——, comp. "1970 ACTFL Annual Bibliography." *Foreign Language Annals* 4(1971):427–90.

116 ——,ed. *The Britannica Review of Foreign Language Education, Volume 2*. Chicago: Encyclopaedia Britannica, Inc., 1970.

117 *Language-Teaching Abstracts*. English Teaching Information Centre and the Centre for Information on Language Teaching,eds. London: Cambridge Univ. Press. [Available: Cambridge Univ. Press, 32 East 57th Street, New York, N.Y.]

118 Lenard, Yvonne. *Jeunes voix, jeunes visages*. New York: Harper & Row, 1970.

119 —— *Jeunes voix, jeunes visages, Teachers Edition*. New York: Harper & Row, 1970.

120 Locke, John L. "The Value of Repetition in Articulation Learning." *International Review of Applied Linguistics* 8(1970):147–54.

121 Logan, Gerald E. "A Totally Individualized High School Program." *Individualization of Foreign Language Learning in America* 1,i(1970):8–10.

122 —— *Kernstufe* (Tentative Title, Level I). Morgan Hill, California: Author, n.d. [Mimeograph.]

123 Malcolm, Andrew H. "Study of Foreign Languages Declines." *New York Times* 23 August (1970):1.

124 Marckwardt, Albert H.,ed. *Linguistics in School Programs, NSSE Year Book LXIX, Part II*. Chicago: National Society for the Study of Education, 1970. [Available: Univ. of Chicago Bookstore, 5701 South Ellis Avenue, Chicago,

Illinois 60637.]

125 Marton, Ilona. *European History in French.* Kensington, Maryland: Albert Einstein High School, n.d. [Mimeograph.]

126 Masciantonio, Rudolph. "Innovation of Classical Programs in The School District of Philadelphia." *Foreign Language Annals* 3(1970):592–95.

127 Mathieu, G. Bording. "Poems in Early Foreign Language Instruction." *MLA/ERIC Focus Report Number 15.* New York: Modern Language Association Materials Center, 1970.

128 Matthews, J.E. "Tape Recorder Projects." *Modern Languages* 51(1970):62–66.

129 McClennan, Robert. "German Language Program Mountain View High School, California." *Individualization of Foreign Language Learning in America* 1,i(1970):6–8.

130 Mengler, Klaus. "Possible Use of the Flannel Board in French Teaching." *Praxis des neusprachlichen Unterrichts* 17(1970):289–303.

131 Meyer, Gertrud E. " 'Career Day' at Whitewater, Wisconsin." *Foreign Language Annals* 3(1970): 554–55.

132 Michalski, John. "News Media as a Source of Culture in the German Classroom." Unpublished paper. [ERIC Document Reproduction Service: ED 042 382.]

133 Mildenberger, Andrea S., and Margarita Mazzeo. "ERIC Documents on the Teaching of Foreign Languages:List Number 4." *Foreign Language Annals* 3(1970):489–502.

134 Minn, Jay Paul. "Pattern Drill 'Schmattern Drill':An Essay on Communication." *The Dialog* 4,iii(1970):2–8. [ERIC Document Reproduction Service: ED 037 147.]

135 *Modern Languages:Teaching and Testing.* Princeton, New Jersey: Educational Testing Service, 1970.

136 Molepske, Jerrold H. to author. Personal communication, n.d.

137 Monka, Carolyn. "ERIC Documents on the Teaching of Foreign Languages:List Number 5." *Foreign Language Annals* 4(1970):313–28.

138 Morel, Stefano. *Total Immersion Language Program.* Albany, New York: State Department of Education, 1970.

139 —— *Total Immersion Language Program: Technical Report.* Albany, New York: State Department of Education, 1971.

140 Mortenson, Gerald A., and Dorothy A. Rhoads. "Latin by Informed Descriptive Linguistics." Pittsfield, Massachusetts: Pittsfield High School, n.d. [Mimeograph.]

141 Morton, F. Rand. "Experimental Approach to the Language Requirement (The College of Artesia Bilingual Program)." *Modern Language Journal* 54(1970):20–25.

142 Mueller, Theodore H. "Research in Progress." Lexington, Kentucky: Univ. of Kentucky, 1970. [Mimeograph.]

143 Nostrand, Howard L., et al.,eds. *Research on Language Teaching:An Annotated International Bibliography, 1945–64.* Seattle: Univ. of Washington Press, 1965.

144 Ollman, Mary J.,ed. *Selective List of Materials for Use by Teachers of Modern Foreign Languages in Elementary and Secondary Schools.* New York: Modern Language Association, 1962.

145 "Oppose NDEA Slavic Studies Budget Cuts." *New York Times* 29 March(1970):3.

146 Orfali, Stephanie. "Der verrückte Deutsch-klub: Eine Lehrübung." *Die Unterrichtspraxis* 3,ii(1970):147.

147 Palmer, Adrian. "Teaching Communication." *Language Learning* 20(1970):55–68.

148 Papalia, Anthony. "A Study of Attrition in Foreign Language Enrollment in 4 Suburban Public Schools." *Dissertation Abstracts International* 30(1970):3199A (State Univ. of New York, Buffalo).

149 Parent, P. Paul. "Toward the Nucleation Stage: An Investigation of Three Methods of Teaching Reading Comprehension in a College Course in Intermediate French." *Dissertation Abstracts International* 31(1970):683A (Pennsylvania State).

150 —— and Simon Belasco. "Parallel Column Bilingual Reading Materials as a Pedagogical Device:An Experimental Evaluation." *Modern Language Journal* 54(1970):493–504.

151 Pill, Geoffrey. "Composition and the Four Skills," Stillwater, Oklahoma: Oklahoma State Univ., n.d. [Mimeograph.] [Department of Foreign Languages, Stillwater, Oklahoma 74074.]

152 Pimsleur, Paul. "New Approaches to Old Problems Through Testing." *Canadian Modern Language Review* 26(1970):23–32.

153 —— *C'est la vie:Lectures d'aujourd'hui.* New York: Harcourt Brace Jovanovich, 1970.

154 Politzer, Robert L. *Foreign Language Learning:A Linguistic Introduction.* Definitive edition. Englewood Cliffs, New Jersey: Prentice-Hall, 1970.

155 —— and Louis Weiss. *Improving Achievement in Foreign Language.* Philadelphia: Center for Curriculum Development, 1970.

156 —— *The Successful Foreign Language Teacher.* Philadelphia: Center for Curriculum Development, 1970.

157 Pollei, G.E. to author. Personal communication, n.d.

158 Prather, Andy to author. Personal communication, n.d.

159 Probst, Glen W. "Two Basic Methods of Presenting Spanish at the University Level." *Dissertation Abstracts International* 30(1970):4152A (Ohio State).

160 Reichmann, Eberhard,ed. *The Teaching of German:Problems and Methods.* Philadelphia: The American Association of Teachers of German and the National Carl Schurz Association, 1970.

161 Remington, Louise. "Dramatization in the Target Language." Mesquite, Texas: Mesquite Public Schools, n.d. [Mimeograph.]

162 Rivers, Wilga M.,et al. "Techniques for Developing Proficiency in the Spoken Language." Stanford, California: Stanford Conference on Indi-

vidualizing Foreign Language Instruction, 1971. [Mimeograph.]

163 Roe, Clair. *La vie d'un vendeur d'automobiles.* London: Longman, 1970.

164 Ross, L. "Improving the Effectiveness of Language Laboratory Work." *Audio-Visual Language Journal* 8(1970):25–35.

165 Rosselot, Lavelle, Margaret L. Wood, Alain M. Favrod, and Edward F. Wilgocki,Jr. *Je Parle Français.* Second edition. Chicago: Encyclopaedia Britannica Educational Corporation, 1970.

166 Rothfarb, Sylvia H. "Teacher-Pupil Interaction in the FLES Class." *Hispania* 54(1970):256–60.

167 Rundell, George M. *Foreign Language Exploration.* Topeka, Kansas: Topeka Public Schools, 1971. [In press.]

168 "Russian Teaching Films on Language." *Audio-Visual Language Journal* 8(1970):49.

169 Rutt, Theodor. *Der Unterricht im Sprechen und Aufsetzen.* Wuppertal-Elberfeld, German Federal Republic: Henn, 1970.

170 Ryberg, Donald C. "A Learning-Centered Teacher Preparation Program:A Series of Applied Problems," 8–17 and 20–22 in Victor E. Hanzeli and William D. Love,eds., *New Teachers for New Students.* Seattle and New York: Washington Foreign Language Program and the American Council on the Teaching of Foreign Languages, 1970.

171 —— "Student Involvement Flexibility and Individualization." *Washington Foreign Language Program Newsletter* 15 February(1971): n.pag.

172 Sadler, Edward J. "Model for Teacher Behavior in Level I Audio-Lingual Language Programs Based on an Analysis of Current Teaching Methodology and Teacher Preparation." *Dissertation Abstracts International* 30(1970):3839A (Nebraska).

173 Sandberg, Karl C. "Writing Laboratories:A New Approach to Teaching Composition." *Arizona Foreign Language Teachers Forum* 15,iii(1968):5–8. [ERIC Document Reproduction Service: ED 018 799.]

174 Scherer. George A.C. "Programming Second Language Reading," 108–129 in G. Mathieu,ed., *Advances in the Teaching of Modern Languages, Volume II.* Oxford: Pergamon Press, 1966.

175 Schuh, Hermann. "Deutsch als Fremdsprache im Kindergarten der Auslandsschule." *Zielsprache Deutsch* 1(1970):35–41.

176 Schulz, Dora, Heinz Griesbach, and Morten Lund. *Auf Deutsch, bitte.* Munich: Hueber, 1970.

177 Seifman, Eli. "Teaching Strategies," 53–62 in Dwight Allen and Eli Seifman,eds., *The Teacher's Handbook.* Glenview, Illinois: Scott-Foresman, 1971.

178 Semke, Harriet D. "Wie gefällt Ihnen." *Die Unterrichtspraxis* 3,ii(1970):146.

179 Seward, Elizabeth N. "Employment of the Target Language in Learning a Third Language."

Survey response. South Junior High School, Boise, Idaho.

180 Shepherd, W. Everitt. "An Experiment in Individualized French." *Foreign Language Annals* 3(1970):394–99.

181 Silberman, Charles E. *Crisis in the Classroom.* New York: Random House, 1970.

182 Slack, Anne,ed. "Le coin du pedagogue." *French Review* 53(1970):651–52.

183 Smart, John C., Charles F. Elton, and Collins W. Burnett. "Underachievers and Overachievers in Intermediate French." *Modern Language Journal* 54(1970):415–20.

184 Smith, Alfred N. "Strategies of Instruction for Speaking and Writing," 113–31 in Dale L. Lange,ed., *The Britannica Review of Foreign Language Education, Volume 2.* Chicago: Encyclopaedia Britannica, Inc., 1970.

185 Smith, Sidney R. "Teaching the Modified-Adjective Construction." *Die Unterrichtspraxis* 3,ii(1970):52–55.

186 "Spanglish is Spoken Here; And New School Teaches It." *New York Times* 28 December (1970):33.

187 Sosenko, E.U. "Linguistic Foundations for A System of Exercises to Train Oral Communication." *Russkij Jazyk v Škole* 5(1970):71–74. [Title translated.]

188 *Southwest Cooperative Educational Laboratory Mark III Oral Language Program.* Albuquerque: Southwest Cooperative Educational Laboratory, 1970.

189 Spears, Ann, and Julie Lottinville to author. Personal communication, n.d.

190 Spolsky, Bernard. *Getting Down to the Grass Roots:Affiliate Affairs.* Presented at the Fourth Annual TESOL Convention. San Francisco, March 1970. [ERIC Document Reproduction Service: ED 037 709.]

191 Steiner, Florence. "Perfecting Objectives in the Teaching of Foreign Languages." *Foreign Language Annals* 3(1970):579–91.

192 Steiner, Jon, and Beverly White. "Fourth Year French Team." Mercer Island, Washington: Mercer Island High School, n.d. [Mimeograph.]

193 Stockton, Edith B. to author. Personal communication, 1971.

194 Stough, G.,et al. "Video in the Foreign Language Classroom." Cleveland, Ohio: Ford Junior High School, 1970. [Mimeograph.]

195 Strasheim, Lorraine A. "Teaching the Latin Student to Translate." *MLA/ERIC Focus Report Number 17.* New York: Modern Language Association Materials Center, 1970.

196 —— "Teacher Training . . . For What?" 3–7 in Victor E. Hanzeli and William D. Love,eds., *New Teachers For New Students.* Seattle and New York: Washington Foreign Language Program and the American Council on the Teaching of Foreign Languages, 1970.

197 Tamarkin, Toby. "Career Language Program." Manchester, Connecticut: Manchester Community College, n.d. [Mimeograph.]

198 Tate, Robert S. "Teaching French 'à deux' at Duke." *French Review* 54(1970):92–94.

199 Taylor, James S. "Direct Classroom Teaching of Cultural Concepts," 42–50 in H. Ned Seelye, ed., *Perspectives for Teachers of Latin American Culture*. Springfield, Illinois: State Department of Public Instruction, 1970.

200 *Toute la bande*. New York: Scholastic Publications, 1970.

201 Tucker, Mary J. to author. Personal communication, 1971.

202 Tuel, Isis. "Oklahoma Workshop." *Modern Language Journal* 54(1970):426,436.

203 Turner, John D., ed., *Programming for The Language Laboratory*. London: Univ. of London Press, 1968.

204 Turner, Ronald C. "CARLOS:Computer Assisted Instruction in Spanish." *Hispania* 53(1970): 249–53.

205 Turner, Susan C. to author. Personal communication, 1971.

206 Tursi, Joseph A., ed. *Foreign Languages and the "New" Student*. Reports of the Working Committees of the Northeast Conference on the Teaching of Foreign Languages. New York: Modern Language Association Materials Center, 1970.

207 Valette, Rebecca M. "Evaluation of Learning in a Second Language," 815–53 in Benjamin S. Bloom and Hastings Madeus, eds., *Handbook on Formative and Summative Evaluation of Student Learning*. New York: McGraw-Hill, 1971.

208 Wagner, Marybeth. "Mass Media Aid Language Study at University of Illinois." *Champaign-Urbana Courier* (May 16, 1971):n.pag.

209 Walker, Claire. "What is our First Priority in Teaching?" *Slavic and Eastern European Journal* 14(1970):47–53. [Materials available from Friends School, 5114 North Charles, Baltimore, Maryland 21210.]

210 Walker, Jo Ann. "Problem and Answers." *Oklahoma Foreign Language Teachers Association Newsletter* 4,iii(1970):2.

211 Walsh, Donald D., ed. *A Handbook for Teachers of Spanish and Portuguese*. Lexington, Massachusetts: D.C. Heath, 1969.

212* Wells, Gloria. "Individualizing Foreign Language Instruction." Northridge, California: Nobel Junior High School, n.d. [Mimeograph.] [9950 Tampa Avenue, Northridge, California 91234.]

213 Wilson, Robert. "In Danville:Spanish Takes Root in Elementary Schools." *Danville Commercial News* 25 November(1970):n.pag.

214 Wood, Fred H. "The McCluer Plan:An Innovative Non-Graded Foreign Language Program." *Modern Language Journal* 54(1970):184–87.

215 Wolfe, David L. *Curso básico de español*. New York: Macmillan, 1970.

216 Wright, Wendy A. "Testing Examples and Suggestions for Use With Le Français International, Level I." *Canadian Modern Language Review* 27,i(1970):33–43.

217 *Zielsprache Deutsch*. Goethe-Institut(Munich), ed. Munich: Max Hueber Verlag. [8045 Ismaning bei München, Krausstrasse 30, German Federal Republic.]

8

Individualization of foreign language learning: What is being done

Introduction and scope

Ronald L. Gougher

West Chester State College

After the entire *Britannica Review of Foreign Language Education, Volume 2* (Lange, 52) was devoted to individualized foreign language instruction, representing a milestone in foreign language education, it does seem fitting to review briefly just how the interest in individualized foreign language instruction has expanded, how theory has developed and crystallized, as well as to determine what consensuses about individualized instruction have begun to develop among the members of the foreign language teaching profession in 1970 and early 1971. Then, too, the practicing foreign language teacher will want to review how and where foreign language instruction is being individualized in America, including a survey of the problems, potentials, and limitations.

Raising the issues

Although it appeared only in the waning days of 1970, the most inclusive treatise of the year on individualized instruction was the *Britannica Review of Foreign Language Education, Volume 2* (Lange, 52). The different chapter authors provided the profession with a review of literature and expert comment about the major aspects of individualized foreign language instruction. Such a comprehensive and potentially influential volume is certainly worthy of special attention.

Strasheim (95) leads off well as she explains the rationale for diversification and personalization in a truly student-centered pedagogy.

A rationale for individualization

In Volume 2, as in most current discussions about individualized instruction, the issue of behavioral objectives plays a prominent role. Steiner (91) provides a very detailed analysis. Although educators appear to be divided on whether behavioral objectives are helpful or harmful, there does seem to be a very convincing case for performance objectives as aids to students and guides to curricular development in individualized programs.

Behavioral objectives

Individualization of language learning/Gougher

Adequate preplanning is essential for successful use of performance objectives in individualized instruction. Both the teacher and the student must know what each is expected to do within acceptable time limits in each individual, practical school situation. Objectives must state clearly what linguistic and humanistic goals are to be reached by the student, as well as what the teacher might do. It is likewise important that testing and evaluation be based only on those objectives set in advance in a performance curriculum for individualized pacing.

Jarvis (46) reviews strategies for inculcation of listening and reading skills, while Smith (83) surveys strategies of instruction in reading, speaking, and writing skills. Listening and reading are classified as receptive skills, whereas speaking and writing are labeled productive skills. Both chapters concentrate on what the authors believe are basic pedagogical truths related to the skills in question, including the implications for individualizing instruction.

Instructional strategies

One of the most important reviews for the teacher of foreign languages interested in individualizing instruction is the survey of curricula for individualized instruction. Logan (55) points out that there are at least seven categories of individualized foreign language instruction, ranging from self-pacing (the most common type), independent study, and interest- and ability-grouping to combinations based on these three. Materials used fall, too, into categories, including standard texts, programmed materials, computerized programs, learning packets, and so forth. With reference to learning packets, a doctoral dissertation is now being completed wherein the author (Teichert, 99) compares the effectiveness of learning via learning packets with the effectiveness of learning in the conventional classroom.

Curricula for individualized instruction

In addition, Logan (55) offers practical suggestions about scheduling, curricular development, sources of material, adjustment of facilities, and proper articulation. It is emphasized that communication and discussion among the members of the foreign language teaching profession are essential to enhance development of effective individualized instruction in America.

With increased individualization of curricula and the inevitable varied approaches, a need for more numerous combinations in the use of educational media arises. Arendt (6) provides the profession with an excellent survey of literature concerning the use of hardware as well as software in foreign language teaching. He relates his topic to various individualized programs and

Use of media

offers the profession a thorough basis for thought and planning for the use of media.

With the change in philosophical approach toward individualized learning has come an alteration in attitudes about the use of language laboratories. Smith (87) states that machine-aided instruction is effective in intensive language learning. Such instruction is of special theoretical and practical value to teachers wanting to individualize, in semi- or totally individualized learning programs. Although more research is needed to assess the full effectiveness of innovative equipment, it seems clear that more portable equipment is needed to facilitate individualized language learning in the schools.

Use of language laboratories

Altman & Weiss (5) discuss the latest trends in foreign language teacher education, projecting that the new emphasis on attention to the individual student will inevitably affect the training of teachers to guide the students. Reviews of some innovative graduate teacher-training programs offer a source of information for those interested in keeping abreast of developments in foreign language teacher education.

Teacher education

The teaching of Latin and Greek has begun to undergo some changes in the direction of individualization, although there is still much teacher resistance to changing older, traditional methods of teaching the classics. Reports of several innovative approaches present real alternatives for the teacher interested in individualizing classics curricula in the schools (Erickson, 27).

Teaching of Latin and Greek

In his review of the status of TESOL (Teaching English to Speakers of Other Languages), Spolsky (90) concludes that related programs have the potential to answer the need for relevance for large groups of students in America.

TESOL

Although some chapters in Volume 2 deal only in part with individualized foreign language instruction, most do provide needed insights and helpful hints for teachers wanting to learn about individualizing foreign language learning in America. The issues have begun to be presented more succinctly because of this major contribution to foreign language education.

The profession inquires — growing interest and evidence of a need for change

Growing interest in both the theory and the practice of individualized instruction is well documented throughout pedagogical literature in 1970 and early 1971.

Individualization of language learning/Gougher

One sign of increased interest was the positive reaction and nationwide attention accorded *Individualization of Foreign Language Learning in America*, a newsletter devoted to individualized instruction, printed and distributed by the Foreign Language Department of West Chester State College, Pennsylvania. The editors (Bockman & Gougher, 16) have received hundreds of requests for copies, even after a fairly wide audience was reached by using mailing lists available to the profession. This newsletter has been reviewed and mentioned in many well-known state and national journals, too numerous to mention here. *Foreign Language Annals* is now supporting a permanent column on individualized instruction to be edited by Bockman & Gougher (15). The decision to support such a column was endorsed publicly by a prominent foreign language educator, Wilga Rivers, and her working committee at the Stanford Conference on Individualized Instruction in May, 1971. The MLA/ERIC Clearinghouse on Foreign Languages has accessioned this newsletter into the ERIC system.

A newsletter and a column in Foreign Language Annals

The Northeast Association for the Individualization of Instruction (68) continues to be active. It also produces a newsletter encouraging individualized learning in many subject areas.

Many foreign language conferences in 1970 and early 1971 were devoted, at least in part, to individualized instruction. The University of Kentucky Foreign Language Conference sponsored a special meeting on Individualized Instruction in Foreign Language Teaching (Altman, 3; Gordon, 33; Jakobovits, 44). The Delaware Council on the Teaching of Foreign Languages devoted much effort and time to individualized foreign language instruction in 1970 and early 1971 (Bryant, 21; Sohodski & Bohning et al., 88; Villa & Robbins, 105). Among numerous others, the Utah Foreign Language Association (Logan, 56), St. Joseph's College, Emmittsburg, Maryland (Kincaid & Flinton et al., 49), and the Wisconsin Department of Public Instruction (42) hosted conferences devoted to individualized instruction. There is no doubt that interest in theory and practice is growing rapidly.

Conferences and papers on individualized instruction

The most prestigious of the conferences on individualized foreign language instruction was held in early May, 1971, at Stanford University, supported by a United States Office of Education grant. The conference and the work done there will have to be evaluated and discussed for years to come. An assessment of its full impact is not possible at this time. With competent, well-known members of the profession participating, the issues be-

The Stanford University conference

224

came clearer; and there was a spirit of cautious optimism at the end of the conference. However, many still retained a "wait and see" attitude after the summit at Palo Alto.

Topics related to individualization in professional literature, conference papers and reports, and in-service workshops show that much of the increased interest was motivated by the desire to establish needs for a change to individualized instruction as well as to define the concept.

Being concerned about each individual and how he learns are not really new ideas in education. Private secondary schools have emphasized for years that their students will benefit from more individual attention. Tutorials on the college level have allowed many gifted and well-motivated students to learn at their own pace and within their own academic areas of interest and concentration. For a long time independent study in its many forms has been on the American educational scene. Even in the old one-room schoolhouse there was by necessity an abundance of individualized instruction (Steiner, 92; Logan, 55).

Individualization of instruction is not a new concept

What appears to be new in America is the increased need for individualized instruction based on the desire of many students for more self-identity, self-orientation, and self-direction (Strasheim, 95). These student desires and the subsequent personal queries have produced an increased awareness that much of teacher-centered instruction in foreign languages is highly inadequate. There is a growing feeling that the schools may be educating students for the type of world that will not exist a few years from now. As a result, each student must participate in determining who he is, what he is doing, and where he is heading (Steiner, 92).

Increased interest based on desires of students

The individual needs an opportunity to prepare for the future in an innovative American society (Gardner, 31). Politzer (71) contends that the trend toward individualization is a reaction against a curriculum that tended to neglect individual differences. This reaction is in line with present trends that stress the learner's role rather than that of the teacher. Many professional educators have reacted to students' individual needs for the present and beyond by criticizing many present and past practices and suggesting some changes for the immediate future. Such is the case partly because students desire and request a larger role in planning learning activity and partly because teachers recognize that students need more experience in planning their own destinies (Gordon, 33; Raubinger & Row, 72;

Student and teacher roles may change

Individualization of language learning/Gougher

Shofstall, 81). The disillusionment caused by an inadequate and perhaps outdated teaching-learning model has become increasingly disturbing to serious, concerned educators (Roberts, 74). As a result many such educators are acting to change the situation.

The teaching-learning model in any case relies on the roles of the elements and people involved. First let us discuss the role of the teacher. Many educators (Barrett & Phelps, 9; Bockman & Gougher, 15; Jakobovits, 44; Keller, 48; Kincaid & Flinton et al., 49; Raubinger & Row, 72; and Sutton, 97) believe that the traditional teacher's role as dispenser of knowledge and authority figure must change. The teacher no longer need be the center of the learning process; he should no longer merely present information and evaluate how well the student learns that information within the specifically set time limits. Some authors point out that the teacher's main function should be to supply the students with recorded tapes, learning packets, textbooks, and programmed materials. In that manner the teacher dispenses the information to be learned and presents it to each individual student. In addition, the teacher's task is to state clearly what the performance objectives are and suggest possible ways of achieving them, acting as the student's guide and counselor in the process (Duda, 24; Estarellas, 28; Lohnes, 58; Steiner, 93).

The teacher's role

The "new" teacher's role will require him to encourage some students to change their thinking about learning, as well as to help them learn individually. In this new role the teacher will become a long-range planner, organizing language learning materials in such a way that each student will be able to use them independently and effectively to reach acceptable levels of linguistic performance. In addition, the teacher will want to provide guidance for the students' understanding of humanistic concepts (Gougher, 34,35,36).

Teacher tasks

Since not all individualized instruction is carried out on a one-to-one basis, the teacher must also learn how to plan and organize small group activities to facilitate interaction in the target language (Logan, 55; McClennan, 60).

Since individualized programs require good record-keeping, the "new" teacher will have to develop and maintain precise record-keeping systems to determine the extent of each student's progress (Steiner, 92). He must also learn to become an effective guidance counselor (Rogers, 75) for the students who will need him in that capacity. And finally the teacher must be available as a motivator (Gougher, 38), as well as a diagnostician

Record-keeping and counseling

and flexible prescriber (Steiner, 93). Although these goals are idealistic, teachers can, indeed, succeed at individualizing foreign language instruction (Sutton, 96).

All the needed and suggested activities are aimed at the "new" teacher's role of reaching all the students effectively (Hugot & Caldwell et al., 41; Ryberg, 76; Sandstrom & Pimsleur, 77), helping each student to learn, making him sense that *he* is responsible for his *own* learning (Eisenhardt, 26), and providing him with the tools to do it. This "new" role creates a colleaguial instead of an adversary relationship between student and teacher.

In the present period of change that education is experiencing, the teacher is required to continually assess his professional as well as his personal strengths and weaknesses (Jersild, 47). The *Teachers need continual self-assessment* changes that are taking place in our profession indicate a greater need for more teacher training, especially in individualizing instruction. At least two members of the profession have developed teacher-training courses devoted to individualized instruction, one at San Francisco State College (89) and one at San Jose State College, California. Altman & Weiss (5) believe teacher training will move more and more in the direction of preparing students to teach in programs that individualize instruction.

The major contributions that administrators can provide for *Contribution of administrators to individualization* individualizing instruction are time and assistance for the teachers to prepare materials, expert help in selecting resources and arranging the learning facilities available, and a forum in which the teachers can communicate to the community what the school is trying to do for the students (Steiner, 92). Some administrators (102) are encouraging development of in-service seminars and workshops to clarify aims, methods, and curricula for individualized programs (Bockman, 14) and to make suggestions for their management. One eminent foreign language educator believes that text-adoption policies governed by the state foreign language administrators must be made more flexible to allow for easier and more effective individualized foreign language study in America (Smith, 85).

Just as there is a need for the teacher to change—to become guide, evaluator, assistant planner, counselor, and diagnostician in terms of the individual student—so there is a great need for the student to become more and more aware that he is, in fact, *The student's role* his *own* keeper. In the language learning situation he must share the teaching role with the classroom teacher and become

227

more responsible for his own decisions (Barrett & Phelps, 9; Bockman & Gougher, 16; Keller, 48; Jakobovits, 45).

The "new" student needs to face each task himself. He must *Student must know self* come to know each type of learning activity for which he is responsible. He must learn to discover his own weaknesses and strengths. He must learn how much time it takes him to achieve certain performance objectives. This "discovery" of self leads to a different approach to learning and growing, which has implications far beyond the learning of a foreign language (Steiner, 92).

There is an underlying need for learning excellence, itself, expressed in the literature. Several scholars and teachers believe that individualization will provide opportunities for more students to achieve excellence in the form of higher levels of performance relative to their own abilities and motivation (Bohning, 17; Keller, 48; McClennan, 62; McDonald, 63; Steiner, 93).

Excellence as a goal in foreign language education and life does not *necessarily* imply that only the top-notch, intelligent, well-motivated student will be allowed to develop his talents, thereby achieving to the disadvantage of the majority. On the contrary, there is a need for programs in which many students can achieve excellence when they learn what they need and want to learn at their own optimum rate. Gardner (30) believes American society and education can engender excellence by encouraging all to do their best individually. It is a raising of the *What is excellence?* tone of thinking and behaving. It is a recognition that the goal of excellence, *if* it is at all attainable, is so *only* if all individuals are, in fact, *trying*. But, then, the individual must be given the *opportunity* to try. And that is precisely what many educators who are attempting to individualize foreign language instruction are doing: providing the individual with an opportunity to learn a foreign language.

A few basic reasons why the profession should seek to help *Why help students achieve* students achieve excellence in individualized performance cur- *excellence?* ricula are put forth by Steiner (93). Among those reasons are: (*1*) the student can measure and know exactly what he has done; (2) he can develop to his highest potential with reference to foreign language study and learning in general; (3) he will learn *how to* learn, a fact that may be very important 20 years from now.

Says Steiner, "That is why we teach!"

Defining individualized instruction — a pluralistic concept

Although one observes increased interest and expansion of theory and practice, not until very recently have educators really attempted to define individualized foreign language instruction. It has been evident that many educators find it difficult to explicate the term *individualized instruction* when called upon to do so. One *now* finds professional literature attempting to define or describe in writing what individualized foreign language instruction actually means.

Altman (1,2,3) and Gougher (36,37) believe we can only provide philosophical bases *toward* defining individualized instruction. Altman states that no one definition has been sufficient to provide clues to the teacher for practical classroom application. It is suggested that there are several basic *characteristics* of an individualized foreign language program, including:

Basis for a definition of individualization of instruction

1 Students are free to proceed at their own pace.
2 Students are tested at given intervals on only that about which they expect to be tested.
3 When students need help to progress in their learning, they work individually with their teacher. The teacher compensates the student for the impediment to his learning by giving needed assistance.
4 Students always know the nature of their learning task. They know what they must be able to do and to what degree of accuracy to be able to move ahead.
5 It is not necessary for all students to have different texts. Many students may profit from learning the same material and participating in the same activities because they are studying foreign language for similar reasons.
6 Some group activity is necessary. No one can expect a teacher to work on a one-to-one basis with each student.
7 Special scheduling and grading systems are not absolutely necessary. Altman & Morrey (4) believe that failure can be eliminated entirely. Gougher (34,38) disagrees slightly. He believes that some time limitations are necessary, and, therefore, some failure will still occur in a practical sense.

Bockman & Gougher (16) assert that individualized instruction does not eliminate structured teaching strategies. The student and the teacher share the roles of teaching in the individualized learning process.

At least two members of the profession (Bourque, 18; Gougher, 37) indicate that the practicing foreign language teacher must seek out his own definition by reading the literature available and then forming his own concepts as they apply best in his local school situation. The individual abilities of the teacher will determine, to a great degree, what his definition of individualized instruction will be. The new situation, individualized instruction in the schools, will demand a careful evaluation and utilization of individual abilities of teachers. It could be a serious mistake not to include the teacher and his goals and aptitudes in the individualization process (Politzer, 71).

Need for the teacher to apply concepts to the local situation

It is obvious that past and present efforts to define individualized foreign language instruction have resulted in a pluralistic picture of individualization. This writer believes that the very diverse nature of the American school system militates against anything but a pluralistic definition.

Bases for operation — review of practical theories

At least one member of the profession (Bourque, 18) stresses that each foreign language teacher should read in the literature that concerns itself with the theory of individualized instruction. Then the teacher should consider implementing an individualized learning program in his own practical situation, using the literature as a basis for decision-making. When an interested teacher looks to the available literature in 1970 and early 1971, he finds a great variety of theory to absorb.

At least three general works provide help to teachers interested in individualization (Bishop, 10; Jakobovits, 45; Veatch, 104). Bishop does not deal specifically with individualized foreign language instruction, but his work provides many insights into theory upon which one might base an individualized program, as does the work of Veatch. In a part of his work, *Foreign Language Learning*, Jakobovits discusses individualized language learning or, as he calls it, "compensatory foreign language learning." He elucidates with sharp, concise insights some of the major issues in learning and teaching a foreign language, as well as the nature of the individual learner and the learning factors involved in second-language acquisition.

Three general works on individualization

In order to review other literature dealing with theory and the individualization of foreign language instruction, it is well to divide the discussion into ten basic areas:

Ten elements of individualization

1 Multimedia programs
2 Programmed learning
3 Small group work
4 Mini-courses
5 Individually prescribed instruction
6 Self-pacing and performance objectives
7 Independent study
8 Interest and relevance
9 Computer-assisted instruction
10 Differentiated staffing

Multimedia programs

Logan (55) states that multimedia approach materials are needed to permit widespread individualization of foreign language learning to take place in the schools. The multimedia approach can take some of the burden away from the teacher, saving him time to guide and plan learning activities. Arendt (6) gives a thorough account of theory based on the use of media in foreign language instruction. He indicates how and why visuals, sound recordings, slides and filmstrips, the overhead projector, television, films, and learning packets can be used and relates their use to individualized instruction. His critical comments and evaluations about theories of multimedia instruction are worthwhile for the profession to consider.

Smith (87) illustrates how the language laboratory, cassette recorders, and combinations of listening devices can be used effectively. Yarbro (108) has carefully outlined the use of a multimedia approach to French in Anne Arundel County, Maryland.

The Peace Corps has developed multimedia materials for learning Portuguese. In this program, it is believed that students will learn language more efficiently when they are given an opportunity to choose from several different individual "tracks," using multimedia materials that make provision for each person's learning strengths and weaknesses (Smith, 84). Similar attempts at multimedia individualization have been made in preparation of materials for teaching of African French in the Peace Corps (Smith & Sparkman, 86).

Programmed learning

Arendt (6) provides a good, short overview of programmed learning materials as they fit into the theory of individualized instruction, including a critical look at negative and positive aspects. Barrett (8) insists that programmed materials can be very effective if used appropriately. She concludes that there

231

must be a variety of activities presented to the student as a source of interest, and that interest will help to produce success in an individualized program based on programmed learning. Estarellas (28) and Arendt (6) state, however, that programming is still in a somewhat primitive state in second-language learning.

The value of small-group learning in individualized instruction is clarified by several educators experienced in the field. They all indicate how very important this aspect can be for development of successful programs in individualized foreign language learning (Altman, 1; Barrett & Phelps, 9; Bishop, 10; Gougher, 39; Logan, 55; Sutton, 97; Terwilliger, 100).

Small-group work

One-to-one teacher to student ratios and independent study do not always provide enough opportunity for speaking the foreign language and communicating in the target language with other students. The general consensus is that small group instruction gives each student an opportunity to interact with his fellow students, a highly desirable condition for best educational results. A good combination of independent study and small group work produces the best results, according to the literature available. (See listed items in paragraph above.)

The "mini-course" seems to be at least a partial answer for individualizing learning in small classes at more advanced levels. Moore (64) has outlined a "mini-course" curriculum for German III and German IV that capitalizes on individual student interest and personal motivation for studying the language. With enrollments dwindling in some schools, the "mini-course" may provide a practical answer to effective motivation and individualization.

Mini-courses

Duda (24) and Scanlon (79) believe individually prescribed instruction can be effective in the schools as a system of individualized instruction, *if* managed properly and expanded on a carefully controlled basis. It must include: (*1*) detailed specifications of educational objectives, (2) organization of methods and materials to attain these objectives, (3) careful evaluation of each student's present competence in a given subject, (4) daily evaluation and guidance of each pupil on an individual basis, (5) frequent monitoring of student performance, (6) continual evaluation to inform both the pupil and the teacher of progress toward a set objective.

Individually prescribed instruction

Appropriate tests are necessary in such a program. At least one publisher (22) has produced a series of language tests designed to help the teacher to diagnose learning problems, teach

232

for mastery, allow for remedial exercises, and encourage use of a performance curriculum. Such tests are helpful to provide for easier individualization of foreign language instruction.

Self-pacing or allowing individuals to learn at their own optimum rates continues to be the most popular basic philosophy in individualization of foreign language learning. Several basic characteristics of self-pacing programs are suggested by members of the profession (Bohning, 17; Bourque, 18; Gougher, 38; Keller, 48; LaLeike, 51; McClennan, 62; Reinert, 73; Ryberg, 76; Scherer, 80; Steiner, 91,93; Terwilliger, 100). Some basic tenets are:

Self-pacing and performance objectives

1 A student is permitted to move through a course at a speed commensurate with his own ability, interest, and motivation.
2 The student moves ahead to new material only after demonstrating near mastery of that which preceded.
3 There is as much one-to-one contact between teacher and student as time allows.
4 Credits are based on proficiency levels achieved according to preset performance objectives, not on time spent or *exposure* to language study.

Independent study is recommended most often for use in schools where there are very small enrollments in some languages, yet enough interest to motivate teachers and administrators to offer the languages on a small-scale basis. Such schools often individualize out of *necessity*.

Independent study

Independent study is important, too, for providing an opportunity for students to learn the uncommonly taught languages. Bockman (12,13) describes an experimental program for learning German and Russian at the junior high school level in Tucson, Arizona. These two languages are not as common as Spanish in Arizona. Perkins (69) describes the basic aims, methods, and curriculum of a self-instruction program in Japanese in Garden City High School, New York, and Kopp (50) outlines the course offerings in critical languages on an independent study basis at the Pennsylvania State University. Boyd-Bowman (20) has issued a helpful manual meant to assist program directors who are responsible for managing self-instruction in the non-Western languages, while Stevick (94) has developed a manual to aid professionals in the task of adapting language materials for purposes of individualizing instruction in the uncommonly taught languages.

Successful individualized foreign language programs based on student interests are not very prolific. Theoretically perhaps, the most idealistic of individualized programs based to a great degree on student interest are those at Live Oak High School, Morgan Hill, California, and Marshall-University High School in Minneapolis, Minnesota.

Interest and relevance

Logan (57) outlines courses to fit almost every possible interest a high school student studying foreign language might show — German for Fun, Commercial German, Conversational German, and so forth. Logan theorizes that every student of German at Live Oak High School should have his own personalized, individualized program.

Ryberg (76) espouses total curricular flexibility in the individualized foreign language program at Marshall-University High School. Theoretically the student is to be given a chance to engage in a wide variety of interest areas or to emphasize learning any one of the language skills he wishes to acquire.

The basic theory of Computer-Assisted Instruction is outlined well by Arendt (6) and Logan (55). Both indicate that CAI is really very new and not accessible to the vast majority of foreign language teachers. Turner (103) outlines a fine CAI program for learning Spanish at Dartmouth College, and Scanlon (78), of the University of Illinois, indicates how a CAI program might be set up for Latin study. He states that CAI will certainly be an important factor in individualizing foreign language instruction in the future. Some basic characteristics of a CAI program include:

Computer-assisted instruction

1 Each student proceeds at his own rate of speed.
2 The student responses are judged immediately.
3 Each student may stop at any point in his lesson and proceed later from that juncture.
4 The student can choose the areas in which he wishes to work at any one particular time.
5 Testing is a learning experience unlike that in a conventional classroom. Wrong answers do not carry with them the stigma of immediate embarrassment or bad grades. They merely indicate to the student that he must try again.

Differentiated staffing can be used in all or a combination of programs employing some of the theoretical categories discussed above. Logan (55) reviews some of the most common ways of using differentiated staffing to facilitate individualized instruction. Some activities for which various members of the

Differentiated staffing

234

staff – teachers, paraprofessionals, community volunteers – can be responsible are: (1) motivational, recreational, and group activities leader, (2) laboratory director, (3) conversation leader, (4) producer of materials, (5) diagnostician, (6) tutor, (7) phonetician, (8) librarian, (9) locator and purchaser of materials, (10) counselor in charge of individualizing student contracts. Wells (106) and Levy (53) "experimented" with differentiated staffing, assigning some of the duties mentioned above to various members of the foreign language department.

Although the Northeast Conference, 1971, took place late when one considers the purposes of this review, the author suggests that readers may well profit from reading the Conference Report (Hugot & Caldwell et al., 41). A few very helpful theories are suggested in relating innovative curricula to individualized instruction.

Implementation in the schools – practice and problems

As is true with many other educational developments a lag exists between discussion and development of any theory about individualized instruction *and* actual implementation in the schools. One might truthfully say that practice has lagged awesomely. When one considers the vast number of schools and colleges in America, the comparative number individualizing foreign language instruction seems, indeed, to be small; however, there are *some* schools individualizing, and the numbers are increasing slowly as members of the profession take a greater interest in theory.

Theory and implementation

Logan (55) cites a number of developing programs with various types of individualized learning. This writer will cite some of the more recent pilot experimental programs at the high school level and then some of the more established programs, hoping to provide the readers with insights into how programs are being implemented and the problems related to their implementation.

It must be emphasized that most programs are *still* based on adjusting curricula to learning rates, as Logan (55) reported for programs in 1969. One rather "new" experiment is being attempted in Portland (Maine) Public Schools (Thompson, 101). Again, the program is not new in theory, but new in *practice* in that particular school district. It is an example of a slowly developing pattern of individualization in American foreign lan-

The Portland (Maine) program: new in practice

guage teaching. Simply stated, the school district wants to change Spanish I from a course based on time spent to one based on performance criteria alone. In the beginning stages all students meet in a group with the teacher. The purposes of large group meetings in the initial stages are to achieve (1) instruction in the basic skills of the language learning process, (2) group practice leading to a good background in pronunciation and listening-comprehension skills, (3) development of the attitude and self-discipline necessary to language learning, and (4) training in procedures to be followed in the continuous learning phase of the program.

Beginning stage: large group meetings

After completing this introductory phase of the program, the student takes a pretest. Successful completion of the pretest means he is ready to enter the second phase of the program in which he will proceed at an individualized rate. He then advances according to his performance in prescribed tests. Now and then he will meet with larger groups of students to discuss topics for cultural enrichment. Small groups of students whose language learning levels are similar meet from time to time to use the target language for communication. The teacher supervises individual and group work with the help of teacher assistants and advanced Spanish students.

Pretest and second stage

A survey has shown that other, similar programs with variations, of course, are found in beginning or experimental stages in various cities and towns throughout America. By reviewing the schools and locations one can easily see that the development is widespread, at least geographically. Some one dozen examples are listed below:

Other programs

1 John Dewey High School in New York City (Levy, 52)
2 Montgomery County, Maryland (Arsenault, 7)
3 Eagle Rock High School, Los Angeles (Irwin & Casey, 43)
4 Lincoln High School, Manitowoc, Wisconsin (Mortwedt & Troupe, 65)
5 Bangor High School, Bangor, Maine (Economu, 25)
6 Independence High School, Independence, Ohio (Gesinsky & Cardina et al., 32)
7 Brighton High School, Salt Lake City, Utah (Gubler, 40)
8 Anne Arundel County Schools, Maryland (Yarbro, 108)
9 Ithaca Public Schools, Ithaca, New York (Teetor, 98)
10 Charles Town Senior High School, Charles Town, West Virginia (Lorenz, 59)
11 Capuchino High School, San Bruno, California (Shurk, 82)

12 Gaithersburg High School, Gaithersburg, Maryland (Colburn, 23)

Very few individualized programs in American schools are operating on anywhere near a full-scale basis. There are some that could classify as "full-scale" programs, i.e., they include most students in most levels of instruction with the staff and materials to support them. Most such programs are either heavily funded or are led by very dedicated teachers who are willing to expend much time and effort to make the programs work.

Few "full-scale" individualized programs

Costs of some large-scale individualized programs have been reported to be discouragingly higher than the costs for conventional classroom instruction (Steiner, 92; Thompson, 101; Yarbro, 108). It is rare that members of the profession will spend the time necessary to develop good individualized programs when they are not aided properly. Both the problems of funding and time for development of curricula loom as potential roadblocks to large-scale individualized foreign language instruction.

Costs, time, and effort

Some prime examples of programs in a more developed stage include the Individualized Foreign Language Program in the West Bend Schools, Wisconsin, (LaLeike, 51) and the McCluer Plan for Individualized Small Group Learning in Ferguson-Florissant Schools, St. Louis County, Missouri, (Barrett & Phelps, 9; Wood, 107). Two programs nurtured and guided by dedicated teachers are the German programs at Mountain View High School, Mountain View, California, (McClennan, 60,61) and Live Oak High School, Morgan Hill, California, (Logan, 54,56,57).

Highly developed programs

They are all cases in point. West Bend and McCluer have required heavy funding. Both programs seek more financial aid. The profession will have to *wait* to see if large-scale, expensive programs *can* exist in many American schools on a wider basis. Without men such as Logan and McClennan to give up hours and hours of time to keep totally individualized learning going, the programs, quite frankly, are in trouble. This writer has seen potentially good individualized programs collapse when dedicated teachers committed to individualized learning have left a school. In summary then, energy and cash are going to be big items that will determine, to a large extent, whether large-scale individualized foreign language instruction survives in some schools and develops in others.

Large programs are heavily funded

It is not only in the secondary schools that individualized foreign language instruction is causing a stir but also at the college and university levels. The evidence available indicates that two

237

popular types of individualized programs are combinations of self-instruction or independent study and optimal learning-rate programs.

Some representative samples follow. Florida Atlantic University supports a Self-Instructional Foreign Language Program (Estarellas, 28). The State University of New York at Buffalo will begin a pilot program in independent study of Spanish, including small-group work and team teaching, in September 1971 (Boyd-Bowman, 19). The University of California at Berkeley has begun a program for learning German at optimum rates (Mueller, 66). The University of Kentucky has encouraged a program for placing responsibility for learning on each student's shoulders (Mueller, 67). A program for learning languages at optimum rates is described by Keller (48) at Arizona State University. Prince George's Community College in Maryland has proposed a program for learning French at optimum rates (Blanco, 11). West Chester State College in Pennsylvania (70) and Lafayette College at Easton, Pennsylvania, (McDonald, 63) are considering pilot programs for learning of German at optimum rates. Obviously, many of the colleges are interested. It must be remembered, though, that much individualization has taken place *in the past* at many colleges in the form of tutorials and independent study.

Perusal of the literature describing many of the programs in practice at all levels shows that they are at many varied stages of implementation. This fact might lead one to ask just what the best road to implementation might be. To say there is any one *best* way for the implementation of an individualized program is to give an absurd answer; however, at least one noted foreign language educator (Steiner, 92), who has shown that she sees the problems and issues of individualized instruction very clearly and can also communicate those insights to colleagues, suggests a concise list of guidelines for implementation, including:

1 Establish purposes for each course. Review these within the department to be sure they are in line with department philosophy.
2 State behavioral or performance objectives for each course.
3 Specify a variety of activities and resources by which individual students can achieve the performance objectives.
4 Develop proper evaluative instruments to measure each objective.

5 Develop pre-entry tests to measure the knowledge and abilities needed for success in a given course. These tests may be diagnostic in nature.
6 Develop pretests that will measure whether or not a student has already mastered objectives contained within the course.
7 Develop a series of feedback instruments so that student interests and needs can be measured as the program develops.
8 Develop proper communicative instruments for parents, students, and the community.
9 Start the program gradually. Let those students and teachers who are willing lead the way. Be prepared for some failure and give support to those teachers who are acting as pioneers.
10 Devise and implement a program of in-service training that will enable the staff to feel more comfortable with the new program.
11 Appropriate changes in schedule and facilities should be made.
12 Evaluate the program carefully, making sure that all information and feedback are given consideration.

Logan (55), too, considers many of the problems to be faced when implementing individualized programs, and offers partial solutions. He includes the difficulties of (1) oral work, (2) packaging the curriculum, (3) providing a sufficient variety of materials, (4) scheduling, (5) articulation, (6) classroom space and arrangement of furniture, and (7) using staff most efficiently.

Problems of individualization

Obviously, there are advantages and disadvantages to individualized foreign language instruction. Steiner (93), again, provides the profession with a thought-provoking list of disadvantages and advantages of individualized foreign language learning.

Some of the disadvantages are: (1) administrators are not always committed to the program, (2) teachers are loath to change their role, (3) teachers frequently make mistakes in judgment during the early implementation period, (4) time and money are lacking for teachers to prepare the necessary instructional materials, (5) in-service programs cost money, (6) students and parents are loath to change a system in which they have been successful, (7) time and money are lacking for the

Disadvantages of individualized foreign language instruction

239

necessary public relations work, (8) resources for adopting the facilities and for more instructional equipment may be unavailable, (9) articulation is difficult, (10) commercial materials are not yet available.

On the other hand, Steiner (93) provides a challenging list of practical advantages of individualized foreign language instruction, a fitting list with which to close this review of individualized foreign language instruction in 1970. If a teacher can pass the initial stages of implementation *he may* well see the advantages clearly. Some of them are:

Advantages of individualized foreign language instruction

1 Students will learn responsibility. They will not be able to hide within a group.
2 Students will receive more individual attention in areas where they most need it.
3 Students will learn to diagnose their own learning habits and soon find out how they learn best.
4 Teachers will become helpers, friends, counselors, rather than a threat.
5 Teachers will learn to diagnose, to help students learn, to take the student where he is and teach him.
6 Failure will disappear. This writer realizes that goal is hard to achieve.
7 Students will be much better prepared for college. They will know their own strengths and weaknesses and know better how to make decisions.
8 Greater flexibility in course offerings will be possible.
9 The profession can begin to give direction to the type of commercial materials it wishes to see prepared.
10 This system allows accessibility to all and, yet, can and should preserve quality education.

Summary and conclusions

(1) Interest in the theory and practice of individualizing foreign language instruction is growing rapidly at the beginning of the decade. The quantity and quality of contributions to the literature in the field are both increasing, and the number of conferences and seminars including individualized foreign language instruction as a topic for discussion is mounting rapidly.

Administrators, teachers, and students are beginning to show more and more concern about justifying and establishing a need for change from "conventional" foreign language instruction to individualized learning. Along with the attempt to clarify the need for change has come a concerted effort on the part of some professionals to explicate the concept of individualized foreign language instruction.

(2) The fervor over individualized instruction has also encouraged educators to look to the past for older ideas—independent study, programmed learning, tutorials, and so forth—and to relate these concepts to the new "trend" toward individualization. Indeed, many syntheses of something "old," "new," and "borrowed," are beginning to appear in theory and practice.

(3) Individualized foreign language instruction has emerged as a pluralistic concept. There is no one way to implement it, since so much depends on students, teachers, and their abilities, as well as schools and communities in the traditional locally controlled American school districts.

(4) There is a growing feeling that foreign language instruction in the past has been grossly inefficient; with all the "new" developments have arisen again three important pedagogical questions with reference to the student as the *center* of the learning situation. Exactly what should the student learn? What does he have to do to learn it? What can we, as teachers, do to facilitate that learning and help to make the learning process more efficient?

(5) The majority of the programs in practice are still small, many in the pilot, experimental stages; most are based on self-pacing or language learning at individual optimum rates. Some "full-scale" individualized programs are developing, but they are in the extreme minority. It is quite evident that the development of individualized programs at present depends mostly on two ingredients—dedicated, energetic teachers and/or increased financial support.

(6) In the past year it has also become increasingly fashionable for the colleges and universities to develop individualized programs or extend those already started.

(7) In the future the profession might expect to hear of many programs called "individualized instruction"; many will be *asked* to individualize and personalize learning in their schools. Many questions about the issues brought forth in this review will have to be faced head-on and fathomed by

teachers and scholars involved in individualizing instruction. Arriving at satisfactory answers will demand thoughtful contemplation and then careful planning, as well as credible activities aimed at implementation.

(8) To be successful in American schools, the goals of individualized foreign language instruction will have to suggest an acceptable balance between linguistic proficiency based on a performance curriculum and relevant cultural and humanistic concepts that can be acquired from the study of foreign languages.

(9) Teacher training for individualized foreign language instruction is beginning to emerge as an important trend. At the core of it all remain the concepts of teacher/student in the learning process, but within a different framework. That being the case, much more training and retraining of teachers aimed at facilitating individualized instruction will be necessary, if this important concept is to fulfill its potential promise for the foreign language students in American schools.

References, Individualization of foreign language learning: What is being done

1 Altman, Howard B. "Individualized Foreign Language Instruction:What Does It Mean?" *Foreign Language Annals* 4(1971):421–22. [See also: *Individualization of Foreign Language Learning in America* 2(1971):14–16. (West Chester State College, West Chester, Pennsylvania.)]

2 ——— "Toward a Definition of Individualized Foreign Language Instruction." *American Foreign Language Teacher* 1,iii(1971):12–13.

3 ——— "Toward a Definition of Individualized Foreign Language Instruction." Unpublished lecture given at Foreign Language Conference, University of Kentucky. Lexington, Kentucky, 24 April 1971.

4 ——— and Robert Morrey. *Individualizing Instruction in Foreign Languages:Theory and Practice*. Rowley, Massachusetts: Newbury House, 1971. [Forthcoming.]

5 ——— and Louis Weiss. "Recent Developments in the Training and Certification of the Foreign Language Teacher," 239–73 in Dale L. Lange, ed., *Britannica Review of Foreign Language Education, Volume 2*. Chicago: Encyclopaedia Britannica, Inc., 1970.

6 Arendt, Jermaine D. "Media in Foreign Language Teaching," 157–89 in Dale L. Lange,ed., *Britannica Review of Foreign Language Education, Volume 2*. Chicago: Encyclopaedia Britannica, Inc., 1970.

7 Arsenault, Philip E. "Self-Pacing Programs in Foreign Languages." Survey response. Rockville, Maryland: Montgomery County Public Schools, 1 May 1971. [See Garfinkel, Chapter 7, p. 190.]

8 Barrett, Kathleen. "Programmed Modules for Teaching French." *American Foreign Language Teacher* 1,i(1970):40–43.

9 Barrett, Martin, and Florence Phelps. *The McCluer Plan for Individualized and Small Group Learning*. Florissant, Missouri: Innovative Curricula, 1969.

10 Bishop, Lloyd K. *Individualizing Educational Systems*. New York: Harper & Row, 1971.

11 Blanco, Marjorie. *Proposals Regarding French 101–102 Courses at Prince George's Community College*. Largo, Maryland: Prince George's Community College, 1971. [Mimeograph.]

12 Bockman, John F. *A Three-Year Research Project on Individualized Foreign Language*

Learning Based on Programmed Instruction and on Management by Consultation – Summary of Rationale and Principal Findings. Tucson, Arizona: Tucson Public Schools, 1970. [Mimeograph.]

13 —— Comments in Summary and Evaluation of Independent Study and/or Individualized Instruction Management Seminar Series. Tucson, Arizona: Tucson Public Schools, 1971. [Mimeograph.]

14 —— *Tentative Syllabus Mini-Course in the Preparation of Control Instruments and Techniques for Independent Study Programs.* Tucson, Arizona: Tucson Public Schools, 1971. [Mimeograph.]

15 —— and Ronald L. Gougher. "An Editorial Comment." *Foreign Language Annals* 4(1971): 420. [See also: *Individualization of Foreign Language Learning in America* 1(1970):1.]

16 —— "Editorial Comment." *Individualization of Foreign Language Learning in America* 2(1971):1.

17 Bohning, Elizabeth. "Position Statement." *Individualization of Foreign Language Learning in America* 1(1970):3–4.

18 Bourque, Jane M. "Individualized Learning." *Accent on ACTFL* 1,iii(1971):2–4.

19 Boyd-Bowman, Peter. "A Pilot Project for Achieving Economy in Our Basic Spanish Courses." Unpublished report on independent study at State University of New York at Buffalo, 19 March 1971.

20 —— *Self-Instruction in the Non-Western Languages: A Manual for Program Directors.* Pittsburgh: University of Pittsburgh, 1969.

21 Bryant, Priscilla. "A Self-pacing Program in French." Unpublished paper read at Delaware Council on Teaching of Foreign Languages Convention. Caesar Rodney High School, Delaware, 6 February 1971.

22 *The CCD Language Skills Testing Program.* Philadelphia: The Center for Curriculum Development, 1971.

23 Colburn, Jean H. "An Individualized Program in German II and III." Survey response. Gaithersburg, Maryland: Gaithersburg High School, 1 April 1971. [See Garfinkel, Chapter 7, p. 190.]

24 Duda, Mary J. "A Critical Analysis of Individually Prescribed Instruction." *Educational Technology* 10,xii(1970):47–51.

25 Economu, Efthim, "Model Schools Project." Survey response. Bangor, Maine: Bangor High School, 1 April 1971. [See Garfinkel, Chapter 7, p. 190.]

26 Eisenhardt, Catheryn. "Individualization of Instruction." *Elementary English* 47(1971):341–45.

27 Erickson, Gerald M. "Classics: The Teaching of Latin and Greek and Classical Humanities," 275–321 in Dale L. Lange, ed. *Britannica Review of Foreign Language Education, Volume 2.* Chicago: Encyclopaedia Britannica, Inc., 1970.

28 Estarellas, Juan. "A Psycholinguistic Model for Second Language Learning: New Prospects for Programmed Instruction." *Actes du Xe Congrès International des Linguistes Bucarest, 28 Août –2 Septembre 1967.* Bucarest: Congrès International des Linguistes, 1970.

29 —— *The Self Instructional Foreign Language Program at Florida Atlantic University.* Boca Raton, Florida: International Teaching Systems Corporation, 1969.

30 Gardner, John W. *Excellence – Can We Be Equal and Excellent Too?* New York: Harper Colophon, 1962.

31 —— *Self Renewal – The Individual and the Innovative Society.* New York: Harper Colophon, 1965.

32 Gesinsky, William J., and Joseph Cardina, et al. *Emulation and Independent Study in Modern Foreign Languages.* Independence, Ohio: Independence High School, 1971.

33 Gordon, Barbara. "The Speech Community of the School and Individualized Instruction." Unpublished lecture given at Foreign Language Conference, University of Kentucky. Lexington, Kentucky, 24 April 1971.

34 Gougher, Ronald L. "A Practical Approach to Individualized Instruction in Foreign Languages." Unpublished paper presented at Ohio Chapter, American Association of Teachers of German Meeting. Columbus, Ohio, 27 March 1971.

35 —— "Individualized Instruction." Unpublished lecture delivered at Middle Atlantic States Foreign Language Teachers Association Meeting. Atlantic City, New Jersey, 7 November 1970.

36 —— "Individualized Instruction in Foreign Languages." Unpublished lecture delivered at Rochester Branch, New York Modern Foreign Language Teachers Association Meeting, Rochester, 13 March 1971.

37 —— *Individualization of Foreign Language Learning in America – A Practical Guide for Teachers in American Schools.* Philadelphia: Center for Curriculum Development, 1971. [Forthcoming.]

38 —— "Learning of German at Optimum Rates." *Unterrichtspraxis* 3,i(1970):142–43.

39 —— "Motivation and Materials for Learning German at Optimum Rates." *The Bulletin of the Pennsylvania State Modern Language Association* 48,ii(1970):5–7.

40 Gubler, Marilyn. "Individualized French." Survey response. Salt Lake City: Brighton High School, 1 April 1971. [See Garfinkel, Chapter 7, p. 190.]

41 Hugot, Francois, and Genelle Caldwell, et al. "Innovative Trends in Foreign-Language Teaching," 91–141 in James W. Dodge, ed., *Leadership for Continuing Development.* Reports of the Working Committees of the Northeast Conference on the Teaching of Foreign Languages. New York: Modern Language Association Materials Center, 1971.

42 "Individualizing Instruction in the Foreign Language Program." Unpublished papers read at Seventh Annual Whitewater Foreign Language Conference. Whitewater, Wisconsin, 27 March 1971.

43 Irwin, Jean, and Helen Casey. "Individualized

Instruction in Foreign Languages." Survey response. Los Angeles: Eagle Rock High School, 1 April 1971. [See Garfinkel, Chapter 7, p. 190.]

44 Jakobovits, Leon A. "Compensatory Foreign Language Instruction." Unpublished lecture given at the Foreign Language Conference, University of Kentucky. Lexington, Kentucky, 24 April 1971.

45 —— *Foreign Language Learning:A Psycholinguistic Analysis of the Issues.* Rowley, Massachusetts: Newbury House, 1970.

46 Jarvis, Gilbert A. "Strategies of Instruction for Listening and Reading," 79–111 in Dale L. Lange,ed., *Britannica Review of Foreign Language Education, Volume 2.* Chicago: Encyclopaedia Britannica, Inc., 1970.

47 Jersild, Arthur T. *When Teachers Face Themselves,* New York: Teachers College Press, 1955.

48 Keller, Fred S. "Good-bye Teacher". *Journal of Applied Behavior Analysis* 1(1968):79-89.

49 Kincaid, Thomas, and Sister Margaret Flinton,et al. "Involving Language Teachers and Students in Innovation." Unpublished papers read at Foreign Language Conference, St. Joseph's College, Emmittsburg, Maryland, 1 May 1971.

50 Kopp, W. LaMarr. *Critical Languages Program.* University Park, Pennsylvania: Pennsylvania State University, 1971. [Mimeograph.]

51 LaLeike, Fred. *Individualized Foreign Language Program.* West Bend, Wisconsin: Joint School District No. 1, 1970. [Mimeograph.]

52 Lange, Dale L.,ed. *Britannica Review of Foreign Language Education, Volume 2.* Chicago: Encyclopaedia Britannica, Inc., 1970.

53 Levy, Stephen L. "Adapting Foreign Language to New Educational Designs." *Language Federation Bulletin* 22,ii(1971):5-7. [The New York State Federation of Foreign Language Teachers.]

54 Logan, Gerald E. "A Totally Individualized High School Program." *Individualization of Foreign Language Learning in America* 1 (1970) 8-9.

55 —— "Curricula for Individualized Instruction," 133-55 in Dale L. Lange, ed., *Britannica Review of Foreign Language Education, Volume 2.* Chicago: Encyclopaedia Britannica, Inc., 1970.

56 —— "Individualization of Instruction." Unpublished lecture given at Utah Foreign Language Convention. Salt Lake City, Utah, 27 March 1971.

57 —— *1971–72 German Curriculum Guide and Catalogue of Courses.* Morgan Hill, California: Live Oak High School, 1971. [Mimeograph.]

58 Lohnes, Walter F.W. "Comment." *Individualization of Foreign Language Learning in America* 1(1970):1.

59 Lorenz, Jean M. *A Continuous Progress Program of Individualized Instruction in the Study of Spanish.* Charles Town, West Virginia: Charles Town Senior High School, 1970.

60 McClennan, Robert. "German Language Program, Mountain View High School, California." *Individualization of Foreign Language Learning in America* 1(1970):6–8.

61 —— *German Studies Student Handbook.*

Mountain View California: Mountain View High School, 1970. [Mimeograph.]

62 —— "How Do We Allow Students to Learn at Optimum Rates?" *American Foreign Language Teacher* 1,iii(1970):8–11.

63 McDonald, Edward R. *Elementary German:An Individualized Approach.* Easton, Pennsylvania: Lafayette College, 1971. [Mimeograph.]

64 Moore, Merriam. *Suggested "Mini-Course" Curriculum for German IV and German V.* Ridgefield, Connecticut: Ridgefield High School, 1971. [Mimeograph.]

65 Mortwedt, Dianne, and Jack Troupe. "Individualized Instruction in French." Survey response. Manitowoc, Wisconsin: Lincoln High School, 1 April 1971. [See Garfinkel, Chapter 7, p. 190.]

66 Mueller, Klaus, "Individualized Instruction." Unpublished report delivered at Stanford University Conference on Individualized Instruction. Palo Alto, California, 7 May 1971.

67 Mueller, Theodore, "Individualized Instruction at the University of Kentucky." Unpublished mimeographed outline distributed at Stanford University Conference on Individualized Instruction. Palo Alto, California, 7 May 1971.

68 *Northeast Association for the Individualization of Instruction–Reports.* Wyandanch, Long Island: Wyandanch Public Schools, 1970.

69 Perkins, Daniel N. "Self-Instruction in Japanese I and II, Garden City Senior High School, Garden City, New York." *Individualization of Foreign Language Learning in America* 2(1971):2–5.

70 "Pilot Program of Individualized Instruction." *The Bulletin of the Pennsylvania State Modern Language Association* 49,iii(1970–71):30.

71 Politzer, Robert. "Toward Individualization of Instruction." *The Modern Language Journal* 55(1971):207–12.

72 Raubinger, Frederick M., and Harold G. Row. *The Individual and Education–Some Contemporary Issues.* New York: MacMillan, 1968.

73 Reinert, Harry. "Practical Guide to Individualization." *The Modern Language Journal* 55(1971): 156–63.

74 Roberts, Alfred D. "Position Statement." *Individualization of Foreign Language Learning in America* 1(1970):3.

75 Rogers, Carl R. *On Becoming a Person.* Boston: Houghton Mifflin, 1961.

76 Ryberg, Donald C. "Student Involvement, Flexibility, and Individualization." Unpublished paper presented at Oregon Association of Foreign Language Teachers' Fall Meeting. Portland, Oregon, October 1970.

77 Sandstrom, Eleanor L., and Paul Pimsleur,eds. "Foreign Languages for All Students?" 105–33 in Joseph A. Tursi,ed., *Foreign Languages and the New Student.* Reports of the Working Committees of the Northeast Conference on the Teaching of Foreign Languages. New York: Modern Language Association Materials Center, 1970.

78 Scanlon, Richard T. "Computer-Assisted Instruction in Foreign Languages at the University of Illinois." *Foreign Language Annals* 4(1971): 423.

79 Scanlon, Robert G. "Individually Prescribed Instruction:A System of Individualized Instruction." *Educational Technology* 10,xii(1970):44–46. [See also: *Individualization of Foreign Language Learning in America* 2(1971):6–7.]

80 Scherer, George A.C. "Toward More Effective Individualized Learning," 112–14 in Eberhard Reichmann,ed., *The Teaching of German Problems and Methods.* Philadelphia: National Carl Schurz Association, 1970.

81 Shofstall, W.P. "Changes Needed." *Individualization of Foreign Language Learning in America* 2(1971):7–8.

82 Shurk, J.A. *German Handbook.* San Bruno, California: Capuchino High School, 1971. [Mimeograph.]

83 Smith, Alfred N. "Strategies of Instruction for Speaking and Writing," 113–131 in Dale L. Lange,ed., *Britannica Review of Foreign Language Education, Volume 2.* Chicago: Encyclopaedia Britannica, Inc., 1970.

84 Smith, Philip D. "Peace Corps Materials Project Toward Individualization." *Individualization of Foreign Language Learning in America* 1(1970):10–11.

85 —— "Text Adoption Policies Inhibit Individualization." *Individualization of Foreign Language Learning in America* 2(1971):13–14.

86 —— and Lee Sparkman. *Dialogue Africain Contemporain.* Philadelphia: The Center for Curriculum Development, 1971.

87 Smith, W. Flint. "Language Learning Laboratory," 191–237 in Dale L. Lange, ed., *Britannica Review of Foreign Language Education, Volume 2.* Chicago: Encyclopaedia Britannica, Inc., 1970.

88 Sohodski, Lidia, and Elizabeth Bohning,et al. "Selfpacing of Instruction." Unpublished panel discussion given at Delaware Council on the Teaching of Foreign Languages Convention. John Dickinson High School, Delaware, 30 October 1970.

89 *Special Foreign Language Program.* San Francisco: San Francisco State College, Summer, 1971.

90 Spolsky, Bernard. "TESOL," 323–40 in Dale L. Lange,ed., *Britannica Review of Foreign Language Education, Volume 2.* Chicago: Encyclopaedia Britannica, Inc., 1970.

91 Steiner, Florence. "Behavioral Objectives and Evaluation," 35–78 in Dale L. Lange,ed., *Britannica Review of Foreign Language Education, Volume 2.* Chicago: Encyclopaedia Britannica, Inc., 1970.

92 —— "Individualized Instruction." Unpublished paper read at Central States Conference on the Teaching of Foreign Languages. Detroit, Michigan, April 1971.

93 —— "Performance Objectives in the Teaching of Foreign Languages." *Foreign Language Annals* 3(1970):579–91.

94 Stevick, Earl. *Adapting Language Materials.* Washington,D.C.: Foreign Service Institute, 1970. [Mimeograph.]

95 Strasheim, Lorraine A. "A Rationale for the Individualization and Personalization of Foreign-Language Instruction," 15–34 in Dale L. Lange,ed., *Britannica Review of Foreign Language Education, Volume 2.* Chicago: Encyclopaedia Britannica, Inc., 1970.

96 Sutton, Donna E. *A Feasibility Study on Individualized Foreign Language Program in the High Schools of the United States.* Unpublished Ph.D. dissertation. Columbus: Ohio State University, 1971.

97 —— "A Short Bibliography for Individualizing Foreign Language Instruction." *Individualization of Foreign Language Learning in America* 2(1971):8–12.

98 Teetor, Will Robert. "Individualized Instruction in Ithaca." Unpublished lecture delivered at Rochester Branch, New York Modern Foreign Language Teachers Association Meeting. Rochester, New York, 13 March 1971.

99 Teichert, Herman U. *An Experiment Comparing Individualized Instruction via Learning Packages and Conventional Instruction in Beginning College German.* Ph.D. dissertation in progress. Athens, Georgia: University of Georgia, 1971. [Mimeograph.]

100 Terwilliger, Ronald I. "Multi-Grade Proficiency Grouping for Foreign Language Instruction." *Modern Language Journal* 54(1970):331–33.

101 Thompson, Nancy A. *Special Approach to Spanish.* Portland, Maine: Portland Public Schools, 1970. [Mimeograph.]

102 "Tucson (Arizona) Educators Mobilize for Individualized Instruction." *Foreign Language Annals* 4(1971):424. [See also *Individualization of Foreign Language Learning in America* 2(1971):2.]

103 Turner, Ronald C. *CARLOS:Computer-Assisted Instruction in Spanish at Dartmouth College.* Hanover, New Hampshire: Dartmouth College, 1968. [ERIC Document Reproduction Service: ED 025 972.]

104 Veatch, Jeannette. "Individualizing," 90–99 in Virgil M. Howes,ed., *Individualization of Instruction:A Teaching Strategy.* New York: MacMillan, 1970.

105 Villa, Hector, and Royce Robbins. "Demonstration of a Self-pacing Program in Spanish." Unpublished discussion held at Delaware Council on the Teaching of Foreign Languages Convention. Caesar Rodney High School, Delaware, 6 February 1971.

106 Wells, Gloria T. "Individualized Instruction Through Differentiated Staffing." Survey response. Northridge, California: Nobel Junior High School, 1 April 1971. [See Garfinkel, Chapter 7, p. 190.]

107 Wood, Fred H. "The McCluer Plan:An Innovative Non-Graded Foreign Language Program." *Modern Language Journal* 54(1970):184–87.

108 Yarbro, Bernice. "Multi-Media French." Unpublished paper presented at Middle Atlantic States Foreign Language Teacher's Association Meeting. Atlantic City, New Jersey, 7 November 1970.

9

In-service programs in foreign languages at elementary and secondary levels

Introduction[1]

Robert I. Cloos

*University of Missouri—
St. Louis*

In-service education—the continuing professional growth and development of educational personnel—has played an ever expanding role as it has responded to the growth and the increasing complexity of American public education. The idea has now become generally accepted that teacher training is a continuous process. McArdle (26) describes the in-service program as providing a supplementary type of training, while McKim in Hanzeli & Love (21) maintains that local school districts are involved in in-service work in an effort at retraining as a result of the inadequacy of colleges. Andrews (5) finds present in-service programs unsatisfactory and proposes lengthening the present sequence of teacher preparation. Altman & Weiss (3) prefer the term "advanced study" in referring to the continuous training that professionals receive in their areas of specialization. In Moir's view (28) the seventies can be expected to bring outward, visible signs of change in our schools. More significant, however, will be *inner* changes that occur in the thinking of educators—especially in their readiness to experiment. It is more important than ever that teachers have a clear vision of the magnitude of the task of keeping abreast, and that *they* are the ones who develop structures for doing so.

What is in-service?

Time and cost for in-service programs are certainly important considerations. They are crucial factors in the further development of the professional teacher. It has been a goal of the National Education Association—by supporting salary policies, professional and sabbatical leaves, scholarships, and income tax deductions for educational expenses—to encourage teachers to maintain and improve their professional competence (23). Fulfillment of requirements for certification is another of the major concerns of in-service education at elementary and secondary levels. In the fall of 1965, it was reported by state departments of education that there were 81,000 full-time teachers with less

Importance of time and cost

---

1 Editor's note: Uncredited programs discussed in this chapter were described in response to a special questionnaire designed by the author and are not given in the list of references.

than standard certificates. Teachers with less than standard credentials numbered 30,100 in secondary schools, while in elementary schools the number was 51,600 (Schloss, 39). The *NEA Handbook* for 1970–71 (31) states that "to assure leadership in education, the NEA must support programs for professional development of teachers through in-service and pre-service education, and continuous development of professional standards and self-governance of the profession. . . . Every effort shall be made to effect state and local certification renewal and advanced certification credit for professional training received through participation in in-service training programs."

The following representative list may call to mind the wide variety of ways in which in-service education is now being carried out: course work (evening, summer, extension, correspondence), research, conferences, workshops, institutes, teacher exchanges, travel, committees, study groups, staff meetings, field trips, intervisitation, professional organization work, and the reading of professional literature. In-service programs may be promoted by individuals, departments, schools, school districts, commercial enterprises, professional organizations, institutions of higher education, by city, county, state, or national governments. In addition to all this diversity in means and sponsors, one must also recognize the infinite variety produced by situational factors of time, place, and the uniqueness of individual participants. Such an array of possibilities prompts two observations: (1) the greater the number of in-service options open to a teacher, the higher the probability that he will be attracted by some of them and find activities that suit his particular needs; and (2) an effective in-service program—one that produces measurable improvement in professional competency—is rarely a product of chance. Elements essential to success include an awareness of need, care in the selection of an appropriate format, and, most important of all, personal involvement of each participant in every phase of the program from planning, through implementation, to an objective evaluation. In-service education aids in the achievement of institutional purposes, such as orientation of new teachers, curriculum improvement, development of emergent leadership, and introduction of innovative practices. Its ultimate goal, however, remains the improvement of professional competency in teaching, which is defined by Pulley & Veri (37) as:

1 A capacity to interact with students in a manner which

Ways in which in-service programs are being carried out

Two important observations

Ultimate goal of in-service education

produces a learning atmosphere and retains the human dignity of both the teacher and the student,

2 A variety of teaching skills necessary to enable students to achieve the desired learning behaviors, and

3 A broad knowledge of the subject area so that the teacher can make valid judgments concerning content.

Each of the programs to be described seeks to bring about improvement in one or more of these aspects of teacher competency.

It would, of course, be impossible to consider in this chapter the vast number of formal college-level courses that are offered, although academic study does remain the most important facet of in-service education (36). Foreign study and travel programs, so indispensable to foreign language teachers, must also be excluded from this review. What the reader will find is a survey of some other recent in-service activities in the United States, beginning at the national level and continuing through regional, state, area, district, and local levels, then a look at in-service training as it relates to the individual teacher. In the latter segments, references to contributions from outside the foreign language field are included. This is done because the contributions are appropriate and useful, and also because there has been a tendency for foreign language teachers to stay within their discipline.

Chapter overview

National in-service programs

Although NDEA (National Defense Education Act) Institutes in the commonly taught languages have become history, the effects of this massive in-service effort—587 institutes, attended by more than 30,000 elementary and secondary school teachers—will be felt for years to come. Andersson (4) is critical of certain aspects such as an underemphasis of FLES (Foreign Language in Elementary School), decisions based on political rather than educational considerations, and the lack of a clear policy for the selection of participants. He concludes that the institutes contributed materially to the upgrading of foreign language education but were impeded by professional inertia. King (24) agrees with Axelrod (6) in attributing a large part of the success of the institute program to the fact that it was conducted outside of the established "System." Among the weaknesses he cites are the relative inexperience of institute directors with the real needs of teachers in the schools, and an un-

Contributions of the NDEA Institute Program

imaginative approach to the culture component. He believes the impact of the institutes has been considerable, primarily because they provided for ten years a basis for improved communication among language teachers and fomented a greater sense of professional solidarity. Prince (35) describes the success of the institutes in pulling participants from the rut into which some of them had fallen, and in helping to break with tradition, which had dictated the contents of most teacher preparation programs in foreign languages.

The NDEA Institutes offered incentives to travel, stipends to alleviate financial burdens, and, often, academic credit. Best of all, they provided a magnificent opportunity at the national level for leaders to exercise leadership. Unfortunately, the participants all too often found it difficult to translate their new experiences into desired change once they returned to their own classrooms. The selection of *local* participants in later programs appears to have reduced this problem. Smith & Castro (40) report that the spirit of the NDEA Institute is alive in Virginia. During the summer of 1970 more than 30 teachers of French, German, Spanish, and Latin were enrolled in a productive four-week workshop in cooperation with the Virginia State Department of Education, at Old Dominion University, Norfolk, Virginia. The participants, all of whom were local, received scholarship grants from the Virginia State Department of Education. Lange & Hammers (25) describe the EPDA (Education Professions Development Act) Institute in German for cooperating teachers and teacher trainers, which was conducted at the University of Minnesota during the 1969–70 academic year. The overall objectives of the Institute were to develop a *model* classroom teacher-college relationship, which would give the classroom teacher an important place as a co-professional in planning foreign language teacher-training programs, and to develop the very important function of cooperating teacher in the student-teaching program. The 14 participants (4 teacher trainers and 10 secondary teachers) lived within commuting distance of the University. After a two-week preschool workshop in August, 1969, the participants met on alternating Saturdays throughout the school year. Two evaluations, one carried out by the participants and the other by Frank M. Grittner, State Supervisor of Foreign Languages for the Wisconsin State Department of Public Instruction, both rated the Institute as highly effective. In Grittner's opinion it was an exemplary institute, which with minor adjust-

Carrying on the "spirit" of NDEA institutes

An EPDA institute at the University of Minnesota

250

ments in format, could well become the model for restructuring in-service and pre-service education for foreign language teachers in the schools of America.

During the 1969–70 academic year, the School of Languages and Linguistics of Georgetown University conducted its second EPDA Experienced Teacher Fellowship Program in the Teaching of Standard English to Speakers of Other Languages or Dialects (SESOLD). The Program consisted of 11 courses totaling 34 semester hours and leading to a Master of Arts degree. It was designed to increase the effectiveness of 20 elementary and secondary school teachers and supervisors working with pupils who were not native speakers of English or who were handicapped by nonstandard language habits. Fellowship stipends were $4,000 plus $600 per dependent (tax exempt), and no tuition fees were charged. During the academic year 1970–71 and the following summer, Georgetown offered an EPDA Program to ten graduate students participating in a model teacher preparation program in English as a Second Language and Bilingual Education. Scholarships consisted of tuition and fees. There was no other fiscal support attached to the scholarship. The fact that the program will not be funded for the 1971–72 academic year is indicative of the general trend in federal financial support for in-service programs in foreign language education.

A special EPDA experienced teacher fellowship program at Georgetown University

The problem of bilingual education is recognized as a serious one in several areas of the United States—particularly in New England, New York City, Florida, and the Southwest. Through the 1967 amendment to the Elementary and Secondary Education Act (ESEA) of 1965, bilingual education is one of the few remaining foreign language programs that continue to receive federal support. Specialized curricula and instructional materials are being developed, while teachers are being retrained to use them as effectively as possible. In Greenville, New Hampshire, the Mascenic Area Bilingual Program is one of over 130 federally financed projects under ESEA Title VII to develop the oral language skills and to reinforce the traditional cultural values of the regional ethnic community through innovative educational programs at all levels of instruction. The Project is under the direction of Normand Robitaille and is centered in L'école du Sacré-Coeur in Greenville. The primary goal of the Project is to provide all children in the "target area" with increased educational opportunity. The program has as its basic aims the development of greater competence in English for the children with limited En-

Bilingual education continues to receive federal support

251

glish-speaking ability, who come from a Franco-American subculture, as well as the development of literacy in French for the
English-speaking child. An analysis of curricular system components has indicated at least ten strategic areas that permit identification of teacher performance behaviors necessary to the implementation of the bilingual program. Development of these
performance behaviors in teachers is the immediate goal of the
program.

Another ESEA Title VII bilingual education program is in operation in Frenchville-St. Agatha and in Lewiston, Maine. The
project is being expanded to include the elementary school in
Fort Kent, St. Thomas (public) School of Madawaska, and St.
John (public) School in Van Buren. The program is being directed by Omar Picard of Madawaska. Donald Dugas is the program
adviser and linguistics consultant who is preparing materials
and assisting with teacher training.

While federal support for foreign language teacher education
is, in several dimensions, being reduced, there is a noticeable
increase in the activities of foreign language professional organizations at all levels. The American Council on the Teaching of
Foreign Languages combined efforts with the National Council
of State Supervisors of Foreign Languages to conduct a three-
day symposium on foreign language teacher training preceding
the 1970 ACTFL Annual Meeting in Los Angeles. Lester McKim,
President of ACTFL and Foreign Language Coordinator of
the Bellevue (Washington) Public Schools, and Joanna Breed-
love Crane, 1970 President of the National Council of State
Supervisors of Foreign Languages, served as Co-Chairmen
of the Symposium. More than a hundred participants, from all
parts of the United States, met to consider the topic "The Supervisor's Role in Foreign Language Teacher Training." The meetings reflected the widespread professional concern for the state
of foreign language teaching today. There was a general call for
closer cooperation among local and state supervisors and college
teacher trainers, since supervisors are more involved in foreign
language teacher training than ever before, especially at the
post-B.A. level. Among eight recommendations that were endorsed by two or more of the discussion groups, two that are of
special interest in the present context are: (1) that ACTFL continue its efforts to upgrade teacher competence and to help
teachers grow as professionals; and (2) that continuing effort be
devoted to giving recognition to effective teachers by encourag-

*Increased activity
of professional
organizations*

1970 ACTFL Annual Meeting

ing them to conduct in-service classes and to publish their favorite "tricks-of-the-trade" (1). The Opening General Session of the 1970 ACTFL Conference had as its theme "Teachers as Students," and numerous meetings in the course of the Conference dealt with the pre-service and in-service training of foreign language teachers. In many respects such a meeting constitutes an extensive and highly significant in-service program at which leaders of national stature have an opportunity to set forth their views. The timeliness of discussion topics and the general excellence of presentations have made the annual ACTFL Conference an event that deserves the enthusiastic support and participation of every foreign language educator.

Regional in-service programs

Regional conferences in different parts of the country serve as a leading factor in in-service programs for foreign language teachers. Two of these conferences are discussed in the following paragraphs.

The Northeast Conference on the Teaching of Foreign Languages grew out of the Yale-Barnard Conference on the Teaching of French, which met alternately on the two campuses for four years (1950–53). In 1954 the scope of the Conference was enlarged, geographically and linguistically, and the first Northeast Conference was held in the spring of 1954. It has met each spring since then, usually in New York City, occasionally in Boston, Philadelphia, or Washington. Despite its regional title, the Conference has become one of the largest and most widely attended meetings in the United States to concern itself with foreign language education. Due to growth in attendance, the 1970 Conference was held twice, once in Boston and once in Washington. What distinguishes the Northeast Conference from other pedagogical conferences are the *Reports of the Working Committees*, which grow out of a series of meetings of each committee throughout the year. The deliberations and findings of each committee are written down in a report. The reports, printed and distributed to pre-registrants in advance of the Conference, serve as a basis for open discussion by the whole Conference (33). In an effort to assist teachers to meet the challenges of the 1970s, the Working Committees for the 1970 Conference chose to investigate three major topics under the title of *Foreign Languages and the "New" Student* (Tursi, 44). The first was a ques-

The Northeast Conference on the Teaching of Foreign Languages

253

tionnaire for use as an aid in understanding what the *student* believes would be a relevant foreign language curriculum. The second area of exploration was the nature and role of motivation in foreign language learning. The third dealt with the issue of expanding foreign language education to include *all* students. One of the committee recommendations was that teachers participate in in-service programs and colloquia in which ideas are shared and expanded, particularly with a view to cooperating with adminstrators in planning and implementing innovative programs. These reports, which conclude with the text of Nelson Brooks's address, "The Rung and the Ladder," are so current and insightful that they provide essential, rewarding professional reading for everyone who has an interest in foreign language education.

The Central States Conference on the Teaching of Foreign Languages (Grittner & Arendt, 20), which has grown with the support and encouragement of the Northeast Conference, met in St. Louis in April, 1970. The Conference theme was "The 70's: Focus on Change." General Session topics dealt with systems approach to foreign language teaching and with bilingual education. An especially interesting segment of the Conference was provided by the Separate Language Sessions in French, German, Italian, Latin, Russian, and Spanish. Participants were invited to discuss, in the language, practical teaching techniques: "Things I Have Used in the Classroom That Have Worked."

Central States Conference on the Teaching of Foreign Languages

State in-service programs

An example of the forward-looking leadership being exercised by state foreign language consultants and supervisors may be seen in the proceedings of the Seattle Symposium on the Training of Foreign Language Teachers, which have been published by Hanzeli & Love (21) and are available from the Modern Language Association Materials Center, 62 Fifth Avenue, New York, New York 10011. The Symposium was sponsored by the Washington Foreign Language Program, which (like the Indiana Language Program) is supported by the Ford Foundation. On October 5–6, 1970, more than 80 participants were present for the discussion of the future direction of foreign language teacher training in the United States. In his report of the Symposium's program, Altman (2) includes a concise summary of the presentation made by Leo Benardo, Director of Foreign Lan-

The Washington Foreign Language Program and the Seattle Symposium

254

guages, New York City Schools, who spoke about the problems of in-service education for foreign language teachers. Benardo dealt with the need for innovative in-service training, especially for inner-city teachers of foreign languages. The latter, being typically white and middle-class, find it difficult to communicate with their frequently nonwhite, non-middle-class students. Most importantly, in-service programs are needed that help teachers learn how to persuade the local communities and their school administrators of the value of foreign language learning. New York City has introduced short-term courses in Spanish for policemen and firemen, and the New School for Social Research lists in its fall, 1970, catalog a course in *Spanglish* for civil servants who find it necessary in their jobs to communicate with Puerto Ricans in *el barrio*. Benardo strongly advocated the development of such practical courses to meet local needs. He concluded that in-service education will take on new importance in the 1970s, and that the impetus for innovative programs will probably have to come from the public schools.

In-service in New York City

In surveying in-service-related work that is being done at the state level, one encounters a wide range of activities on the part of state departments of education and state foreign language teacher organizations, with a strong role being played by highly competent and dedicated foreign language consultants and supervisors. In several states the preparation of teacher guides or handbooks provides useful study and discussion materials for local workshops. In the fall of 1970, the Foreign Language Department of the Wyoming State Department of Education sent the rough draft of a state foreign language handbook to 80 teachers of modern foreign languages, soliciting reaction to the content of the book. The final, revised, edition is scheduled for publication in 1971, at which time all Wyoming foreign language teachers will receive a copy (47).

A wide range of activities at the state level

Wyoming

Under the direction of Elliot C. Howe, Specialist in Foreign Language Education for the Utah State Board of Education, a new state guide, entitled *Foreign Language, Key to Understanding in a Jet-Age World,* has been prepared. It was introduced in a series of seven regional workshops held in various centers of the state in the fall of 1970. It is available by writing to the Utah Board of Education in Ogden, Utah.

Utah

Robert W. Cannaday, Jr., who is now Program Specialist in Foreign Languages for the Hawaii State Department of Education, has produced—under earlier sponsorship of the Pennsyl-

Hawaii

255

vania Department of Public Instruction—a *Viewer's Guide* to accompany the film series, *Successful Use of the Language Laboratory*. It is, in reality, a workshop guide for both director and participants. Used with the films, it provides a succinct, yet detailed, guide for in-service activity in this area. The *Guide* and film series are available for preview through Walter G. O'Connor Co., 100 North Cameron Street, Harrisburg, Pennsylvania 17126.

The Georgia Educational Television Network, a service of the Georgia State Department of Education, in Atlanta, telecasts an in-service series for foreign language teachers. It was produced by Ruth Keaton, Foreign Language Consultant, and has the title "Teaching Modern Foreign Language in Georgia Schools." This telecourse, consisting of eight 30-minute programs, includes a teacher's study guide and is intended to serve teachers of modern foreign languages as regularly scheduled departmental meetings throughout the year. The format of the programs is *Georgia* based on informal panel discussions with the state consultant, special guests, and school personnel and with film clips or actual demonstrations inserted to show the methodology in action. It is recommended that all teachers of modern foreign languages meet to view each telecast together and to participate in a half-hour follow-up discussion. This phase of the session permits teachers to review the highlights of the presentation and to relate the material to their own local teaching situation.

The Liaison Committee on Foreign Language of the California Articulation Conference undertook the investigation of the training of teachers of foreign languages in California's colleges and universities, publishing its findings in 1970 under the title *Teacher Training Practices in Foreign Language Instruction* (42). The report presents the results of (1) a survey of the provisions of teacher-training programs in the colleges and universities; and (2) an opinionnaire completed by 934 active foreign language teachers, representing a sample from every region of *California* California. Literature courses were listed as by far the most frequently taken postcredential course work, although they were described as one of the least helpful types. In regard to in-service programs as opposed to formal courses, teachers listed as most helpful: methods workshops, workshops offered by publishing companies or by school districts in the use of particular textbooks, training sessions in the preparation of tapes and other audiovisual materials, and training in the use of nonacademic instructional techniques (e.g., games and songs). Respondents emphasized that in-service programs should (1) be available to them during released time; (2) be of a practical nature; and (3) be conducted by experts in the field.

The California State Advisory Committee was recently charged with producing a curriculum framework for foreign language instruction. In its completed form, the framework will provide a philosophical as well as a technical guide for teachers, curriculum specialists, and administrators who are concerned with developing or maintaining foreign language programs. Included will be such topics as "Planning for Effective Articulation," "Individualizing Instruction," "Cultural Understanding," "Instructional Objectives," and "The Process of Improving Instruction." One of the major concepts contained in the framework is that foreign language teachers have the responsibility to improve their own instruction through participation in in-service education activities and to improve foreign language education in general by contributing to the professional association in their field (17). As an inspiring demonstration of what active participation in professional organizations can accomplish, Gries (19) reports the development of the California German Teachers' Workshops (GTWs). They began as the result of one of the proposals for action formulated at a two-day conference in May, 1969, sponsored by the Northern California Chapter of the American Association of Teachers of German. All of the 11 geographical regions of Northern California now have functioning GTWs, whose purpose is to provide an opportunity for informal in-service training and professional collaboration for all teachers of German. They grew out of a sense of urgency for action and the desire to seek a way to stimulate genuine enthusiasm for their language among language teachers. Following the formation, in 1969, of the United German Clubs (UGC) of Santa Clara County—the student counterpart of the GTWs—teachers have brought with them to the workshop meetings students who were UGC officers. At each meeting an adjacent room is provided for the UGC members. Factors found to be unimportant to the GTWs are geographical region, socioeconomic status of a community, or availability of metropolitan resources. They are not interested in large attendance, high-pressure tactics, or insistence upon formal structure, according to Gries, preferring a gentle approach to grass-roots involvement and professionalism.

Since coming to the Missouri State Department of Education

A curriculum framework for foreign language instruction: a guide to in-service work

Teachers' workshops

United German Clubs

as Modern Foreign Language Consultant in September, 1968, William O. Clapper (in 27) has conducted in-depth in-service programs, through the program of NDEA Title III for foreign language teachers in St. Louis, Kansas City, Springfield, and Cape Girardeau. Two series of these programs are conducted annually, one beginning in the latter part of September, the other beginning in January. Each in-service program runs ten weeks, one two-hour session per week, with a maximum enrollment of 33 participants permitted. The workshops may be scheduled through the district's superintendent of schools, the requests being directed to Carleton B. Fulbright, State Director of NDEA Title III. The service is provided to the local school district without cost other than the providing of meeting facilities and the recruitment of a number of participants adequate to justify the program. A certificate is issued to each participant indicating the extent of the individual's participation. Local in-service credit in regard to salary credit consideration is usually granted by the sponsoring district.

Missouri

From June 1–5, 1970, foreign language teachers in North Dakota had an opportunity to participate in a one-week foreign language Media Workshop, directed by LeRoy A. Oberlander, at Dickinson State College (32). Funds for the Workshop were made available through the State Department of Public Instruction and two quarter-hours of graduate credit were granted by North Dakota State University. The Workshop was short, but participants indicated they gained much that they would be able to use in the classroom. Focusing a short workshop on a few specific areas in media can be educationally fruitful and reduce the cost—important elements of this program. The daily plan of the Workshop was basically this: Workshop participants first met in large groups for general demonstrations and lectures on a specific area in media. These presentations were made by a media specialist in education. Next followed smaller group lab periods to give each participant an opportunity to discuss and to practice the various procedures and techniques observed in the group demonstrations. In the case of films and filmstrips, each language group (German, French, Spanish, and Latin) viewed materials that could be used in their classrooms. Various media areas demonstrated and discussed during the week included the use of films and filmstrips in language teaching, the use of the overhead projector, and the preparation of various types of transparencies that could be used on it. A discussion and demon-

North Dakota

stration of various types of picture mountings were also included. Extensive displays added to the educational aspect of the Workshop, and longer feature films for each language provided some evening entertainment for the participants.

Area in-service programs

A special foreign language workshop in German was conducted for five elementary school teachers of language arts and social studies—who had had no prior foreign language training or contact—from June 3 to June 19, 1970, at East Texas State University. The Workshop, which offered three hours graduate credit, was co-directed by William J. Harvey, of the Department of Foreign Languages, and Donald R. Coker, of the Department of Elementary Education. The goals of the Workshop were (1) to use contact with foreign languages to increase awareness of the nature of language in general and of language differences; and (2) to use experiences with foreign language in order to achieve cross-cultural insights that would be valuable to the teacher in introducing students to other cultures and in developing student awareness of cultural differences. Such in-service training should enable the participants to work more effectively with FLES and bilingual programs. Often there is little understanding of the significance of FLES instruction on the part of fellow teachers in other areas. The Workshop was regarded as a success and all participants reported classroom applications during the following year. Another such workshop, concentrating on Spanish, is scheduled during the summer of 1971.

East Texas State University: for FLES teachers with no prior training

Two four-week workshops for elementary and secondary foreign language teachers were conducted during the summer of 1970 in Whitewater, Wisconsin, at Wisconsin State University at Whitewater. The French Workshop, directed by Roland Durette, had 14 participants, and the German Workshop, directed by Hans C. Kayser, had 13. Each workshop carried three hours graduate or undergraduate credit in education. The main objectives were the cultural aspects of foreign language teaching and the improvement of language competence.

Wisconsin State University at Whitewater

In Maryland, public schools are administered on a county-wide basis. Philip E. Arsenault is one of two foreign language supervisors for Montgomery County, which lies just north of Washington, D.C. An idea of the scope of the supervisors' task, which has become quasi-administrative, may be gained from school popu-

Montgomery County, Maryland

lation figures provided by Arsenault: 27,000 students in grades 7–12, and 240 teachers of French, German, Spanish, and Latin in 48 secondary schools—with 4 new junior high schools scheduled to open in the fall of 1971. For the past ten years a pre-school workshop has been conducted for the orientation of new teachers. Workshop activities include the text programs, supplementary materials, their procurement and use, practice sessions using the texts and materials, interaction analysis, and ending with administration, i.e., where the new teacher may turn for help. During the 1969–70 school year a variety of excellent classroom situations were videotaped, such as the teaching of dialogs, the introduction of reading, effective use of drill materials, directed dialog, vocabulary development, and conversation at the upper levels. The tapes cover Levels I through V of the different languages, including a tape on the audio aspects of Latin instruction. Once the tapes were produced, edited, and ready to use, scheduled showings in the schools were announced to the teachers. The demonstration teacher on tape was present at each showing in order to answer questions in the discussion period that followed the viewing. Although attendance at these meetings was voluntary, Arsenault describes attendance as good, with much lively participation by teachers in the meetings.

Orientation program for new teachers

Another type of in-service activity which the teachers in Montgomery County appreciate is the opportunity to spend a day visiting a colleague in one of the other schools in order to observe classes and confer on matters of mutual professional concern. The supervisor's role here is to distribute to all teachers the schedules of the teachers who are doing something special about matters such as grouping, or individualizing instruction. The administration has cooperated by providing substitute teachers, all arrangements being made in the local schools. The Department of Supervision and Curriculum Development has also made it possible, from time to time, to invite consultants to visit the County's schools. Their most recent guest was Ronald L. Gougher, of West Chester State College, Pennsylvania, who spent a day observing some classroom situations and then met with all interested teachers to discuss individualizing instruction in the foreign language program.

A visitation program

Special consultants

Anne Arundel County, another of Maryland's more populous counties, lies to the east bordering Chesapeake Bay, and includes Annapolis, the political and executive capital of the State.

Anne Arundel County, Maryland

Virginia S. Ballard, Supervisor of Foreign Languages, conducts an annual two-week in-service program during the latter half of August for non-tenure teachers. Its purpose is to provide an opportunity for participants to learn about the program and teaching techniques needed to implement their curriculum. A per diem stipend is paid for attendance, which is required of all new teachers. A certificate is awarded at the conclusion of the program, and the State Department grants two workshop credits, provided all conditions are met. Specific textbook reading is assigned from day to day, so that participants will have a common source for discussion during group sessions. The morning and afternoon meetings are carefully scheduled. The first afternoon, teachers visit their respective schools to meet administrators, learn their schedules, and pick up instructional materials. The wide range of topics covered during the remainder of the program includes use of the language laboratory, behavioral objectives, micro-teaching, problems in teaching pronunciation, pattern practice, interaction analysis, standardized and informal testing, the reading lesson, dictation, the preparation of bulletin board displays, the daily lesson plan, using a course of study and guidelines for long-range planning, the use of the audiovisual equipment, and the pre-text unit for Level I teachers. The Modern Language Association Proficiency Tests for Teachers and Advanced Students are administered to participants. Time is also provided for conversation groups by languages (French, German, and Spanish). Four activities are carried out at the end of the program: (1) a test is administered that deals with the work that has been accomplished; (2) the pronunciation of each participant is evaluated; (3) checkouts are given, in which participants demonstrate skill in the operation of a tape recorder; and (4) participants evaluate the program. A system of behavioral-objective rating is used by Ballard, and visiting specialists, in analyzing the competencies of foreign language teachers both during the in-service program and during the school year. The system includes professional objectives and objectives involving general content. It applies, as appropriate, to all languages, skills, and levels.

*A two-week program
for non-tenure teachers*

District in-service programs

The development of theory and the process of research in in-service education are especially suited to the school district level, where they have their most practical application. Pulley & Veri (37) summarize the work performed by five committees of professional educators toward the building of a theoretical model in-service program for schools. Included were university professors, representatives of the Missouri State Department of Education, school administrators, supervisors, classroom teachers, school board members, community leaders, parents, and expert consultants from outside Missouri. The project was designed for two major purposes: (1) to supplement, complement, and stimulate further development of the existing in-service program in the Parkway School District, located in Chesterfield, Missouri; and (2) to provide the initial phase of models for the development of programs for school personnel and policy makers who are engaged in administering and servicing public education. The first committee dealt with the development of an in-service model for instructional personnel by identifying a set of assumptions, each of which carries specific implications. The implications, in turn, are the source of questions that enable decision making in either instituting or evaluating in-service programs.

The implementation of a theoretical model: Chesterfield, Missouri

Two elementary schools in upstate New York provided Carline (9) with teachers for his study of the effect that in-service training in interaction analysis might have on teacher behavior. One objective of the study was to test the hypothesis that an intensive in-service training program would significantly alter teacher verbal behavior. Twenty-three teachers in one school participated in the training program and were designated as the experimental group. The 20 teachers in the other, comparable, school did not participate and constituted the control group. Pupils of experimental and control teachers in grades 1 through 5 were the subjects whose achievement in mathematics was studied. The Flanders *Technique and Category System of Verbal Analysis* was used as the observation technique for all 43 teachers. Fourteen teacher-training variables or verbal patterns were examined. During the course of the study, formal and informal training sessions were conducted with the experimental group in an attempt to "train-in" seven of the variables and "train-out" the seven others. Results indicated that the "positive" approach was more effective, since all of the train-out variables were rejected, while five of the train-ins were accepted at the .01 level. The results provide evidence that an intensive in-service training program can significantly change teacher behavior.

Effects of interaction analysis on teacher behavior

Although numerous studies in interaction analysis have been conducted in other curricular areas, very little experimental research has been done in analyzing the verbal behavior of foreign language teachers. Moskowitz has modified the Flanders system in applying it to foreign language teaching by dividing the ten categories of behavior into two types of influence: indirect (i.e., expanding student participation) and direct. She reports a study that compared foreign language student teachers who were trained in interaction analysis with others who were not. Foreign language student teachers trained in interaction analysis used a variety of indirect teaching patterns, and the patterns appeared to be more in keeping with the goals of the lessons (30). At the annual meeting of the Colorado Congress of Foreign Language Teachers in the fall of 1970, Moskowitz, in (10), presented an explanation of her approach to interaction analysis by dividing the audience into two groups. She then demonstrated a teacher-dominated class and one in which student participation was encouraged. This was followed by a comparison of the two approaches in terms of interaction analysis. As a follow-up, the audience was sent to various conference rooms according to language for practice in interaction analysis using tapes prepared by Moskowitz. She has produced a set of materials, entitled *The Foreign Language Teacher Interacts*, which are well suited to foreign language in-service education. The set includes a programmed text, tapes (in French, German, Spanish, Italian, Latin, and English as a Foreign Language), and 12 unmounted transparencies. The set is available from the Association for Productive Teaching, 5408 Chicago Avenue South, Minneapolis, Minnesota 55417.

Moskowitz' work with interaction analysis applied to foreign languages: the Colorado Congress

While the improvement of competency has been stressed as the major goal of in-service education, there is another function of an institutional nature that is growing steadily in importance, that of articulation. Two events at opposite ends of the United States will serve to highlight developments in this direction. Fairfield University, in Fairfield, Connecticut, sponsored a Curriculum Symposium in Foreign Languages on April 15, 1970. Participants were members of the Fairfield University Department of Modern Languages, the Fairfield Preparatory School Department of Foreign Languages, and the Department of Foreign Languages of the Fairfield Public Schools. Topics brought into discussion included college-level curriculum revision, new trends in teacher preparation, comparison of college and secon-

Fairfield, Connecticut: articulation stressed in in-service education

dary school methodology, college expectations of foreign language achievement by high school students, rating of oral work at the college level as opposed to reading, motivation of students and teachers of foreign languages, and the placement of incoming freshmen at the University. Those in attendance felt that a worthwhile exchange of ideas had taken place, and that the meeting itself constituted an important contribution to better articulation (14).

The California Foreign Language Teachers Association (CFLTA) reported that public school foreign language supervisors and college teachers of foreign language methodology were to "break bread and knock heads" in a two-day exchange of ideas at the Monterey Institute of Foreign Studies on March 19–20, 1971. The event was sponsored by the CFLTA as part of its program of improving foreign language instruction. Participation in the conference was free, and all teachers interested in foreign language education were invited to participate. The first session was devoted to a day-long demonstration and explanation of an audiovisual foreign language teaching method. During the second day, conferees joined in a series of group discussions on a wide range of topics, such as the teaching of culture, performance objectives, individualizing instruction, and the use of video tape for instructional improvement (18).

California: a two-day exchange of ideas

Among the many in-service programs for foreign language teachers was one in Greeley, Colorado, which was conducted by Lynn Sanstedt, Foreign Language Coordinator for the District. It included ten three-hour weekly sessions, beginning September 24 and ending December 10, 1970. The sessions were conducted on Thursday afternoons from 3:30 to 6:30 P.M. Three hours of salary increment credit were granted to those teachers who completed the program. In addition to several topics of the type already listed, five that illustrate the possible dimensions of such programs were: (1) foreign language programmed material; (2) nongraded foreign language classes; (3) teaching foreign language to the slow learner; (4) maintaining foreign language skills for the student who is unable to enroll in advanced language courses; and (5) using radio to develop and maintain foreign language competence. Two foreign language consultants, one from Holt, Rinehart and Winston, and one from Harcourt Brace Jovanovich, gave special demonstration classes. ERIC Focus Reports were used as a source of inexpensive and up-to-date information (15).

Greeley, Colorado: ten three-hour sessions

To help teachers meet language needs brought about by an influx of Spanish-speaking citizens into the community, the Lancaster (Pennsylvania) School District conducted a conversational Spanish course for approximately 150 elementary and secondary teachers in the District during the first half of 1971. In the selection of participants, preference was given to those teachers from schools with a high percentage of Spanish-speaking children. Six classes, which met once a week for two hours, were taught by professors of Spanish from Franklin and Marshall College and from Millersville State College. The classes did not follow a coordinated curriculum, each professor being free to conduct the course in his own way. Attendance was mandatory for those teachers who enrolled in the course, and the District granted two semester hours of in-service credit to all who successfully completed the course. The credits counted toward the teachers' permanent certification and also for salary increments.

Lancaster, Pennsylvania: a conversational Spanish course

The Department of Foreign Languages of the Washington, D.C., Public Schools provides abundant opportunity for in-service training, according to Judith LeBovit, Supervising Director for the Department. Teachers of French, Spanish, and Latin in the elementary schools begin the school year with two weeks of orientation meetings. These meetings present methodology, text materials, and general guidelines for effective teaching. Demonstrations of various techniques are also presented by veteran teachers. For all foreign language teachers, workshops are regularly scheduled throughout the year. Secondary teachers meet for in-service training by geographical area, as well as by language. Exchange visits are arranged for teachers of all levels within the District and also with teachers of the greater metropolitan areas.

Washington, D.C.: a regular schedule

As Spanish Consultant for the Des Plaines (Illinois) School District, Dorothy S. Bishop is concerned with the teaching of Spanish to children in the middle grades. She believes that in-service programs should be planned and conducted in response to specific needs. Over the past eight years she has conducted programs dealing with a variety of topics such as psychological aspects of foreign language teaching and learning, techniques for teaching foreign languages to children, the place of Spanish culture in the curriculum, and articulation of FLES high school courses. One of her special interests is the teaching of Spanish phonics as an important step in the development of reading skill in grade 6. A teacher's guide, *La primera fonética*, and its corre-

Des Plaines, Illinois: FLES

265

sponding pupil workbook, *Mi primera fonética*, have been published by her and her associate, Alice A. Mohrman, and serve as the basis for the in-service sessions on phonics. These and other of Bishop's publications are available from National Textbook Company, 8259 Niles Center Road, Skokie, Illinois 60076.

Local in-service programs

Feldman (16) points out that rapid change is characteristic of foreign language teaching today: new concepts in textbook preparation and classroom procedures, the proliferation of materials, technical aids, and innovative practices, to list but a few examples. Both the new and the experienced foreign language teacher are finding themselves inadequately prepared to deal with these changing conditions. As Feldman sees the situation, the solution to the dilemma of keeping pace lies largely in in-service education. Even the most ideal preprofessional curriculum would not be enough. In fact, he asserts, the more a well-designed pre-service curriculum has given the student a sense of professional responsibility and academic curiosity, the more he will, as a teacher, demand meaningful in-service opportunities. Feldman believes that the federal government should play a part in improving foreign language instruction, most significantly by providing a stimulus and a core of trained personnel. The broad front of in-service training must be developed at the local level.

In-service the key to continued teacher competence

Moir (28) also contends that the school must become the focal point of in-service education. Tracing the historical development of school organization, he describes how the concept of group efforts to upgrade competence and improve curricula has gradually developed. Departmentalization and team teaching, as well as many current in-service programs have come into vogue to enable teachers to work together and to help one another. Teachers prefer well-planned in-school training programs, according to Moir, because they represent training best suited to their needs. He views supervisors as catalysts rather than organizers in the operation of local in-service programs, for it is more important for the initiative to be in the hands of the teachers — even if errors and omissions occur — than for all fields to be covered in an equitable manner.

In-service helps teachers work together

Turner (43) finds that many in-service programs seem to be causing as many problems as they are solving. Not only are

266

teachers upset by "central planning," in which they have little or no part, but they are resisting the traditional end-of-the-day scheduling of programs. He believes that much of the feeling of being "talked down to" may result from mixing beginning and experienced teachers, especially in programs just prior to the beginning of the school year. In arranging in-service training, the consumers must be considered and the product must be directly tailored to suit their needs. A suggestion offered by Turner is that, under most circumstances, improvement will result from developing programs for three separate groups: (1) beginning, untenured teachers; (2) more experienced teachers; and (3) veteran teachers. Teacher needs and supervisory tasks differ for each group. The beginning teacher will need help in classroom management, teacher-student relations, and the utilization of materials. The more experienced teacher is more apt to be interested in innovations or more formal study. The veteran teachers represent the well-trained, most experienced portion of the staff, although they, too, will need refresher sessions from time to time. They can provide an important reservoir of talent and expertise. In carrying out a comprehensive in-service program, Turner states that the supervisor must (1) provide the means for retraining participants in any innovative program; (2) keep his colleagues informed as the innovating develops; (3) insure that teachers are able to remain competent in the use of the changing technology; (4) remain alert to better ways of reaching individual students and of providing for their needs; (5) encourage teachers to continue serious study of their own discipline; and (6) take the lead in establishing a high level of involvement opportunities at every stage of planning and performance.

Teachers want to be considered in planning for in-service

Supervisor's role

    In his discussion of in-service training programs for teachers of disadvantaged children, Buskin (8) finds most of past programs inadequate. He refers to several new programs, supported by the federal government, whose evaluation requirements call for setting predetermined, specific goals for teachers—and for their students—and then testing to see if those goals have been reached. Buskin points to an intensive, in-depth study of in-service training by Louis J. Rubin, at the Center of Coordinated Education, University of California at Santa Barbara. Rubin (38) identified a set of characteristics that any good, meaningful in-service program should have. Among these were: (1) the program should be flexible enough so that a teacher can begin at his own level of ability and progress at his own rate; (2) pro-

Characteristics of a meaningful in-service program

grams should be conducted during teachers' paid time; (3) programs should be compulsory; (4) retraining should not interfere with individual styles of teaching, as long as performance and effectiveness is not damaged; and (5) outstanding classroom teachers should conduct in-service programs for other teachers.

Chalmers (11) emphasizes the importance of the role an audiovisual supervisor should play in the in-service training of teachers in materials, equipment, technology, and methodology that did not exist when the teachers themselves were undergraduates. Five of the areas of audiovisual management that contribute to media competency and that can be dealt with in in-service training are: (1) selection of materials and equipment; (2) utilization of media for effective teaching; (3) production of instructional materials; (4) evaluation of the use of media in the light of teaching objectives; and (5) distribution procedures of materials and equipment. Chalmers recommends using media to teach about media as an effective means of presentation and of saving time and effort on the part of the supervisor. The synchronized slide-tape set and video tape are particularly well-suited for this purpose. Special publications may be prepared as another means of keeping teachers informed on specific topics such as the preparation of transparencies or the use of the overhead projector.[2]

Role of audiovisual supervisor

Vinson (45) investigated the relative importance of problem areas from the point of view of teachers and supervisors by analyzing data from questionnaire responses obtained from 144 foreign language teachers and 13 foreign language supervisors in six states. The purpose was to draw comparisons between the perceptions of: (1) beginning teachers and supervisors; and (2) first-year teachers and third-year teachers. In reference to the first of these comparisons, she found that the most difficult problems in the view of beginning teachers, as they related specifically to foreign language teaching, were: (1) student attitudes toward foreign language learning; (2) acquiring and using satisfactory equipment and materials; (3) organizing and planning for individual differences; (4) applying the latest research findings; and (5) teaching writing skills. The foreign language supervisors strongly disagreed with the teachers as to which problems deserve greatest attention. As they saw them, the problems were: (1) language laboratory and audiovisual use; (2) helping

Problems of beginning teachers

The supervisor's point of view

2 Editor's note: For a broad discussion of media in foreign language teaching and learning, see Chapter 7, by Jermaine D. Arendt, in the *Britannica Review of Foreign Language Education, Volume 2.*

the teacher evaluate his own effectiveness; (3) promoting articulation among and within language levels; (4) obtaining and adapting textbooks; (5) keeping informed and applying the latest research findings; and (6) preparing lesson plans. In the comparison of first-year teachers with third-year teachers, Vinson found that the third-year teachers were more aware of problems due to (1) administration and community attitude toward the foreign language program; and (2) lack of articulation among and within language levels. She concluded that awareness of problems probably increases with teaching experience. Among several interesting observations made by Vinson are: (1) teachers see their problems as "minor" and ask for little help, while supervisors see them as "major"; and (2) teachers generally seem to regard the supervisor as a consultant who should provide the teacher with information; they request little help with methodology, planning, or their own language competency, such as an inservice program could provide. Vinson's recommendations concerning supervision and in-service training include the following: (1) supervisors should inform beginning teachers how they, the supervisors, can be of assistance; (2) supervisors should not wait for beginning teachers to request help but should schedule conferences; (3) supervisors should try to build the beginner's self-confidence by encouraging the improvement of his language skills; and (4) supervisors should provide in-service training in the use of media in lesson presentation.

Problems of third-year teachers

In-service education and the individual teacher

One justification that can be given for the development of in-service programs to meet needs of individual teachers is that resultant changes can be expected to be longer-lasting. Wilson (46) points out that imposed change in the schools has had only short-lived value and that, due to resistance from various sources, many practices that had proved to be of high value have been aborted. He proposes a concept of involvement that has proved highly successful in bringing about lasting changes in many schools. The basic assumption underlying the "Wilson Model" for change is that personnel within a school are different. Not only do they play different roles, they also have different needs, dispositions, knowledge bases, and expectations. Five steps, as they apply to teachers, are involved in the Model:

The "Wilson Model" of in-service for the individual

1 At the beginning of the school year, an individual confer-

ence is held with each teacher by the change agent. The purpose of the conference is to outline *long-range goals* that the teacher wishes to accomplish during the school year, with the teacher being the authority on his own needs. Together, the teacher and change agent define strategies to meet those needs, with the change agent acting as recorder and communication catalyst.

Five steps

2 Every two weeks throughout the school year, the change agent meets with the teacher to help him in identifying *short-range objectives* that he, the teacher, wishes to accomplish. These objectives are placed in priority order, with the procedures that may be expected to accomplish them also being defined. A copy of the objectives and procedures is kept by both the change agent and the teacher.

3 An additional copy of the objectives is sent to the principal or superintendent. It is that administrator's responsibility to review the objectives and *facilitate* their accomplishment in every way possible.

4 *Fulfillment of objectives* may be achieved in a wide variety of ways, including such activities as professional reading, visiting consultants, or small-group instruction.

5 *Evaluation* of progress and results are made at each successive conference.

There is no doubt that such an individualized counseling process would be demanding in terms of time and personnel, but the concept does deserve consideration as a productive procedure for involvement and for a systematic approach to change through in-service education. Further, it is important because it gives the teacher needed direction for professional growth.

Another entirely different approach to in-service training makes use of a device that lends itself to the direct observation and analysis of the teacher's classroom performance: the video-tape recorder. The use of videotape recordings in student-teacher training is rapidly becoming a common practice. For the experienced teacher, however, video technology is often a new idea that is accompanied by a number of unstated and unexplored anxieties. Steward & Steward (41) explain that there are several reasons why experienced teachers are disturbed when they are faced with the prospect of being videotaped. For one thing, experienced teachers are seldom observed critically by competent observers and then provided with useful feedback. For another — a reason that holds both the problem and the promise of video —

Direct observation: the videotape recorder

the videotape recording shows situations and people exactly as they are, providing nearly total feedback. The Stewards point out that finding out how other people see us is a highly important and personal matter—one that takes some getting used to. They find that the beginning teacher, who has so many other kinds of problems to face, is not as perturbed by the presence of videotape equipment in the classroom as is the experienced teacher, who has become comfortable in the classroom setting and skilled in the observation of his students. For him the main concern is how *he* is going to look on TV. One of the real difficulties in helping the experienced teacher overcome his reluctance about being taped is that the first viewing often contributes to his anxiety rather than helping to overcome it. The Stewards believe that the teacher deserves all possible help in getting through this experience, and they recommend that every teacher who is videotaped as a part of an in-service training program be given a period of time to view himself in private—simply to get used to seeing himself, to get acquainted with his body image. They recognize the emotional difficulty of beginning to use this personal source of information, and believe that teachers can be introduced to it in such a way that they can endure the anxiety and reap the rewards of substantial increase in awareness of their own professional performance.

Difficulties in using this machine

Rubin (38) regards the video camera as a powerful aid in analyzing teacher performance, since it can provide an exceedingly valuable experience in extending the teacher's perception of his role and in helping him assess the variance between his intent and the results he obtains. In his consideration of the self-evolving teacher, Rubin describes the dilemma posed by the processes of manipulation in bringing about alteration in human behavior. He contrasts operant conditioning, and its reward-punishment approach, with "sanative experience"—experience that increases insight, deepens awareness, enlarges one's sense of options, or that reduces the anxiety of change. Videotape recordings of teaching episodes are one effective means of providing "sanative experience," but the extent to which a teacher can evaluate his own performance is still unclear. Some experimental programs now underway provide the teacher with a structured guide for self-analysis while others make use of a trained collaborator. As a result of experiments he has conducted, Rubin believes that regular diagnosis can be made a routine part of professional life.

"Sanative experience"

In-service programs and innovation

Moore & Mizuba (29), in their study of innovation diffusion, state that *what* is worthy of belief and *who* is worthy of belief probably are key influences in the individual's acceptance or rejection of an idea. In a school situation, the initiator—in our present context the foreign language supervisor—regards himself and the innovative idea as being credible. The problem of successful diffusion, then, is to "transfer" this attitude to the teachers he supervises. Moore & Mizuba point out two distinct levels of credibility within the complex of cultural, situational, and personal factors that lead to successful diffusion: (*1*) the nature of the innovation; and (2) the nature of the person acting as change agent. It seems that one tends to believe people one can trust. The authors suggest three conditions for successful innovation: (*1*) an acceptable image of the initiator needs to be established; (2) the objectives and functions of the innovation need to be communicable; and (3) the nature of the receiver must be incorporated into the diffusion process.

Successful diffusion, innovation

An interesting example of an innovative in-service idea that was developed through involvement and negotiation may be seen in the Scarsdale (New York) Teachers Institute, which is described by Breslow & Dempsey (7). A committee of the Scarsdale Teachers Association conceived the idea of the Institute as a means of offering current information on a variety of subjects, maintaining an atmosphere of intellectual excitement, and throwing full light on any problem of immediate professional concern to teachers. Teachers responded to a questionnaire, circulated by the committee, by endorsing the concept and making numerous suggestions for courses, speakers, and procedures. The Executive Board of the Association then established a committee composed of teachers from the seven schools in the system to organize and operate the Institute, which has gained the support of the National Education Association and the New York State Teachers Association. Teacher suggestions determined the 11 after-school and evening courses offered during 1969–70, the first year of the Institute's operation. Although the teachers run the Institute, the community has become involved through the Educational Advisory Committee, a group of 14 prominent citizens who meet periodically with the Institute teachers to help plan courses, suggest possible speakers, and

The Scarsdale Teachers Institute

provide useful advice. As a result of negotiations between the board of education and the Scarsdale Teachers Association, the board has agreed to provide funds for those Institute courses that are approved for salary credits—the Institute retaining the option of offering other courses without such credit. The school administration, too, has many functions in the operation of the Institute. An accreditation committee of three principals and three teachers reviews courses and makes recommendations for salary credit. The superintendent of schools and the director of curriculum and research serve as official consultants to the Institute. In concluding their report, Breslow & Dempsey indicate three important results of the Institute: (1) the high quality of the courses is broadening educational horizons for the teachers and making their classrooms a more stimulating environment for learning; (2) a greater sense of harmony and credibility has been established between the teachers and the community; and (3) the prospects of productive negotiations have been improved by the increased assumption of professional responsibility by the teachers.

Patterson (34) reports the development of an in-service program somewhat similar in format to the Scarsdale Teachers Institute but much less formal and more flexible. He describes the Grants Pass (Oregon) Public School District Micro-College, held on a Saturday from 9 A.M. to 3 P.M. at North Junior High School. The invitational event drew a majority of the District's teachers, grades 1–12, and administrators. Approximately 50 different Micro-College classes, lasting from 15 minutes to an hour, were scheduled—five or six at a time—during the six-hour period. Some 75 teachers and administrators volunteered to serve as "professors" in offering a variety of courses including teaching demonstrations (using local students) of individualized instruction, panel discussions with representatives from the news media, and elementary counseling techniques. Most of those who attended the one-day Micro-College pronounced it a success, although criticism of its being conducted on Saturday rather than on a workday was included in the feedback. Patterson recommends the Micro-College approach to in-service education because it is adaptable to many situations, not only for teachers but also for other members of the community.

A micro-college

Hartung & Gelman (22) describe an entirely different technique for in-service education that has been worked out by the English Department of University Extension, the University of

Wisconsin. The idea began in 1965, when Extension offered continuing education programs over the Educational Telephone Network, allowing participation by groups widely scattered about the state. The English Department began its Workshop for English Teachers in 1967. From the beginning, efforts were made to avoid conventional lecture-type programs and to provide, instead, informal exchanges of a type that junior and senior high school teachers could shape to their needs. Enrollment has grown from about 80 to 230, despite the fact that many teachers must travel 20 or 30 miles to a telephone station. The stations are located in hospitals, clinics, courthouses, and on 15 University of Wisconsin campuses. Each is equipped with a loudspeaker and a telephone. In order to speak, the listener need only lift the telephone receiver, since the line is already connected to the studio on the Madison campus where the programs originate. The programs are presented once a month and last for an hour and a half. Each program is presented in two sessions separated by a five-minute break. The first session is a panel discussion carried on by four to six teachers, University faculty members, or guests. The second encourages informal response from participants in the form of comments and questions to the panel. Reading material is mailed to participants in advance and, after each program, the teachers fill out reaction sheets as a continuing means of evaluation. Each program is taped and made available to anyone who has missed a meeting. Hartung and Gelman believe that the format is more productive than the usual type of workshop. They point out that the Workshop (1) allows questioners to remain anonymous; (2) prompts teachers to open up in discussing new approaches they have found useful; (3) aids articulation by bringing various educational levels into closer contact; (4) enables guests from all parts of the United States to participate conveniently; and (5) best of all, provides an opportunity for teachers in smaller, relatively isolated communities to discuss their problems. The authors find that teachers have accepted the new medium with enthusiasm, but that program planners feel they have only begun to realize its potential in in-service education.

An educational telephone network in in-service

Innovative ideas may be introduced not only to improve and expand existing curriculum components, but also to establish entirely new ones. In Minnesota, a program teaching the Chippewa Indian language is underway at the Vineland Elementary School on the Mille Lacs Indian Reservation. The project began

A workshop for teachers/teacher aides for Chippewa

in July, 1969, with a week-long workshop conducted by Percy Fearing, Modern Foreign Language Consultant for the Minnesota State Department of Education, to develop teaching materials and to give the Indian aides training in teaching methodology. The principal of the school and the Vineland Board of Education invited the State Department of Education to pilot the project in the first and second grades because the children had had an introduction to language study during their Head Start program and were motivated to continue. After an assessment of the pilot year, another workshop was conducted during July, 1970, to develop another level of materials. This resulted in a set of tape lessons with accompanying visuals and lessons plans to be used during the 1970–71 school year in grades 3 and 4. It is hoped that a third and final elementary level can be developed during the summer of 1971 and that in succeeding years the materials and curricula for the secondary schools can be prepared (12,13).

In Concord-Carlisle (Massachusetts) High School, half of the 12 foreign language teachers have elected to work during July, 1971, under the local 210-day (or "eleven month") contract, to lay the groundwork for diversification of their foreign language curriculum in a way that fits the needs of their own students. Elaine DeCicco, Foreign Language Department Chairman, explains that Concord-Carlisle is a four-year high school that receives its students from three area schools, each of which has multi leveled foreign language offerings. The high school foreign language teachers believe they can deal more effectively with the many different levels of achievement by adding numerous options to their present "traditional," audiovisual foreign language courses. They proposed to work during the summer of 1971 toward the development of their own individualized study program. By the end of a three-year period they hope to expand their foreign language curriculum further to include mini-courses of varying duration, depending on the content, the teacher, and the students. By that time, it is anticipated that the school will be an extended-day, open-campus operation, with students able to work at any time of the day or evening. Members of the Foreign Language Department have distributed the Northeast Conference Foreign Language Student Questionnaires to their students and have invited students to help in the project. The school is fortunate, according to DeCicco, to have a sympathetic administration and to serve a community that is receptive to this type of innovation.

A contracted in-service program

275

Conclusions

1 The process of in-service education is continuous and includes all educators. Its primary goal is the improvement of professional competence.

2 The diversity in American schools is reflected in the great variety of possibilities and opportunities that are offered for in-service education.

3 Responsibility for in-service education is shared equally by the educator and the school system by which he is employed.

4 In-service education at the national level provides exposure to excellence. In-service training at the local level provides exposure to reality.

5 Individualization, motivation, and behavioral objectives are just as important to in-service education program participants as they are to students in the classroom.

6 Foreign language teachers, as communications specialists, should seek the expansion of opportunities for in-service education through every technological means, including telephone networks, radio, and television.

References, In-service programs in foreign languages at elementary and secondary levels

1 "ACTFL Symposium on FL Teacher Training." [Alabama State Department of Education.] *Foreign Languages* Spring (1971):10–11.

2 Altman, Howard B. "The Seattle Symposium on the Training of Foreign Language Teachers." *Modern Language Journal* 55(1971):229–32.

3 ——— and Louis Weiss. "Recent Developments in the Training and Certification of the Foreign Language Teacher," 239–74 in Dale L. Lange, ed., *Britannica Review of Foreign Language Education, Volume 2.* Chicago: Encyclopaedia Britannica, Inc., 1970.

4 Andersson, Theodore. "From NDEA to EPDA: Can We Improve?" *Hispania* 52(1969):357–61.

5 Andrews, L.O. "Initial Preparation of the Career Teacher:An Approach to the In-Service Phase." *Educational Leadership* 27(1970):553–55.

6 Axelrod, Joseph. "NDEA Foreign Language Institute Programs:The Development of a New Educational Model." *PMLA* 82,iv(1967):14–18.

7 Breslow, Doris G., and Vincent Dempsey. "The Scarsdale Teachers Institute." *Today's Educa-*

tion:*The Journal of the National Education Association* 59,ii(1970):56–57.

8 Buskin, Martin. "Putting the Screws to Inservice Training." *School Management* 14,ix(1970):22–24.

9 Carline, John L. "In-Service Training—Re-examined." *Journal of Research and Development in Education* 4,i(1970):103–15.

10 "CCFLT Fall Meeting." *PEALS* 11,i(1971):2. [Newsletter of the Colorado Congress of Foreign Language Teachers.]

11 Chalmers, John J. "Audiovisual Inservice Training." *Audiovisual Instruction* 15(1970):60–63.

12 "Chippewa Language Project." Minnesota State Department of Education. *Foreign Language Items* 3,i(1969):1.

13 "Chippewa Language Workshop." Minnesota State Department of Education. *Foreign Language Items* 4,i(1970):5–6.

14 Connecticut State Department of Education. *FL News Exchange* 16,v(1970):7.

15 "ERIC Reports Used in Greeley." *PEALS*

11,i(1971):3. [Newsletter of the Colorado Congress of Foreign Language.]

16 Feldman, David M.,ed. "In-Service Training," 478–83 in Eberhard Reichmann,ed., *The Teaching of German:Problems and Methods*. Philadelphia: National Carl Schurz Association, 1970.

17 "FL Framework Proceeds According to Schedule." *Newsletter* 2,ii(1971):1,4. [Newsletter of the California Foreign Language Teachers Association.]

18 "FL Methods Teachers and Supervisors to Share Views." *Newsletter* 2,ii(1971):3. [Newsletter of the California Foreign Language Teachers Association.]

19 Gries, Frauke. "A Model for In-Service Education." *The American Foreign Language Teacher* 1,ii(1970):5,43–44.

20 Grittner, Frank, and Jermaine D. Arendt. "Proceedings of the Central States Conference on the Teaching of Foreign Languages." *Modern Language Journal* 54(1970):605–10.

21 Hanzeli, Victor E., and William D. Love,eds. *New Teachers for New Students:Proceedings of the Seattle Symposium on the Training of Foreign Language Teachers*. Seattle and New York: The Washington State Foreign Language Program and the American Council on the Teaching of Foreign Languages, 1970.

22 Hartung, George, and Rena Gelman. "Something Different in In-Service Education." *Today's Education:The Journal of the National Education Association* 59,v(1970):24–25.

23 *Inservice Education of Teachers:Research Summary 1966–71*. Washington,D.C.: National Education Association, 1966.

24 King, Charles L. "A Decade of NDEA Language Institutes." *Hispania* 52(1969):361–68.

25 Lange, Dale L., and James Hammers. *Final Report on the EPDA Institute in German for Cooperating Teachers and Teacher Trainers at the University of Minnesota:August 11, 1969, to June 15, 1970*.

26 McArdle, Richard J. "Teacher Education, Qualifications, and Supervision," 259–80 in Emma M. Birkmaier,ed., *Britannica Review of Foreign Language Education, Volume 1*. Chicago: Encyclopaedia Britannica, Inc., 1968[1969].

27 *Modern Foreign Languages:In-Service Program, National Defense Education Act, Title III*. Jefferson City, Missouri: Missouri State Department of Education, n.d.

28 Moir, Carmen F. "The School:Focal Point of In-Service Education." *Education Canada* 10(1970): 15–17.

29 Moore, Samuel, and Kiyoto Mizuba. "Innovation Diffusion:A Study in Credibility." *Educational Forum* 33(1969):181–85.

30 Moskowitz, Gertrude. "Interaction Analysis." *The American Foreign Language Teacher* 1,i(1970):10–15.

31 *NEA Handbook for Local, State, and National Associations:1970–71*. Washington,D.C.: National Education Association, 1970.

32 "North Dakota FL Workshop." *Accent on ACTFL* 1,ii(1971):8.

33 "Northeast Conference." *Unterrichtspraxis* 1,i(1968):150–51.

34 Patterson, Wade N. "In-Service Micro-College." *Today's Education:The Journal of the National Education Association* 60,ii(1971):53.

35 Prince, J. Roy. "An Institute Director Looks Back." *Hispania* 52(1969):368–75.

36 *Progress of Public Education in the United States of America 1968–1969*. Report for the Thirty-Second International Conference on Public Education, Sponsored by the United Nations Educational, Scientific and Cultural Organization, International Bureau of Education. Washington,D.C.: United States Office of Education, 1970.

37 Pulley, Jerry L., and Clive C. Veri,eds. *In-Service Education Models for Schools:A Summary*. Normandy, Missouri: Extension Division, University of Missouri–St. Louis, 1970.

38 Rubin, Louis J. "The Self-Evolving Teacher," 263–76 in Louis J. Rubin,ed., *Improving In-Service Education: Proposals and Procedures for Change*. Boston: Allyn & Bacon, 1971.

39 Schloss, Samuel. *Fall 1965 Statistics of Public Elementary and Secondary Schools*. Washington,D.C.: Government Printing Office, 1966.

40 Smith, Gloria N., and Angel A. Castro. "The Spirit of the NDEA Institute is Alive in Virginia: Summer 1970 Workshop Report." *Accent on ACTFL* 1,ii(1971):6–7.

41 Steward, Margaret S., and David S. Steward. "Teacher, Teach Yourself." *Audiovisual Instruction* 15(1970):26–27.

42 *Teacher Training Practices in Foreign Language Instruction*. Prepared by the Liaison Committee on Foreign Language of the California Articulation Conference. Sacramento: California State Department of Education, 1970.

43 Turner, Harold E. "Improved In-Service:A Challenge for Supervisors." *Clearing House* 45(1970): 116–19.

44 Tursi, Joseph A.,ed. *Foreign Languages and the "New" Student*. Reports of the Working Committees of the Northeast Conference on the Teaching of Foreign Languages. New York: Modern Language Association Materials Center, 1970.

45 Vinson, Sharon S.W. "Problems of Beginning Secondary School Teachers of Foreign Languages with Implications for Supervision and In-Service Education." Unpublished Ph.D. Dissertation. Tallahassee: Florida State Univ., 1969 [1970].

46 Wilson, Alfred P. *Individualized In-Service Training*. Paper presented at the meeting of the Association for Supervision and Curriculum Development in St. Louis, Missouri, on March 7, 1971. [Self-Instructional Packages for Inservice Education, presented at this Conference, may be obtained from Video Inservice Program, P.O. Box 10, Milford, Nebraska 68405.]

47 "The Wyoming Foreign Language Handbook." *The Lasso:Wyoming Foreign Language Bulletin* 33(December 1970):7. [Bulletin of the Wyoming Foreign Language Council and Wyoming State Department of Education.]

10

Modern foreign language teaching in the uncommonly taught languages

Introduction

This chapter differs from the others in this volume in two important ways. Whereas the theme of pluralism is uniquely relevant to the role of the neglected languages in American education, this chapter will not be limited in scope to interpretation or review of the most recent literature in the field, but will provide historical perspective where necessary, while concentrating on the developments of the past decade. It will also provide a comprehensive overview of the state of the art in the teaching and learning of uncommonly taught languages.

There is no generally accepted terminology to refer to the subject of this chapter. These languages have been referred to alternately as neglected, unusual, uncommonly taught, exotic, hard, critical, non-Western, non-cognate, and even funny. The most precise definition is categorical listing – all languages other than French, Spanish, German, and Italian, with Russian wavering on the edge. The term used in this chapter is *uncommonly taught languages*.

The uncommonly taught languages are perhaps more commonly taught than one might at first imagine. Chinese, for example, formerly the purview of a small number of highly trained scholars in a handful of highly specialized graduate programs, has developed into a major national resource. Enrollments (Kant, 20) have risen dramatically, with as many as 1,844 registered at institutions of higher education in 1960; 5,061 in 1968; and, according to preliminary results for the 1970 Modern Language Association survey, registrations are up significantly again. The picture in the schools (Kant, 19) is similar, with Chinese having enrollments of over 2,000 in 1968. A survey is presently under way at the Modern Language Association to provide current information for 1970. Higher education enrollments for Swahili, to take another example, have risen from 4 in 1958 to 608 in 1968, and, according to a Modern Language Association report in May, 1971, there are presently 64 colleges and universities offering Swahili to 1,571 students.

Richard T. Thompson

United States Office of Education

(This article was written by Richard T. Thompson in his private capacity. No official support or endorsement by the United States Office of Education is intended or should be inferred.)

Selecting a term

Examples of enrollments in the uncommon languages

One major source of support for the uncommonly taught languages has been the National Defense Education Act (NDEA) of 1958. The history, functions, and achievements of the NDEA will be covered at length in this chapter.

NDEA support

The purpose of this chapter will be to survey the field of the uncommonly taught languages, analyzing the historical perspectives, with emphasis on the role of the government and private funding agencies and organizations, and the professional area association and societies. It will describe the development of language methodology in the field of modern foreign language teaching and the special role that linguistics and the teaching of non-cognate languages has played in this development, and measure the growth of language teaching materials, centers, and programs both at home and abroad, as well as the preparation of specialists in these languages. It will present the state of the art in the teaching and learning of uncommonly taught languages by world area, and evaluate the effect of the recent crises in the schools and colleges, the elimination of degree requirements, and the production of language specialists for the neglected languages, with a view toward developing a more rational understanding of the special role of these languages and related areas studies in order to plan for their continued growth at all levels of American education.

Purpose of this chapter

Some historical perspectives

It is especially appropriate for the unique purposes of this chapter to present the reader with an historical perspective of the development of non-Western studies in this country, tracing the influences from several sources and evaluating their impact on the teaching of the uncommonly taught languages today.

Development of non-Western studies in U.S.

As mentioned above, by and large, what little competence existed in this country in non-Western studies was limited to a handful of scholars in a few selected institutions of higher education at the graduate level. It was also generally restricted to the traditional premodern languages, including Chinese and those of the Middle East, including Arabic.

The isolationism that characterized American foreign policy in the post-World War I period directly affected this country's linguistic outlook. The resulting linguistic isolation came to an abrupt end when the outbreak of World War II ushered in a new era in foreign language study. For the first time in history, large numbers of linguists turned language teachers attempted to apply the findings of linguistics to the field of language teaching. For an excellent general discussion of the early development of linguistics and the uncommonly taught languages see Haas (15) and Moulton (30).

World War II and after: Major programs

American Council of Learned Societies

The American Council of Learned Societies (ACLS), under the foresight and initiative of its executive secretary, Mortimer Graves, established an Intensive Language Program (ILP) early in 1941. J. Milton Cowan assumed the Directorship of the program and by the following summer there were in operation 56 courses in 26 languages at 18 universities, involving a total of 700 students. ILP intensive language courses were based on sound linguistic analysis of the language and were concerned primarily with the uncommonly taught languages.

World War II intensive language programs

The philosophy of language teaching that underlay this program was eventually to serve as the foundation for the development of much of what has become the audiolingual method. The influences of the Intensive Language Program were especially great upon the armed forces programs.

After World War II, and the closing of the military programs, the American Council of Learned Societies determined to continue the work that had been begun through its Committee on the Language Program (CLP). This program became an organization of national scope.

After World War II: Committee on the Language Program

The Committee on the Language Program sponsored linguistic research, provided fellowships to the linguistic institutes, and encouraged the application of linguistics to language teaching. A "Spoken Language" series was initiated to meet the needs of the military. After World War II these manuals were republished through Henry Holt & Co. and made available to the academic community. Eventually the list grew to include 22 different languages: Iraqi Arabic, Burmese, Mandarin Chinese, Danish, Dutch, Finnish, French, German, Greek, Hindustani, Hungarian, Italian, Japanese, Korean, Malay, Norwegian, Portuguese, Russian, Serbo-Croatian, Spanish, Thai, and Turkish. The authors of these manuals read like a *Who's Who* of American linguists (Bloomfield, Block, Dyen, Hockett, Hodge, Moulton, and Sebeok, to name a few).

Uncommonly taught languages/Thompson

In 1952, with a Ford Foundation grant of $500,000, the Committee on the Language Program inaugurated a Program in Oriental Languages designed to make a major effort in developing a national linguistic competence in oriental languages and to prepare the necessary tools of access for these languages, including descriptive analysis, introduction to the writing system, elementary text and exercise books, graded readers, and a student's dictionary.

During the initial six years of this program, research was initiated on 36 languages or dialects and 43 books were published or near publication. The languages included Arabic (modern literary, Egyptian, Iraqi, Moroccan), Armenian (Eastern and Western), Azerbaijani, Berber, Burmese, Cambodian, Chinese (literary, Amoy, Mandarin, Shanghai), Hindi, Indonesian, Javanese, Kannada, Karen, Kazakh, Khasi, Korean, Kurdish, Lao, Marathi, Mongol, Pashto, Persian, Sindhi, Telugu, Thai, Tibetan, Uigur, Urdu, Uzbek, and Vietnamese.

Ford Program in Oriental Languages

For further discussions of the Intensive Language Program, Committee on the Language Program, Program in Oriental Languages, and the wider role and significance of the American Council of Learned Societies in the development of the uncommonly taught languages, see Moulton (30), Graves & Cowan (14), Mildenberger (28), Cowan (9), Diekhoff (10), and ACLS (23).

Army Specialized Training Program

The armed forces were quick to appreciate the need for people trained in foreign languages to serve not only in Europe but also in parts of the world that represented gaps in American education – in Asia, the Middle East, Africa, and Oceania.

In April, 1943, the Foreign Area and Language Studies program of the Army Specialized Training Program (ASTP) was established. This was the largest and most significant of all the area and language programs.

ASTP Foreign Area and Language Studies

Given the recent experience of the ACLS Intensive Language Program and the audiolingual orientation of the program, it was only natural that the Army Specialized Training Program should turn to the American Council of Learned Societies as a model for development. Drawing upon the advice, experience, and cooperation of ACLS, the Army program had 15,000 soldiers in training at 55 colleges and universities in 27 different languages. ASTP helped develop a new kind of language teaching that came to be known as the linguist-informant method and which, surprisingly enough, still characterizes much of the language teaching methodology in the uncommonly taught languages in the United States today. This topic will be specially treated later in this chapter.

The contracts for research and training deriving from the Army Program, in cooperation with ACLS, provided a major impetus for the introduction of the uncommonly taught languages and area studies at American institutions of higher learning.

Major impetus for the uncommonly taught languages

The "Spoken Language" series mentioned above was developed through the Army Specialized Training Program in cooperation with the American Council of Learned Societies and especially the Linguistic Society of America, an example of the cooperation of linguistics and language teaching that characterized much of foreign language teaching in the uncommonly taught languages for the next three decades.

The "Spoken Language" series

For a review of the considerable amount of literature on ASTP see especially Moulton (30), Ornstein (31), Carroll (8), and (41).

Modern Language Association Foreign Language Program

The Modern Language Association (MLA) inaugurated an important Foreign Language Program (FLP) in the fall of 1952 under the direction of MLA's Executive Secretary, William Riley Parker, and with the aid of a Rockefeller Foundation grant. The purposes of the Foreign Language Program were to encourage the study of foreign languages at all levels of American education —in elementary and secondary schools, as well as in the colleges and universities. The early stages of the program were characterized by fact-finding and data collection to ascertain the state of the art, and by attempts to unify a profession seriously divided over goals and methods of language teaching.

The Foreign Language Program: purposes and development

Important to these goals was the necessity of bringing together language teachers, linguists, professional educators, and foundation and government officials. *PMLA* (*Publications of the Modern Language Association*) included several articles describing the application of linguistics to language teaching, of which Marckwardt (24) is an example. Articles were also published that summarized some of the more outstanding examples of this application at universities such as Cornell (Moulton, 29) and Georgetown (Dostert, 11). Parker's guide (32) provided the profession with an excellent account of the origins and development of linguistics in this country and urged that linguists and

Professional unity

language teachers join in a cooperative attempt to improve language teaching.

In September, 1956, the MLA Foreign Language Program steering committee adopted a nine-point statement document on FLP policy. Since this committee comprised representatives of the professional language teaching professions, it constituted a position paper by the profession. Although the Foreign Language Program was almost exclusively concerned with the commonly taught languages (and Russian), and since the representative teachers' associations for the uncommonly taught languages had not yet been constituted, the work of this committee is nonetheless relevant to the purposes of this essay because the MLA Foreign Language Program served an important leadership role as a source of continuity in transmitting much of the methodology that grew out of contact with the uncommonly taught languages during the World War II period until the National Defense Education Act (1958).

Foreign Language Program policy statement

Prominent among the statements of the committee were many of the salient features of the American Council of Learned Societies and Army Specialized Training Programs: initial emphasis on listening and speaking, followed by reading and writing; intensive oral drill; small classes; and the allotment of more hours to foreign language study.

In 1957, on the occasion of the 5th Anniversary of the Foreign Language Program, the Modern Language Association initiated a five-year plan designed to: (*1*) encourage more Americans to study foreign languages, (2) improve and modernize foreign language institutions at all levels of instruction, (3) encourage the study of the uncommonly taught languages by the creation of new programs and scholarships, (4) foster more research and experimentation in language learning and the development of new tests and teaching materials, (5) establish pilot programs in selected states to serve as delivery systems for the new methodology.

The Foreign Language Program: the five-year plan

Although the five-year plan failed to receive the requested support from the Ford Foundation, it cannot be regarded as a failure, since most of the planning and thinking laid the groundwork for an important part of what was to become the National Defense Education Act. The only part of the original plan to be implemented was the establishment of a Center for Applied Linguistics, which received an initial grant of over $5 million.

National Defense Education Act

An excellent discussion of the Modern Language Association's

Foreign Language Program and its relationship to the National Defense Education Act can be found in Diekhoff (10); see also Moulton (30), Parker (32), and (12).

Center for Applied Linguistics

The Center for Applied Linguistics (CAL), grew out of the combined interests of the Modern Language Association's Foreign Language Program and the Fulbright steering committee for linguistics and English language teaching, which passed a resolution in the fall of 1957 urging the establishment of such a nongovernmental body.

Finally, in February of 1959, aided by a Ford Foundation grant, the Center for Applied Linguistics was formed. Although the Modern Language Association served as the fiscal and administrative agent of the grant and agreed to oversee the activities of the Center, the Center for Applied Linguistics was quite independent from the beginning. It was located in Washington, D.C., and invited Dr. Charles A. Ferguson, a nationally regarded linguist with a background in the uncommonly taught languages, to serve as its first Director, with Raleigh Morgan, Jr., as Associate Director.

Funding and organization

The Center was originally established to serve a number of interrelated purposes. It functioned in an advisory capacity to government agencies on problems of teaching English as a second language and language development. It trained or aided in the training of Americans in the uncommonly taught languages, and assisted in the preparation or dissemination of language-teaching materials, bibliographies, study guides, and films for the uncommonly taught as well as the commonly taught languages. It served to advance the improvement of cooperation and communication between linguists, language teachers, and psychologists, and functioned as a clearinghouse of information for the field.

Purposes of the Center for Applied Linguistics

In order to accomplish the clearinghouse function, the Center for Applied Linguistics inaugurated a newsletter-journal, the *Linguistic Reporter*. In 1966, the clearinghouse function at the Center for Applied Linguistics (CAL) received a shot in the arm when, with the aid of a United States Office of Education grant under the National Defense Education Act, an Educational Research Information Center (ERIC) program was established at CAL, as well as at the Modern Language Association. MLA/ERIC was devoted primarily to the commonly taught languages

The clearinghouse function

and English, while CAL/ERIC generally concentrated on linguistics, the uncommonly taught languages, and English as a second language.

Recent funding constraints within the Office of Education have resulted in the reduction of the two clearinghouses to a single ERIC Clearinghouse on Language and Linguistics. This newly formed clearinghouse is located at the Modern Language Association in New York.

With the exception of some minor activities carried out under the Foreign Language Programs in its early days, the Modern Language Association paid only nominal attention to the uncommonly taught languages. With its new responsibility as the sole clearinghouse for all languages and linguistics, including the uncommonly taught languages, MLA will have to retool for a major new effort in this field. To accomplish this critical task, it will have to add the required new staff, reorient its leadership, and appeal to a new constituency, that of the Center for Applied Linguistics.

Nominal attention given to the uncommonly taught languages

The Center for Applied Linguistics has made significant contributions to the study of the uncommonly taught languages through the publication of state-of-the-art papers for Chinese (Wrenn, 44), Arabic (Abboud, 1), Hindi/Urdu (Kelley, 21), and Japanese (Martin, 26); by publication of selected and annual bibliographies on the uncommonly taught languages (Bauman, 3; Blass, Johnson & Gage, 5; Kocher, 22; Prochazka, 34; Teoh, 42); and by serving as a focal point for the sharing of ideas and discussions on the uncommonly taught languages (see Gage, 13; Hodge, 17; Thompson, 43). For a general discussion of the Center see also Moulton (30) and Marckwardt (25).

Contribution of the Center fo Applied Linguistics to the teaching of the uncommonly taught languages

National Defense Education Act

"The NDEA Language Development Program is obviously a many-splendored thing," wrote John S. Diekhoff in a MLA publication in 1965 (12). The National Defense Education Act (NDEA) of 1958 was the largest and most critically massed attack on modern foreign language research and training in history. It was more important than any of the earlier programs that preceded it, yet it owed its very existence to the efforts of all the linguists, foreign language teachers, and education specialists who contributed to the major foreign language programs described above, as well as to the thousands of teachers and facul-

Importance of NDEA

ty in the colleges and universities throughout the country who supported and participated in the various programs under NDEA Title VI.

The fabric out of which NDEA was woven came primarily from the separate threads of the several concerned programs and interests that had represented both the commonly and uncommonly taught languages in the pre- and post-World War II periods. The following list of key dates provides a checklist of important activities:

A list of important dates leading to NDEA

1941   Intensive Language Program of the American Council of Learned Societies

1943   Army Specialized Training Program

1952   Program in Oriental Languages of the American Council of Learned Societies

1952   Foreign Language Program of the Modern Language Association

1956   Nine-point Statement of Foreign Language Program Policy of the Modern Language Association

1957   Foreign Language Program Five-year Plan and consequent establishment of the Center for Applied Linguistics (in 1959)

1957   Sputnik shocked American education

1958   August 31, President Dwight D. Eisenhower signed the National Defense Education Act

The General Provisions of the National Defense Education Act established that the security of the nation required the fullest development of the mental resources of the country. They set forth to correct as rapidly as possible the existing imbalances in educational programs that had led an insufficient proportion of the nation's population into the study of science, mathematics, and modern foreign languages.

Provisions of the Act

Title VI of NDEA provided extensive aid for language development in the form of (*1*) Language and Area Centers; (2) National Defense Foreign Language Fellowships; and (3) Research and Studies.

Title VI

Language development

During fiscal year 1970 nearly $170 million was set aside to support these activities under NDEA Title VI. Initially some small support was provided for the preparation of the Audio-Lingual Materials (A-LM) for the teaching of French, German, Italian, Russian, and Spanish in the secondary schools, and for the preparation of tests to measure the qualifications of teaching of these languages. However, by far the largest share of the funding was allocated for the support of the uncommonly taught languages, and the major efforts were in higher education. For an in-depth report on the first five years of NDEA see Diekhoff's excellent study, *NDEA and Modern Foreign Languages* (10).

Language and area centers

Section 601(a).[1] The Secretary is authorized to arrange through grants to or contracts with institutions of higher education for the establishment and operation by them . . . of centers for the teaching of any modern foreign language with respect to which the Secretary determines that individuals trained in such language are needed by the Federal Government or by business, industry, or education in the United States. Any such grant or contract may provide for instruction not only in such modern foreign language but also in other fields needed to provide a full understanding of the areas, regions, or countries in which such language is commonly used, to the extent adequate instruction in such fields is not readily available, including fields such as history, political science, linguistics, economics, sociology, geography, and anthropology. Any such grants or contract may cover all or part of the cost of the establishment and operation of the center with respect to which it is made, including the cost of grants to the staff for travel in the foreign areas, regions or countries with which the subject matter of the field or fields in which they are or will be working is concerned and the cost of travel of foreign scholars to such centers to teach or assist in teaching therein and the cost of their return, and shall be made on such conditions as the Secretary finds necessary to carry out the purposes of this section.

The Act establishes language and area centers

The groundwork for the NDEA Language and Area Centers was laid early. It took as models the Foreign Area and Language Studies of the Army Specialized Training Program and the advice and experience of the Intensive Language Program of the American Council of Learned Societies. The language and area centers combined language teaching with instruction, not merely in literature as had been and still remains largely the case with the commonly taught languages (Diekhoff, 10), but

Used ASTP and ILP as models

1 National Defense Education Act of 1958, actual text.

also in the history, arts, economics, and broader cultural aspects of a people, nation, and geographical region.

It was only natural that NDEA VI should adapt the model of the earlier programs. One simple but revealing change was made in the wording—*area and language* was changed to *language and area*. This change reflects the significance of the efforts of the language teaching profession in the work of the Foreign Language Program of the Modern Language Association in securing funding for NDEA. The language teaching profession was convinced that knowledge of the language was the core to any significant understanding of an area—a position which is still questioned by some scholars.

The language and area centers under NDEA were designed to provide opportunities for advanced, interdisciplinary study of languages and civilizations that have traditionally been neglected in the American educational system, and to provide the nation with a corps of highly trained specialists in modern foreign languages, area studies, and world affairs. Each center offers a program of instruction dealing with one or more of the following world areas: East Asia, South and Southeast Asia, Inner Asia, the Middle East, Soviet and Eastern Europe, Africa, Latin America, and Northwestern Europe.

Purpose of language and area studies centers

In the fall of 1969, for example, approximately 4,000 courses were offered at the 107 NDEA language and area centers in over 75 modern foreign languages, and in other fields such as the art, history, or economic policy of the regions where these languages are spoken. About 2,000 faculty members were engaged in instruction at the centers; and graduate and undergraduate enrollments in the fall of 1969 totalled over 100,000. For a world area breakdown, see Table 1, *NDEA Language and Area Studies Enrollments and Degrees Awarded, by World Area, 1969–70*, and for a breakdown by discipline, see Table 2, *NDEA Language and Area Studies Degrees Awarded, by Discipline, 1969–70*. (Tables for this chapter are found on pages 305–308.)

Results from NDEA support

Instruction in 27 languages, which for the most part are official languages of independent nations, is offered only at NDEA centers. In addition, at least 40% of the total U.S. course enrollments in 15 other languages are concentrated in NDEA programs. The centers have also served as structural and operational models for international studies programs in schools throughout the country. The interdisciplinary approach to the study of specialized areas, drawing upon students and faculty from a

289

wide variety of academic departments of the institutions, has proven to be academically and administratively feasible.

The centers supported by the National Defense Education Act are the primary source for the training of foreign language and area specialists to serve in educational institutions, federal agencies, business, and public service organizations. In 1969–70, approximately 5,000 Bachelor of Arts, 2,000 Master of Arts, and 800 Doctor of Philosophy degrees were awarded to students specializing in language and area studies at the NDEA programs. Since 1959, when the first NDEA centers were established, over $45 million have been allocated to these centers. In that time, the centers have awarded more than 29,000 Bachelor of Arts, 12,000 Master of Arts, and 4,200 Doctor of Philosophy degrees in non-Western studies varying from Asian to African to Middle Eastern studies, in disciplines such as linguistics, history, anthropology, and literature. It should be noted that these figures do not include the ever increasing number of programs that operate with other sources of support.

Centers train foreign language and area specialists

The number of centers has grown from 19 in 1959-60 to 107 centers in 1969–70. The following breakdown shows the number of centers by major world area: Asia and Asia-East Europe, 8 centers; East Asia, 22 centers; South and Southeast Asia, 15 centers; Middle East, 12 centers; Soviet and East Europe, 20 centers; Northwest Europe, 1 center; sub-Sahara Africa, 13 centers; and Latin America, 16 centers. For a distribution of funds by world area see Table 3, *Distribution of NDEA, Title VI, Support to Language and Area Centers, by World Area*. For a list of the locations of the present centers (1970) see Table 4, *NDEA Centers, by World Area*.

Growth of centers

For a detailed discussion of the concept of language and area centers and their development out of the earlier Army programs see Diekhoff (10), Axelrod (2), Bigelow & Legters (4), and Matthew (27).

Summer intensive language programs

An important component of the National Defense Education Act center programs is the Summer Intensive Language Program, which, in the summer of 1970, provided over $500,000 in Federal support for 21 instructional programs. The summer programs provide the means to accelerate the lengthy process of developing competence in the uncommonly taught languages, and provide access to a wide range of language offerings for students from institutions where academic year offerings are limited. Student enrollments at these programs, which have been funded since 1960, have ranged from 4,000 to over 6,500 in the last four years.

Due to the reduction in NDEA Title VI allocations for fiscal year 1971, no summer intensive language programs were supported during that summer. However, the availability of U.S.-owned excess foreign currencies under Public Law 83–480 permitted support of overseas-based summer intensive language programs for advanced students. Nine programs were supported in summer 1971: in the United Arab Republic, Tunisia, and Morocco for classical, modern standard, and other dialects of Arabic; in Poland; Yugoslavia; and in India for Hindi/Urdu, Marathi, Tamil, Malayalam, Bengali, and Kannada.

No summer intensive programs for fiscal 1971

In addition to these overseas summer programs, academic-year language programs are presently being carried out in the United Arab Republic, through the Center for Arabic Studies Abroad at the American University of Cairo, and at the Stanford University-operated interuniversity programs in Taiwan and Japan. For a discussion of the summer intensive language programs, see Diekhoff (10).

Academic-year programs

National defense foreign language Title VI fellowships

Section 601(b).[2] The Secretary is also authorized . . . to pay stipends to individuals undergoing advanced training in any modern foreign language (with respect to which he makes the determination under subsection [a]), and other fields needed for a full understanding of the area, region, or country in which such language is commonly used, at any short-term or regular session of any institution of higher education, including allowances for dependents and for travel to and from their places of residence, but only upon reasonable assurance that the recipients of such stipends will, on completion of their training, be available for teaching a modern foreign language in an institution of higher education or for such other services of a public nature as may be permitted in regulations of the Secretary.

Whereas Title IV of the National Defense Education Act also provided for foreign language and linguistics fellowships under its broad categories, the fellowship program under Title VI was

---

2 National Defense Education Act of 1958, actual text.

Uncommonly taught languages/Thompson

designed exclusively for students who study an approved foreign language as part of their formal educational program.

The Secretary determined early in the program that languages eligible for support would exclude the commonly taught languages. The rationale for this remains largely unchanged today—those languages and areas that were already well-represented in American education did not suffer the same kind of imbalance referred to in the General Provisions of the Act, nor did they need the same level of stimulus to encourage their growth. Whereas American education was largely based upon a cultural and ethnic heritage shared with Western Europe, non-Western studies constituted a major gap in our educational system at all levels. The decision to limit support to the uncommonly taught languages of Asia, the Middle East, the U.S.S.R. and Eastern Europe, Africa, Latin America, and Northern Europe has been vindicated by the recent developments in the commonly taught languages affecting both enrollments and the job market, and by the demonstrated steady growth of the uncommonly taught languages in the United States.

Commonly taught languages excluded in Title VI fellowship program

According to a preliminary report (June 1, 1971) of the MLA's fall 1970 survey of foreign language registrations and student contact hours in U.S. institutions of higher education, in comparison with 1968, registrations are down in French, German, Russian, Latin, and Ancient Greek; up slightly in Italian and Spanish, but up nearly 30% in the uncommonly taught languages. The discouraging figures of the MLA's 1970 "Manpower Survey" (as reported in the MLA Newsletter of November, 1970, and based upon questionnaires answered by over 900 foreign language department chairmen) represent almost exclusively the present job market situation for Spanish, French, German, Italian, and Russian. The job market for the same period for the uncommonly taught languages was in no way adversely affected by the dropping of language requirements—enrollments are, in fact, on the rise. This rate of growth cannot continue unabated, however, and future surveys of the kind carried out by the Modern Language Association will continue to provide the information necessary to assist in the allocation of fellowships in the most critically needed languages.

1970 survey shows increased enrollment in the uncommonly taught languages

From 1959 to 1970 over $57 million has provided support for nearly 17,000 fellowships. The following world-area profile shows numbers of graduate awards by major geographical/linguistic area: Southeast Asia, 605 awards; South Asia, 1,460 awards; Near and Middle East, 2,211 awards; Latin America, 2,305 awards; Eastern Europe and the U.S.S.R., 2,907 awards; East Asia, 3,668 awards; and Africa, 1,130 awards. In addition to these graduate fellowships, 2,793 undergraduate awards have been awarded during the period from 1963 to 1970 in 35 languages for study at intensive summer language programs. Diekhoff devotes a whole chapter to a detailed presentation of the Title IV and Title VI fellowships for graduate and undergraduate study (see Diekhoff, 10, Chapter 6). *Distribution of awards*

Language and area research and studies

Section 602.[3] The Commissioner is authorized, directly or by contract to make studies and surveys to determine the need for increased or improved instruction in modern foreign languages and other fields needed to provide a full understanding of the areas, regions or countries in which such languages are commonly used, to conduct research on more effective methods of teaching such languages and in such other fields, and to develop specialized materials for use in such training, or in training teachers of such languages or in such fields.

Since the enactment of the National Defense Education Act, over $30 million has provided support for research and studies by contract with colleges, universities, and organizations. In the early days of NDEA, little information was available on the uncommonly taught languages, fewer specialists were trained in these languages, and almost no tools of access existed. Research on 141 separate languages or dialects has led to the development of specialized materials, including 110 basic courses, 60 readers, 40 dictionaries, and 50 grammars, in addition to surveys and basic research on language and language learning. For a list of 542 separate items of completed research, studies, and instructional materials up to 1968, see Petrov (33). *Research and studies*

Research under NDEA is classified under six broad headings: (1) surveys and studies; (2) conferences; (3) methods of instruction; (4) specialized materials for commonly taught languages; (5) specialized materials for uncommonly taught languages; and (6) foreign area studies. *Broad research headings*

Surveys and studies. In accordance with the legislative authority of Section 602, the Office of Education conducts periodic

---

3 National Defense Education Act of 1958, actual text.

surveys to ascertain the status of foreign language and area studies at all educational levels in the United States. For example, the Modern Language Association surveys on higher education and secondary school registrations are supported under this Section of the Act (Kant, 19,20). The most comprehensive survey of the language and area studies field ever made is presently being completed under an Office of Education contract with the Social Science Research Council and the Association for Asian Studies (Steinberg & Lambert, 40), representing the six major professional area associations: the African Studies Association, the American Association for the Advancement of Slavic Studies, the American Oriental Society, the Latin American Studies Association, the Middle East Studies Association, and the Association for Asian Studies. This major assessment will provide the Office of Education with a data base for decision-making in the 1970s. The survey includes: (*a*) language and area centers, (*b*) individual competencies of members of the six area associations, (*c*) former graduate students, and (*d*) present graduate students. Out of the cooperation that resulted from the stimulus of the survey was formed a Council of Executive Secretaries of Area Associations. It should be stressed that the major focus of the survey is the uncommonly taught languages and their relationship to area studies, a major component of NDEA programs. A provisional survey of materials for the study of uncommonly taught languages (Blass, Johnson, & Gage, 5) appeared as a Center for Applied Linguistics publication in 1969. This survey contains over 2,000 entries representing 382 languages and dialects. It includes limited-access materials such as those prepared by the Peace Corps, the Defense Language Institute, and the Foreign Service Institute, in addition to National Defense Education Act and privately supported materials. Up to 1968, some 68 studies and surveys had been completed under this section of the National Defense Education Act. For a complete listing, see Petrov (33).

Conferences. As required, the Office of Education provides a limited amount of funds to support conferences to help determine needs and priorities in the Title VI programs and for the field at large. Twenty-two such conferences had received support by 1968, including a Conference on Psychological Experiments Related to Secondary Language Learning, Flexible Scheduling and Foreign Language Instruction, Conference on Critical Languages in Liberal Arts Colleges, and most recently a confer-

Examples of surveys

Content of the Social Science Research Council survey

Materials survey

Examples of conferences under NDEA, Title VI

ence on Individualization of Foreign Language Instruction held at Stanford University. Information on the availability of the proceedings and reports of these and other conferences are available in Petrov (33).

Methods of instruction. This category of support has encouraged basic and applied research on the nature of language, fundamental questions on the psycholinguistic bases of secondary language acquisition, and foreign language skill measurement and analysis. Outstanding examples of this kind of research include the work of Pierre Delattre on the general phonetic characteristics of languages, all the extensive research carried out at the Center for Research on Language and Language Behavior of the University of Michigan, Scherer's experimentation with German language acquisition, and other important research by Suppes, Carton, Pimsleur, Hocking, Mueller, and Politzer. One major study receiving much attention recently is the Pennsylvania project, "A Comparison Study of the Effectiveness of the Traditional and Audio-lingual Approach to Foreign Language Instruction Utilizing Laboratory Equipment." Nearly 50 basic studies had been completed by 1968. For information on availability of the above reports, see Petrov (33).

Examples of research in methods of instruction

Specialized materials for commonly taught languages. Although the main focus of the NDEA Language Development Program was the uncommonly taught languages, this focus did not preclude support for the commonly taught languages. In fact, the Audio-Lingual Materials (A-LM), developed in the early sixties for French, German, Italian, Russian, and Spanish, were supported under Title VI, as were the Modern Language Association Foreign Language Proficiency Tests. In all, some two dozen research products for the commonly taught languages have received support. A complete listing of these studies can be found in Petrov (33).

Curricular materials for the commonly taught languages: A-LM

Specialized materials for uncommonly taught languages. Over 350 separate specialized materials representing 141 languages received support under Title VI. Although the exact format and plans of execution of the materials were left to the proposer and depend in part upon the language and dialect under study, the materials tended to fall into the categories of basic, intermediate, and advanced intensive and nonintensive courses, tapes, readers, dictionaries, and student reference grammars. The languages for which teaching materials were prepared include the same geographic/linguistic categories formed under

Curricular materials for the uncommonly taught languages

the Centers and Fellowships section in this report and range from Chinese, Japanese, Korean, Vietnamese, Lao, and Cambodian to Turkish, Telugu, Tamil, and Twi. For a list of the completed materials see Petrov (33), and for an annotated review see Blass, Johnson, & Gage (5).

Foreign area studies. For the most part area studies research needed little outside stimulus. This aspect of academic research had always been more highly regarded than the preparation of language teaching materials. Promises of promotion and tenure were sufficient to insure completion of materials dealing with cultural and historical aspects of a people or nation. Nevertheless, only a small number of area studies materials of a general nature were prepared, which dealt with India, Central Asia, Japan, and Indonesia, among others, including bibliographies. The Jelavich (18) survey of East Central and Southeastern Europe is one outstanding example.

The Social Science Research Council Survey, mentioned above, includes information on the utilization of NDEA-supported materials at 82 reporting institutions in 50 languages. Table 5, *Utilization Survey of NDEA Section 602 Language Materials for Selected Languages,* shows that for some languages (e.g., Hindi/Urdu, Bengali, Turkish, and Indonesian/Malay) only NDEA-supported materials are being used.

Materials created from area studies programs

Some high priority gaps remain for the uncommonly taught languages. These will be the targets for more action in the future. Recent developments in language teaching research suggest some important trends for the seventies (Thompson, 43):

Trends for the 1970s

1 Some shift in emphasis from text development toward research into second-language acquisition. This is not to suggest that new materials should not be prepared. Developments in linguistic theory and language change urge modernization of language teaching materials. The sad fact is that in the absence of empirical evidence on how language is acquired, teaching methods remain highly speculative. The format of a text, the sequencing of the linguistic structures, and intensity of presentation still remain in no small part beyond present understanding.

2 Concentration on data collection in the form of "case histories" or "linguistic files" on a massive scale for foreign language learners. Only after significant amounts of data have been gathered, computerized, and analyzed can any meaningful conclusion be drawn.

3 Development of criterion-referenced testing devices. The question of what it is to know a language is not yet well understood, and consequently the language proficiency tests now available (and there are few for the uncommonly taught languages) are inadequate in that they attempt to measure something that has not been well defined. Until tests are made available on a national scale, research on effective learning and teaching strategies will remain largely theoretical for lack of adequate empirical validation through appropriate measurement. General demands for accountability in education will sift down to the language teaching profession and provide an added impetus for the development of these tests.

4 The movement toward self-instruction (Boyd-Bowman, 6) and the adaptation of existing materials (being prepared by Earl Stevick at the Foreign Service Institute) will be of considerable importance.

For a discussion of research and the uncommonly taught languages, see Brown (7), Diekhoff (10), Gage (13), Hodge (17), Mildenberger (28), and Thompson (43). For a detailed discussion of the current state of the art in selected languages with bibliographies, see Arabic (Abboud, 1), Chinese (Wrenn, 44), Hindi/Urdu (Kelley, 21), and Japanese (Martin, 26). The *Current Trends in Linguistics* series, edited by Sebeok, provide an especially valuable introduction to the languages and linguistics of the major world areas for the specialist and nonspecialist alike. To date the following relevant volumes have appeared: *Soviet and East European Linguistics* (35); *Linguistics in East Asia and South East Asia* (36); *Ibero-American and Caribbean Linguistics* (37); *Linguistics in South Asia* (38); and *Linguistics in South West Asia and North Africa* (39). The following volumes are either in planning or preparation: *Linguistics in Sub-Saharan Africa; Linguistics in Oceania; Linguistics in Western Europe;* and *Linguistics in North America.*

State of the art

The area-oriented professional associations

A major difference in the teaching of the common and the uncommon languages derives from the widely differing organizational patterns of the two fields. In the case of the teaching of such languages as French, Spanish, German, and Italian, much of the focus has been on a more narrowly interpreted introduc-

A major difference in teaching common and uncommon languages

tion to the culture through literature (Diekhoff, 10). With the uncommonly taught languages this focus was not possible since, unlike the case of Western European culture, little or no instruction has traditionally been available in the history, economics, politics, and culture of the countries and areas under study. Therefore, it was possible to introduce a broader interpretation of culture in the teaching of the uncommon languages. The area associations grew out of a material need for an interdisciplinary approach to a full understanding of these areas and regions. The various area associations are jointly represented by a Council of Executive Secretaries of the Area Associations. For more details, see Steinberg & Lambert (40). The area-oriented professional organizations discussed here are: the African Studies Association, the American Association for the Advancement of Slavic Studies, the American Oriental Society, the Association for Asian Studies, the Latin American Studies Association, and the Middle East Studies Association.

Area-oriented professional associations

African Studies Association

Established in 1957, the African Studies Association represents one of the most recently organized area associations. For the most part, African studies came into existence at the graduate and undergraduate levels in 1955. Since that time, more than 70 programs in African studies have been established at colleges and universities throughout the country. The Association laid forth its purposes at the first meeting in New York with Melville J. Hershovits as the first president:

Purposes

1 to facilitate communication among African studies scholars;
2 to provide a clearinghouse function;
3 to encourage and assist in the collection of documentation;
4 to provide international liaison for scholars;
5 to provide consultation services to colleges and organizations;
6 to assess bibliographical, research, and training needs.

To help accomplish these goals, the Association first published the *African Studies Bulletin* and subsequently added a *Newsletter*. It further organized committees on languages and linguistics, archaeology, archives and the library, oral data, and African literature, among other subjects. Chapter two in Steinberg & Lambert (40) contains a history of the Association which reviews its development.

Publications

American Association for the Advancement of Slavic Studies

On December 29, 1960, in New York, William B. Edgerton was elected president of the newly formed American Association for the Advancement of Slavic Studies (AAASS). The Association states its purposes as a nonprofit, nonpolitical group of scholars organized to encourage the study and teaching of the U.S.S.R., Eastern Europe, and the Communist bloc, and to provide a forum for the exchange of ideas and information. There were four main functions:

Functions

1 to sponsor a revised and enlarged journal;
2 to distribute an annual bibliography;
3 to sponsor annual meetings and conferences;
4 to provide a newsletter and establish a secretariat.

In order to better effect the above functions, the Association established a publications plan that included *The Slavic Review: American Quarterly of Soviet and East European Studies*, the twice-yearly *Newsletter*, and four editions of a *Directory of Members*. The organizational links function is carried out in part through the *Newsletter* and national meetings, and in part through the establishment of several committees: (*1*) the Joint Committee on Slavic and East European Studies; (*2*) affiliates based on the disciplinary professional associations (economics, geography, history, language and literature, library science, and political science); and (*3*) affiliates having a geographical basis.

Publications

For a history of the Association, see Steinberg & Lambert's third chapter (40).

American Oriental Society

The oldest of all of the area-oriented professional associations, the American Oriental Society (AOS) was founded in 1842 in Boston. The Society's publications and activities reflected a predominant interest in the ancient civilizations of Egypt and Mesopotamia, and Islamic and Sanskritic studies. By the turn of the century ancient Chinese civilization was included, and more recently the Society's sphere of influence spread to Middle Eastern (Persian and Turkic) and Japanese studies. The major focus of the Society today remains almost exclusively philological and premodern.

The goals of the Society, as set forth in 1842, were stated as follows:

1 the cultivation of learning in the Asiatic, African, and Polynesian languages;

Goals

2 publication of works relating to these languages;

3 collection of library resources.

It is interesting to note the extremely wide interpretation given to the term *Oriental* as indicated in the organizational name and purpose one, above.

The Journal of the American Oriental Society first appeared in 1843 and remains one of the Society's strongest assets. The extremely long history of the American Oriental Society precludes giving attention to many of the interesting facets of the organization. Some of the special committees established include the Committee for the Promotion of Oriental Research, established in 1934, which was designed to encourage research and publication of research and to seek sources of support for such research. For a detailed and fascinating discussion of the establishment of the American Oriental Society, see Steinberg & Lambert's (40) chapter four.

Its journal

Association for Asian Studies

The Association for Asian Studies is the largest learned society in the world devoted to promoting scholarly interest in the study of the civilizations and cultures of East, Southeast, South, and Inner Asia. Its membership is nearly 5,000 and its annual meetings attract up to 2,000 registered participants.

An outgrowth of the Far Eastern Association, which dated back to 1941, the Association for Asian Studies was founded in 1956 with the stated objectives:

Objectives

1 to form a scholarly, nonpolitical association of persons interested in the Far East;

2 to promote the scholarly study of the Far East;

3 to encourage publication of research and materials;

4 to promote cooperative activities and exchange of information about the Far East, nationally and internationally.

In order to accomplish its goals, the Association for Asian Studies publishes the *Journal of Asian Studies* (formerly the *Far Eastern Quarterly*), a *Newsletter*, and the *Bibliography of Asian Studies*. The Association has been very active in publishing monographs and papers. It holds annual national meetings as well as regional meetings and conferences. Chapter five in Steinberg & Lambert (40) contains a detailed history of the Association. For Japanese studies, see also Hall (16).

Publications

Latin American Studies Association

The Latin American Studies Association was founded in 1966 by a concerned group of area specialists in Washington, D.C., in order to provide a professional organization that fosters the concerns of scholars and individuals interested in Latin-American studies, to encourage effective teaching, research, and training in this field, and to provide a forum for dealing with matters of common interest to the scholarly professions and individuals concerned with Latin-American studies.

Objectives

The Association publishes a *Latin American Research Review*, a *Newsletter*, and holds annual meetings. As with the other area associations, much of the work of the organization is accomplished through the various committees. Important in the Association is the Committee on Area Studies Programs, which convenes national meetings and has a membership of 245 institutions. In addition to these activities the Association is closely associated with several related regional councils. Chapter six of Steinberg & Lambert (40) contains a brief history of the Association.

A newsletter

Middle East Studies Association

The Middle East Studies Association was created at a meeting of the Social Science Research Council/American Council of Learned Societies Joint Committee on Middle East Studies in 1966 in New York. The announced purposes of the Association are:

Purposes

1 to promote high standards of scholarship and instruction in the area;
2 to facilitate communication among scholars through meetings and publications; and
3 to foster cooperation among persons and organizations concerned with the scholarly study of the Middle East.

To help carry out these purposes the Association publishes a *Journal of the Middle East Studies Association*, a *Bulletin*, and an *International Journal of Middle East Studies*. It also holds annual meetings, and generally provides a variety of informational services to its membership. As with the other associations, the Middle East Studies Association has established a variety of committees, such as the Research and Training Committee, with subcommittees on Bibliography, Language and Instruction Resources, and Library. The Language and Instruction Resources

Publications

301

subcommittee actively sought out Office of Education, and private, support to prepare language teaching materials for modern standard Arabic and are completing an intermediate course at the present time. Chapter seven of Steinberg & Lambert (40) contains a history of this Association.

A sketch of methodology for the teaching of uncommonly taught languages

Several separate movements influencing the development of the methodology of foreign language teaching in this country converged at the outbreak of World War II. These influences include developments in the field of linguistics, the experiences of applied linguists working in the field of teaching English as a second language at the University of Michigan, and the sudden need for intensive short- and long-term language training for the armed forces (Moulton, 30; Marckwardt, 25). *Influences on methodology*

Experience gained from carrying out linguistic field work, initially with the American Indian languages during the first decades of this century, and then on the languages of Oceania, Asia, and the Middle East during World War II, greatly influenced language teaching for these languages. The linguistic techniques (field methods) for analyzing a language unknown to the investigator carried over to help create a new system of language teaching that was actively adopted at many universities — the linguist-informant method. Under this method a linguist, who often never learned to speak the language (Haas, 15) and may never have even learned to read or write the language (obviously justifiable for the preliterate languages), was placed in charge of the language training with the aid of a native speaker of the language. *Linguistic techniques*

Another influence on language teaching, finding its origins in linguistic theory, is the teaching of reading and traditional orthography. At the time when linguistics was having its initial and most effective influence upon language teaching, linguistic theory had reached the stage of having excluded orthography from linguistic consideration. Language was defined in various ways by American linguistics, but in almost every case it included the use of "vocal symbols." This definition presents no problems for languages which do not possess a traditional orthography and hence no literature. For these languages linguists devised phonemic transcriptions. However, the concept was in- *Linguistic theory* discriminately applied to languages with well-developed writing systems and extensive literature (e.g., Russian and Chinese). For such languages romanization systems were developed. This resulted in an arbitrary and harmful delay in the introduction of the writing systems of many languages. In some cases the delay was one semester, in others a year, while in some programs the traditional writing system was never taught at all.

When one realizes that the linguists in charge of these programs, who initially wrote the materials used in them, could for the most part neither read nor write the language under study, one can better understand the lack of concern with orthography *Lack of concern* that permeated not simply the teaching of the uncommonly *for orthography* taught languages but also that of some of the more commonly taught languages.

Another major influence derived from the early work of linguists and applied linguists during the forties was the linguistic approach to teaching vocabulary. Until quite recently linguists have de-emphasized the role of vocabulary in language and have concentrated their attention on the relations that hold between the units—morpho-syntax. Whereas the linguist was most willing to recognize the entire inventory of phonemes as linguistic units, and even some closed classes in the morphology, yet when describing lexemes or word classes of nouns, for exam- *Teaching vocabulary* ple, the abstract symbol N took on *only* linguistic significance. Since a given language is defined by the units and relations that compose it, we can no longer relegate vocabulary to such a distant role. It is suggested that this influence has negatively affected research into vocabulary acquisition and appropriate teaching methodologies. This is not such a serious problem in teaching languages related to English, but in languages which are not cognate with English, such as Chinese, the problem is magnified enormously.

Summary and conclusions

Teaching the uncommonly taught languages received initial impetus during World War II and major financial support from the Ford Foundation and the Office of Education through the National Defense Education Act. Enrollments have increased dramatically, as have the number of institutions offering these languages. The language and area concept has been proven successful in teaching the uncommonly taught languages and area studies. Recent decisions to eliminate foreign language and other requirements in schools and colleges seem to have had little effect on the teaching of the uncommonly taught languages, and the job market problems faced by the commonly taught languages do not exist for the neglected languages.

In the next decade, for the uncommonly taught languages and area studies:

1 The emphasis in foreign language research will shift from text development to research into second-language acquisition theory.

2 Self-instruction and a "learning orientation" will replace the present emphasis on "teaching."

3 Linguistic files or case histories on individual language learners will be gathered, computerized, and analyzed.

4 New attention will be paid to the development of criterion-referenced testing devices which measure native-speaker competence.

5 The model for language and area studies developed for the uncommonly taught languages and area studies will be applied to the modern languages of Western Europe.

6 The greatest impact of the uncommonly taught languages for the next decade will be at the secondary school level.

7 The influences of linguistics on modern foreign language teaching, rooted in the linguistic thinking of the thirties and forties, are rapidly changing, especially with respect to teaching writing systems and vocabulary.

World area	No. of centers	Enrollments (Fall 1969)	Degrees			
			B.A.	M.A.	Ph.D.	Total
Asia						
General	6	13,115	592	253	52	897
East	21	10,612	849	225	72	1,146
South and						
Southeast	3	1,752	163	53	18	234
Southeast	2	547	3	19	9	31
South	10	4,047	113	90	57	260
Inner	1	122	0	3	4	7
Asia–East Europe	1	1,252	15	22	2	39
Middle East	12	8,567	394	136	99	629
U.S.S.R. and						
East Europe	21	19,522	1,018	357	123	1,498
Northwest Europe	1	935	40	8	4	52
Africa	13	6,436	590	269	114	973
Latin America	16	33,218	1,696	593	254	2,543
Total	107	100,125	5,473	2,028	808	8,309

Table 1. NDEA language and area studies enrollments and degrees awarded, by world area, 1969–70

Discipline	Degrees			
	B.A.	M.A.	Ph.D.	Total
Language and literature	1,096	402	144	1,642
Linguistics	72	65	41	178
Area studies	549	336	15	900
American studies	0	3	0	3
Anthropology	329	112	59	500
Economics	218	83	32	333
Fine arts	135	32	20	187
Geography	98	54	32	184
History	897	272	160	1,329
International relations	24	60	5	89
Music	1	2	1	4
Natural sciences	169	22	13	204
Philosophy and religion	123	26	13	162
Political science	647	202	119	968
Psychology	139	2	3	144
Sociology	285	64	34	383
Agriculture	12	25	24	61
Architecture	39	7	0	46
Business	69	34	0	112
Education	309	129	55	493
Engineering	16	2	2	20
Forestry	0	1	0	1
Health	26	13	4	43
Journalism	67	13	2	82
Law	8	23	8	39
Library science	7	28	0	35
Public administration	0	0	1	1
Social work	0	1	0	1
Speech	1	0	0	1
Unspecified	137	15	12	154
Total	5,473	2,028	808	8,309

Table 2. NDEA language and area studies degrees awarded, by discipline, 1969–70

Table 3. Distribution of NDEA
(Title VI) support to language
and area centers, by world area

World area	1959–69		1969–70		1970–71		Totals		
	Federal support	%	Federal support	%	Federal support	%	Federal support	%	No. of centers
Asia and									
Asia–East Europe	$2,640,016	8	$ 415,921	7	$ 337,830	7	$3,393,767	8	8
East Asia	6,603,576	20	1,297,750	20	1,069,100	21	8,970,426	20	22
South and									
Southeast Asia	6,241,592	18	1,174,690	18	934,488	18	8,350,770	18	15
Middle East	4,348,541	13	731,550	12	632,912	12	5,713,003	13	12
Soviet and									
East Europe	6,446,328	19	1,159,019	18	936,410	18	8,541,757	19	20
Northwest									
Europe	142,365	(.4)	38,190	(.5)	32,035	(.6)	212,590	(.4)	1
Sub-Sahara									
Africa	2,888,045	9	680,750	11	546,155	11	4,114,950	9	13
Latin America	4,375,197	13	882,130	14	696,070	13	5,953,397	13	16
Total	$33,685,660	100%	$6,380,000	100%	$5,185,000	100%	$45,250,660	100%	107

N.B. Dollar figures are composites, including federal support both to the academic year programs at the centers and to the separately contracted intensive summer programs. Number of centers refer only to academic year programs. The number of centers has grown as follows: 1959–60, 19 centers; 1960–61, 46 centers; 1961–62, 52 centers; 1962–63, 53 centers; 1963–64, 55 centers; 1965–66, 98 centers; 1967–68, 106 centers; and 1969–70, 107 centers.

Asia	South Asia (cont'd.)	Middle East (cont'd.)
Arizona (Oriental)	Michigan State	Harvard, *Mass.*
Harvard (E. Asia)	Minnesota	Johns Hopkins, *D.C.*
Hawaii	Missouri	Michigan
Illinois	Pennsylvania	New York U.
Texas	Rochester, *N.Y.*	Pennsylvania
U. of Washington	Wisconsin	Portland State, *Oregon*
East Asia	*Southeast Asia*	Princeton, *N.J.*
Brown, *R.I.*	Cornell, *N.Y.*	Texas
Bucknell, *Pa.*	Yale, *Conn.*	Utah
Chicago	*Soviet and E. Europe*	*Africa*
Colorado	Boston Col., *Mass.*	California, Los Angeles
Cornell, *N.Y.*	California, Berkeley	Columbia, *N.Y.*
Columbia, *N.Y.*	Chicago	Duquesne, *Pa.*
*Dartmouth, *N.H.*	Colorado	Florida
*Earlham, *Ind.*	Columbia (Soviet), *N.Y.*	Howard, *D.C.*
Iowa	Columbia (Uralic), *N.Y.*	Indiana
Kansas	Fordham, *N.Y.*	*Lincoln, *Pa.*
*Manhattanville, *N.Y.*	Harvard, *Mass.*	Michigan State
Michigan	Illinois	Northwestern, *Ill.*
*Oakland, *Mich.*	Indiana	Ohio
*Oberlin, *Ohio*	Kansas	Stanford, *Cal.*
Pittsburgh, *Pa.*	Louisiana State	Texas Southern
Princeton, *N.J.*	Michigan	Wisconsin, Madison
Rochester, *N.Y.*	Ohio State	*Latin America*
So. California	Pennsylvania	*Antioch, *Ohio*
Stanford, *Cal.*	Pennsylvania State	California, Los Angeles
Washington U., *Mo.*	Portland State, *Oregon*	Columbia, *N.Y.*
Yale, *Conn.*	Princeton, *N.J.*	Cornell, *N.Y.*
Inner Asia	Vanderbilt, *Tenn.*	Florida
Indiana	Virginia	Illinois
South and Southeast	U. of Washington	Miami, *Florida*
Asia	*Sino-Soviet*	New Mexico
American, *D.C.*	George Washington,	New York U.
California, Berkeley	*D.C.*	Stanford, *Cal.*
Michigan	*Northwest Europe*	Texas
South Asia	Minnesota	Tulane, *La.*
Chicago	*Middle East*	Virginia
Cornell, *N.Y.*	California, Berkeley	Wisconsin, Madison
Duke, *N.C.*	California, Los Angeles	Wisconsin, Milwaukee
Kansas State	Georgetown, *D.C.*	Yale, *Conn.*

Table 4. NDEA centers, by world area

*Undergraduate center.

Language	No. of speakers*	Enrollments†		Language courses†	Language faculty†
		NDEA	% of national		
Chinese	500	1,711	34%	191	125
Hindi/Urdu	105	278	76%	60	29
Japanese	100	2,016	47%	145	94
Arabic	95	560	51%	74	52
Bengali	100	18	100%	9	5
Korean	42	57	81%	19	10
Polish	36	119	18%	21	17
Turkish	30	103	87%	36	18
Swahili	20	374	62%	32	23
Indonesian/Malay	14	53	56%	15	7
Hausa	20	62	100%	19	12

Table 5. Utilization survey of NDEA Section 602 language materials for selected languages

Language	NDFL fellowships 1959–1970	Texts supported by NDEA in sets	Schools using 602 materials‡
Chinese	2049 (267†)	40	80% (21 of 24)
Hindi/Urdu	1026 (148†)	33	100% (17 of 17)
Japanese	1303 (146†)	23	52% (12 of 23)
Arabic	1383 (178†)	52	85% (6 of 7)
Bengali	110 (10†)	9	100% (3 of 3)
Korean	112 (10†)	16	66% (2 of 3)
Polish	116 (11†)	3	75% (3 of 4)
Turkish	276 (40†)	8	100% (2 of 2)
Swahili	541 (88†)	8	88% (8 of 9)
Indonesian/Malay	296 (53†)	5	100% (1 of 1)
Hausa	236 (45†)	8	33% (2 of 6)

Table 5 (continued)

Note: Table is based on Social Science Research Council program inventory, 82 programs responding in 50 languages.

*In millions, projected to 1969.
†1968 only.
‡As reported by SSRC.

References, Modern foreign language teaching in the uncommonly taught languages

1 Abboud, Peter F. *The Teaching of Arabic in the United States:The State of the Art.* Washington,D.C.: ERIC Clearinghouse for Linguistics, Center for Applied Linguistics, 1969.

2 Axelrod, Joseph. "NDEA Foreign Language Institute Programs:The Development of a New Educational Model." *PMLA* 82(1967):14–18.

3 Bauman, Frederick W., Jr. *1968 Index to ERIC Documents in Linguistics and Uncommonly Taught Languages and Selected Bibliography of Related Titles.* Washington,D.C.: ERIC Clearinghouse for Linguistics, Center for Applied Linguistics, 1969.

4 Bigelow, Donald N., and Lyman H. Legters. *NDEA Language and Area Centers:A Report on the First Five Years.* Washington,D.C.: U.S. Office of Education, 1964.

5 Blass, Virgil A., Dora E. Johnson, and William W. Gage. *A Provisional Survey of Materials for the Study of Neglected Languages.* Washington, D.C.: Center for Applied Linguistics, 1969.

6 Boyd-Bowman, Peter. *Self-Instruction in the Neglected Languages: A Manual for Program Directors.* New York: National Council of Associations for International Studies, 1969.

7 Brown, Judith. "The Peace Corps and the Development of Foreign Language Instructional Materials." *Linguistic Reporter* 11(1969):1–3.

8 Carroll, John B. *The Study of Language:A Survey of Linguistics and Related Disciplines in America.* Cambridge: Harvard University Press, 1953. [See especially, "Language Teaching during World War II."]

9 Cowan, J. Milton. "Program in Oriental Languages." *ACLS Newsletter* 10(1959):3.

10 Diekhoff, John S. *NDEA and Modern Foreign*

Languages. New York: Modern Language Association, 1965.

11 Dostert, Léon. "The Georgetown Institute Language Program." *PMLA* 68(1953):3–12.

12 "A Five-Year Program for Improving Modern Foreign Language Instruction in the National Interest." New York: Modern Language Association, 1957. [Mimeographed.]

13 Gage, William. "Uncommonly Taught Languages." *Educational Resources Information Center* 17(1970):1–7.

14 Graves, Mortimer, and J.M. Cowan. *Report of the First Year's Operation of the Intensive Language Program of the American Council of Learned Societies, 1941–42.* Washington,D.C.: American Council of Learned Societies.

15 Haas, Mary R. "The Application of Linguistics to Language Teaching," 807–18 in A.L. Kroeber,ed., *Anthropology Today.* Chicago: Univ. of Chicago Press, 1953.

16 Hall, John. *Japanese Studies in the United States.* New York: American Council of Learned Societies, 1970. [Committee on Japanese Studies.]

17 Hodge, Carleton T. "Response to W. Gage's Article:Uncommonly Taught Languages." *Educational Resources Information Center* 17(1970): 7–9.

18 Jelavich, Charles. *Language and Area Studies: East Central and Southeastern Europe:A Survey.* Chicago: Univ. of Chicago Press, 1969.

19 Kant, Julia Gibson. *Foreign Language Offerings and Enrollments in Public and Non-Public Secondary Schools Fall 1968.* New York: The Modern Language Association, 1970.

20 ———*Foreign Language Registration and Student Contact Hours in Institutions of Higher Education Fall 1968 and Summer 1969.* New York: The Modern Language Association, 1969.

21 Kelley, Gerald B. *The Teaching of Hindi-Urdu in the United States:The State of the Art.* Washington,D.C.: ERIC Clearinghouse for Linguistics, Center for Applied Linguistics, 1969.

22 Kocher, Margaret,ed. *1967–68 Selected Bibliography in Linguistics and the Uncommonly Taught Languages.* Washington,D.C.: ERIC Clearinghouse for Linguistics, Center for Applied Linguistics, 1968.

23 "Language study and American education." *Language* 29(1953):215–18. [Report of the Committee on the Language Program of ACLS.]

24 Marckwardt, Albert H. "The Aims, Methods, and Materials of Research in the Modern Languages and Literatures." *PMLA* 67(1952):4–15.

25 ——— "Teaching English as a Foreign Language," 15–31 in *Language Development.* New York: Ford Foundation, 1968. [Selected papers from a conference on the state of the art.]

26 Martin, Samuel E. *On the Teaching of Japanese: The State of the Art.* Washington,D.C.: ERIC Clearinghouse for Linguistics, Center for Applied Linguistics, 1969.

27 Matthew, Robert J. *Language and Area Studies in the Armed Services:Their Future Significance.* Washington,D.C.: American Council on Education, 1947.

28 Mildenberger, Kenneth. "Teaching and Research on Foreign Languages," 32–39 in *Language Development.* New York: Ford Foundation, 1968. [Selected papers from a conference on the state of the art.]

29 Moulton, William G. "The Cornell Language Program." *PMLA* 67(1952):38–46.

30 ——— "Linguistics and Language Teaching in the United States," 82–109 in Christine Mohrmann,ed., *Trends in European and American Linguistics 1930–1960.* Antwerp: Spectrum, 1963.

31 Ornstein, Jacob. "Structurally Oriented Texts and Teaching Methods Since World War II:A Survey and Appraisal." *Modern Language Journal* 40(1946):213–22.

32 Parker, William R. *The National Interest and Foreign Languages.* Washington,D.C.: U.S. National Commission for UNESCO, Department of State, 1954.

33 Petrov, Julia A. *Completed Research, Studies, and Instructional Materials for Language Development, List No. 6.* Washington,D.C.: U.S. Government Printing Office, [Cat. No. FS 5.212: 12016–69 (1969):144.].

34 Prochazka, Theodore,Jr. *1960–67 Selected Bibliography of Arabic.* Washington,D.C.: ERIC Clearinghouse for Linguistics, Center for Applied Linguistics, 1967.

35 Sebeok, Thomas A.,ed. *Current Trends in Linguistics:Vol. 1, Soviet and East European Linguistics.* The Hague: Mouton, 1963.

36 ——— *Current Trends in Linguistics:Vol. 2, Linguistics in East Asia and South East Asia.* The Hague: Mouton, 1967.

37 ——— *Current Trends in Linguistics:Vol. 4, Ibero-American and Caribbean Linguistics.* The Hague: Mouton, 1968.

38 ——— *Current Trends in Linguistics:Vol. 5, Linguistics in South Asia.* The Hague: Mouton, 1969

39 ——— *Current Trends in Linguistics:Vol. 6, Linguistics in South West Asia and North Africa.* The Hague: Mouton, 1969.

40 Steinberg, David J., and Richard D. Lambert. *Language and Area Studies Review:The Role of Area Oriented Professional Organizations.* Final Report submitted to U.S. Office of Education. Washington,D.C.: U.S. Office of Education, 1970.

41 *A Survey of Language Classes in the Army Specialized Training Programs.* New York: Commission on Trends in Education, The Modern Language Association, 1944.

42 Teoh, Irene. *1966 Selected Bibliography in Linguistics and the Uncommonly Taught Languages.* Washington,D.C.: ERIC Clearinghouse for Linguistics, Center for Applied Linguistics, 1967.

43 Thompson, Richard T. "Uncommonly Taught Languages:Another Perspective." *Educational Resources Information Center* 19(1971):1–5.

44 Wrenn, James J. *Chinese Language Teaching in the United States:The State of the Art.* Washington,D.C.: ERIC Clearinghouse for Linguistics, Center for Applied Linguistics, 1968.

11

Program evaluation:
Accountability

Introduction

P. Paul Parent and
Frederick P. Veidt
Purdue University

The uniqueness of accountability in regard to educational performance can be seen by the fact that its inclusion as a term in the *Education Index* first occurred in the year 1970 (Morris, 50). The novelty of the concept as well as its relationship to industrial terminology has led to some confusion concerning its meaning and application to purely educational endeavors. Although Barro (4), Duncan (17), and Dyer (19) have suggested workable definitions and have outlined principles basic to accountability, perhaps the most succinct explanation of the term has been offered by Professor Leon Lessinger of Georgia State University who is recognized by many as the originator of educational accountability (39). "At its most basic level, it means that an agent, public or private, entering into a contractual agreement to perform a service will be held answerable for performing according to agreed-upon terms, within an established time period, and with a stipulated use of resources and performance standards. This definition of accountability requires that the parties to the contract keep clear and complete records and that this information be available for outside review."

The newness of the term

At this point, it is essential that the distinction between accountability and responsibility be made clear. The kernel of this differentiation is contained in the notion of enforced performance or achievement. As Lopez (42) has indicated, "It is the responsibility of a board of education to insure the effective education of the children in its community. Board members cannot pass this responsibility on to principals and to teachers. But they can hold teachers and principals accountable for the achievement of tangible educational effects *provided* they define clearly what effects they expect and furnish the resources needed to achieve them."

Accountability and responsibility

The origins of accountability

The growing demands for accountability in education appear to emanate from a dichotomous source. On the one hand, the enlarged intellectual requirements and abilities necessary for contemporary employment, the new militance on the part of ethnic and racial minority groups who feel increasingly alienated from and neglected by the educational establishment, and the new visions of social injustices that have been acutely documented by the continuing communications explosion have been delineated as causal factors (Lessinger, 40). On the other hand, the expansion of modern technological theories and the resultant practices have presented a complex variety of efficient business and industrial systems that offer various means of solving specific problems and concerns in many fields of endeavor. Thus, the notion of applying technological management techniques, in the form of product control, to societal dysfunctions in education is rapidly gaining proponents.

Demands for accountability

Contemporary pressures for accountability

The incidence of public demand for workable education programs is high. In a 1970 survey conducted by the Gallup organization, 75% of the respondents indicated that students in local schools should be given national tests so that their educational achievement could be compared with that of students in other communities. Furthermore, 67% of those questioned in the same public poll favored a system that would hold teachers and administrators more accountable for student progress (67). Echoing the desires of his constituents, President Richard M. Nixon, in his 1970 message to Congress on education, discussed accountability and declared that, "School administrators and school teachers alike are responsible for their performance, and it is in their interest as well as in the interests of their pupils that they be held accountable."

Actual public demands

Another cogent reason for the implementation of educational accountability centers around the rising costs of education and the resultant bind on the taxpayer. Duncan (17) points out that past methods of determining educational costs have been primarily based on monetary outlay for educational "input." Included as input are such factors as the amount of money expended per enrollee, the costs of building programs, and the disbursements for special equipment and projects. As a result, the taxpayer, if he is fortunate enough to reside in a school district that feels the necessity to inform the public of such itemized expenditures, often learns how his tax dollars were expended and what he received for them in terms of the number of teach-

Rising costs for the taxpayer

ers with master's degrees, the makes and models of the new automobiles for the driver-education program, and the cost of new plumbing at John Q. Public High School. Now, increasingly, the provider of these revenues wants to ascertain the scope of the "output" obtained by his funds. In other words, what degree of improved student learning, if any, has accrued from the advanced degrees, the new cars, and the renovated drainage system?

McComas (47) asserts that public institutions have always had a moral obligation to be accountable for their effectiveness. Therefore, it is a natural inclination for schools to stress the number of scholarships awarded, the advanced placement rankings earned by college-bound graduates, and the successes of the distributive education program in placing students with local business concerns. Unfortunately, the failures of the schools, as indicated by the rate and number of students who drop out or are graduated with basic educational deficiencies, are often revealed, not by the schools, but by agencies extrinsic to public education.

Moral obligation of public institutions for accountability

A final manifestation of the need for accountability in education can be seen in the disenchantment of the general population with the "experts" (Lessinger, 40). If those who are in charge of public institutions are as capable of error as anyone else, should there not be some degree of control over their actions and performance?

Public distrust of "experts"

The ingredients of accountability

Behavioral objectives

The roles of behavioral objectives, performance criteria, and evaluation, and their relationships to accountability were suggested by Steiner in the preceding volume of this series (71). Therein, Steiner also presents an extremely comprehensive review and discussion of the development and the suggested and applied utilization of performance objectives. It seems, therefore, unnecessary to repeat previous efforts in defining and delineating such objectives except to refer those who are unfamiliar with the concept to the pioneering works of Bloom (9) and Mager (44) and to the more recent assessment edited by Popham (64).

Ingredient number 1

The advent of individualized instruction and its employment

in the field of foreign language instruction largely since 1968 has brought a concomitant increase in the use of performance objectives. The major criticisms that have been voiced in the past regarding the efficacy of these objectives can be summarized as follows:

Use and criticism of performance objectives

1 Performance objectives often tend to deal with overly specific trivialities.
2 The substance of presentation should be subordinate to the manner of presentation.
3 Long-term learning is more desirable than segmented short-term learning.
4 The application of principles by the student is preferable to the retention of facts.
5 Preoccupation with predetermined objectives tends to stifle the timely and relevant digression from a planned sequence of activities.
6 Many important objectives, especially in the humanities, do not lend themselves easily, if at all, to measurement.

Valette & Sherrow (76) feel that teaching for specific objectives in foreign languages is a healthy undertaking provided the instructor spreads his concentration from the lower-level to the higher-level objectives in all learning domains. They warn that the danger inherent in accountability in foreign language teaching is the seductiveness associated with the convenience and ease of using objectives that deal with such skills as vocabulary knowledge, phonological control, and comprehension of specific facts. Furthermore, if the teacher's performance is to be measured in terms of how well he meets his objectives without an evaluation of the objectives themselves, the teacher may elect to teach only those objectives that he is certain of fulfilling. This, in turn, could lead to the misconception on the part of the teacher that lower-level objectives are of primary importance in beginning and intermediate classes, where there may be administrative scrutiny, and that the higher objectives must be held in abeyance until the advanced classes.

Spreading objectives from lower to higher levels

While agreeing that behavioral objectives can be used to improve instructional practices in the humanities, Hoetker (29) questions what he terms the "simple-minded insistence upon the *a priori* specification of all objectives in terms of conveniently observable behaviors." Hoetker divides educational behaviors into three types:

Three types of educational behaviors

1 "Can-do" behaviors are those specific things that a student

314

can do at the end of a particular unit of his education that he could not do at the beginning of it.

2 "May-do" behaviors are things a student may be able to do in a novel or unfamiliar situation because he has mastered certain "can-do" behaviors.

3 "Will-do" behaviors are the choices and preferences that describe the quality of an adult's life, and which are present only fractionally during the school years.

In order to circumvent the charge of undue triviality, Hoetker suggests writing performance objectives only for the higher-level objectives. If these objectives are met, one can assume that the "can-do" behaviors have been achieved also. However, empirical indication that only basic "can-do" behaviors have been attained without a corresponding acquiring of higher-level objectives is a sign of teacher incompetence and a dignifying of the knowledge of quiz-show facts.

Recently, MacDonald & Wolfson (43) have added new criticisms to the use of behavioral objectives. They note that it is possible for the learner to perceive the stated objectives and criteria to be of such little value to him, that he does not even want to bother to demonstrate that he has complied with them. Moreover, many school learning tasks are susceptible to backsliding and forgetting. Given these phenomena, to attempt an interpretation of whether learning has taken place, based purely on performance, can be quite misleading.

New criticism of performance objectives

A detailed study of performance objectives and their ramifications for foreign language teaching has been prepared by Sherrow (69). In this report, the author proposes a classification system based on various behavioral levels. Uses of performance objectives for the improvement of foreign language instruction are discussed. In addition, the major arguments against the utilization of performance objectives are presented and analyzed. Each opposing argument is countered with a positive reply. One such refutation follows:

A future ERIC Focus Report on performance objectives

The emphasis on observable, measurable behavior neglects the abstract, humane values which our schools attempt to inculcate.

Radical answer: If you can't measure it, you haven't taught it.

Moderate answer: A visit to most schools would reveal very little that is humane. Unless teachers are held

315

accountable for achieving higher goals, they will never progress beyond the level of facts, facts, facts.

Conservative answer: Perhaps some of the things we try to accomplish in our classrooms are indeed unmeasurable. Nevertheless, at least some of the goals we have now can be expressed in behavioral terms.

Performance criteria

The second essential ingredient of accountability concerns the specification of definite norms or standards for determining student success or failure in achieving stated behavioral objectives.

Ingredient number 2

Deterline (15) states that education requires a commitment to an established set of criteria and, unless we are willing to make this commitment, no complete and objective evidence can be obtained indicating to what extent our students have or have not learned. "If we don't care about all of our students attaining at least some uniform minimum level of competence, then we can do without criteria, and quality control and accountability. We can then continue to present information and grade on a curve and let it go at that." Deterline further contends that certain academic subjects, including foreign languages, have objective criteria available whose performance components are relatively static regardless of the nature of the real world circumstances to which they are to be applied.

Commitment to established criteria

Hoetker (29) would reduce all standards to binary terms such as pass/fail, occur/not occur, or present/absent. The result would be the complete avoidance of separate levels of student achievement. According to Hoetker, the only element that should be involved in an evaluation concerns mastery or nonmastery in attaining a specified objective. The use of finer gradations is indicative of the desire to rank-order students rather than to teach them. This, however, does not rule out the collection of such data for research purposes, e.g., the computation of the degree of change over a set period of time. With norms of the binary type, it is the teacher who is evaluated as having failed or succeeded.

Binary criteria

Dolmatch (16) warns about misuses in the "measurement game" and declares that the best way to guarantee performance is to establish one's own criteria by designing pre- and post-tests and then creating a program of study that shows measurable improvement between the two evaluative standards. A second approach is to determine beforehand which standardized measure of achievement will be employed by the educational institution and then develop instructional materials that teach the student how to perform on the measures likely to be used. Still another technique to assure achievement is to circumscribe the promised performance to such a degree as to render the guarantee valueless. This can be accomplished by dealing with class achievement rather than individual gain or by dropping those students least likely to achieve.

How to guarantee performance

Perhaps the most equitable approach to establishing criteria is to provide for different norms for students of varying backgrounds, abilities, and circumstances (Wildavsky, 80). In this way, students who are homogeneous on several variables can be compared. Schools within a given area or city would be placed in one of several possible groups. "The five top schools within each subgroup could be taken together and their current achievement and average growth used as the normative standard. In this way participants in each school's activity would know that the norm set for them had in fact been achieved by students in situations comparable to their own." However, Wildavsky cautions that this proposal is not feasible if there exists great heterogeneity within schools.

An equitable approach to the establishment of criteria

Testing

Although Holt (30) is adverse to evaluations of all kinds, pre-testing, continuous evaluation, and post-assessment are a *sine qua non* for accountability. It is not possible to hold anyone— teacher, administrator, or school board—accountable for student progress if effective and precise measurements of entering and terminal capabilities are lacking. Accountability for the unknown or the surmised is a contradiction in terms.

Ingredient number 3

One current problem in ascertaining achievement levels occurs in regard to the type of instrument that will be employed to gauge the degree of student gain. Should said acquisition be determined by the use of norm-referenced (standardized) or criterion-referenced tests? The latter report the proficiency of those being tested in absolute terms on a mastery-nonmastery basis. The student is in competition with himself rather than his peers and his achievement is reflected in the number and the nature of units mastered or controlled.

Wildavsky (80) sees standardized tests as a requirement for a program of accountability. He refutes the charge of cultural bias in such tests and proposes that all standardized testing be done by agencies who have no stake in the results.

Use of standardized tests

Klein (37) and Harmes (25) discuss the limitations of using standardized tests in programs of accountability. Harmes finds that the advantages of such tests, i.e., their specificity and ease of administration, are far outweighed by two major disadvantages: the lack of reliability between any two commercial norm-referenced achievement tests, and the temptation to teach the memorization of specific responses when only a single commercial instrument is employed for both pre- and post-assessment.

Tyler (75) further explains that standardized tests were constructed to furnish scores that will rank-order pupils in terms of their proficiency and, thus, contain primarily questions that 40 to 60% of those tested are able to answer correctly. As a result, the typical standardized test furnishes too few questions to obtain a reliable measure of what students at either end of the normal curve have learned. Furthermore, since these tests do not commence with entering behavior and follow the student through the learning sequence used by his teachers and school to help him acquire the requisite skills, any change between pre- and post-test scores can be attributed to chance. In an experimental evaluation of parallel-column bilingual reading materials as a pedagogical device, Parent & Belasco (60) have called attention to the measurement problem inherent in the use of standardized tests. Although there were no significant differences between groups when a standardized reading test was used, such differences were dramatic when reading comprehension was assessed by criterion-referenced tests.

However, there are also problems associated with the use of norm-referenced evaluative tools that are not solved by recourse to criterion-referenced tests (Millman, 49). The first of these concerns the specification of the universe of relevant content, i.e., exactly what items can be included in the test to achieve the desired content validity. Secondly, the choice of a standard of proficiency, even on a pass/fail basis, is still largely an arbitrary value judgment, albeit to a lesser degree than when performance level divisions between letter grades are required.

Use and evaluation of criterion-referenced tests

In light of these demonstrated advantages and inadequacies in both types of evaluative models, the Office of Economic Opportunity (OEO) plans to undertake a large-scale two-year experiment contrasting and comparing different combinations of both standardized and criterion-referenced tests (31).

Perhaps the most complex task in accountability measurement is the creation of a workable technique for determining the contributions to student performance of individual variables in the educational process. Barro (4) proposes a comprehensive method, based on multiple regression analysis of the relationship between student performance and an array of various pupil, teacher, and school characteristics. He also indicates at least three areas in which his system may be deficient:

The role of individual variables in the educational process

1 Difficulty in attributing results to sources because of ambiguity due to correlations between supposedly independent variables.
2 The omission of unidentified relevant variables that have significant effects on pupil performance and that are not distributed uniformly among classrooms and schools.
3 The simplicity of the model may ignore essential relationships among school inputs and outputs.

This brings us to another related problem. Is it, indeed, possible to measure *all* of the pertinent variables that may be associated with teacher efforts and student achievement? For example, can a postulated behavioral objective dealing with "liberated expression" in a foreign language be assessed by a controlled and contrived measure of the variable? Jarvis & Hatfield (33) conducted an exacting comparison of foreign language drill types in which they distinguished between practice using potentially communicative language and practice in actual communication with particularized referents. After discussing the results, they remind the practitioner that the experiment contrasted behaviors as they occurred in the confined environment of the classroom.

Which variables does one measure?

Veidt (77) contends that the true condition of free or spontaneous expression can be encountered only in a state that is extrinsic to the educational setting. The very fact that the student is operating in a role-playing capacity invalidates true free expression. Free expression and free communication are impeded by the teacher, the teacher's knowledge or intuition as to the thoughts that the learner wishes to convey, the other members of the class and the learner's relationship with them, the textbook, the classroom realia, and even by the educational or school environment itself. The foreign language student, surrounded by his peers and a teacher to whom he can easily express his ideas and feelings at a moment's notice, is not apt to be bound by or to feel the stress of a situation where this exit is not available.

Granted, the concept of "liberated expression" can be delimited in terms of its behavioral objectives and performance criteria so that it can be evaluated in the classroom. But, what degree of circumscription can legitimately be applied to free communication before it becomes only a pale imitation of what was originally intended by the term? Should we not admit that, due to an absence of viable testing instruments, we are unable to teach true free expression and that the maximum that we can attain in this regard is a measure of the reaction of the learner in a contrived classroom setting only marginally similar to genuine foreign language surroundings?

For example: what about measuring "free expression"?

An alternative to determining accountability solely through assessment of student achievement has been suggested by Harmes (25), who advocates instead a system of process evaluation. He deems the appraisal of student performance to be analogous to industrial product output in which guidelines for the quantity and quality of such items as pairs of shoes, transistor radios, and automobile tires are specified. The services of teachers should be similar to those provided by lawyers and physicians who agree to perform certain specified tasks for their clients. Even though they are expected to use the best procedures known to their respective fields of endeavor in an effort to accomplish the objectives of their agreements, the members of these professions are paid whether or not the desired outcomes of the implemented processes are realized. Harmes suggests that the content of the following areas must be identified and delineated: (1) learning objectives for students; (2) characteristics of students for which the program is designed; (3) materials and methods of instruction for reaching the objectives with the intended target population; (4) techniques for assessing student learning; and (5) internal and external management specifications. In order to implement such a program, functional and well-defined classroom monitoring procedures, and penalties for discrepancies existing between program requirements and observed performance must be agreed upon by all parties involved. The author describes an approach in which video tape recordings and interaction analysis are utilized for this purpose.

Accountability through an evaluation process

Parent (59) cautions that product evaluations may be misleading in assessing teacher effectiveness. Rather, he urges teachers to adopt selected strategies calculated to bring about modern foreign language learning not for academically talented students alone, but for all students who feel they can profit from such study. The pluralistic objectives of today's foreign language students require us to look beyond demonstrated achievement on standardized tests as the sole measure of teacher effectiveness.

Cautions in product evaluation

McComas (47) calls for measurement in the affective as well as in the cognitive domain. Seelye (68) provides an answer to this plea for foreign language teachers in an article in which he offers several practical suggestions for measuring the student's "cultural understanding." His recommendations are presented in a hypothetical framework in which proposed salary increments for a group of language teachers are contingent upon demonstrable sensitivity of the students toward cultural manifestations.

Measurement of the affective domain

A final issue pertaining to the role of testing in accountability is the charge of educator preoccupation with "teaching the test" and not the subject matter. Sherrow (69) replies, "If tests are indeed valid measures of your goals, then there is every reason to direct class activities toward them." Wildavsky (80) finds nothing wrong with such a practice if the examinations are good indicators of what the student is to learn. He also distinctly demarcates acceptable and deceptive manipulative procedures. "It is one thing for teachers to prepare students by giving them exercises similar to one on the test; it is another for teachers to feed their students the exact words and phrases that will be used on the test." It was evidence of the latter practice that called into question the ethics and the results of the 1969-70 Texarkana (Arkansas) project, the first private-enterprise-contracted, public school program of accountability (62).

"Teaching the test"

Problems of accountability and foreign language education

Basic versus secondary skills

In discussing foreign language program evaluation in the first volume of this annual series, Hatfield (26) found that evaluation was a relatively innocent-appearing term that had generated considerably more theoretical pondering and prescription than true empirical research. Since then, the appending of the concept of accountability to program evaluation has effectively eliminated any of the innocence that may have formerly accompanied the concept. However, as far as accountability in foreign language instruction is concerned, the emphasis to date has continued to reflect theoretical meditation and recommendations rather than controlled investigation.

Status of accountability in foreign language education

An explanation for the preponderance of studies in accountability with basic skills as the focus and the corresponding absence of programs in other areas can be discovered in the inherent nature of these abilities. Lessinger (40) reminds the reader that there are certain crucial competencies in which we *should* have "Zero Rejects" among our school population. Barro (4) postulates that it is more feasible to pursue accountability in the elementary grades because adequate instruments of educational measurement are readily available for such areas as reading and mathematics. He cites the difficulty in obtaining valid and reliable measurements for secondary subject areas and the general disagreement among specialists concerning the desired objectives as being the basic causes for the general unavailability of acceptable commercial testing devices for these areas. As far as foreign language education is concerned, there would appear to be a sufficient number of adequate instruments available for experimentation with some form of accountability. It goes without saying that foreign language instruction would benefit greatly in several respects if the utilization of available commercial testing instruments was more widespread.

Accountability in basic skills outside foreign languages

Allen (1) transcends the need for purely foundation skills and declares that no one should leave school without sufficient training to enable him to find satisfying employment. The goal of secondary education is seen as competence for all.

According to Dyer (19), there is a threefold danger in limiting programs of accountability to the basic skills area of the student's educational development:

Dangers of limiting accountability to basic skills

1 It encourages the notion that, as far as the school is concerned, training in the basic skills is all that matters in a society where so many other human characteristics also matter.

2 It neglects the fact that, if a school gives exclusive attention to this one realm of pupil development, it may pur-

322

chase student success therein at the expense of failure in other areas.

3 It tends to blind people to the fact that pupil development in one area may be heavily dependent on development in other spheres.

Several educators have recommended or described accountability programs that concentrate on areas other than primary skills acquisition. Roueche (66) reports on several community colleges that have instituted either partial or total policies of accountability. The field of vocational-technical education is seen as an area where learning outcomes can be precisely measured and validated, thus making it an ideal area of the curriculum for the implementation of accountability measures (Straubel, 74). The Dallas Independent School District has submitted a preliminary proposal to the U.S. Office of Education for a dropout prevention program that calls for the use of bilingual materials with Mexican-Americans (79). Mini-grants have been established for teachers so that they can compete with contractors in the development of the project.

Accountability in areas other than basic skills

In a much-publicized experimental program in Gary, Indiana, a private corporation, Behavioral Research Laboratories, has contracted to manage the entire curriculum of the Banneker Elementary School for a period of three years beginning in 1970. The corporation has guaranteed to raise achievement scores or refund its fee for any child who fails. Mecklenburger & Wilson (48) describe the five curricular components for which responsibility has been assumed: (1) language arts; (2) mathematics; (3) science; (4) social studies and foreign language; and (5) enrichment. The last mentioned area includes arts and crafts, music, drama, and physical education. However, to date, the project has concentrated heavily on reading and mathematics. This recalcitrance in moving to other segments of the curriculum has incurred the displeasure of the Gary Teachers Union whose representatives have charged that the project administrators are teaching "only reading and math, *all day long!*"(48).

An experimental program in accountability

Accountability for whom?

The subject of who is to be held accountable for what in the school program does not suffer from lack of opinion, suggestion, speculation, or even controversy among the special interest groups involved. There is a definite lack of initiative and good

323

will in accepting responsibility but a plethora of recommendations as to where such liability should be assigned.

In the previously cited Gallup Poll, 67% of the public declared that accountability should be shared by both teachers and administrators (67). As indicated in another survey, 72% of the administrators, in their turn, would delegate accountability to teachers (38). Wildavsky (80) recommends focusing on school principals because they hold the essential power in, and can be assumed to have a longer-term commitment to, the school system. At least one state, Florida, has initiated some pilot programs in principal accountability (23).

A Gallup Poll on accountability

The idea has also been advanced that the state departments of education are becoming the most powerful elements in the control of education and, hence, should develop their accountability roles (Bair, 3). This suggestion has found concurrence in Florida where the Florida Department of Education is completing "plans to establish conditions for applying accountability techniques to exemplary and innovative educational programs on a state-wide pilot basis" (Daniel, 12). C. J. Donnelly (in 63) contends that those organizations presently engaged in performance contracting are the only groups in the country today that can be held totally accountable for the educational process.

Accountability and state departments of education

Several specialists, among them Deterline (15), Dyer (19), and Barro (4), have espoused the equity of partitioning accountability among the parties involved in the teaching-learning process. Barro states the principle: "Each participant in the educational process should be held responsible only for those educational outcomes that he can affect by his actions or decisions and only to the extent that he can affect them."

Partitioning accountability

Teacher accountability

If it is, in fact, the teachers who are to be called to account for the attainments of their immediate clientele, a precise system of controls and regulations on the processes of accountability must be formulated and instituted (Garvue, 24; Kaufman, 36; Stocker & Wilson, 73). Lessinger's appeal that accountability suggests penalties and rewards and that without redress or incentive it becomes mere rhetoric (39), is disputed by Lopez (42) who remarks that "it must be quite clear from the outset that the purpose of the accountability program is improvement of present role performance. If the measurements and standards developed are used for other purposes—such as discipline, promotion, and

Teacher accountability for program improvement

324

salary increases—the program will fail, positively and absolutely."

Dyer (in Hechinger, 28) and Deterline (15) note that a punitive and/or incentive system would meet with antipathy on the part of instructors. This claim has been substantiated by documented resistance and bitter hostility on the part of teachers toward several recent reward programs (56).

To extend Barro's principle to foreign language education, there exist factors that lie beyond the control of the teacher. For example, Bartley (5) has shown that attitude plays a decisive role in foreign language achievement. Again, DeFrancis (14) questions the effect of varying amounts of outside-classroom study on foreign language proficiency. This problem is succinctly manifested in a discussion of performance objectives in foreign language teaching (Steiner, 72). Students were requested to react to a test and to the performance criteria used to prepare them for the evaluation. Excerpts from the comments of two of the students indicate the importance of the time factor and the lack of teacher control on this element (Steiner, 72):

Student attitude toward learning

Student G: The performance criteria would have prepared me well had I studied for it [the test] regularly. But I studied only about every other night . . .

Student H: The test covered the subject and would have been easy for me if I had more time.

Indeed, a study by Mueller & Miller (52) has presented evidence that learner attitudes toward foreign language study transcend the time element in regard to the rate of learning.

In describing his model for multiple regression analysis, Barro (4) isolated a minimum of 41 separate pupil, teacher, classroom, school, and group characteristics that must be determined and analyzed in regard to their effect on student achievement. But, only a small number of these factors can be either directly or indirectly controlled by the teacher. We are reminded of the remarks of Leon A. Jakobovits in the Working Committee Reports of the 1970 Northeast Conference on the Teaching of Foreign Languages (54). If approximately 86% of student achievement in second-language learning in an average American school can be attributed to a combination of pupil attitudinal, intellectual, and motivational factors, the role played by the teacher would be reduced even more once the large number of applicable contributors envisioned by Barro were added to the list. Given these pluralistic effects, the influence of the teacher appears to be minimal. If the teacher is of no consequence, he cannot be held accountable for learning outcomes at all!

Will the installation of accountability systems have a deleterious effect on teacher morale? Although the New York City based United Federation of Teachers was in the fore in expending cooperative efforts seeking to develop objective criteria of professional accountability (Lieberman, 41), there are many indications that other teacher groups are less than happy with the concept. The American Federation of Teachers has condemned accountability and performance contracting on the grounds that they dehumanize the learning process and subvert collective bargaining procedures (Bhaerman, 7). Furthermore, accountability threatens to establish a monopoly of education by big business and can easily be construed as a gimmick that diverts attention from the real needs of education: smaller classes, an increase in remedial reading teachers, more counselors (63).

Teacher morale and accountability

While registering less disapprobation and opposition, the National Education Association first announced a campaign to establish professional practices boards, by state statute, to grant teachers more control of teacher training, licensure, in-service education, and the ethical conduct of their peers. Once this self-governance is attained, teachers could be held accountable (Bain, 2; Darland, 13). Later the NEA adopted a policy statement cautioning its members against accountability contracting and establishing strict conditions for its use (63).

NEA reaction

The Gary Teachers Union has voiced its displeasure and has even threatened strike action over several alleged contractual violations in that city's agreement with Behavioral Research Laboratories (Mecklenburger & Wilson, 48).

Additional problems

Several miscellaneous problems have developed in initial experimentation and others could arise. The required record-keeping of such projects is immense and will necessitate the collecting, culling, and using of large amounts of information. Durstine (18) has designed a system for the storing and processing of this type of information.

Dyer (19) wishes to dissuade educational institutions from seeking to answer complex questions on the basis of inadequate information and hastily formulated superficial plans. New approaches must make allowances for the semantic problems involved in communicating the nuances of the subject matter to the various participants in the program (21).

Wildavsky (80) warns against the tendency of teachers and even schools to recruit the more talented students and to remove the less apt in an effort to "demonstrate" success. The results would be education for an academic elite.

Parent (57) describes the challenge of making foreign language study relevant to *all* interested students. In this article, the author holds the teacher accountable for dropouts when he fails to take into account the pluralistic demands of his students and favors the intellectual elite. Elsewhere, Parent (58) examines the role of foreign languages in a modern curriculum concerned with education for survival. He considers our present approach to survival as a matter of "national defense" as negative and suggests that we should rather educate young Americans for international survival through world understanding.

Foreign languages for all students

Accountability applied

Until the advent of educational accountability, attempts to increase student achievement in various areas of the curriculum were characterized by a manipulation of sundry input factors both in isolation and combination: methodology, pupil experiences, materials, and hardware. The accountability approach, with an emphasis on assured output, has at least three present manifestations: performance contracting, merit pay, and the voucher system. Each concept requires the careful consideration of the profession so that it is applied appropriately.

Performance contracting

This application of accountability is attributed to Charles L. Blaschke, now president and chairman of the Board of Education Turnkey Systems. Performance contracting can be described in general terms as a formal agreement between a local school board and a group of private or public educators to induce certain specified gains in student performance within an established time period at a predetermined cost (63). Payment is made on the basis of results, i.e., a lack of increase in the level of student achievement brings no reimbursement and a bonus is often granted for performance in excess of the contractual stipulations.

What performance contracting is

The advantages of performance contracting have been delineated as follows (Lessinger, 39):

1 Contracting facilitates the targeting and evaluation of
educational programs.
2 Performance contracting for instructional services could
introduce more resources and greater variability into the
public school sector.
3 The approach allows a school system to experiment in a
responsible manner with low costs and low political and
social risks.
4 Performance contracting can help insure every child the
inherent right to read at his grade level.
5 Performance contracting can play a significant role in
school desegregation.
6 The approach creates dynamic tension and responsible institutional change within the public school system through
competition.

Several legal questions and their ramifications are involved in
the signing of performance contracts. These are discussed by
Martin & Blaschke (45) who conclude that "the principal legal
consequence of performance contracting is educational reform."

An offshoot of performance contracting is the "turnkey" arrangement. This is a provision in the agreement which specifies
that once an educational concern has successfully demonstrated the productiveness of a learning approach the procedures
(keys) for the operation of the program are turned over to the
school system for continued implementation. An important pro-
viso in this arrangement is that conditions for the regular monitoring and updating of the program be stipulated (Blaschke,
Briggs, & Martin, 8).

The National Education Association (63), in an effort to caution its members against the pitfalls of performance contracting, has specified the following as prerequisites to undertaking
any performance contract:

1 Teachers must be involved through their local associations
as a basic condition of the contract. This involvement must
extend from the planning of the contract objectives
through the evaluation of the performance of the contract.
2 Other measurements in addition to the so-called standardized achievement tests must be used as measures of student learning.

3 Learning objectives must be developed with community and professional involvement and must be the basis for the requests for bids on the contract.

4 All contracts must include a provision—the so-called turn-key approach—that will make it possible for all innovative aspects of the contract to revert to the regular staff and program of the school.

5 The contract must provide for the maximum use of school personnel who must be given adequate preparation in the processes related to the contractual objectives.

6 All students must be under the close supervision of professionally trained and certificated personnel.

7 Contracts must be limited to genuinely innovative approaches that are neither likely nor possible within the school's program.

8 Contracts must not be in conflict with negotiated agreements between school boards and local associations and must not violate the established legal rights of teachers.

9 Contracts must assure that no performance contractor may profit by virtue of any privileges given to nonprofit educational institutions or agencies under copyright law in order that there be no conflict with NEA's basic position on copyright law revision.

Merit pay

As Berger (6) has indicated, the idea of bonus payments to educators for the achievement of stipulated educational outcomes on the part of their students has English antecedents dating as far back as 1862. The practice was also attempted in Canada in 1875. Berger suggests that those wishing to embark on similar ventures today might benefit from a perusal of the results of these previous programs.

Voegel (78) envisions a system of faculty commission pay in performance contracting. He indicates basic rules for the operation of the plan and concludes by enumerating some of the advantages and problems inherent in the effectuation of such a system.

In a similar vein, Johnson (35) suggests performance criteria pay for existing staff as an alternative to school performance contracting by private firms. Such a structure is seen as a way of motivating good, experienced teachers to work with students of greater need. With this plan, a teacher would receive remunera-

Elements and detractors of merit pay

tion relative to the number of his students who exceed established individual increments of growth during the preceding academic year.

However, the concept of merit salaries for teacher accountability is not without detractors. Deterline (15) stresses that "Accountability is not a punitive method of assigning blame for failure, or a method of rewarding teachers who work harder."

The voucher system

Still another proposal designed to increase student achievement through accountability involves the use of educational vouchers. Basically, the plan is to provide parents with vouchers that would cover the cost of educating their children. The choice of schools would be a matter of parental selection. Thus, the school is directly accountable to the parents who can withdraw their children and their vouchers if they feel that the chosen school is not discharging its given tasks. This system has not yet been empirically tested in the United States.

A recent study funded by the U.S. Office of Economic Opportunity (OEO) analyzed seven current voucher plan models (22). The "free-market" proposal, which would grant every child an equal amount of money to be used at either a private or a public school is criticized on the grounds that it would increase economic and, thus, racial segregation and that it would intensify the already enormous problems of the public schools. Parents with higher incomes would be in a position to pay a supplement to the voucher and thereby ensure an exclusive private school education for their children. Jencks (34), who was in charge of the OEO study, offers an alternate model that would carefully control the minority group composition of each participating school, would accord children from low-income families vouchers with a higher monetary value, and would require that a certain proportion of the vacancies in each school be filled by a yearly lottery among its applicants.

Voucher plan models and a proposed alternative

Clayton (11) is critical of the Jencks proposal due to its lack of a specific experimental design and controls. He refers to similar programs in Europe and indicates the problems that have resulted there.

Carr & Hayward (10) examine five voucher plans and find that all of them are inadequate in at least these two respects:

Inadequacies of the voucher systems

1 An efficient education in terms of gains in measurable cognitive skills may not be an effective education as far as

societal benefits such as political participation and interpersonal competence are concerned.

2 There is no evidence that production competition in the human sector will yield the same quality control that it does in the manufacturing of material goods.

Finally, these authors note the deficiency of reliable, valid, multiple measures of school effectiveness. Clayton (11) also notes the deficiency and states: "The prospect of implementing voucher proposals without first developing adequate quality measures runs counter to even the least stringent research approaches."

In spite of this warning, Havighurst (27) reports that the OEO has made tentative plans to provide support for a major experiment with the voucher system advocated by Jencks. The project would begin in 1971 and should be carried out over a period of from five to eight years.

Some proposals for implementation

Suggested guidelines and recommendations for the introduction of programs of accountability have emanated from many quarters (Barro, 4; Duncan, 17; Mayrhofer, 46).

Guidelines for the introduction of accountability programs

Deterline (15) lists three elements for beginning a program:

1 No trainee will proceed from training to the job until we have complete and objective evidence that he can do the job according to the established criteria.

2 We must assemble a set of "learning experiences" and evaluation and management procedures that will allow and assist every student to reach that specified criterion or set of criteria.

3 We must rely on obtained data and not on the subjective, intuitive, and experiential judgments of the experts.

Deterline concludes that education must change its orientation from one of time to one of performance. A student will complete a course of instruction when he reaches a specified level of proficiency rather than at the end of a fixed period of time.

According to Lopez (42), to be successful, a program of accountability in education must insure that the behavior of every member of the organization is largely *functional*. This can be accomplished by meeting the following requirements:

Requirements for program functional behavior

1 The program must be an important communications me-

331

dium in a responsive environment through which members are informed of what is to be accomplished, by whom, and how; wide participation in the obtainment of organizational goals must be invited; and the attention of top management must be focused on the accomplishment of the personal goals of individual employees.

2 The program must reflect an organizational philosophy that inspires confidence and trust in all members.

3 The program must be based on ethical principles and sound policies that can be implemented by a set of dynamic, flexible, and realistic standards, procedures, and practices.

4 The program must clearly specify its purposes.

5 The program must be designed primarily to improve the performance of each member in his current job duties.

6 The manner in which the supervisor discusses his evaluation with the subordinate constitutes the core of the process. If this is handled poorly, the program, no matter how well designed and implemented, will fail.

7 To be effective and accepted, both those who use it and those who will be judged by it must participate in the design, installation, administration, and review of the total accountability system.

Lopez then describes three broad interventions aimed at a distinct level of the organizational structure: the top, the middle, and the base (the teachers themselves). Intervention at the top is generally done by a technique referred to in private industry as "Management by Objectives" (Ordione, 55) and in government as the "Planning, Programming, and Budgeting System" (Hughes, 32).

Program interventions

Intervention in the middle requires the establishment of a serious supervisory development program, primarily participative in nature. It is intended to bring about a change in attitudes and to impart specific skills, particularly that of conducting accountability interviews with subordinates (teachers and assistants).

The third phase, intervention at the base, is concerned with the development of specific instruments and techniques to evaluate the manner in which individual members of the school system are performing their assigned roles. It is the most difficult and delicate since it affects the teachers directly.

If individual teachers are to be held accountable, Lopez would set three conditions:

1 Such a policy can be effective only within the context of a program of goal setting and continuous supervisory development in coaching and evaluation interviewing.

2 The purpose of such a program is the improvement of present performance. Rewards and punishment should play no part.

3 The evaluative instruments developed as part of the program should be primarily intended to provide the teacher with feedback on his efforts and to furnish material for mutual discussions with the supervisor of ways to strengthen professional performance.

Conditions for individual teacher accountability

The evaluative instruments or standards of performance measurement must be meaningful and acceptable to the person who is to be assessed by them. In addition, the instruments must permit quantitative consolidation in the form of means, standard scores, and percentiles so that the achievement of departmental, school, and district objectives can be determined.

In order to ensure acceptance of measurement standards, it is essential that the teachers as well as their supervisors participate actively in the research, design, and implementation of these instruments.

Conclusion

Results of current accountability programs

The federally funded dropout prevention project begun in Texarkana, Arkansas, late in 1969 has provided an impetus, or perhaps it would be more accurate to say opened the floodgates, for a nationwide surge in performance contracting. The fact that such moves may be precipitous has not been a deterrent to more than two dozen other school districts throughout the United States that have since concluded similar agreements. Moreover, statewide programs are currently planned for Virginia and New Jersey. In view of this flurry of activity, one would assume the results of the introductory Texarkana program to be explicit and significant.

The Texarkana, Arkansas, project

Elam (20) has presented a detailed account of the project in Texarkana based on personal observations and interviews, and several published sources. The major goal of the program was the prevention of dropouts, primarily by increasing achievement levels in reading and mathematics as measured by the Iowa

Tests of Educational Achievement. The private contractor, Dorsett Educational Systems, utilized programmed materials in Rapid Learning Centers that were staffed by two instructors. These centers were able to accommodate 15-25 students each hour. Pupils selected for the project were diagnosed as potential dropouts and were all at least two grade levels behind in the target subjects. *Design*

In order to stimulate initial achievement, tangible incentives such as Green Stamps, transistor radios, and portable television sets were built into the process. Other rewards, including games, puzzles, popular magazines, and free time, were employed as motivational devices.

A post-test, administered after 120 hours of instruction, showed that students were achieving, on the average, 2.2 and 1.4 grade-level increases in reading and mathematics respectively. However, the use of averages obscured the fact that as many as 32% of the pupils had made *no* progress and that some had slipped back by from .1 to more than three grade levels in one or another subject. *Evaluation*

The project director cited several possible explanations for this occurrence: (1) the existence of testing error; (2) the unreliability of the evaluative instruments; (3) the tendency on the part of a few students to purposely score low so that they could remain in the program; and (4) the lack of compatibility of teaching machines and the learning styles of some children.

On the other hand, significant behavioral changes were mentioned as a result of the project: (1) only one of 301 program participants has voluntarily dropped out of school; (2) vandalism in the cooperating schools has been halved; and (3) community support and participation is high.

In summary, Elam emphasizes that the project is still in the experimental stages and that few of the original objectives have been reached. He mentions that a clause, specifying that students be retested six months after completion of the Dorsett program to ascertain if retention rates were equal to those of the average student within the system, was deleted from the contract at the recommendation of the USOE. Elam notes that it may be that such multimedia projects as the one in Texarkana are best suited precisely for what they are doing: boosting the performance levels of potential dropouts on nationally normed reading and arithmetic achievement tests. In conclusion, he cautions that "Wholesale acceptance of the procedures for other *A critical review* purposes, at least in the present state of our ignorance, will not serve American education well."

In 1970, the School City of Gary, Indiana, contracted with a private educational firm to assume the entire operation of an elementary school on a money-back guaranteed performance basis. Curricular and teacher morale problems in connection with the program have been discussed elsewhere in this chapter. After three months of instruction, preliminary tests were administered to a randomly selected group of students. The assessment has indicated that participants have advanced, on the average, in excess of four months in reading proficiency and math ability (Star, 70). However, since the project is to be carried out for a period of three years, extrapolation from incomplete initial data is unwarranted.

Another accountability program: Gary, Indiana

Information concerning the locations, the educational companies involved, and the varying approaches to instruction that will be utilized in forthcoming accountability projects is available (61, 63).

Due to the tremendous interest in performance contracting in accountability undertakings, the Department of Health, Education, and Welfare has taken steps to aid in the appraisal of performance contractors (63). The RAND Corporation, a nonprofit research group, has been awarded a grant to evaluate all existing projects. The results of this study will be made available to school personnel who are contemplating similar programs. Furthermore, in order to avoid charges of "teaching for the test," the Battelle Memorial Institute in Columbus, Ohio, has been chosen to handle the testing of students in projects funded by the OEO.

A study to appraise performance contractors

Looking ahead

In spite of the general attraction of this most current panacea for our educational maladies, there are some educators who steadfastly refuse to mount the enticing steps of this latest bandwagon.

Nash (53) declares that we are hurrying to adopt a model that is so remote from the contemporary *Zeitgeist* that it has become, "but another unquestioned fetish in the arsenal of pedagogical ammunition." Motzkus (51) parodies accountability by transferring the concept to the local parson who prepares performance objectives in which 90% of the congregation will be able to recite the Ten Commandments with less than 10% error

Accountability remote from contemporary Zeitgeist

in a four-minute time period. This spiritual systems analyst can
also determine his effectiveness in the affective domain, to wit,
"The females of the congregation will appreciate the beauty and
truth of the Seventh Commandment to the extent that the illegit-
imacy rate will decrease 10% per year for the next 10 years."

It would appear that a prerequisite initial step in the establishment of any accountability system is the delineation of a
two-way avenue of communications. The external manifestation
of this is communication with the public, with school personnel
in other subject areas, with parents, and, most importantly, students. The form of the message should be a concise statement as
to what degree of proficiency a student enrolled in a particular
course can reasonably expect to have attained at the end of a
specified period of instruction. If, to use an example from the
cognitive domain, an average foreign language student can be
expected to identify 50 concrete objects, to sing three songs, to
name the days of the week and 10 colors, to excuse himself after
accidentally stepping on someone's foot, and to count up to 100 —
all in the target language after one semester's exposure to instruction — it behooves those responsible to convey this information to the immediate audience, i.e., the students, and to those
who have a vested interest in the pupils and in the educational
processes.

The necessity for communication

The internal communication channel rests on what Lopez (42)
terms the accountability interview. If it is done poorly, the whole
program will flounder; if it is conducted well throughout all
hierarchical levels of the school system, the educational processes will thrive. To be effective, a number of conditions must
exist before, during, and after the interview:

Accountability interview

1 The supervisor must have accounted for his own performance with his immediate superior, usually the principal or
the superintendent. He must have been involved in developing his own area of accountability as well as that of
his school or district. It is essential that both teacher and
supervisor be familiar with all of these areas.

2 Teacher and supervisor must be aware of the goals and
objectives for the department and the school and they
must have agreed previously on the dimensions of the
teacher's role and on acceptable standards of performance.
The supervisor must be trained in interviewing skills and
the teacher must be given adequate time for self-evaluation. Both teacher and supervisor must have reviewed data

from the accountability instruments in current use.

3 During the interview, both discuss material collected on the teacher's performance, analyze teacher strengths, and identify areas for improvement. A plan to develop the needed improvement will be formulated and the resources necessary for its implementation chosen. Agreement is reached on follow-up schedules to determine progress. All of this is then put in *writing* for subsequent review and reexamination.

Given the scantiness of evaluative data on existing programs of accountability, any statement at this point either in favor of or in opposition to the concept would be highly tenuous. As the results of experimentation in the area of accountability accumulate, it may become increasingly clear that performance in this segment of social science is not more predictable or subject to guarantee than in any other branch. Significant changes in achievement may well be attributable to purely local personalities and conditions that resist transplantation. For the present, perhaps the reader should be guided by the admonitions of John Wilson, the director of the OEO's Office of Planning, Research, and Evaluation, who has declared that far too little is known about the concept of accountability to indicate even optimism (63). He terms a commitment at this time "as foolhardy as buying a car without ever having seen or driven it; without ever having discussed its performance with someone who owned one like it; without even knowing its cost!"

The tenuous nature of accountability

Even if no enduring and tangible effects are gleaned from the present and future investigations of this phenomenon, "The debate over accountability and its several manifestations—performance contracting, merit salaries, the voucher plan, etc.—is bound to help many schoolmen think more precisely about what their goals are, how they can be achieved, and how we can reassure ourselves about the degree to which they have been achieved" (Robinson, 65).

References, Program evaluation: Accountability

1 Allen, James E.,Jr. "Competence for All as the Goal for Secondary Education." *Education Digest* 36,i(1970):24–27.

2 Bain, Helen. "Self Governance Must Come First, Then Accountability." *Phi Delta Kappan* 51(1970):413.

3 Bair, Medill. "Developing Accountability in Urban Schools:A Call for State Leadership." *Educational Technology* 11,i(1971):38–40.

4 Barro, Stephen M. "An Approach to Developing Accountability Measures for the Public Schools." *Phi Delta Kappan* 52(1970):196–205.

5 Bartley, Diana E. "The Importance of the Attitude Factor in Language Dropout:A Preliminary In-

vestigation of Group and Sex Differences." *Foreign Language Annals* 3(1970):383–93.

6 Berger, Allen. "Commentary on Reading." *Journal of Reading* 13(1969):233–37.

7 Bhaerman, Robert D. "Accountability:The Great Day of Judgment." *Educational Technology* 11,i(1971):62–63.

8 Blaschke, Charles L., Peter Briggs, and Reed Martin. "The Performance Contracting-Turnkey Approach to Urban School System Reform." *Educational Technology* 10,ix(1970):45–48.

9 Bloom, Benjamin S.,ed. *Taxonomy of Educational Objectives, Handbook I:Cognitive Domain.* New York: David McKay, 1956.

10 Carr, Ray A., and Gerald C. Hayward. "Education by Chit:An Examination of Voucher Proposals." *Education and Urban Society* 2(1970):179–91.

11 Clayton, A. Stafford. "Vital Questions, Minimal Responses:Education Vouchers." *Phi Delta Kappan* 52(1970):53–54.

12 Daniel, K. Fred. "Moving Toward Educational Accountability:Florida's Program." *Educational Technology* 11,i(1971):41–42.

13 Darland, D.D. "The Profession's Quest for Responsibility and Accountability." *Phi Delta Kappan* 52(1970):41–44.

14 DeFrancis, John. "The Time Factor in Language Learning." *Foreign Language Annals* 4(1971):287–92.

15 Deterline, William A. "Applied Accountability." *Educational Technology* 11,i(1971):15–20.

16 Dolmatch, Theodore B. "Who Will Be Accountable for Accountability?" *School Library Journal* 17,ii(1970):19–21.

17 Duncan, Merlin G. "An Assessment of Accountability:The State of the Art." *Educational Technology* 11,i(1971):27–30.

18 Durstine, Richard M. "An Accountability Information System." *Phi Delta Kappan* 52(1970):236–39.

19 Dyer, Henry S. "Toward Objective Criteria of Professional Accountability in the Schools of New York City." *Phi Delta Kappan* 52(1970):206–11.

20 Elam, Stanley. "The Age of Accountability Dawns in Texarkana." *Phi Delta Kappan* 51(1970):509–14.

21 "ETS Active in Assessment, Accountability, Audit, and Performance Contract Evaluation." *ETS Developments* 18,i(1970):1. [ETS-Educational Testing Service.]

22 *Financing Education by Grants to Parents:A Preliminary Report.* Cambridge, Massachusetts: The Center for the Study of Public Policy, 1970.

23 "Florida Accountability Plan Focuses on the Principal." *Nation's Schools* 86,v(1970):54.

24 Garvue, Robert J. "Accountability:Comments and Questions." *Educational Technology* 11,i(1971):34–35.

25 Harmes, H.M. "Specifying Objectives for Performance Contracts." *Educational Technology* 11,i(1971):52–56.

26 Hatfield, William N. "Foreign Language Program Evaluation," 375–88 in Emma M. Birkmaier,ed., *Britannica Review of Foreign Language Educa-*

tion, Volume 1. Chicago: Encyclopaedia Britannica, Inc., 1968[1969].

27 Havighurst, Robert J. "The Unknown Good:Education Vouchers." *Phi Delta Kappan* 52(1970):52–53.

28 Hechinger, Fred M. "Accountability:A Way to Measure the Job Done by Schools." *New York Times* 14 February(1971):7.

29 Hoetker, James. "The Limitations and Advantages of Behavioral Objectives in the Arts and Humanities:A Guest Editorial." *Foreign Language Annals* 3(1970):560–65.

30 Holt, John. "I Oppose Testing, Marking, and Grading." *Today's Education* 60,iii(1971):28–31.

31 "How OEO Will Test." *Nation's Schools* 86,vi(1970):38.

32 Hughes, C.L. *Goal Setting:Key to Individual and Organizational Performance.* New York: American Management Association, 1965.

33 Jarvis, Gilbert A., and William N. Hatfield. "The Practice Variable:An Experiment." *Foreign Language Annals* 4(1971):401–10.

34 Jencks, Christopher. "Giving Parents Money to Pay Schooling:Education Vouchers." *New Republic* 4 July(1970):19–21.

35 Johnson, W. Frank. "Performance Contracting With Existing Staff." *Educational Technology* 11,i(1971):59–61.

36 Kaufman, Roger A. "Accountability, a System Approach and the Quantitative Improvement of Education—An Attempted Integration." *Educational Technology* 11,i(1971):21–26.

37 Klein, Stephen P. "The Uses and Limitations of Standardized Tests in Meeting the Demands for Accountability." *UCLA Case Evaluation Comment* 2,iv(1971):n.pag. [UCLA—University of California, Los Angeles]

38 "Large Majority Favors Teacher Accountability." *Nation's Schools* 86,vi(1970):33.

39 Lessinger, Leon. "Engineering Accountability for Results in Public Education." *Phi Delta Kappan* 52(1970):217–25.

40 ——— "Robbing Dr. Peter to 'Pay Paul':Accounting for Our Stewardship of Public Education." *Educational Technology* 11,i(1971):11–14.

41 Lieberman, Myron. "An Overview of Accountability." *Phi Delta Kappan* 52(1970):194–95.

42 Lopez, Felix M. "Accountability in Education." *Phi Delta Kappan* 52(1970):231–35.

43 MacDonald, James B., and Bernice J. Wolfson. "A Case Against Behavioral Objectives." *Elementary School Journal* 71(1970):119–28.

44 Mager, Robert F. *Preparing Instructional Objectives.* Palo Alto, California: Fearon, 1962.

45 Martin, Reed, and Charles Blaschke. "Contracting for Educational Reform." *Phi Delta Kappan* 52(1971):403–5.

46 Mayrhofer, Albert V. "Factors to Consider in Preparing Performance Contracts for Instruction." *Educational Technology* 11,i(1971):48–51.

47 McComas, J.D. "Accountability:How Do We Measure Up?" *Educational Technology* 11,i(1971):31.

48 Mecklenburger, James A., and John A. Wilson. "The Performance Contract in Gary." *Phi Delta*

Kappan 52(1971):406–10.

49 Millman, Jason. "Reporting Student Progress:A Case for a Criterion-Referenced Marking System." *Phi Delta Kappan* 52(1970):226–30.

50 Morris, John E. "Accountability:Watchword for the 70's." *The Clearing House* 45(1971):323–27.

51 Motzkus, John E. "Accountability and the Reverend Dogwood." *Today's Education* 60,iii (1971):57.

52 Mueller, Theodore H., and Richard I. Miller. "A Study of Student Attitudes and Motivation in a Collegiate French Course Using Programmed Language Instruction." *International Review of Applied Linguistics in Language Teaching* 8(1970):297–320.

53 Nash, Robert J. "Commitment to Competency: The New Fetishism in Teacher Education." *Phi Delta Kappan* 52(1970):240–43.

54 Nelson, Robert J., and Leon A. Jakobovits,eds. "Motivation in Foreign-Language Learning," 31–104 in Joseph A. Tursi,ed., *Foreign Languages and the "New" Student*. Reports of the Working Committees of the Northeast Conference on the Teaching of Foreign Languages. New York: Modern Language Association Materials Center, 1970.

55 Ordione, G.S. *Management by Objectives*. New York: Pitman Publishing Company, 1965.

56 "Outlook for Teacher Incentives." *Nation's Schools* 86,v(1970):51–54.

57 Parent, P. Paul. "Minimizing Dropouts in the Foreign Language Program." *Modern Language Journal* 52(1968):189–91.

58 —— "Modern Languages–Needed for International Survival." *The Clearing House* 42, i(1967):36–38.

59 —— "Selected Teacher Strategies for Modern Language Learning." *National Association of Secondary School Principals Bulletin* 53(1969): 80–89.

60 —— and Simon Belasco. "Parallel-Column Bilingual Reading Materials as a Pedagogical Device:An Experimental Evaluation." *Modern Language Journal* 54(1970):493–504.

61 "Performance Contracting." *Phi Delta Kappan* 52(1970):225.

62 "Performance Contracting:Clouds and Controversy Over Texarkana." *Nation's Schools* 86,iv (1970):85–88.

63 "Performance Contracting:The Issue." *I/D/E/A Reporter* Winter(1971):n.pag.

64 Popham, W. James,ed. *Instructional Objectives*. Chicago: Rand McNally, 1969. [American Education Research Association (AERA) Monograph Series on Curriculum Evaluation, Monograph 3.]

65 Robinson, Donald W. "Accountability for Whom? for What?" *Phi Delta Kappan* 52(1970):193.

66 Roueche, John E. "Accountability for Student Learning in the Community College." *Educational Technology* 11,i(1971):46–47.

67 "Second Annual Survey of the Public Schools 1970." *I/D/E/A Reporter* Fall(1970):n.pag. [Special Issue.]

68 Seelye, H. Ned. "Performance Objectives for Teaching Cultural Concepts." *Foreign Language Annals* 3(1970):566–78.

69 Sherrow, Renée. "Performance Objectives:New Focus in Foreign Language Teaching." Unpublished paper, 1971. [Draft of an MLA/ERIC Focus Report.]

70 Star, Jack. "We'll Educate Your Kids–Or Your Money Back." *Look* 15 June(1971):56–64.

71 Steiner, Florence. "Behavioral Objectives and Evaluation," 35–78 in Dale L. Lange,ed., *Britannica Review of Foreign Language Education, Volume 2*. Chicago: Encyclopaedia Britannica, Inc., 1970.

72 —— "Performance Objectives in the Teaching of Foreign Languages." *Foreign Language Annals* 3(1970):579–91.

73 Stocker, Joseph, and Donald F. Wilson. "Accountability and the Classroom Teacher." *Today's Education* 60,iii(1971):41–56.

74 Straubel, James. "Accountability in Vocational-Technical Instruction." *Educational Technology* 11,i(1971):43–45.

75 Tyler, Ralph W. "Testing for Accountability." *Nation's Schools* 86,vi(1970):37–39.

76 Valette, Rebecca M., and Renée Sherrow. *Individualizing Foreign Language Instruction Through Performance Objectives*. New York: Harcourt Brace Jovanovich, 1971.

77 Veidt, Frederick P. "The Effects of Dialogue Memorization and Oral Presentation on the Ability of Students in Beginning College Russian to Produce Analogous Verbal Responses to Controlled Stimuli." Unpublished Ph.D. Dissertation. Lafayette, Indiana: Purdue University, 1971.

78 Voegel, George H. "A Suggested Schema for Faculty Commission Pay in Performance Contracting." *Educational Technology* 11,i(1971):57–58.

79 "Where the Action Is in Performance Contracting." *Phi Delta Kappan* 51(1970):510.

80 Wildavsky, Aaron. "A Program of Accountability for Elementary Schools." *Phi Delta Kappan* 52(1970):212–16.

Index

Index

343

Index

Index

Index

Index

351

Index

Index

United States Office of Education 285–86
University
  in-service programs 247–76
  interdisciplinary program 142–45
Utah State Board of Education
  Foreign Language Education 255

V

Valencia, Atilano A. 117
Valette, Rebecca M. 314
Van Doren, Mark 44–45
Van Horn High School
    (Independence, Missouri)
  interdisciplinary program survey 149
Veatch, Jeannette 230
Vega, Marie L. 65–66
Veidt, Frederick P. 311–39
  evaluation of curricular programs 7
Verbal-active method
  professional resource materials 205
  texts and teaching materials 187
Veri, Clive C. 248, 262
Victor Electronic Remote Blackboard 198
Videotape
  in-service education 270–71
  instructional strategies 191, 193
Villa, Hector 224
Vinson, Sharon S. W. 268
Virginia Polytechnic and State
    University 151
Visual Element in Language
    Teaching, The (Corder) 210
Voegel, George H. 329
Voices of Children Around the World 201
Von Hofe, Harold 86
Voucher system
  accountability applied 330–31

W

Wachner, Clarence 49
Wagner, Marybeth 190
Wakefield High School (Arlington,
    Virginia)
  interdisciplinary programs 127, 147
Walden Middle School (Atlanta,
    Georgia) 148
  interdisciplinary program survey 148, 150
Walker, Claire 191
Walker, Jo Ann 201
Walsh, Donald D. 102
Walt Whitman High School
    (Bethesda, Maryland)
  interdisciplinary program survey 147

Wardhaugh, Ronald 168
Warriner, Helen P. 125–61
  interdisciplinary programs and activities 4–5
Washington Foreign Language
    Program 254
Was wollen die Deutschen? 21
    Zeitgenossen (Drath) 188
Weinhold, E. Raymond 66
Weiss, Gerhard H.
  folklore and culture 80
  teaching of culture 63
Weiss, Louis 247
  teacher education 223
Wells, Gloria T. 204
West Chester State College
    (Pennsylvania) 260
Wheaton, Marjorie 68, 74
White, Beverly 203
Whiteside, Dale 75
Wildavsky, Aaron 317, 327
Wilgocki, Edward F., Jr. 187
Williams, Frederick 166
Willis, Benjamin C. 26–27
Wilson, Alfred P. 269
Wilson, Donald F. 324, 326
Wilson, John A. 323
Wilson, Robert 201
"Wilson Model" 269
Wisconsin, University of
  in-service education 273–74
Wisconsin State University
  in-service education 259
Wolfson, Bernice J. 315
Wood, Fred H. 203, 237
Wood, Margaret L. 187
Woodford, Protase 188
Woodson-Levey, Roy A. 69
Wrenn, James J. 286, 297
Wright, Louis B. 9, 17
Wright, Wendy A. 199
Writing
  instructional strategies 197–98
Wyoming State Department of
    Education
  Foreign Language Department 255

Y

Yale-Barnard Conferences on the
    Teaching of French 253
Yarbro, Bernice
  funding of individualized programs 237
  multimedia approach to French 231
Young, Nick 142

Z

Zenner, Walter P. 81
Zeydel, Edwin H. 19
Zielsprache Deutsch (journal) 206
Zolar, William 67

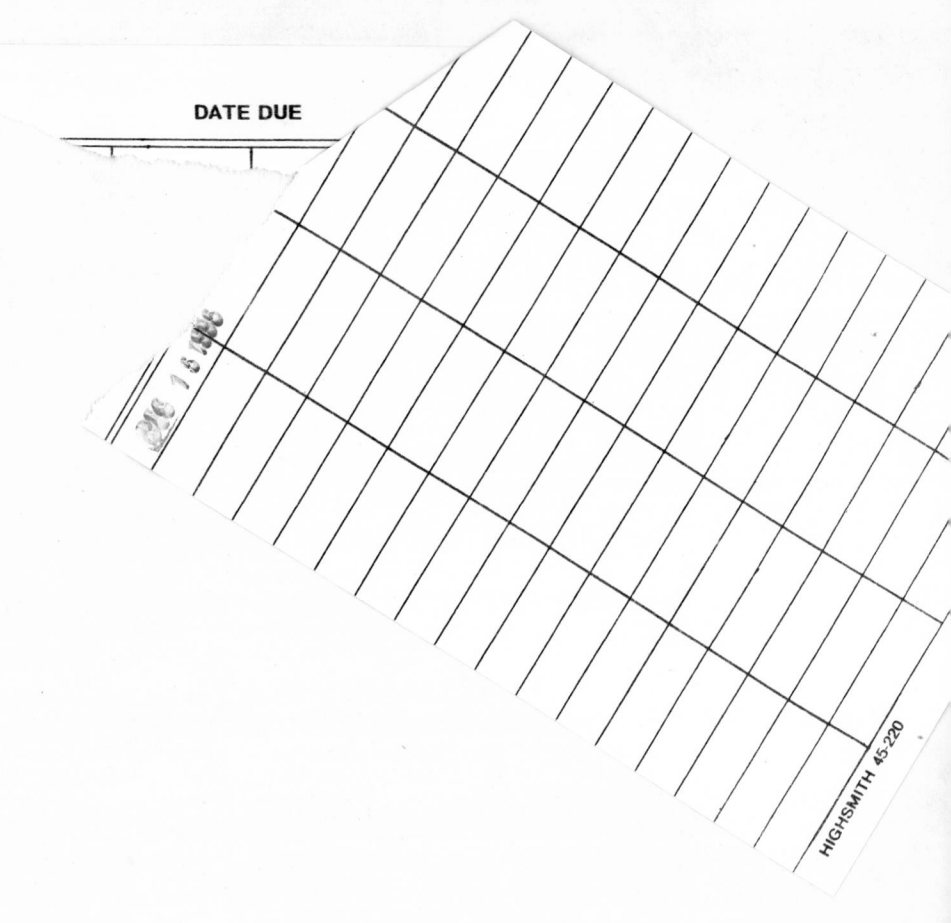